Re-viewing
Fascism

Re-viewing **Fascism**

Italian Cinema, 1922–1943

Edited by Jacqueline Reich
and Piero Garofalo

INDIANA UNIVERSITY PRESS

Bloomington and Indianapolis

This book is a publication of
Indiana University Press
601 North Morton Street
Bloomington, Indiana 47404-3797 USA

http://iupress.indiana.edu

Telephone orders   800-842-6796
Fax orders   812-855-7931
Orders by email   iuporder@indiana.edu

The paper used in this publication meets the minimum requirements of American National
Standard for Information Sciences—Permanence of Paper for Printed Library Materials,
ANSI Z39.48-1984.

Manufactured in the United States of America

ISBN: 978-0-253-21518-5

Library of Congress Cataloging-in-Publication Data

Re-viewing fascism : Italian cinema, 1922–1943 / edited by Jacqueline Reich and
Piero Garofalo.
p. cm.
Includes bibliographical references (p.) and index.

1. Motion pictures—Italy—History. 2. Fascism and motion pictures—Italy—History.
I. Reich, Jacqueline, date II. Garofalo, Piero.
PN1993.5.I88 R45 2002
791.43′0945′09041—dc21
2001003249
1 2 3 4 5   07 06 05 04 03 02

Contents

Contents

Preface

At a 1936 rally announcing massive state intervention in the film industry, Benito Mussolini appeared in front of a large banner that bore the soon-to-be infamous statement: "Cinema is the strongest weapon." Several years later, in front of a group of young film scholars, he answered the question "What is cinema?" in less belligerent terms:

> For me, films are divided into two categories: those during which the audience asks itself how it will end and those during which the same audience asks itself when it will end.[1]

These two statements by Fascism's leader summarize the major tension in the Italian feature film industry during the twenty-year period of Fascist rule: cinema's potential as propaganda versus its value as entertainment. This duality also served as the interpretive paradigm for much scholarship on Italian cinema during the Fascist period up through the 1970s. Studies in Italy and abroad dismissed most of the 700 feature films produced during the era as either blatant indoctrination or mindless drivel.[2]

New research on Fascism in general, however, has revealed the issue to be much more complex than previously assessed, underscoring the contradictions of Fascism and Italian political, social, and cultural institutions. Within this flourishing field of studies, American and European scholars have exposed the intricacies and difficulties inherent in the analysis of this controversial period. Historians such as Renzo de Felice and Zeev Sternhell, who are not without controversy themselves, have examined the composite and paradoxical nature of Fascist doctrine, noting how the party's lack of ideological consistency produced a totalitarian regime rife with conflicts and contradictions. Victoria de Grazia and George Mosse have introduced the categories of gender and sexuality into the arena of Fascist studies, revealing both Fascism's need to construct a gender ideal and its limited success in accomplishing that task. David Forgacs's work on cultural industries and Barbara Spackman's study of rhetoric and virility have exposed the tenuous nature of Fascist cultural policies and practices, as have works on Fascist spectacles by Jeffrey Schnapp, Mabel Berezin, and Simonetta Falasca-Zamponi. Robin Pickering-Iazzi's investigation of women's literary production, Karen Pinkus's study of advertising, Marla Stone's work on arts patronage, and Ruth Ben-Ghiat's analysis of Fascism and modernity all further question and ultimately disprove the myth of Fascist cultural hegemony.[3]

Re-viewing Fascism: Italian Cinema, 1922–1943 draws on these exciting contributions to Fascist studies by applying their insights into history, gender, sociology, culture, and literature to the feature film production of the era. The works gathered here represent new research by historians, film scholars, and cultural theorists of Fascist culture from the United States, Great Britain, and Italy. To varying degrees, they reflect an engagement with archival research, film distribution, spectatorship, theories of national formation and national identity, postcolonial studies, and the representation of gays and lesbians. The anthology addresses such groundbreaking subjects as the diachronic relationship between pre- and post-Fascist cinematic production; the constructions of sexuality, gender, and race in important texts of the era; the star system; and the Venice Biennale's role in exhibition.

Re-viewing Fascism begins with the premise that culture, and in this case cinema, is a site of power and governing but not one easily or even necessarily controlled by the state. Cinema during the Fascist period was indeed a cultural practice, a cultural institution, a cultural technology organized through government. The effects of cinema in Italian life, however, supersede these terms. The growing consumerism of society reshaped both social space and individual desire. Changing gender and sexual roles complicated traditional cultural constructions. The presence of American and European production models circulated divergent images that had the potential to undermine Fascist ideology.

Re-viewing Fascism opens with the first of three parts, "Framing Fascism and Cinema," which explores the relationship of films produced under Fascism with pre- and post-Fascist film production. The four essays included in this part address issues of film historiography of the silent, early sound, and neorealist periods in order to expose the continuities between the various stages and to challenge the assumptions of definite aesthetic and political demarcations. Jacqueline Reich's "Mussolini at the Movies: Fascism, Film, and Culture" surveys the history of Italian cinema during Fascism as well as the cultural debates that circulated during the *ventennio*. She notes how Italian cinema, in eschewing more overt propaganda and in relying instead on the classical Hollywood formula as its primary industrial and textual guide, opened itself up to potential deviations and subversions from Fascist ideological constructs. She studies the genre of the "woman's film," in particular the maternal melodrama, and how the representation of motherhood therein sharply contradicted the regime's ubiquitous maternal discourse. Through a critical examination of the nature of Fascist ideology, Italian cinema as Fascist cultural industry, and a survey of previous scholarship on the period, Reich reveals the many contradictions inherent not only in Fascist ideology but also in its cultural practices.

Giorgio Bertellini's contribution, "Dubbing *L'Arte Muta:* Poetic Layerings around Italian Cinema's Transition to Sound," studies Italian cinema's transition to sound in light of both the regime's cultural politics and contemporary theoretical debates on the sound film. In his archeological examination of Italian and European film theorists, Bertellini reveals how Italian film culture before, during, and after Fascism struggled in its attempt to establish a national popular tradition through cinema. Bertellini focuses on the work of such prominent thinkers as Gabriele D'Annunzio, Ricciotto Canudo, Sebastiano Arturo Luciani, Roberto Paolella, the Futurists, and Luigi Pirandello. His insightful analysis into the relationship between music, sound, and cinema constitutes a unique approach to this field of study.

On the other end of the temporal spectrum, Ennio Di Nolfo's research addresses the waning years of Fascism and its importance in the emergence of a neorealist aesthetic. "Intimations of Neorealism in the Fascist *Ventennio*" challenges the notion that a cinematic rupture produced the neorealist movement. Through a detailed analysis of cinematic production in Italy between 1938 and 1943, Di Nolfo exposes the maturation of those filmic techniques that would appear to be so revolutionary after the war. In this way, Di Nolfo demonstrates how the term *neorealism* and its subsequent foreign, and in particular American, critical acclaim have origins in limited familiarity with historical developments in the Italian film industry. International perception rather than national reality generated the myth of a new realism.

Part 1 concludes with James Hay's study "Placing Cinema, Fascism, and the Nation in a Diagram of Italian Modernity." As a formal, iconic feature of these films, the white telephone was said to have displayed and fetishized the social privilege of a modern bourgeois ethos. The historical relationship between the "cinematic" and the "telephonic," however, has not been emphasized either in film studies or in histories about the modern formation of the nation. Hay links recent political theories and developments in the construction of Italy as a nation and discusses how cinema and telephony constituted two interdependent "concrete assemblages" through which the Italian nation has been conceived and regulated as a territory from the Fascist era up through the present.

The second part, "Fascism, Cinema, and Sexuality," addresses issues of gender and representation; specifically, the actual subject of sex as depicted in the films, homosexuality, and the intersections between female spectatorship and colonial discourses. David Forgacs's essay, "Sex in the Cinema: Regulation and Transgression in Italian Films, 1930–1943," takes issue with previous film histories and their dismissal of Italian films on sexual themes as trivial and conservative. He argues that the openness of the market to imported features meant that audiences were constantly confronted with stories, star personae, and images that disturbed or transgressed the official sexual codes of Fascist and Catholic Italy. Drawing on contemporary written and oral accounts of film spectatorship, Forgacs examines the cinema of the period as a site of desire and transgressive fantasy and looks at how films are crisscrossed by conflicting models and images of sexual desirability and propriety.

William Van Watson's "Luchino Visconti's (Homosexual) *Ossessione*" critiques heterocentrist readings of *Ossessione* because they have neglected to consider the director's open homosexuality. In his reading, which differs from Forgacs's discussion of the film, Watson argues that Visconti transposes illicit homosexual love into adulterous heterosexual love. In this manner, the heterosexual framework of the narrative serves to disguise the director's sensibility, allowing him to light, costume, and image the male protagonist in a manner that (homo)eroticizes him. Watson links this self-censure to patriarchy and shows that while *Ossessione* removes the patriarchal figure from the narrative, the residue of privilege remains.

Robin Pickering-Iazzi's essay "Ways of Looking in Black and White: Female Spectatorship and the Miscege-national Body in *Sotto la croce del sud*" investigates questions about Italian female spectatorship and the differences gender makes in the representation of racial identities in Guido Brignone's *Sotto la croce del sud* (*Under the Southern Cross*, 1938). In order to theorize female spectatorship in relationship to cinematic colonial discourse, she examines opinions expressed by women of the 1930s on their film-viewing practices as well as writings on the roles envisioned for women in the construction of the Italian colonial empire. Pickering-Iazzi also explores problems arising from the application of current theories of spectatorship to colonial cinema. She argues that through an appropriation of the "native" for the white gaze, the other is performed, drawing attention to the artifice of cinematic constructions of difference.

The concluding part, "Fascism and Cinema in (Con)texts," situates the era's cinematic production within different cultural influences and practices: consumer culture, Bolshevism, the star system, performance, and spectacle. Piero Garofalo's study "Seeing Red: The Soviet Influence on Italian Cinema in the Thirties" explores the circulation of Soviet filmic and written texts in Italy. Garofalo examines the ambiguous relationship that the Fascist regime had with the Soviet Union and how the texts of Dovzhenko, Eisenstein, Pudovkin, and Vertov circulated in Italy via literature, cinema, and cultural critics. He demonstrates how cinema integrated cultural discourse with political discourse and the inherent contradictions that ensued. Italian engagement with Soviet directors exposes the fallacy of continuing to consider cinematic production under Fascism provincial and reveals the contradictory spaces formed through attempts by the state to appropriate competing discourses.

Marcia Landy's essay "Theatricality and Impersonation: The Politics of Style in the Cinema of the Italian Fascist Era" examines how Italian popular cinema disseminated modern folklore under Fascism. She considers this dissemination a form of politics—a politics of style rather than one of doctrinal and polemical substance. Through attentive readings of several films, Landy shows how these texts are self-reflexive about performance, self-reflexive in their play with intertexuality, and self-reflexive in their emphasis on fictional narratives drawn from drama, opera, and literature. While traditional interpretations of popular cinema have trivialized the films as escapist, Landy expands the notion of "escapism" by exploring how cinema, as a producer of commodities, announces its commodification couched in the language of escapism. Landy shows how these popular films are self-conscious about their status as entertainment and how they share these attitudes with the audience.

Barbara Spackman addresses the question of the relationship between Fascism and consumer culture as it played out in relation to women and gender. In "Shopping for Autarchy: Fascism and Reproductive Fantasy in Mario Camerini's *Grandi magazzini*," Spackman argues that this seemingly apolitical film in fact attempts to resolve the fundamental contradiction between Fascism's rural mother and capitalism's urban female consumer through a specifically Fascist fantasy of autarchy. Yet this resolution conflicts with the consistent association, in Fascist discourse, of city life with prostitution, an association thematicized in the film's sexual harassment sub-plot. To mediate the inconsistencies, Spackman argues that the film produces a ghost narrative centering on the transformation of the actors into mannequins and a fantasmatic attempt to represent the mannequins themselves as capable of reproduction, producing the children of the autarchic urban consumer.

Marla Stone's contribution, "The Last Film Festival: The Venice Biennale Goes to War," details the dictatorship's challenges to the social boundaries of high culture in the context of the 1942 Venice Biennale of International Art. The Biennale provides a case study of how the regime appropriated and adapted the cultural capital of elite culture through a reconfiguration of its content. For Stone, the 1942 Festival reflected both Fascism's attempt to unify its culture and ideology with Nazism and the ruptures already evident in that alliance. As evidence of those fractures, Stone examines the prize-winning Italian films of 1942 and how they expose apprehension and dissension in the face of the national struggle. The officially coordinated evolution of the Biennale, then, reveals the Fascist transformation of fine arts (re)presentation in the face of modernity, consumer capitalism, and, ultimately, war.

Stephen Gundle's essay "Film Stars and Society in Fascist Italy" both theorizes and examines empirically the star system in Italian society. Using a substantial range of sources, Gundle constructs a model of stars and stardom, drawing attention to the way in which some (mainly American) aspects of star culture were rejected while certain more national features were encouraged. By examining male and female stars, both foreign and domestic, and their linkages to politics, fashion, and style, Gundle presents a complex picture that sheds light on Italian Fascism, Italian cinema, and the role of the star in that cinema.

The contrasting approaches and readings in this volume constitute a sub-dialogue within a broader reassessment of Italian film studies on Fascism. These essays raise questions of gender, sexuality, and representation; of postcolonialism, nation formation, and national identity; and of industrial production and exhibition that expand on previous investigations in order to expose the relationships between the political and cultural spheres. These interdisciplinary strategies investigate Fascism and cinema as signifying practices while emphasizing the process of negotiation over representation. In presenting these often contrasting views (for example, the different interpretations of Visconti's *Ossessione*), our aim is to broaden both the field of Italian film studies and engage students and scholars in recent debates about Italian Fascism and cultural representation.

We opened this discussion by positing the false dichotomy of cinema as weapon versus cinema as entertainment. The ambiguity of cinema's status reflects the difficulties inherent in the study of Fascism. We believe, however, that the issues raised in this volume are germane to the challenges that contemporary society must confront, especially given the rise of right-wing politics in Italy over the last decade. Weapons stronger than cinema defeated Fascism, but Fascism's victims know that those weapons are not strong enough. In the author's preface to *Se questo è un uomo* (*Survival in Auschwitz*), Primo Levi writes: "[The Laager] is the product of a conception of the world brought to its consequences with rigorous coherence: as long as the conception exists, the consequences threaten us."[4] For us, Fascism remains a relevant and vital area of study in order both to comprehend the past more clearly and to challenge the present more effectively. By understanding the ways in which politics and culture interact to mediate meaning, we might be in a better position to refute the conception and to say "never again."

Notes

1. Quoted in Luigi Freddi, *Il cinema. Miti, esperienze e realtà di un regime totalitario,* 2 vols. (Roma: L'Arnia, 1949), 1: 387–400. Unless otherwise noted, all translations are ours.

2. The counterculture movements of the 1960s also manifested themselves in cinema studies in reaction to a critical establishment accused of prematurely dismissing the developments of the film industry during the Fascist period for purely political reasons. This renewed interest with the Fascist period, among both Italian filmmakers and film critics, led to a retrospective in Pesaro, Italy in 1975, followed a year later by another in Ancona, Italy, in which these long-neglected films could be reevaluated. It was not until the 1980s, thanks in large part to the comprehensive studies of Elaine Mancini, Marcia Landy, and James Hay, that these important developments in Italian film historiography gained a voice in the United States. Elaine Mancini, *Struggles of the Italian Film Industry during Fascism, 1930–1935* (Ann Arbor: UMI Research Press, 1985); Marcia Landy, *Fascism in Film: The Italian Commercial Cinema, 1930–1944* (Princeton: Princeton University Press, 1986); and James Hay, *Popular Film Culture in Fascist Italy: The Passing of the Rex* (Bloomington: Indiana University Press, 1987).

3. Renzo de Felice, *Le interpretazioni del fascismo* (Bari: Laterza, 1989); Zeev

Sternhell with Mario Snajder and Maia Asheri, *The Birth of Fascist Ideology: From Cultural Rebellion to Political Revolution*, trans. David Maisel (Princeton: Princeton University Press, 1994); Victoria de Grazia, *How Fascism Ruled Women: Italy, 1922-1945* (Berkeley: University of California Press, 1992); George Mosse, *Nationalism and Sexuality: Respectability and Abnormal Sexuality in Modern Europe* (New York: Howard Fertig, 1985); David Forgacs, *Italian Culture in the Industrial Era, 1880-1980: Cultural Industries, Politics and the Public* (Manchester: Manchester University Press, 1990); Barbara Spackman, *Fascist Virilities: Rhetoric, Ideology, and Social Fantasy in Italy* (Minneapolis: University of Minnesota Press, 1996); Jeffrey Schnapp, *Staging Fascism: 18BL and the Theater of Masses for Masses* (Stanford: Stanford University Press, 1996); Mabel Berezin, *Making the Fascist Self: The Political Culture of Interwar Italy* (Ithaca: Cornell University Press, 1997); Simonetta Falasca-Zamponi, *Fascist Spectacle: The Aesthetics of Power in Mussolini's Italy* (Berkeley: University of California Press, 1997); Robin Pickering-Iazzi, *Politics of the Visible: Writing Women, Culture, and Fascism* (Minnesota: University of Minnesota Press, 1997); Karen Pinkus, *Bodily Regimes: Italian Advertising under Fascism* (Minneapolis: University of Minnesota Press, 1995); Marla Stone, *The Patron State: Culture & Politics in Fascist Italy* (Princeton: Princeton University Press, 1998); and Ruth Ben-Ghiat, *Fascist Modernities: Italy, 1922-1945* (Berkeley: University of California Press, 2001).

4. Primo Levi, *Se questo è un uomo* (Torino: Einaudi, 1976), 7.

Acknowledgments

Several individuals and institutions deserve much thanks for helping us bring this project to life: the contributors, for their superb essays and indulgent patience; Michael Lundell and the staff of Indiana University Press for their interest in the project and their unwavering help in bringing it to fruition; the two anonymous reviewers for their insightful comments; the Museum of Modern Art Film Stills Archive for their assistance with illustrations; Umberta Brazzini and the Mediateca Regionale Toscana for facilitating our research with their accessible resources and solicitous attention; the University of New Hampshire, particularly the Center for the Humanities, and the State University of New York at Stony Brook for financial assistance with both research and publication; and Matthew de Ganon, Sean de Ganon, and Karen DuBois for their unquestioning support. We dedicate this volume to the memory of Gian Paolo Biasin, invaluable mentor to us and to generations of scholars.

PART I
Framing Fascism and Cinema

1

Mussolini at the Movies

Fascism, Film, and Culture

Jacqueline Reich

An examination of the body of films produced in the 1930s and early 1940s suggests that the principle of film as entertainment certainly appeared to be the rule. Italian commercial cinema focused on cinema's capacity to delight and enthrall. Comedies, melodramas, and literary adaptations dominated feature film production during those years. The film industry's reliance on cinema's entertainment value formed the basis for a cultural politics of evasion. What the industry wanted were not feature films that functioned as overt, dogmatic political mouthpieces. The task of the directors, scriptwriters, and performers involved was not to make the spectator think, but rather to induce him or her to forget.

This politic of temporary social amnesia, however, often wound up thwarting its own intentions. In looking for a guaranteed model of financial and artistic success, Italian commercial cinema turned to the United States, and to Hollywood in particular, for industrial and aesthetic inspiration. Seeking in part to exploit Italy's fascination with the myth of the American dream, these Italian films deliberately relied on the images of pleasure, wealth, beauty, and opportunity that permeated Hollywood imports. The fundamental difference, then, between Hollywood and Cinecittà was not so much textual as contextual. When Italian cinema refashioned these American texts, new models of proper male and female subjectivity appeared on the screen, which contrasted strongly with the masculine and feminine ideals promoted by the regime and propagated in other forms of mass media.

It is my contention that Italian feature film production of the Fascist

3

period was rife with other conflicts and contradictions which superseded its often self-defeating reliance on American cultural production. These films reflected the greater inconsistencies inherent in Fascist ideology itself. Contradictory and ambiguous visions of "reality" appear in the films, revealing the many cultural and political conflicts which characterized Italian Fascism. Furthermore, the publicity materials created to help promote the films in the marketplace often deliberately made recourse to these conflictual and non-conformist elements in selling the films to the audience. Thus, most feature films produced during the Fascist period wound up publicizing and displaying a picture of life under Fascism in which contrast and contradiction rather than harmony and unity came to dominate.

The aim of this particular essay is thus both theoretical and historical. I will analyze how Italian Fascism in general and its cultural politics in particular (or rather the lack thereof) created conditions of interpretive plurality. My critical examination of the Italian film industry under Fascism follows much the same line of argument: there existed much space for maneuvering in between the lines of government intervention, and the American industrial and artistic models were the means that made these cinematic negotiations possible. As a textual example of this cultural ambiguity, I will examine Luigi Chiarini's 1942 film *Via delle cinque lune* (*Five Moon Street*), a film which draws on both Hollywood and national models in its problematic representation of deviant female subjectivity.

Fascism and Culture

An exploration of various interpretations of Fascism, while it is a "fascinating" subject, is not the purpose of this study.[1] Explanations differ in scope from the psychoanalytical, for which Fascism served as the depository of childhood's ideal self as well as the expression of all that is irrational in human beings; the Marxist, for which Fascism was a defense of the social order by industrialists and landowners against the rising threat of working-class solidarity; the parenthetical, which saw Fascism as an aberration, a parenthesis in Italian history; or the consequential, in which the Fascist rise to power was directly connected to the failures of post–World War I liberalism.[2]

Historians now tend to agree that Italian Fascism represented not one political ideology but rather a synthesis of various ideological and political positions, implying constant negotiations between political factions, social institutions, and popular support. According to Roland Sarti, the Fascist movement was born out of "competing and often in-

5

compatible" ideologies and philosophies, including liberal capitalism, revolutionary syndicalism, democratic revisionism, and anarchism. Fascism's roots can be traced, in Zeev Sternhell's view, to a conglomeration of an anti-materialist and anti-rationalist strain of revisionist Marxism (which in Italy assumed the form of revolutionary syndicalism), tribal nationalism (which contributed the cult of the powerful leader), and Futurism (providing its avant-garde element). Alexander De Grand uses the term "hyphenated Fascism" to denote the ideological fragmentation behind the façade of unity, stressing the fact that much of Fascism's popular appeal can be attributed to this very plurality: since Italian Fascism, unlike Marxist-Leninism or Nazism, did not limit itself to one coherent ideology, it attracted a broader camp of supporters. Mussolini thus assumed the guise not so much of charismatic leader as that of "charismatic negotiator" who, particularly in Fascism's early days of consolidation, attempted to reconcile the various factions and not alienate his base of support.[3]

As a consequence of these ideological and political conflicts characteristic of Italian Fascism, gaps emerged between government self-proclamations of total domination and the actual state of the state. Instances of deviations from the Fascist ideal emerged across a wide variety of cultural practices, including cinema. The relationship between the Fascist regime and culture was constantly in flux, a "negotiated relation" in which intellectuals assumed the role of "brokers" or "mediators" between their own interests and those of the political power.[4] These notions of reciprocity, negotiation, and conflict take into consideration the imperfectly totalitarian and fluctuating nature of Fascist power. The mediations between culture and Fascism had the potential to exploit the conflicts in the dominant discourse and to maneuver between its inherent gaps and fissures, often with the effect (if not the explicit intent) of thwarting ideological hegemony.

Facilitating such an interpretation is the fact that Italian Fascism, unlike National Socialism, lacked a clear-cut cultural policy or dominant artistic style with respect to high culture. In the regime's grandiose plans, art, architecture, literature, and theater would serve to exalt the glory of the third Roman Empire through the propagation of certain myths and images. Certainly there were artists, such as Mario Sironi and Ardengo Soffici, who came to be associated with a Fascist style which in turn corresponded aesthetically with many of the regime's ideological imperatives: a cultural representation which was cemented in the social and/or political world of Fascism and based on a spectacular and mythic vision of Fascist reality.[5]

On the whole, however, culture under Fascism can be characterized by Marla Stone's pertinent phrase as one of "hegemonic pluralism," encompassing works from such diverse cultural tendencies as Futurism, modernism, neo-classicism and the *Novecento* school.[6] Although there was censorship with respect to the arts, the Fascist government, particularly during its first decade in power, tended toward inclusivity rather than exclusivity when it came to cultural policy. In fact, there were many such "free zones" in Italian cultural life, some of which were temporary, others of which were permanent, and many of which continued even as the government cracked down on all forms of deviation. Notable instances of cultural tolerance included the contribution of non-Fascist and anti-Fascist scholars to the *Enciclopedia italiana* (*Italian Encyclopedia*), staged productions of Bertolt Brecht's plays, and screen distribution of Chaplin's *Modern Times*.[7] These vacillations indicate that Fascist cultural policy was far from stable and solid. Instead, it left room for incorporation of a plurality of artistic experimentations and points of view.

Low, or popular, culture attempted to serve more of a propagandistic purpose, with the intent of creating consent through the dissemination of recurring words and images that would serve to glorify the Fascist empire and deify its leader. Organization of cultural activities, often in conjunction with the OND (Opera Nazionale del Dopolavoro), the Fascist organization created to regulate lower-middle-class and working-class leisure time, became the means by which the regime attempted to build consent for its policies among the masses. The idea was to bridge the gap between the state apparatuses and the people through the media, popular literature, theater, and film. The press, along with radio, was the government's most useful weapon in reaching its audience. The Fascist party directly controlled such newspapers as *Il popolo d'Italia*, and its input and influence was felt in other non-government-controlled dailies.[8] Just as with high culture, however, the results often did not meet government expectations. Cinema in particular was wrought with contradictory goals that were subject to negotiation among a variety of concerns and, as a result, far from solidly conformist in its production. It constantly had to reconcile and appease the individual interests of hard-line party members, private industrialists, and intellectuals, who all played integral roles in the restructuring and reshaping of the Italian film industry in the 1930s.

Italian Cinema during the Fascist Period

When approaching Italy's cinematic production between 1922 and 1943, the first issue to confront is one of terminology. In referring to the body of films as a whole, should one use the term "Fascist cinema," implying intentional service to and direct correspondence with Fascist ideological and cultural imperatives? Or should the more general and generous phrase "the cinema of the Fascist period" be applied, implying a margin of freedom and independence framed within the confines of Fascist structures and institutions? In order for the first term to be appropriate, cinema as both art form and institution/industry must have a clearly elaborated cultural policy, rigid control over film production, distribution, and exhibition, and a keen eye for deviations from these firmly established boundaries. Although the regime did infiltrate some aspects of the feature film industry, Italian Fascism never had a far-reaching and all-encompassing control over the film industry. The reasons for this lack of total domination are several. First, given the fact that Fascism could not achieve the status of a monolithic totalitarian power, it is not surprising that the various cultural figures involved could neither agree upon nor implement a lucid, fixed cultural program with regard to the propagandistic potential of feature film production.[9] Second, the regime was late in realizing the enormous potential of feature film as a capable means of creating cultural consensus. Keen on the ideological use of documentary, the government was quick to generate propagandistic newsreels (*cinegiornali*) and educational and/or patriotic short subjects under the auspices of the Istituto LUCE (L'Unione Cinematografica Educativa—the Educational Film Institute), established in 1924.[10] Another significant reason for this rather slow start was the state of total economic, technical, and financial disarray in which the feature film industry found itself in the 1920s and early 1930s. The Italian film industry virtually collapsed after its so-called Golden Age before World War I. It was unable to keep pace with foreign (particularly American) competition, it lagged behind technologically, and it faced high exportation tariffs abroad as well as growing production costs and poor management at home.[11]

To refer to the entire body of feature films produced during the *ventennio*—the roughly twenty-year period of Fascist rule—as "Fascist cinema" is clearly erroneous. Nevertheless, to say that it was not politically or ideologically oriented is equally misleading. With its penchant for melodramatic love stories, banal comedies, and costume epics, the *ventennio*'s cinematic production did not reflect an open agenda of ideological saturation via cinematic images. The primary modus operandi of the films of this period was entertainment and enjoyment, from the moment the spectator entered the darkness of the movie house or the reader avidly began consuming the pages of numerous fan magazines. Moreover, in projecting this image of "kinder, gentler" Fascism, these films, as Mino Argentieri and others have noted, reflected a general complicity with the regime: its imperial ambitions, its social values, and even some of its political policies.[12]

In this cultural gap between collusion and diversion, there arose occasions for deviations and even subversions. In order to best analyze and comprehend this fundamental friction, it is necessary to examine the historical, economic, and social development of the complex and constantly shifting relationship between the state and the film industry during the Fascist period.[13] Initially, the regime did not recognize commercial cinema's potential and advantages as a cultural tool. Before 1930, much of the power and influence over the industry rested in the hands of one man: Stefano Pittaluga. His company, the Società Anonima Stefano Pittaluga (SASP), with the help of capital from the Banca Commerciale Italiana, took control of the government's flailing production trust, L'Unione Cinematografica Italiana (UCI), and set about rebuilding the industry. In 1929, Pittaluga acquired the Cines studio and officially reopened it in the following year, producing several films, including Italy's first sound film, Gennaro Righelli's *La canzone dell'amore* (*The Song of Love*, 1930). Two important legislative pronouncements concurrently supported Pittaluga's personal initiatives: in order to combat the pervasive presence of foreign (specifically American) films on Italian soil, the Regio Decreto Legge no. 1121 stated that 10 percent of all films shown in theaters in Italy must be of Italian origin; and under Regio Decreto Legge no. 1117, LUCE films became required viewing, to precede the main feature films screened in all theaters. The introduction of the LUCE films into commercial theaters illustrates the separation of film as education and film as entertainment. Although united in the process of filmgoing, these two types of film constituted distinct cultural industries producing radically different products for consumption.

It was the addition of sound to cinema that convinced the regime to act quickly in aiding Pittaluga and others, including Emilio Cecchi, in reviving the film industry. Legislation was both constructive and prohibitive. In 1931, Regio Decreto Legge no. 1121 specifically set forth the concept of Italian cinema, offering a precise definition of what constitutes an "Italian" film: 1) the story must either be written by an Italian or adapted from a foreign source by an Italian; 2) the majority of filmmakers involved in all phases of product production, distribution, and exhibition must be Italian; and 3) all scenes must be shot on Italian soil.[14] In 1933, laws further curtailed foreign imports. The required number of Italian films exhibited per theater increased, so that one out of every four films screened had to be Italian, all imports faced higher tariffs, and all foreign films had to be dubbed into Italian, initiating a practice which still flourishes in Italy today. Films dubbed outside of Italy faced a supplemental tax as well.

The motivations behind this early financial assistance, however, were not to use commercial film as propaganda. As Giuseppe Bottai, the minister of corporations, who initially oversaw this initial government intervention, explained in a 1931 speech:

> I rarely go to the movies, but I have always observed that the audience becomes bored when the cinema wants to educate them. The audience wants to be entertained, and it is precisely on this terrain that we would like to help the Italian [film] industry today.[15]

Thus, government involvement in feature film production from its preliminary stages focused on its entertainment value, not on its potential service to the state. LUCE films were responsible for the cinematic education of the masses. With these early initiatives, the regime was not only attempting to solidify a position in a growing industry but also to define its national cinematic production.

A journalist by the name of Luigi Freddi would play an integral role in reconstructing the Italian film industry. In 1933, Freddi had the opportunity to go to the United States to cover Italo Balbo's long-distance flight from North America back to Italy. During that trip, he also proposed to his editors a detour to Hollywood, where he planned to stay for ten days. Instead, he remained there for two months, keenly observing the American film industry at work. He came to the conclusion that Italian cinema trailed other national cinemas in terms of industrial organization, technical capabilities, artistic criteria, and public relations. After Freddi wrote a series of articles decrying the sorry state of Italian cinema, an intrigued Mussolini invited him to devise a plan to help revive the Italian film industry.

The principal missing link, Freddi discerned, was massive state intervention.[16] He proposed government participation in film production, exhibition, and distribution based on capitalist models of financial control. His plan involved a fusion of both public and private moneys that would be backed by regulatory legislation. Culturally, he wanted a cinematic production which would appeal to a wide audience, would be nonpolitical, and yet would still offer an image of a solid, permanent, Fascist nation. Thus, for Freddi and the Fascist regime, there were two fundamental concerns: 1) to rebuild the Italian film industry in order to exalt the artistic merits and cultural glories of the third Roman Empire to those at home and abroad; and 2) to use film as an indirect tool in the creation of consensus among the masses (particularly the lower middle class, or *piccola borghesia*) by aligning it ideologically with the regime's politics and policies.

On 24 September 1934, the Fascist government established the Direzione Generale per la Cinematografia (The General Film Office) with Luigi Freddi as general director. It fell under the auspices of the Ministero per la Stampa e la Propaganda (The Press and Propaganda Ministry), directed by Mussolini's son-in-law, Galeazzo Ciano. The Press and Propaganda Ministry aimed for the greater centralization and coordination of state authority in cultural matters. Although journalism was its primary tool, it oversaw the administration of over sixteen cultural institutions, including theater, publishing, and cinema. Its purpose, as summarized in one of Ciano's speeches to the Senate, was to create a national popular Italian culture by echoing its glories, capturing the essence of its people, and highlighting its natural beauty.[17] In 1936, Ciano, off to Africa to oversee colonial expansion, passed control over to Dino Alfieri, a fervid Fascist with a penchant for propaganda. In the following year, the ministry underwent a face-lift in both name and orientation. Now called the Ministero della Cultura Popolare (The Ministry of Popular Culture), commonly known as the Minculpop, it envisioned a larger role for itself in the everyday lives of Italian citizens. While its major focus up to that point had been censorial, it would now operate more as a coordinator of popular culture. This change signaled a shift in Fascist cultural policy. Instead of focusing solely on the static repression of cultural deviations, the new agenda emphasized the dynamic construction of a new Fascist culture in which cinema was to play an extremely central role.

Even though they predated Alfieri and the Minculpop by some three years, Freddi's own plans for the Direzione and the film industry coincided with the Minculpop's subsequent agenda of active participation rather than repression. He divided his plan into five principal areas of state intervention: 1) organization (i.e., legislation); 2) financial assistance; 3) prizes and awards; 4) control (i.e., censorship); and 5) artistic and commercial encouragement and incentives.[18] The focus rested primarily on production. Regio Decreto Legge no. 1143, enacted on 13 June 1935, set up an autonomous division of the national bank (Banca Nazionale del Lavoro) that would help finance motion pictures with money from private industry. Of course, a film would have to receive the go-ahead from the Direzione before it could receive financing. Between 1934 and 1939, over 300 scripts passed through Freddi's office, which served not only to regulate and politically align potential films but also to boost production numbers (and hence profits) through financial assistance. In fact, the number of Italian films made during the period increased drastically. In 1937, only 40 were released; by 1942, that number had reached 117.[19]

A good example of how cinema, under Freddi, became a tool through which the government promulgated its policies was language. The regime's agenda of Italianization manifested itself on a linguistic as well as a geographic plane. The standardization of language, spearheaded by Achille Starace, became an integral component of collective unification. The attempt to eliminate the use of regional dialects in favor of "standard" Italian, to decontaminate the "standard" of barbarisms, and to substitute the personal pronoun *"Voi"* for the Spanish-influenced *"Lei"* in formal situations all aimed to purify the Italian spirit and abolish difference. These initiatives directly affected the film industry. Tuscan pronunciation, in accordance with the use of Florentine as standard Italian, became the regulated norm. The Direzione forbade the use of dialects in films in 1934, and *Voi* became the pronoun of preference in 1937. Here, under Freddi, cinema, like other mass media, became a tool through which the government promulgated its policies.[20]

Freddi resigned as director of the Direzione in 1939 following a long disagreement with the Minculpop over the latter's new emphasis on quantity over Freddi's dictum of quality.[21] Nevertheless, many of his policies and initiatives in the film industry proved lasting. He helped establish Italy's premiere film school, the Centro Sperimentale di Cinematografia (CSC) and contributed to its subsequently influential publication, *Bianco & Nero* (*Black and White*). He created the Cineguf, a university cinema club linked to the Fascist party, and helped foster another important periodical, *Cinema* (under the firm editorial hand of Vittorio Mussolini). His greatest innovation by far, however, was coordinating the construction and establishment of *La Città del Cinema*, or Cinecittà. Officially inaugurated on 28 April 1937, it contained on its vast property the most technologically advanced facilities needed for filmmaking: sets, costumes, editing and dubbing facilities, sound stages, and the possibility of constructing ample exterior sets. Although its primarily concern was modernizing the industry and centralizing the means of production, the promotional campaign concentrated instead on its impending role in glorifying the Italian empire through diffusion of its cultural production.[22] Financed by state money, it nevertheless remained under private ownership until 1939, when the state assumed total control of its administration. Cinecittà gradually became the center of the film industry: between April 1937 and July 1943, approximately 300 full-length feature films (over two-thirds of total production) were in some part made or produced on its premises.[23]

State intervention in exhibition and distribution revolved around the

formation of one agency, the ENIC (L'Ente Nazionale Industrie Cinematografiche), which began its operations in 1935 funded by the IRI
(Istituto per la Ricostruzione Industriale). Its aim was to stimulate production and to defend those national products through guaranteed distribution and profit minimums. The ENIC first began by buying up the
theaters themselves from the previous autonomous film agency (SASP),
at first owning only 29 in 1935 and gradually building up to 95 by 1941.
It managed to distribute on average only 16–18 percent of total film
production: private companies and studios released the remaining films.
The films under its wing did not differ much in character from the general trend of light-hearted films. The ENIC even lent its hand to production, eschewing overtly propagandistic films.[24]

Apart from ENIC's involvement in theater management, most of the
new policies concerning exhibition centered on curbing foreign imports,
specifically American ones. In 1935, the government placed a ceiling of
250 on the number of American films allowed into Italian theaters. In
1938, Alfieri sponsored a law giving the ENIC a monopolistic control
over the importation and distribution of foreign films, aimed primarily
at American films, which controlled 80 percent of the market. He found
cause for this initiative by accusing Hollywood of monopolistic practices and citing incongruities with Italy's own autarchic policies. As a
result, the "Big Four" American studios (Warner Brothers, Twentieth
Century Fox, MGM, and Paramount) withdrew their films in Italy. Between 1938 and 1942, the number of Hollywood imports shrank from
187 to a mere eight. By 1942, all foreign imports were reduced to a total
of 127, Italian films dominated the market, and the number of Italian
productions and their box-office receipts rose significantly.[25]

Another important aspect of the feature film industry during the entire Fascist period was the question of censorship, in which not only the
Direzione but also Mussolini as film spectator played a large role. Drawing on existing Liberal-era policies, legislation introduced in September
1923 made it obligatory for the few films being produced in the 1920s
to have government approval. The most significant early development
was the constitution of a censorship board one year later, which would
decide which films, both domestic and foreign, were appropriate for Italian viewers. The board initially consisted of an official from the Office
of Public Security, a magistrate, and an Italian mother—presumably the
voice of true morality. It fluctuated in size, membership, and influence
during the *ventennio*, gradually evolving in its directives from the moral
and the political to the administrative and the political. By 1935, control
had passed from the Ministry of the Interior to the Ministero per la
Stampa e la Propaganda (the Press and Propaganda Ministry). Now

comprised only of ministers and party representatives, its objective also changed. Initially it merely partially or totally censored those scenes it deemed inappropriate. After it passed to the Ministero per la stampa e la propaganda (and later the Minculpop), the censorial emphasis shifted to the dual project of control and encouragement. Nevertheless, while the board did play an important role in pre- and post-production censorship, the real power rested with the men in charge: Freddi, Alfieri, and, of course, Mussolini, who, functioning in the capacity of supreme censor, privately viewed almost all films before the general public could see them.[26]

It is remarkable, however, how few times the board actually censored feature films from 1930 to 1944. Dubbing was a way to evade dubious elements in foreign films: it was easy to change dialogue that denigrated Italy in any way or could pose other potential menacing influences.[27] Hollywood films, however, did not suffer any particular prejudice, since they too were subject to the comprehensive restrictions of the Production Code. Of the 700 or so Italian films completed between 1930 and 1944, only one was never released at all (Ivo Perilli's 1933 *Ragazzo*).[28] Few were subject to minor changes: Mario Camerini was forced to remove all jokes about dictators and unfair taxes in his 1935 film *Il cappello a tre punte* (*The Three-Pointed Hat*) and to use the *Voi* in his screen adaptation of Manzoni's *I promessi sposi*.[29] A few films which had evaded the censors were later withdrawn from circulation: Goffredo Alessandrini's version of Ayn Rand's *Noi vivi / Addio Kira* (*We the Living / Goodbye Kira*, 1942) for its sympathetic portrayal of a Communist official, and Luchino Visconti's *Ossessione* (*Obsession*, 1942) for its sexual and political undertones.

There are several reasons for the relatively inactive censorship process during the Fascist period. First, rejection occurred in the pre-production phase, since films would not get financial assistance without official approval. Both Alberto Lattuada's attempts to adapt Alberto Moravia's significant novel *Gli indifferenti* (*The Time of Indifference,* 1929) into a film and Visconti's similar desire to bring Giovanni Verga's work to the screen failed at this stage of development.[30] Second, as Lino Micciché concludes, the filmmakers' most effective weapon was to not be overtly propagandistic or militaristic. As a result, the space of permissibility would be more expansive and not easily delineated by specific regulatory parameters.[31] Third, there was what Cesare Zavattini, a frequent collaborator to many films during the era, described as "self-censorship."[32] The various artists involved (writers, directors, and producers) knew which projects they could and could not propose. In order to avoid confrontation and detrimental reverberations, they chose not to pursue certain treatments or abandoned them at the first sign of reluctance. Finally, after Freddi's dismissal from the Direzione, censorship became decidedly more relaxed, since the main preoccupation was with increasing production numbers in order to fill the gap created by the exclusion of most Hollywood imports.

An important external influence upon the moral constitution of Italian cinema was the Catholic Church. Throughout the *ventennio*, the church assumed two rhetorical positions with respect to the growing industry: it either professed a repugnance toward cinema in general, deeming it an immoral vice, or tolerated films, especially if they aspired to high moral principles. Although the Church rarely intervened at the production stage, it remained a force which exerted both conscious and unconscious influence on all levels of the film industry. The Catholic Church voiced its official pronouncements on the cinema in a series of outlets which often paralleled but did not necessarily interfere with the government's own plans of intervention. Acknowledging the propagandistic potential of film, it established its own theaters (*sale parrocchiali*), exhibiting films which it deemed possessed the appropriate ethical and spiritual values and excluding those which were morally degenerate. On the other hand, the Church voiced its campaign against cinema's moral degeneracy through written pronouncements: in an encyclical letter of 1929, a *Vigilanti cura* in 1936, and a 1936 article published in *Cinema* by Padre Agostino Gemelli, "Enciclica e cinematografia" ["Encyclical and Cinema"].[33] Each treatise advocated a "moral and moralizing" cinematic production, one which corroborated many Fascist moral and political imperatives, had Christian principles at its guide, addressed the masses and not the individual, taught by positive and not negative example, and promoted justice and virtue.

In 1934, the Catholic Church established the Centro Cattolico Cinematografico (The Catholic Film Center, or CCC) with its own censorship board, designed to complement the government agency with an emphasis on moral and religious values. Its annual publication, *Segnalazioni cinematografiche*, circulated the CCC's moral ratings for each film, deciding for whom the film was appropriate and if it could be screened in their *sale parrocchiali*.[34] Their judgments were quite severe, but they did not actually deter spectators from flocking to the movies. For example, they scolded Mario Camerini's 1939 film *Grandi magazzini* (*Department Store*) for "too many clear references to illicit relationships, and a vague sense of amorality [that] pervades the story." It was, nonetheless, one of the most popular films of the year. Even a film such as *Scipione l'Africano* (*Scipio the African*, Carmine Gallone, 1937), a production supervised by Mussolini himself, received an advisory rating—the CCC said that it was fine for the *sale pubbliche* but would need "some touches in order to eliminate a few scenes with too much of a heathen flavor."[35]

What were most of the films produced during the Fascist period like? Most opted for images of beauty, glamour, wealth, and luxury. The majority of Italian feature films released in the 1930s evidenced little or no trace of the regime's constant presence in the daily lives of Italian citizens. For example, in the many schoolgirl comedies produced during the 1930s and 1940s, the obligatory portrait of Mussolini does not hang on the wall, nor do the students read the many Fascist revisionist textbooks published during the era.[36] In Fascism's waning years, for instance, it was as if the war did not exist. Ferdinando Maria Poggioli's 1942 film *La bisbetica domata* (*The Taming of the Shrew*), a modernized version of the Shakespeare original set in contemporary Italy, contains one of the only allusions to the detrimental consequences of the conflict. It actually refers both to the effects of repeated bombings on Rome and features a scene where the characters seek refuge from an air raid in a bomb shelter.

Among the most popular films were the so-called white-telephone parlor comedies, which were closely associated with the bourgeois theatrical tradition and labeled as such due to their opulent living-room settings featuring the obligatory status symbol of the white telephone.[37] Other genres included films showcasing new comic talents such as Totò and Macario; sentimental love stories; melodramas, including a series of four films by Mario Mattòli with the telling catchphrase "Films which speak to your heart"; historical epics; and literary adaptations from Italian and other sources (particularly French). This is not to say that there were no political feature films at all. There were several, such as *L'Assedio dell'Alcazar* (*The Siege of the Alcazar*, Augusto Genina, 1939) and *Bengasi* (Genina, 1941), both heavily promoted by the film industry and lauded at the annual Venice film festival. During the war years, filmmakers such as a young Roberto Rossellini began making realist documentary-like films, indicating a future trend which would come to characterize post-Fascist Italian production. Important players in the Italian film industry during the Fascist period, other than those mentioned above, included the directors Alessandro Blasetti, Mario Camerini, and Vittorio De Sica (one of the most popular actors as well); the actors Amedeo Nazzari, Fosco Giachetti, and Gino Cervi; and the actresses Isa Miranda, Alida Valli, and Assia Noris.[38]

Italian commercial cinema did not differ greatly from the cinematic productions of other countries. In fact, it drew much of its inspiration from them, especially from Hungarian and American cinema. Hungarian literature, theater, and cinema proved politically and morally non-threatening in both form and content with their evasive and escapist principles and innocent (hence non-sexual) love stories.[39] Hollywood functioned as industrial model and artistic spark. With their conscious imitation of settings and characters typical of Hollywood films, Italian films attempted to take advantage of the established popularity in Italy of Hollywood products. According to James Hay's *Popular Film Culture in Fascist Italy,* America projected an almost "divine power" which captivated Italian audiences. With respect to cinema, it was the myth of America as propagated by Hollywood which entranced the Italian populace: the images of opulence, extravagance, and splendor; the triumph of good over evil and right over wrong; and the attraction of exotic adventure.[40]

It is important to compare Italian cinema during the Fascist period not only to American and Hungarian cinema but also with the feature film production of its closest ally: Nazi Germany. In his recent study of Nazi cinema, Eric Rentschler places the commercial cinema of National Socialism in several important contexts: 1) the totalitarian state's attempt to create a culture industry in the service of mass deception by controlling production, distribution, and exhibition; 2) the significant role that entertainment, as opposed to propaganda, played in the creation of Nazi culture; and 3) the pervasive influence of Hollywood cinema, not just Nazi "kitsch," as a model for that entertainment. He dispels the myth that propaganda films dominated German cinema of the era; they constituted only 153 out of a total of 1,094 feature films.

Despite the similarities between Italian and German cinema of the era, there remain crucial differences between the film industries of the two axis powers. Although Luigi Freddi, during his tenure at the Direzione, was the man in charge of all things cinematic, the breadth of his power never reached the scope of Joseph Goebbels's control. Furthermore, although most German films produced in the 1930s and early 1940s were "escapist" in nature, the Nazis placed more emphasis on the feature film as a tool of propaganda conditioning.[41]

Thus, despite the many rules and regulations that Freddi and his associates enacted in order to overhaul and oversee the film industry, the relationship between regime and filmmakers remained more a question of the regime's influence rather than its absolute control over filmmakers, at least in the arena of production. If the word *control* is applicable at all, it is most appropriate to the more commercial aspects of the industry, such as film distribution and exhibition. Certainly, the influence the regime exerted in script selection, financial incentives, and cultural accolades reverberated in the films produced and released during the *ventennio.* However, this influence was not static or fixed. In fact, it varied by degrees chronologically, taking a decidedly more lax turn after Freddi's departure, and individually, allowing many questionable films to squeak by without a problem.

Furthermore, there existed a remarkably open artistic environment within the film community, in which many anti-Fascist intellectuals and Jews continued to participate, even after the 1938 racial laws. Aldo de Benedetti, one of the most prolific screenwriters of the era, continued to collaborate on many screenplays without receiving screen credit. In other instances, ongoing participation depended on a quick name change, as was the case with the Jewish actress Anna Proclemer, the future wife of Vitaliano Brancati, who simply took the stage name of Anna Vivaldi. Ultimately, many of Freddi's initiatives in attempting to cultivate an intellectual cinematic climate worked against him. Both the CSC and the Cineguf turned into anti-Fascist breeding grounds, with the regime fully aware of the dissent being fostered but electing, as it often did with intellectuals, to look the other way. Filmmakers and intellectuals such as Roberto Rossellini and Giuseppe De Santis nurtured their interest in cinema through those very institutions.[42]

Another fundamental contradiction centers on both text and context, in that it involves Italian commercial cinema's artistic dependence upon and Italy's cultural fascination with Hollywood. It was Freddi's openly declared goal to mold Italian films along the lines of "Hollywood masterpieces." In fact, many films do appear as inferior American imitations (although this is not always the case). However, what Freddi and others failed to consider were the implications of employing these American models out of context. American films showcased on the whole a greater sense of social liberty, economic mobility, and financial prosperity. Consequently, Italian films based on popular Hollywood configurations often presented images of everyday life which conflicted strongly with the way in which the regime was attempting to dictate the lives of its citizens. Many of these feature films explicitly contradict state-circumscribed modes and codes of behavior for ideal Fascist subjects. Hollywood models could thus prove potentially disrupting to the government undertakings of constructing proper Fascist subjectivity through mass media. The cultural ministries allowed them to flourish because of the popularity (and revenues) they guaranteed.

This wide diffusion of oppositional models and images has important consequences for the construction of subjectivity, and female subjectivity in particular, in both cinema and Fascist society. In Italian versions of such American genres as the shop-girl film and the schoolgirl comedy, a decidedly liberated portrayal of gender subjectivity emerges.[43]

The representation of the feminine does not necessarily correspond with the Fascist ideal. Rather, it is multiplicity and non-conformity which reigns in both the cinematic and extracinematic arenas, providing not one but rather many models of behavior for women during the Fascist period.

Fascism, Melodrama, and Subversion

The Italian maternal melodrama offers a window into the machinations of ideology, gender subjectivity, cinema, and subversion. The maternal melodrama speaks, in E. Ann Kaplan's words, to the "unconscious Oedipal needs, fears and desires" of both the male and female spectator.[44] Goffredo Alessandrini's *La vedova* (*The Widow*, 1939) is an Italian maternal melodrama in which a mother's obsessive love for her dead son results in her malicious and unforgiving attitude toward his impoverished and bereaved widow. An Oedipal drama from a mother's point of view, the film depicts the consequences of those mothers who take their roles to extremes: a woman's intense maternal devotion becomes eerily sexually neurotic. The mother/son bond grows only stronger in death, for the mother has reciprocated the child's Oedipal desires while the son has successfully transferred his desires into heterosexual norms.

Similarly, the maternal woman's film is more aware of and concerned with motherhood's social and political role. It contains a decidedly female point of view which, for Annette Kuhn, "specifically addresses the female spectators and resists dominant ideology."[45] The American maternal woman's film usually has as its subject a strong mother-daughter relationship that resists patriarchal constructs. In an Italian film such as *Catene invisibili* (*Invisible Chains*, Mario Mattòli, 1942), for example, the mothers are the rebels who transgress socially prescribed boundaries of conduct. In the end, some form of patriarchal authority returns them to their traditional roles.

What emerges in the Italian women's films are depictions of mothers who deviate strongly from the image propagated by the Fascist government. The regime's demographic politics played an integral part in its deliberate attempt to construct gender roles and to reinforce its own power over the general populace. Fascism aimed to control male and female sexuality, "absorb and tame" new sexual attitudes, and create a "passionless" sexuality of its own in its quest to create norms of respectability.[46] The prestige of the fatherland was tied to the Fascist image of Italy as a virile, productive, and reproductive nation. Italian men and women had to conform to traditional gender roles in order to achieve this goal. Masculinity was directly linked to sexual prowess and

fecundity, femininity to the predestined call of marriage and motherhood. The role of dutiful wife was the first phase in securing a woman
her correct place in the social and sexual economy of Fascist Italy.[47] Several feature films dealing with motherhood counter this ubiquitous propaganda, showcasing women who are independent, sexual beings who
disregard the social and moral limits imposed upon them. The mother-
daughter bond between the characters is far from cohesive and resists
the dominant ideology, for any lack of maternal instinct necessarily
counters the Fascist position of motherhood as a woman's natural and
sole destiny.

Via delle cinque lune is an example of a film that challenges this Fascist belief. Set in nineteenth-century Rome, the film tells the story of
Ines, a pious and innocent young woman who works as a seamstress at
her local convent. Ines's father dies, leaving her at the mercy of the un-
scrupulous Teta, her stepmother. Interested in money and profit at all
costs, Teta takes over the family watch business, turning it into a pawn-
shop/usury front. Meanwhile, Ines has fallen in love with Checco, a
handsome young assistant to a sculptor; they plan to marry. Teta, once
again thinking of potential profit, fiercely opposes her stepdaughter's
marriage to an impoverished worker. Checco deliberately charms Teta,
persuading her to accept him. Her motives, however, are far from pure,
as she now desires Checco for herself. She hires him at the pawnshop,
gives him spending money, and, arousing the gossip of her neighbors
and the jealousy and suspicion of Ines, openly flirts and cavorts with
him in public. Ines, believing that Checco is giving in to temptation,
retreats into the convent for eight days to pray for their souls, during
which time Teta's seduction of Checco is complete. Upon hearing that
Ines has decided to enter the convent permanently, Checco begins to
realize the error of his ways and rejects a bitter Teta. After their reconciliation, Ines and Checco celebrate their engagement. Teta, seemingly
converted, even sells the pawnshop and returns the items to their right-
ful owners, but her passion for Checco remains. One evening, when
Checco and Ines fail to meet through a miscommunication, Checco
winds up alone with Teta in her apartment. Ines returns home to discover them in Teta's bedroom. In a delirium, Ines plunges to her death
from the stairwell balcony.

Through the veil of the past, *Via delle cinque lune* offers a critique of
existing social conditions, in particular the sexual construction of woman
as mother. The film was one of the few produced entirely by the CSC,
the film school under Chiarini's direction. Chiarini's intention was to
intermingle content and form and create meaning not only through the
events themselves but also through the formal elements of cinema: the

sets, the costumes, the cinematography, and the acting.[48] This emphasis on film form places *Via della cinque lune* in the category of films by the so-called calligraphers or formalists, including filmmakers such as Mario Soldati, who brought versions of Fogazzaro's *Piccolo mondo antico* (*Old-Fashioned World*, 1941) and *Malombra* (1943) to the screen.[49] In order to avoid the formulaic Hollywood-style comedies and melodramas typical of the era, these directors forged their own artistic path through high stylization, attention to detail, and composition. Their focus was on the surface and decoration, including, in the case of *Via delle cinque lune*, with its elaborate construction of the arched stairwell from which Ines commits suicide, magnificent production design. The efficacious lighting constantly fills Checco and Ines's scenes together in dark shadows while angelic close-ups in soft focus dominate Ines's images. Commentative parallel editing and transitions highlight diegetic contrasts (for instance, the peace and tranquillity of the convent versus the rowdy theater crowd indulging in pleasure). Intricate camera work and extra-diegetic music heighten the dramatic tension and foreshadow the tragic consequence of the characters' actions.

This refuge into the formal had political implications. Fused with this predilection for the formal were realist, even pre-neorealist, elements, such as the psychological veracity of the characters.[50] Characterized by a heightened eroticism, the characters' sexual transgressions serve to counter more than just bourgeois and Catholic morality. They also implode the gender constructions of male and female sexuality that the regime attempted to propagate. Chiarini's film portrays Teta as a mother who defies the female ideal of motherhood: she is self-serving as opposed to self-sacrificing, greedy and materialistic, sexually non-conformist, and ultimately responsible for her daughter's death.

For Chiarini, *Via delle cinque lune* was a cinematic manifestation of the true artistic and spiritual essence of the Matilde Serao short story, "O Giovannino o la morte" ("Give Me Giovannino or Give Me Death").[51] The film strategically exaggerates the Serao story's character dichotomies by increasing the stepmother's culpability and decreasing the daughter's autonomy. It also deepens the polarities between the female characters and heightens the subversive portrait of the mother figure. While in the novella the stepmother's primary preoccupation is with money, she is not the primary figure of reproach that she is in the film. Giovannino (aka Checco) is fully complicit in the affair, not a casualty of monetary and sexual seduction. A loafer, he sees mother and daughter as his meal ticket and must work to keep both happy. Chiarina (Ines) is more independent, diffident, and defiant than her cinematic counterpart: it is she who declares, "O Giovannino o la morte." Her relegation to innocent victim status in the film serves to enhance the mother's infraction of her "intrinsic" maternal nature. Consequently, a complex portrayal of a deviant mother dominates a large part of the film's narrative space, contrasting sharply with the official image propagated by the regime of woman as self-sacrificing mother in service to her family and to the state.

Although, as one character aptly puts it, "a stepmother is not a mother," Teta self-fashions that role, referring to herself as Ines's mother and to Ines as her daughter more than once in the course of the film. Thus, her transgression of that role is all the more resonant, for it is a duty which she consciously accepts. However, it is a part that she plays on her own terms. The first time the spectator sees Teta in the film is in the watch shop as she attempts to cheat a customer. One moment she is a grieving widow at her husband's funeral, hours later she partakes in a full-fledged feast complete with shady commercial wheeling and dealing. Her job as *strozzina* (literally, a choker) involves profiting from the misery of others: as she prepares to go to the theater, she wonders, after one desperate client has dared to come to her home, why "these people" must ruin her evening. She openly flaunts her relationship with the much younger Checco as they parade publicly arm in arm through the town's streets and attend the theater side by side. Her relationship with Ines is wrought with tension and contradiction from their first scene together. Cruelly authoritarian in her treatment of Ines, Teta refuses to allow her stepdaughter any degree of freedom, slapping her in the face and telling her: "I will teach you to respect me!"

Chiarini also infuses the text with a clear moral reproach of Teta as mother from a decidedly Catholic point of view. The filmmakers elaborate on the pervasive religiosity of the original text by clearly delineating between good and evil. The figure of the mother comes to personify everything un-Christian and immoral: she is a symbol of temptation, sin, and corruption.[52] In this film, sexual deviance from accepted social norms is connected to greed: avarice and adultery are both sins of the flesh. Chiarini and the filmmakers use commentative transitions to accentuate their point. Teta and Checco's first love scene concludes with a shot of Teta's body covering Checco's. The next scene takes place in a church, where Ines and others in the convent listen to a sermon about the weakness of flesh. The priest declares that "the strength of the spirit must defeat the weakness of the flesh" and says that the young women must "stamp out with faith and prayer the evil desires which bring us to sin." Throughout the homily, the film features Madonna-like close-up shots of Ines and others in prayer, contemplating the words. In one group shot, the priest's shadow "reprimands" the female congregation below. One parishioner faints from the force of his words. Ines, prominently featured in this scene, is a symbol of Christian piety and devotion throughout the film: the addition to the film of Ines's convent life, which is not present in the Serao story, reinforces her spirituality. In her innocence, Ines blames money, not lust, as the root of all evil. Believing that Checco succumbed to greed, she tells him they can survive through hard work and faith in God. It is Ines's faith and her desire to devote herself entirely to God that brings Checco to see the error of his "disgusting" ways.

On the surface, it appears as though Teta as well has seen the light as she decides to liquidate the pawnshop and return to her duties as mother. However, her conversion to proper female subjectivity is incomplete: her passion for Checco is overwhelming, and it is their final tryst that literally sends the innocent Ines over the edge. The final scene is an artistically efficacious sequence as the camera follows Ines on her fatal discovery. The spectator sees an extreme close-up of eyes, shadowed on all sides, slowly revealed by an opening door. Ines's horrified reaction seals the mother's (and lover's) complicity in the daughter's death. The film's last words, shouted by the grief-stricken and guilt-ridden Checco, resonate through the closing images, further placing responsibility on the mother: "It was she who killed her!" The punishment and judgment end there.

Ines's suicide, however, is not just an object lesson for spectators in the audience. By remaining sexually and socially deviant to the tragic end, the figure of Teta presents a portrait of motherhood that not only does not conform to Fascist and Catholic norms but also persists in resisting those very norms to the end. Linda Williams, in her interpretation of the similar conclusion to a Hollywood maternal melodrama, King Vidor's 1937 *Stella Dallas*, notes that this type of tragic ending reflects the consequences of a woman's attempts to be "something else besides a mother," that is, to break down the parameters of her socially prescribed maternal role. The female spectator would thus identify with Stella's "heroic attempt to live out the contradiction" between socially constructed roles and personal desire.[53] Such is the case with *Via delle cinque lune*. Teta, with her deviation from "acceptable" female behavior, personifies the very contradiction Stella faces with social expectations of motherhood. Moreover, when placed in the context of Fascist Italy, her divergence from culturally propagated and legislatively reinforced norms assumes a greater importance. Far from the de-sexualized image presented in such LUCE films as *Madri d'Italia* (*Mothers of Italy*, 1935), which portrays motherhood as personally, socially, and politically fulfilling, Teta sets forth a maternal figure whose open sexuality counters those very ideals.[54]

The conditions for open readings such as the one I suggest for *Via delle cinque lune* existed despite Fascism's attempts to dictate and regulate the consumption and interpretation of its gender constructions. How this and other films "spoke" to their audience varied greatly from those constructions for several reasons. Since the state elected not to impose a comprehensive cultural policy and/or style, the ensuing tolerance of an aesthetic pluralism at the levels of high and low culture allowed for a greater variety of forms and structures of expression. Cinema benefited from this lack of systematic repression, in which the various government offices and officials influenced rather than controlled its feature film production. As a result, the film industry also experienced a relatively large margin of freedom, as evidenced in part by the relatively few seditious scandals that took place in the 1930s and 1940s. Furthermore, in relying on Hollywood for both structural and artistic inspiration, Italian feature film production transposed the textual body of American films, which were decidedly more permissive, even with their own codes and modes of repression, into the context of a more repressive and regulated Italian society. Consequently, these cultural translations, much like the literary translations of American works that proliferated during the Fascist period, offered a multitude of new subject positions to their audience; from the unconventional consumer to the rebellious schoolgirl to the socially and sexually deviant mother. The remaining essays in this volume address the many areas of the film industry in which text, audience, and ideology interacted during the Fascist period, from the star system to consumer culture to the colonies, and the wildly varying responses to these encounters.

Notes

1. I chose to bracket the word "fascinating" with quotation marks because in the world of scholarship about Fascism, it has come to symbolize the appeal both Italian and German fascism held for its contemporaries as well as the attraction it wields now for those engaged in academic research. The term originates in Susan Sontag's now canonical essay "Fascinating Fascism," anthologized in *Movies and Methods* (Berkeley: University of California Press, 1976), I: 31–43, and was used as a title for the symposium "Fascinating Fascism," held at Stanford University in October 1993.

2. For the best survey of the historiography of Fascism, consult the most recent edition of Renzo De Felice's *Le interpretazioni del fascismo* (Bari: Laterza, 1989), with a revised preface/introduction (v–xxiii). More psychologically and/or psychoanalytically oriented interpretations are proposed by Wilhelm Reich, *The Mass Psychology of Fascism*, trans. Vincent Carfagno (New York: Farrar, Straus & Giroux, 1970); and Simona Argentieri, "Il ridicolo e il sublime," *Risate di regime. La commedia italiana 1930–1944*, ed. Mino Argentieri (Venezia: Marsilio, 1991), 19–33. Alice Yaeger Kaplan also notes how it is possible to explain and understand Fascism's appeal through mother-bound rather than father-bound desire, in which "recognizing oneself as manly and safeguarding mother-nation go together." Alice Yaeger Kaplan, *Reproductions of Banality: Fascism, Literature, and French Intellectual Life* (Minneapolis: University of Minnesota Press, 1986).

3. Roland Sarti, "Introduction," in *The Ax Within: Italian Fascism in Action*, ed. Roland Sarti (New York: New Viewpoints, 1974), 2–5; Zeev Sternhall with Mario Snajder and Maia Asheri, *The Birth of Fascist Ideology: From Cultural Rebellion to Political Revolution*, trans. David Maisel (Princeton: Princeton University Press, 1994); Alexander De Grand, *Italian Fascism: Its Origins and Development*, 2nd ed. (Lincoln: University of Nebraska Press, 1989), 137–145.

4. David Forgacs, *Italian Culture in the Industrial Era, 1880–1980: Cultural Industries, Politics, and the Public* (Manchester: Manchester University Press, 1990), 1–11, 55–82.

5. Guido Armellini, *Le immagini del fascismo nelle arti figurative* (Milano: Fabbri, 1980); Walter Adamson, "Ardengo Soffici and the Religion of Art" and Emily Braun, "Mario Sironi's Urban Landscapes: The Futurist/Fascist Nexus," both in *Fascist Visions: Art and Ideology in France and Italy*, ed. Matthew Affron and Mark Antliff (Princeton: Princeton University Press: 1997), 25–45 and 101–133, respectively.

6. Marla S. Stone, "The State as Patron: Making Official Culture in Fascist Italy," in *Fascist Visions*, 205–238; and Marla S. Stone, *The Patron State: Cultural & Politics in Fascist Italy* (Princeton: Princeton University Press, 1998).

7. Renzo De Felice, "Fascism and Culture in Italy: Outlines for Further Study," *Stanford Italian Review* 8, nos. 1–2 (1990): 5–11.

8. Phillip Cannistraro, *La fabbrica del consenso. Fascismo e mass media* (Bari: Laterza, 1975); Victoria de Grazia, *The Culture of Consent: Mass Organization of Leisure in Fascist Italy* (Cambridge: Cambridge University Press, 1981); Forgacs, *Italian Culture in the Industrial Era*, 55–82; and Edward Tannenbaum, *The Fascist Experience: Italian Society and Culture, 1922–1945* (New York: Basic Books, 1972), 219–225. For more on the press and the publishing industry during Fascism, see Paolo Muraldi, *La stampa del regime fascista* (Bari: Laterza, 1986).

9. Christopher Wagstaff notes how the regime acted almost as mediator between various positions regarding the function of culture in the regime's overall politics. See "The Italian Cinema Industry During the Fascist Regime," *The Italianist* 4 (1984): 160–174.

10. For a discussion of LUCE films and their role in the regime's cultural policies, see Mino Argentieri, *L'occhio del regime. Informazione e propaganda nel cinema del fascismo* (Firenze: Vallecchi, 1979); James Hay, *Popular Film Culture in Fascist Italy: The Passing of the Rex* (Bloomington: Indiana University Press, 1987), 201–232; and Elaine Mancini, *Struggles of the Italian Film Industry during Fascism, 1930–1935* (Ann Arbor: University of Michigan Press, 1985), 121–160.

11. Gian Piero Brunetta, *Storia del cinema italiano: Il cinema muto 1895–1929* (Roma: Riuniti, 1993), I: 231–259.

12. See Mino Argentieri, "Dal teatro allo schermo," in *Risate di regime*, ed. Mino Argentieri, 71; and Gian Piero Brunetta, "Mille lire (e più di mille lire) al mese," in *Risate di regime*, 98–99. See also Gianfranco Casadio, et al., *Telefoni bianchi. Realtà e finzione nella società e nel cinema italiano degli anni quaranta* (Ravenna: Longo, 1991), 13–14. Brunetta: "In effect, Fascism preferred the middle road of emotions and situations, geared toward a middle-class audience to excessive and exasperated propaganda." *Intellettuali, cinema e propaganda fra le due guerre* (Bologna: Patrón, 1972), 127.

13. I base my historical analysis on the following sources: Cannistraro, *La fabbrica del consenso*, 273–322; Claudio Carabba, *Il cinema del ventennio nero* (Firenze: Vallecchi, 1974); Jean Gili, *Stato fascista e cinematografia. Repressione e promozione* (Roma: Bulzoni, 1981); Mancini, *Struggles of the Italian Film Industry during Fascism*; Lorenzo Quaglietti, *Storia economica-politica dalle origini ad oggi* (Roma: Riuniti, 1980), 13–33; and Wagstaff, "The Italian Cinema during the Fascist Regime," 160–174.

14. Reprinted in Gian Piero Brunetta, *Cinema italiano tra le due guerre. Fascismo e politica cinematografica* (Milano: Mursia, 1975), 107–108.

15. Reprinted in Brunetta, *Cinema italiano tra le due guerre*, 106.

16. "Since we are dealing with an industry which directly involves the dignity, love and the economic and moral interests of the State with its products, I do not hesitate to declare that it is finally necessary for the State to intervene directly, imposing on the solution its authoritarian and severe mark of intervention and control. Where states have had the authority to impose intervention, they have done it. And it has not impeded the development of a flourishing, effective, profitable, and leading state film industry." Luigi Freddi, *Il cinema. Miti, esperienze e realtà di un regime totalitario*, 2 vols. (Roma: L'Arnia, 1949), I: 70.

17. See Ciano's "Discorso al Senato sulla cinematografia fascista" of 22 May 1936, reprinted in Carabba, *Il cinema del ventennio nero*, 123–125. For a developmental history of the Ministry of Popular Culture, see Cannistraro, *La fabbrica del consenso*, 101–171; and Teresa Maria Mazzatosta, *Il regime*

fascista tra educazione e propaganda (1935-1943) (Bologna: Cappelli, 1978), 27-28.

18. Luigi Freddi, "Nascita della Direzione Generale della Cinematografia," in Carabba, *Il cinema del ventennio nero*, 120-123.

19. See Massimo Mida e Lorenzo Quaglietti, *Dai telefoni bianchi al neorealismo* (Bari: Laterza, 1980), 48.

20. For one of the few discussions of cinema's linguistic policies during Fascism, see Paola Micheli, *Il cinema di Blasetti parlò così . . . Un'analisi linguistica dei film (1929-1942)* (Roma: Bulzoni, 1990), 19-42.

21. Freddi felt that he was forced out of his position. See *Il cinema. Miti, esperienze e realtà di un regime totalitario*, 2: 153-176.

22. For more on Cinecittà, see G. Paulucci di Calboli, "La Città del cinema," *Cinema* 1, no. 1 (10 luglio 1936): 12-14.

23. The accomplishment attains greater significance when one considers the number of short films produced (85) and foreign films dubbed (248) on the premises. See Freddi, *Il cinema. Miti, esperienze e realtà di un regime totalitario*, 2: 287-294.

24. Gili, *Stato fascista e cinematografia*, 100-109, and Freddi, *Il cinema. Miti, esperienze e realtà di un regime totalitario*, 2: 361-375.

25. Brunetta, *Storia del cinema italiano*, II: 22-23; and Mida and Quaglietti, *Dai telefoni bianchi al neorealismo*, 50. See also an interview with Dino Alfieri from *Corriere della sera* (20 novembre 1938), reproduced in Carabba, *Il cinema del ventennio nero*, 133-136.

26. The two best sources on film censorship during the Fascist period are Mino Argentieri, *La censura nel cinema italiano* (Roma: Riuniti, 1974); and Gili, *Stato fascista e cinematografia*. All subsequent information on Fascism and censorship is derived from these sources, unless otherwise noted.

27. Guido Fink notes that the authorities found the gangster films' portrayal of Italian Americans as gangsters particularly offensive and had some of the names de-Italianized through dubbing. Guido Fink, "Orgoglio e pregiudizio: stereotipi hollywoodiani e doppiaggio di casa nostra," *Cinema & Cinema* 11 (gennaio-marzo 1984): 26-35.

28. Intended to be a picaresque tale of Fascist enlightenment, *Ragazzo* recounts the story of a working-class orphan boy who eventually learns the error of his criminal ways through conversion to the Fascist cause. In attempting to make the story realistic, Ivo Perilli opted to shoot much of the film on location in Rome, particularly in the poorer sections and among the delinquents, aspects of daily life that the regime said no longer existed. Furthermore, the fact that a model Fascist could arise from a criminal gang of hooligans was certain to displease Fascist officials. In fact, after being reviewed by the censorship commission and Mussolini himself, *Ragazzo* was banned from all Italian screens. Gili, *Stato fascista e cinematografia*, 31-33.

29. Mussolini's sons Vittorio and Bruno accused Camerini of being both anti-Fascist and anti-Italian. The film was re-edited and released but was soon withdrawn from theaters to avoid further criticism. See Francesco Savio's interview with Mario Camerini in *Cinecittà anni trenta. Parlano 116 protagonisti del secondo cinema italiano (1930–1944)*, 3 vols. (Roma: Bulzoni, 1979), 1: 211–212, and Gili, *Stato fascista e cinematografia*, 55.

30. Visconti got his wish after the war, when Verga's *I Malavoglia (The House by the Medlar Trees)* became the basis for his classic 1948 neorealist film *La terra trema (The Earth Shakes)*.

31. Lino Miccichè, "Il cinema italiano sotto il fascismo. Elementi per un ripensamento possibile," in Argentieri, *Risate di regime*, 41.

32. Cited in Gili, *Stato fascista e cinematografia*, 55.

33. The latter two pieces are anthologized in Carabba, *Il cinema del ventennio nero*, 157–167. See also his discussion of Church attempts to intervene in the film industry, 27–28.

34. Gili, *Stato fascista e cinematografia*, 121–122. Another important periodical was *La rivista del cinematografo*, which, before the publication of the first volume of *Segnalazioni cinematografiche*, functioned as the Church's mouthpiece on all that had to do with cinema. It continued on with its Catholic orientation even after 1934, publishing such articles as "La produzione cinematografica italiana" and "L'apostolato diretto e il cinematografo," both in no. 11, 1938.

35. *Nuovi materiali sul cinema italiano, 1929–43*, Quaderno 71 (Pesaro: Mostra del cinema di Pesaro, 1976), 77.

36. For more on the schoolgirl comedy, see Jacqueline Reich, "Reading, Writing, and Rebellion: Collectivity, Specularity, and Sexuality in the Italian Schoolgirl Comedy, 1934-1943," in *Mothers of Invention: Women, Italian Fascism, Culture*, ed. Robin Pickering-Iazzi (Minnesota: University of Minnesota Press, 1995), 220–251.

37. Many of these white-telephone comedies were adapted from past and contemporary theatrical successes, including works by Pirandello (*Ma non è una cosa seria* and *Pensaci, Giacomino*), Aldo De Benedetti, and Alessandro De Stefani. For more on the relationship between cinema and theater, consult Mino Argentieri, "Dal teatro allo schermo," in Argentieri, *Risate di regime*, 67–95; and Cristina Bragaglia and Fernaldo Di Giammatteo, "Dal teatro al cinema: L'Italia in commedia," article housed in the collection of the Mediateca Regionale Toscana, Firenze.

38. For more on the types of films produced during the Fascist period, see Fabio Carpi, "Il cinema rosa del ventennio nero." *Cinema nuovo* 6, no. 109 (15 giugno 1957); Casadio, *Telefoni bianchi*, and his *Il grigio e il nero. Spettacolo e propaganda nel cinema italiano degli anni trenta (1931-1943)* (Ravenna: Longo, 1991); Carabba, *Il cinema del ventennio nero*, 29–65; Francesco Savio, *Ma l'amore no. Realismo, formalismo, propaganda e telefoni bianchi nel cinema italiano di regime (1930-1943)* (Milano: Sonzogno,

1975); Argentieri, *Risate di regime;* and Riccardo Redi, ed., *Cinema italiano sotto il fascismo* (Venezia: Marsilio, 1979).

39. Francesco Bolzoni, "La commedia all'ungherese nel cinema italiano," *Bianco & Nero* 49, no. 3 (1988): 7–41.

40. Hay, *Popular Film Culture in Fascist Italy*, 66–72; Lucilla Albano, "Hollywood: Cinelandia," in Redi, *Cinema italiano sotto il fascismo*, 219–232; Casadio, *Il grigio e il nero*, 9; and Casadio, *Telefoni bianchi*, 11–30.

41. Eric Rentschler, *The Ministry of Illusion: Nazi Cinema and Its Afterlife* (Cambridge, Mass.: Harvard University Press, 1996). Linda Schulte-Sasse bases her approach on Slavoj Žižek's theories on politics and fantasy in *Entertaining the Third Reich: Illusions of Wholeness in Nazi Cinema* (Durham: Duke University Press, 1996). See also Tom Reiss's article on the Lincoln Center Film Society series of German films produced between 1933 and 1945: Tom Reiss, "How the Nazis Created a Dream Factory in Hell," *The New York Times*, 6 November 1994, 2: 15–16.

42. Brunetta, *Cent'anni del cinema italiano*, 188–190; Luisa Quartermaine, "Tempo di storia e tempo di miti: teoria e prassi nel cinema durante il fascismo," in *Moving in Measure: Essays in Honour of Brian Moloney*, ed. Judith Bryce and Doug Thompson (Hull: Hull University Press, 1989), 152–168.

43. Reich, "Reading, Writing, and Rebellion"; and Reich, "Consuming Ideologies: Fascism, Commodification, and Female Subjectivity in Mario Camerini's *Grandi Magazzini*," *Annali d'Italianistica* 16 (1998): 195–212.

44. E. Ann Kaplan, "Mothering, Feminism and Representation: The Maternal in Melodrama and the Woman's Film 1910-40," in *Home Is Where the Heart Is: Studies in Melodrama and the Woman's Film*, ed. Christine Gledhill (London: British Film Institute, 1987), 113–137.

45. Annette Kuhn, "Women's Genres: Melodrama, Soap Opera and Theory," in Gledhill, *Home Is Where the Heart Is*, 339–349.

46. George L. Mosse, *Nationalism and Sexuality: Respectability and Abnormal Sexuality in Modern Europe* (New York: Howard Fertig, 1985), 10.

47. Victoria de Grazia, *How Fascism Ruled Women: Italy 1922–1943* (Berkeley: University of California Press, 1993); and Maria Addis Saba, "La donna 'muliebre,'" in *La corporazione della donna. Ricerche e studi sui modelli femminili nel ventennio*, ed. Maria Addis Saba (Firenze: Vallecchi, 1988), 1–71.

48. R. Mastrostefano, "Via delle cinque lune," *Bianco & Nero* 6, no. 5-7 (maggio-luglio 1942): 5–16.

49. Other films which belong to this category are Alberto Lattuada's *Giacomo l'idealista* (*Giacomo the Idealist*, 1943); Renato Castellani's *Un colpo di pistola* (*Pistol Shot*, 1942); two other Chiarini films, *La bella addormentata* (*Sleeping Beauty*, 1942) and *La locandiera* (*The Innkeeper*, 1943); and Ferdinando Maria Poggioli's *Gelosia* (*Jealousy*, 1943).

50. Marcia Landy, *Fascism in Film: The Italian Commercial Cinema 1930–1944*

(Princeton: Princeton University Press, 1987), 276–277; and Brunetta, *Cent'anni di cinema italiano*, 257–261.

51. Even though he transposed the setting from Serao's Naples to Belli's Rome in the film and changed the characters' names, Chiarini had to struggle with the censorship board in order to maintain fidelity to the short story's tragic conclusion of Ines's suicide, since any mention of suicides was prohibited. However, a verse of a poem by Belli which alluded to poverty was cut from the film, prompting Jean Gili to remark how the regime was more accommodating in dealing with cinematic depictions of moral problems than it was in dealing with economic problems. Gili, *Stato fascista e cinematografia*, 64–65, and Francesco Savio's interview with Luigi Chiarini in *Cinecittà anni trenta*, 1: 322–330. "O Giovannino o la morte" can be found in Matilde Serao, *All'erta, Sentinella!* (Milano: Baldini, 1904), 309–366.

52. Landy, in her discussion of the film, elaborates on Checco's role as vulnerable victim in Teta's hands. Landy, *Fascism in Film*, 298.

53. Linda Williams, "'Something Else Besides a Mother': Stella Dallas and the Maternal Melodrama," in Gledhill, *Home Is Where the Heart Is*, 314.

54. Leslie Caldwell, "*Madri d'Italia*: Film and Fascist Concern with Motherhood" in *Women and Italy: Essays on Gender, Culture and History*, ed. Zygmunt G. Baránski and Shirley W. Vinall (London: Macmillan, 1991), 59–61.

2

Dubbing *L'Arte Muta*

Poetic Layerings around Italian Cinema's Transition to Sound

Giorgio Bertellini

Tout pour l'oeil, rien pour les oreilles.
　　　　　　　　　　　　　—Charles Baudelaire

Images are images, and images cannot talk. . . . That silence has been broken. It cannot be restored again.
　　　　　　　　　　　　　—Luigi Pirandello

Neorealism and Its Silences

In the spring of 1950, in a contribution published in the film periodical *Bianco & Nero,* director Alessandro Blasetti wrote:

> For me, one cannot speak of a musical factor in the movies because *cinema is music.* Even in the rendering of sound atmospheres or dialogues, in order not to lose the efficacy and clarity of the spectacle, everything relates to the laws of rhythm, volumes, and tones which are the laws of harmony, that is of music. Films are always born, if not from music, within music.[1]

Toward the end of the neorealist season, this short passage on the artistic affinities between music, rhythm, and the cinematic language did not spur much interest or controversy. It probably seemed to display the sort of formalist comfort and ideological complacency which marked —according to the still-influential critics of the defunct periodical *Cinema*—film production under Fascism.[2] After all, Blasetti was regarded as a figure belonging to the past and involved in a different *kind* of cinema. With the exception of a very few works, which were supposedly "proleptic" of neorealist artistry, such as *1860* (1933) and *A Walk in the Clouds* (1942), his film production was considered as somewhat disengaged from the common people who fell victim to a dictatorship and a self-destructive war. By the same token, Blasetti could not and did not consider himself a neorealist director, as his provocative definition of the nature of filmmaking attested. What I find most striking and worth exploring is that behind his rhetorical assimilation of *film images* and *music* lurked an erstwhile attitude toward the medium that was germane to Italian silent film theory and practice. Still fairly widespread in the 1930s film discourse, that very early film poetics had slowly been disowned and eclipsed due to the arrival of synchronized sound and neorealist ideology.

During the 1910s and the 1920s, in fact, the artistry of the film image was forcefully emphasized by frequent analogies with music's expressiveness. To preserve the creativity and ingenuity of artists, Italy's century-old aesthetic culture had attempted to master the modern visual novelties of cinema and photography by emphasizing their "constructedness," linguistic texture, and ontological differences from "reproduced reality." In so doing, an entire generation of film and cultural critics strove to resist and tame cinema's photographic indexicality, its unmastered naturalness, and its unprecedented realism. Accordingly, most of Italy's silent film production, from historical epics or aristocratic melodramas to studio comedies or well-choreographed actualities, performed this redeeming task: high-brow models of artistry inspired notions of cinema as a silent and yet supremely musical flow of images, an *arte muta*. A remarkable exception was constituted by Neapolitan cinema, which from the mid-1910s to the late 1920s had adopted a peculiar and disturbing idea of cinema, developing it as a forthright reproduction of common and poor people's passionate lives and stories. Its poetic orientation differed even from standard documentary practices, which, before and after Fascism came to power, aimed to show Italy's architectural landmarks, official army parades, and national pastimes, thus displaying a measured, ideal, and touristic image of Italy.

From the early 1930s, however, cinema was called to a different poetic task, inspired by the challenges of poetic realism that were emerging in literature and theater. The modern necessities of a "patriotic and realist cinema" implied major communicative and rhetorical differences from the past. At issue was not just a renewal of standard artistic practices. Films had to develop a closer, yet still officially sanctioned, kinship to Italy's everyday reality, people, and stories. The challenge, in Giulio Bollati's words, was whether "there existed an Italian way to modernity."[3] If the visuals of such new poetics were not too difficult to render or command, the aurals posed the major challenges, since the nation lacked a true spoken language common to all Italians—an issue Antonio Gramsci has famously termed *la questione della lingua*.[4] How would a conversation sound among common people in a "verisimilar" Italian story? What lexicon or accent would one hear from a young housewife or an aged blue-collar worker? What kind of dialogue would one expect from a peasant?

Facing the structural challenge of synchronized sound, cinema during Fascism achieved mixed results: it exposed nationwide the average urban prose of secretaries, white-collar workers, and delivery men, but frequently and awkwardly it combined their common language with old literary wordings. And yet, these efforts were never acknowledged by the neorealist enterprise. According to a renowned and acquiescing Crocean assessment, in fact, Fascism was said to have constituted a perverse parenthesis in Italian history and culture. The aesthetic endeavors and accomplishments of the *ventennio* then had to be dismissed as deceptive, inadequate, or even irrelevant—including cinema's crucial shift to sound.

Initiating a lasting historiographical tendency, neorealist film critics were very clever in disputing any serious cultural or artistic consistency in film production during Fascism.[5] As a result, early Italian sound cinema, that is, the film production critics blindly considered heavily influenced by the regime, was utterly and polemically disregarded both from a historiographical and archival standpoint.[6] Such an obscuring move was performed through rancorous polarizations: truth versus falsehood, revelation versus concealment, the common people versus the dictatorship, and, most important, the Italian nation versus the Fascist state. Interestingly, this adversarial scenario silently postulated that Italy's cultural unity somehow and ipso facto existed or that it had never constituted a real question.

My intention here is not to provide a linguistic overview of Italian cinema during its transition to sound.[7] Although the verbal exchanges, songs, and intertitles are crucial to my analysis, my aim is more archeologically that of recuperating a particular portion of *Italian film discourse* of those years, which was embedded with cherished habits of artistic and universal ambitions and still distant from modern patterns of "national-popular representations." My discussion is articulated through three interrelated areas. First, I will examine Italian film production of the 1910s and 1920s—which was composed of decadent melodramas, serial detective stories, historical films, and the "realist" Neapolitan cinema—in their *prolonged* aesthetic obsolescence. Standard studies about "cinema during Fascism" have consistently dealt with those genres only within introductory chapters and have all-too-neatly segregated this production from what occurred after 1930.[8] Second, I will briefly give an account of the European debate on the transition to sound to illuminate the specificity of the Italian critical scene. Third, I intend to report examples of Italy's film discourse on images and sounds developed since the early 1910s by different figures such as poet and writer Gabriele D'Annunzio; critics Ricciotto Canudo, Sebastiano Arturo Luciani, Roberto Paolella; the Futurists; and playwright Luigi Pirandello.

My more general contention is that Italian film culture before, during, and even after Fascism often resorted to a Romantic aesthetic and (even economic) approach to the medium of film. Blasetti's 1950 remark about music and cinematic language was symptomatic of an earlier conception of cinema, which neorealist discourse had silenced with hostile indifference as a politically suspicious obsoletism. By the same token, orthodox neorealist criticism was much more inclined to grant aesthetic value to "realistically coded" *visual* renderings than to emphasize the still-deep linguistic divisions of a country in need of a new political and cultural leadership. Rossellini's *Paisan* (1946) recorded (actually dubbed) the sound of different dialects, but it combined them in the single narrative of the country's liberation from the Germans. The rhetorical assumption, originating in literature, that the Italian nation had always existed was left untouched.

In early twentieth-century Italy, where mannered literary speech had traditionally been kept isolated from daily life for centuries and where common people could sing arias of Verdi's operas and a few *canzonette d'amore* (love songs) but were still illiterate about their national language, a realist and audiovisual aesthetic had to be more inventive than mimetic. If cinema during Fascism was to become a popular audiovisual form of entertainment and propaganda, then the real challenges surrounded the meanings of "popular" and "national." Inevitably, the projects of ambitious directors and engaged critics, caught between the desire for high art and parochial representations, clashed with the lack (indeed a structural absence) of an established national and popular culture that the regime and the audience could easily embrace and appropriate.[9]

Mute Art and Open Air: Decadence and *Sceneggiate*

Since their inception in 1905, Italy's main film companies, located in Milan, Turin, and Rome, structured their output on international demands in terms of both film genres and style. Historical-mythological films, comedies, and the so-called *melodramma dannunziano*—embodied in convoluted plots crowded with femmes fatale, ruined aristocrats, and immoral dandies—appeared to constitute the most representative examples of national film production until the Great War.

World War I suddenly and unexpectedly destroyed the rich commercial routes between Italy, the rest of Europe, and the Americas. The consequences were disastrous. In 1914 the total number of films produced in Italy was 1,027; in 1915 that figure dropped to 563 and it steadily decreased to 295 in 1919, while their estimated average length more than doubled—following a tendency toward longer feature films pioneered by prewar Italian movies.[10] However, despite the war and the increase in the length of films, Italian producers behaved as if nothing had changed. They continued to cling to old narrative and visual routines, which by the mid-1910s had already begun to demonstrate their obsolescence, both domestically and internationally. Utterly disregarding audience responses, producers worked to financially reinforce their antiquated output by centralizing part of the national film industry through aggregation and standardization. This consolidation led to the creation in 1919 of Italy's first film trust, UCI (Unione Cinematografica Italiana), a great example of a commercially fatuous and geographically biased conglomerate.[11]

UCI symbolized the lowest moment of an industry that was in crisis regarding stylistic identity and creativity and incapable of rationalizing its investments or predicting domestic market expectations. It also displayed Italian producers' serious managerial and cultural limits. During the 1920s, the enormous waste of energy, investments, and labor reached its peak: films were produced to be accumulated as stock capital and not necessarily to be distributed or exhibited. Actors and directors emigrated abroad.[12] The commercial misunderstanding of the medium's constituency and exploitability could not have been more menacing.[13] From its beginning, film manufacturing in Italy had not regarded its object-product as an *industrial commodity* that was conceived for recurring, long-term consumption, and even less as a *national* one. Compared to American work and marketing standards, Italian films were often produced as a kind of "artistic entertainment," mostly made for an international market through entrepreneurial ingenuity or serendipity made possible by rich sponsors' generosity and the very low cost of unskilled labor and extras. Between 1920 and 1931, 1,316 films were produced, but they were as many as 415 in 1920, and as few as 2 in 1931.[14]

Meanwhile, Italian audiences were mainly consuming and applauding American and French films—which increasingly after World War I came to constitute the principal source of income for Italian distributors and exhibitors. The only domestic film genres that enjoyed great popularity among the national audience were the crime-story serials featuring Emilio Ghione in the role of *Za-la-Mort* (1914–1922) and the so-called athletic-acrobatic film, featuring "strongmen" such as Maciste, Saetta, Ercole, and Sansone (1913–1926), which narrated and glorified the hero's male body.[15] In the 1920s, historical films were far less numerous and popular than one might expect; they combined worn ambitions of spectacular magnificence with a mannerist taste for antiquity, but their stylistic rigidity and sermonical expressivity could not compete with the narrative pace and ease of Hollywood westerns and exotic adventures.[16] The rest of the domestic productions, however, maintained the narrative and stylistic features successfully exported abroad before the war. The most evident examples of this were the exorbitant contracts that *dive* such as Francesca Bertini, Pina Menichelli, Leda Gys, Lyda Borelli, Italia Almirante Manzini, Maria Jacobini, and Lina Cavalieri still commanded despite the shrinking of popularity of their films.[17] It is symptomatic that Italian fiction films of the 1910s and 1920s hardly left the studio. Very few scenes were shot on location, as standard "national" narrations mainly revolved around past imperial glories or the morbid attractions of urban life.[18]

The only tradition that consistently devoted its poetics to a real-life rendering of ordinary, often destitute, people was the Neapolitan cinema. Here, "ordinary" refers not merely to a "setting" that was spatially and culturally distant from the mannerly and urbanite style of the 1930s white-telephone tradition but also to a particular way to reproduce a specific local humanity. Since the first decade of the century, Neapolitan production companies such as Partenope Film, Vesuvio Films, and Films Dora resorted to a cinema *en plein air* by adopting "open-studio" sets and including documentary footage (*vedute, immagini dal vero*), thus disclosing the picturesque and plebeian world of back streets, urchins, popular festivities, and underclass *masques,* all of which were typical of Naples popular culture.[19] The display of morbid scenes of passion, death, and revenge, the excessive and irreverent *realism* of such "ethnic" cityscapes, which were crammed with nonprofessional actors and viscous symbolism and used live vernacular songs, were consistently reprimanded and marginalized within the exhibition outlets of central and northern Italy.

Since the late 1910s, Neapolitan cinema had uniquely enriched its exhibition style with *sceneggiate,* that is, narrative stagings of songs.[20] Films were presented with live accompaniment by singers and, at times, by a full orchestra. Neapolitan film companies consistently emphasized their close relationships with the music industry by casting famous local tenors, by titling the film after a popular song (obviously, in dialect), or by using the film narrative as a mere pretext for musical collage.[21]

Sceneggiate were intrinsically Neapolitan. As Giuliana Bruno explained, not only did they display "intertwined pathologies of everyday life, dark dramas of *vita vissuta,* that is, lived experience, and scenes of

1. Maria Jacobini,
publicity postcard.
Giorgio Bertellini
Collection

2. Pina Menichelli (second from right), from *Il romanzo di un giovane povero* (Rinascimento Film, 1920), directed by Amleto Palermi and adapted from Octave Feuillet's *Le roman d'un jeune homme pauvre* (1858).
Giorgio Bertellini Collection

3. Italia Almirante
Manzini as Countess
Turchina in *La
maschera del male,* also
known as *La chiromante*
(Fert Film, 1922),
directed by Mario
Almirante.
Giorgio Bertellini
Collection

city (low) life," but they also gave an artistic dignity to the vernacular
language of the marketplace, the boisterous musicality of the urban dialect, and the cursing or hyperbolizing of its expressive excesses.[22] Both
filmic and theatrical *sceneggiate* activated an intense spectatorial involvement, a collective one, since the stories of passion and revenge were familiar to most members of the underclass—*il popolo*—caught between
passionate sentimental affairs and caustic social and religious restrictions. Because of the architectural intricacies of Naples, the alternating
small squares and narrow alleyways, interclass contacts and confronta-
tions were as common as the mixing of the private and public concerns
of individuals. The socio-psychological entanglements of Neapolitan
cinema, especially in their constantly sensualized tensions, were quite
distant from the regime's idea of gender relationships, public morality,
and social order. As a result, Neapolitan realism was not critically and
industrially allowed to become a viable synecdoche for the much-
awaited new Italian cinema of the 1930s.

In the long run, technology would censor *sceneggiate* more effectively than state bureaucracy. Modern sound synchronization and equipment came to Naples only in the mid-1930s, and by then, the centralization of film production embodied administratively by Direzione Generale per la Cinematografia in the Ministry of Popular Culture and practically by the advanced technological resources of Cinecittà had already tamed its unacceptable cultural difference.[23] Furthermore, in the early 1930s, the representation of regional destitution became utterly unacceptable to the nationalistic and Apollonian demands of the Fascist cultural project.[24] The city's despicable poverty and neglect for its children could not be part of the new "visual system," which was proudly, but abstractly, *nazional popolare,* and the melodramatic resonances of Naples could not be assimilated into the 1930s need for a national "sound score."[25]

Silent Cinema, *Cinégraphie,* and the "Musical Analogy"

The industrial transition between silent and synchronized film constituted a traumatic passage for filmmakers and critics alike. Cinema had long struggled to gain the widespread status and recognition of an art form, so that when sound came about at the end of the second decade of the century, the practitioners and admirers of the recently acclaimed "mute artistry" experienced the shift as a radical disruption.[26] The change from silent to sound cinema, far from being clear cut or circumscribed, spanned a period of countless technological trials, patent suits, and commercial negotiations over national quotas; it was also filled with production experiments with "canned theater," new genres such as the dance musicals, the backstage story, and new film types, including multilingual and, especially in Italy, dubbed films. Before examining the Italian theoretical scenario, however, it is important to briefly mention the contributions of a few European figures who affected, largely without credit, Italy's speculative debate.

With the arrival of sound film, film theorists and directors such as Arnheim, Kracauer, Eisenstein, Pudovkin, Balázs, Clair, Gance, and Epstein lamented the loss of an almost perfected poetic expressivity—that of the mute cinema. Interestingly, their disapproval was not against the use of sound per se, which in the form of music (orchestras, pianos, singing, or even silence) had long accompanied "silent" cinema's performative style. What they opposed were the "talkies," that is, the employment of naturalistic dialogues, which sounded unaesthetic because it was too similar to everyday life conversations. What was lost, in their opinion, was the distinctiveness of poetic language which separated art from reality, poetry from prose, creativity from mere reproduction. Silence and music were excellent vehicles for achieving the poetic prominence of pure form, understood as a sort of rhythm—visual, aural, or both. Plain spoken dialogues were not understood in this way.

Romantic ideals of artistic creation could be defended through counter-strategies such as *asynchronous* and *contrapuntal* strategies that were aimed at emphasizing the dialectic opposition between image and sound. The plastic, synesthetic, and non-naturalistic connections between sight and music were praised by critics and filmmakers (and not just avant-garde artists) even, or especially when, no sound or voice was actually heard.[27] Throughout the 1920s, in fact, European criticism had perfected an idea and a practice of "pure cinema," according to which the cinematic image retained an artistic and peculiar access to the realms of beauty, lyrical expression, and truth. French critics, in particular, in their privileging of an elitist ambition to achieve high art and Romantic creation (Canudo, Vuillermoz, or Dulac), of popular realism (Delluc and Moussinac), and of cineplastic or analytic endowment (Faure and Epstein) devoted a close and convergent attention to the *specificity* of film language.

In their approach, the distinctiveness of the cinema related not simply to the film's basic unit, the single shot, in its expressive capacity to frame and lighten the mise-en-scène (*photogénie*), but it also pervaded the "photogenic mobility" of the images (Epstein), their cadence and vibration, inside or between the shots. Such mobility was termed, with a linguistic metaphor, *cinégraphie*. Movement of objects, changes of framings, and editing patterns defined the cinema's most peculiar feature, the *rhythm*, which made the visual film medium artistically closer to an aural one, that is, to a musical composition.[28] Hence, the audiovisual dynamics of film were to be experienced not only through the classical terms of storytelling—as these critics polemically described American movies—but they also had to be understood eclectically, since cinema's eloquence relied on various other domains (emotional, plastic, poetic, *and* musical). A similar multisensorial approach was also voiced by Soviet filmmakers, most prominently by Dziga Vertov, who envisioned a new film aesthetics that combined visuality with radio wireless transmissions.[29]

What should be noted here is that rhythm and musicality were recurring terms and concepts used to describe and designate film's specific language at a time when the transition to sound had not yet occurred. The coming of the talkies would eventually dismiss silent cinema's musical poetics as inconsistent or inapplicable. Yet, the "musical analogy," as David Bordwell aptly defined the critical tendency to stress film's formal structure and nonrepresentational qualities, had been constantly used in European film theory and criticism: at first to master cinema's lack of perfect realism, later to tame its reproductive excesses.[30]

In the early 1910s, the use of musical references was a reaction to (and a continuation of) long-standing platonic anxieties over the imitative proficiency of the photographic image and its apparent lack of formal construction. Cinema's link to reality was reduced to an imperfect copy, a silent, pale shadow.[31] Accordingly, the perception of the *flawed reproductive nature* of film's mechanical visuality long threatened the application of artistic attributes (genius, creation, *poiesis*) to the moviemaking process. How could a cinematic representation be described as a work of art when it lacked accuracy, formal structure, an author's invention, and, due to its reproductive mechanics, even ontological *presence*?[32] In the long run, however, the judgment was turned upside down. The very limits of the film image, its technical imperfection and its highly selective photographic process, represented a mark of artistic expression and directors' creativity. Rudolf Arnheim's 1933 discussion of the dangers of the perfect reproduction (which he called "the complete film") due to the introduction of sound, colors, and three-dimensional film, best conceptualized this position.[33]

In short, cinema's imperfect photographic reproduction was first an indication of film's lack of artistry, then became the very sign of it. The aesthetic structure of films, their acknowledged freedom from a realistic obligation, was described with lexical borrowings from the musical realm, not from the visual one. The most frequent term was that of *rhythm*, which was invariably vaguely defined. Rhythm appeared to retain the universal appeal of music, poetry, and art in the broadest sense. In Italy, the articles by Sebastiano Arturo Luciani, published since 1913, and Pirandello's criticism of sound film represent the best examples of this critical tendency. And yet, an Italian account of the *transition* from silent to sound film cannot entirely coincide with the cosmopolitan *vulgata* I briefly traced above. Italy's cultural situation—namely, its lack of a linguistic unity—posed unique challenges to Italian sound cinema.

From a broad perspective, the most pressing questions about the new kind of cinema had to do with three aesthetic realms: vision, sound, and spoken words—which were each differently perceived in their relations with art, technology, and knowledge. Vision had been repeatedly accompanied by a sense of *uneasiness*—when optical reproductions were perceived either as exact or as flawed—so that vision could hardly constitute a sole guarantor of knowledge, truth, and artistic value. Sound, instead, understood as pure music or as a chain of phonic-rhythmic resonances, had been equated to poetry, a polysemic density of artistic

signification leading to a superior gnosis and connected to the most ar-
cane and inexpressible realms of reality. Lastly, spoken words, at least in
their first appearance, had been regarded as an impure flow of normal
language, or language-as-vehicle. Their employment in early sound cinema constituted a major source of anxiety about the medium's artistic
destiny, its potential obligations to a realist aesthetics, and its link to
national languages and specific cultural traditions.[34] Concerns about the
possible loss of *artistic legitimacy* was in fact accompanied by the quick
acknowledgment that cinema was losing its *linguistic universality*—
which was traditionally praised as its own specificity and as the Esperanto of the modern industrial era.

In Italy, the challenge of realism was furthered by the difficulties of
its aural practicability. In the past, music, and not any other language,
had constituted the discursive analog to define art as well as any form
of national-popular communication. Italian culture in fact had had
quite a singular approach to the value of sound and music, as Gramsci's
discussion of "operatic taste" demonstrated.

> In Italian popular culture music has to some extent substituted
> that artistic expression which in other countries is provided by the
> popular novel and . . . musical geniuses have had the kind of popu-
> larity which writers have lacked. . . . Why did Italian artistic "de-
> mocracy" have a musical and not a "literary" expression? Can the
> fact that its language was not national, but cosmopolitan, as music
> is, be connected to the lack of a national-popular character in the
> Italian intellectuals?[35]

Due to a long-standing linguistic separation between intellectuals
and common people, the *conundrum* of how to represent common people
speaking in a national tongue—instead of in their more natural dialect—was also intensified by the need in the early 1930s to develop an
unprecedented realistic and nationalistic aesthetics. Until then, Italy
had been a nation dominated by worldly cultural traditions (and tongues),
which had struggled to repress regional or local theater, literature, and
cinema as minor, worthless, or even aberrant—as the case of Neapolitan
cinema showed. During Fascism, very few voices, apart from Gramsci,
questioned "the rhetorical prejudice (originating in literature) according to which the Italian nation ha[d] always existed, from ancient Rome
to the present day." Additional difficulties in developing a modern idea
of cinema came from the pervasiveness of Croce's idealism, which
viewed "content" as extrinsic to art and urged a separation between the
"history of art" and the "history of culture." As Gramsci emphasized,
these "totem[s] and intellectual conceits, although politically 'useful' in

the period of national struggle as a means of stirring up and concentrating energies, are critically inept and become, ultimately, a weakness because they do not permit a correct appreciation of the effort of those generations who really fought to establish a modern Italy."[36]

Accordingly, when a realist film aesthetic became a political and an expressive need, the problematics of a national-popular culture became apparent. The most conservative alternative, but also the one whose resilience is worth documenting here, was to resort to the Italian film discourse of the 1910s and 1920s. At the time, film and art critics had been mainly focused on clarifying the defining *artistic materiality* of the cinema, which was appreciated not only for its fantastic and exotic visual displays but also for its musical and silent enticement (and not for its verbal signification). Before sound, film visuality was understood as a musical vibration of spaces and figures, aphasic and logophobic, which was quite distant from the candid transparency claimed a few years later.

In the critical debates of the 1930s and 1940s, in fact, the majority of contributions that insisted on cinema's realistic vocation tended to avoid any "musical analogy" to describe the peculiar language of movies. (Neo)realist critics naturally resorted to film's photographic indexicality (not just for propaganda purposes, but also for pedagogical ones) to proudly exhibit Italy's contemporary reality. Sound metaphors would have emphasized cinema's universal formality and its non-mimetic qualities—two features that are politically disengaging and ineffectual. And yet, here and there, a few critics or directors still voiced ideas of art and cinema utterly untouched by the rhetorics of realism.

Art, Musicality, and Pantomime: Cinema as a Form of Universal Expression in 1910s and 1920s Film Discourse

Italian cinema did not enjoy regular critical coverage in national dailies or cultural periodicals until the early 1910s.[37] Associated with popular fairs, traveling shows, and Grand Guignol, cinema was long regarded among intellectual circles as a vulgar exhibition of modern taste. Early opinions about film varied widely; they ranged from technical judgments to journalistic inquiries, from moralistic allusion to sociological insights and, quite remarkably, scattered aesthetic notes appeared as firm as definitive theoretical assessments. At first, the emphasis was on the novelty and success of the film show in general (the composition, behavior, and movie-going habits of the audience), but few references were made to specific films. Novelists, journalists, and poets (Gozzano,

Deledda, Verga, but also D'Annunzio and Pirandello), who were usually engaged in highly respectable but financially unrewarding practices, regarded the cinema as a quick opportunity to raise their income. They lent their talents, but restricted their official, public involvement.[38] Initially, even Gramsci did not show a particular interest in the new medium, defining it as a "visual curiosity, a distraction" and a cheaper form of "vulgar theater."

Cinema's adverse reputation explains the consistent efforts of movie producers to upgrade the medium to a higher level of public décor and narrative respectability.[39] From the start, Italian film companies had capitalized on the one hand on the traditional association of Italian culture with highbrow art, splendid antiquity, and atemporal classicism while on the other they exploited the easy availability of historical and natural sceneries and cheap labor. That led to a remarkable success among international markets. However, marketing Italian cinema within Italian culture appeared to constitute a much harder job.

It took the release of *Cabiria* in 1914, produced by Turin-based production company Itala, to endow movies with an illustrious and artistic character. Apart from its international success and its unprecedented visual achievements (i.e., special optical effects and unseen tracking shots), *Cabiria* constituted an outstanding cultural moment in Italy, for it marked the much-advertised entree of *il vate* Gabriele D'Annunzio and composer Ildebrando Pizzetti—the two most celebrated "artists" of the time—into the "foreign" industrial world of the cinema.[40] After *Cabiria*, the debate surrounding the artistry of the cinema reached a new level: cinema began to be regarded as something more than a circus-like entertainment or an exotic postcard.[41] The question of what *kind* of art cinema was became deeply intertwined with the question of who a film's author was and whether movies were going to replace theater tout court.[42] These discussions made their way into national newspapers and cultural periodicals that were heavily dominated by literary critics of Crocean, formalist ideology (which was often of erudite and antiquated taste), thus receiving a wider and singular endowment. Once the artistic merits were granted, then a series of unprecedented (and anti-Crocean) problems arose: if cinema was an art, what was its specific character and which relationship and differences did it entertain with other arts—especially theater and literature?

In Italy, D'Annunzio was the first and most influential figure to formulate what looked like a full-fledged idea of cinema, which he elaborated in comparison to the theater. In his rare contribution on film theory, D'Annunzio described the contemporary crisis of theater as a "crisis of the word," and recognized the stage's new possibilities in

4. The Temple of Moloch in Carthage. *Cabiria* (Itala Film, 1914),
directed by Giovanni Pastrone.
Courtesy of The Museum of Modern Art Film Stills Archive

pantomimic performances accompanied by music.[43] Because it is capable
of rendering the deepest nature of things—the poet added—music
should not lose its elementary purity by mixing it with theater's traditional wordings. Instead, he continued, only cinema offered music a
unique possibility of expressive freedom and sovereignty. Cinema, for
D'Annunzio was the realm of fantastic transfigurations, surprising
metamorphoses which could visually articulate melodic waves and fas-
cinate even the simplest minds of the masses.[44]

How could D'Annunzio talk about the musicality of film's images
when, apparently, they were mute, since only at premieres or at special
screenings was the film spectacle accompanied by a full orchestra? The
answer that a simple piano accompaniment (more rarely an orchestra)
was very often present at film exhibitions is not sufficient; it is also necessary to unearth what is now a lost perception of early film shows: the
mere rhythmical succession of images and the pantomimic performance
of actors and actresses. By equating cinema with the "art of silence,"
the Italian poet meant to stress the speechless uniqueness of an optical

5. The imprisonment of Maciste, the faithful African slave, played
by Bartolomeo Pagano. *Cabiria* (Itala Film, 1914), directed by
Giovanni Pastrone. D'Annunzio named Maciste after Hercules'
ancient nickname.
Courtesy of The Museum of Modern Art Film Stills Archive

flow which still displayed phonic features in the musical stream of its
shifting tableaux.

To epitomize his position, D'Annunzio coined the key expression
arte muta, which by 1915, together with *teatro muto, scena muta*, or
dramma muto, was already commonly used to describe and designate
film's specific language.[45] What is interesting in these locutions is that
they speculatively seem to postulate an approach to silent film language
in terms of a *double textuality*, differentiating between, and converging,
visuality and verbal language. In *Cabiria*, as in most film *dannunziani*
(i.e., *Ma l'amor mio non muore* [1913] and *Carnevalesca* [1918]), the use
of learned intertitles produced a semantic and symbolic overcharge of
objects, gestures, and expressions already emphasized by the histrionic
acting style of the characters. Poetry and pantomime were the reciprocal equivalents (from verbal to gestural and vice versa) of grandiose
spiritual displays. Their performative redundancy was, supposedly, an

6. **Lyda Borelli in *Carnevalesca* (Cines, 1918), directed by
Amleto Palermi.
Giorgio Bertellini Collection**

unmistakable sign of artistry and universality.[46] Such a conception of
the film medium—a lasting one, as we will see—could not have been
more elitist and distant from the late 1920s necessity for a truly national
and realistic film production.

D'Annunzio was not alone in theorizing film poetics. His long-time
friend, film and art critic Ricciotto Canudo, who was born in Italy but
was educated and active in France, had included the cinema among the
most important arts in a famous essay titled "La naissance d'un sixième
Art. Essai sur le Cinématographe," published in 1911.[47] Although it is
not clear to what extent D'Annunzio "adopted" his friend's speculations, and although Canudo's influence is still underestimated within
Italian film criticism, the cultural affinities between *il vate* and *le baré-
sien* are unmistakable. That year, Canudo wrote:

> [The sixth art] will be a superb conciliation of the Rhythm of
> Space (the Plastic Arts) and the Rhythms of Time (Music and Po-
> etry). The theater has so far best realized such a conciliation, but
> in an ephemeral manner because the plastic characteristics are al-
> ways different. The new manifestation of Art should really be more
> precisely a *Painting and a Sculpture developing in Time,* as in music
> and poetry, which realize themselves by transforming air into
> rhythm for the duration of their execution. . . . The cinemato-

graph is thus the theater of a new Pantomime, consecrated *Paint-ing in motion*. It constitutes the complete manifestation of a unique creation by modern man. As the modern Pantomime, it is the new *dance of manifestations*.[48]

The inevitable comparison with theater identified cinema both as a medium lacking an audible verbal expression (although words were written and read in the intertitles) and one which could turn its silence into a more intense means of expression. The post-Romantic attraction for indeterminate and secret correspondences or symbolist terrains of significations appropriated pantomime as its preferred means of expression and as the cipher of poetic or artistic realms. Conceiving of art as the terrain of secret knowledge, silent features, and the utterance of words (not just their meaning), Canudo invites the spectator to entertain a special connection to the secrets and souls of the characters.

Throughout the second half of the 1910s and into the 1920s, this position would be perfected by various contributors, music and art critics, Futurists, writers, and playwrights. Mostly of them were Crocean; that is, they had a keen (and elitist) urgency to preserve art isolated from everyday life and to prevent cinema's marvelous illusions from being confused with an industry or a mass medium.

A crucial theoretical contribution on the relationships between cinema, music, and theater came from Sebastiano Arturo Luciani (1884–1950), a versatile critic who was mainly interested in music and was also briefly engaged as a screenwriter and film director. Like Canudo, Luciani was in tune with idealistic aesthetics; he vigorously distinguished between the means of photographic *reproductions* and the means of photographic *expression*. If the former would convert the film medium simply into a positivist device, the latter would turn it into a form of art.[49]

From his first contributions, which were published in 1913, Luciani was concerned with cinema's artistic predicament, which he lucidly located in the capacity of film to combine imaginary subject matters, mute acting style, and musical accompaniment. In "Il cinematografo e l'arte," published in the cultural periodical *Il Marzocco* on 10 August 1913, Luciani responded to an article published in the same periodical a week before on 27 July, written by theater critic Luciano Zuccoli. Zuccoli had described cinema as an inferior and parasitic form of art which was illegitimately luring narrations and audiences away from established literary and theatrical productions.

Luciani acknowledged cinema's poetic immaturity, but noted that the pantomimes performed in the movies were rather different from the traditional ones. If in the latter, he claimed, actors attempted to replace the word with their expressive gestures, in the cinema, gestures did not substitute for the word, they accompanied it. For Luciani, that occurred although no spoken word was heard: speechless gestures per se did not exhaust film's unique expressivity. Thus, the silence of the cinema called for a necessary musical accompaniment; the aural emptiness of the film image had to be filled with sound, and the end result constituted cinema's unique and modern artistic form.[50]

By 1916, he had begun to describe such expressivity with various (and complex) locutions such as "modern pantomimic musical drama" (*dramma mimico musicale moderno*), "musical stage drama" (*dramma scenico musicale*), and "impressionistic drama" (*dramma impressionista*). With them, and through examples from the stage representations of Wagner, Luciani emphasized cinema's unique synthesis of musical rhythm and well-choreographed mise-en-scène. As in D'Annunzio's Ovidian assessment, the purely reproductive burden of movies could have not been more explicitly discarded.

The need to define cinema as an art and to distinguish it from theater dominated Luciani's analysis throughout the following years. His books, *Verso una nuova arte. Il cinematografo* (1920), *L'antiteatro. Il cinematografo come arte* (1928), and *Il cinema e le arti* (1942), helped him develop his earlier intuitions in a more systematic and extensive fashion. Relying on the Crocean notion of art as "pure expression" and a "transfiguration of reality," and granting the "artistic cinema" (distinguished from the documentary one) such aesthetic endowment, Luciani tirelessly stressed the difference between cinema and theater:

> Theater, since it is generated from [the] lyric, is verbal, static and tends toward exterior movement, which is theatricality. . . . Cinema is visual and dynamic and through its exterior movements tends to enhance an interior lyricism, often translated in the character's dialogue or intertitles.
>
> Theater and cinema are, as anybody can see, two forms of art essentially different: since one performs from the inside to the outside, the other from the outside to the inside.[51]

D'Annunzio felt that because of its "centripetal" force, only the cinema uniquely enhanced the inner musicality of human facial expressions: the rhythmical sequence of film close-ups was capable of turning the human face into visual scenery and dramatis personae altogether, thus conveying true animated psychological portraits.[52] As a multisensorial form of art, cinema was thus able to reveal the musical overtones of reality through its careful manipulation of light and shadow.[53] So far, however—he insisted music had been added to images as a mere accompaniment. Film artists had not realized that producing a film script should be more like composing a symphony than writing a drama. A film ought to be more an experience of tempo, duration, eurythmy than one of intellectual concepts or ideas. That is why Luciani praised *The Big Parade* (K. Vidor, 1925) and the *Ballets Russes* of Sergei Diaghilev for their synthesis of aural and visual strategies and criticized the musical strategies of *Rapsodia satanica* (Nino Oxilia, 1917) by Pietro Mascagni, *Frate Sole* (Mario Corsi, 1918) by Luigi Mancinelli, and *Fantasia bianca* (Alfredo Masi & Severo Pozzati, 1919) by Vittorio Guito for their accessory use of the music.[54]

> They have composed their music by trying to comment on the main action, scene by scene, detail by detail, when music, instead, should determine the action, not just follow it: it could evoke images, not just translate them into sound. It is from the world of sounds that one has to arrive at the one of images.[55]

If a film has to be born from music, or through music—as Blasetti would identically phrase it in 1950—what kind of film was to be truly "cinematic"? Luciani mentioned a few foreign examples: Disney's *Silly Symphonies* (1929–1935), which were particularly noteworthy for their perfect synchronism of musical and visual scores; Walter Ruttmann's *In der Nacht* (1931) for its use of Schumann; and Max Reinhardt's *A Midsummer Night's Dream* (1935) for its use of Mendelssohn. The only Italian film discussed was Franco Casavola's *Le sintesi visive* (1924). Inevitably, in such audiovisual poetics of bringing together musical resonances with human or natural figures, sounds with colors and shapes, the cinema Luciani envisioned was resolutely *non-realistic* and *logophobic*.

Because his critical interventions continued for more than a decade after the introduction of sound cinema—Luciani's last study was published in 1942—it is quite interesting to register his detailed account of sound films. It shows the extent of Luciani's attachment to premodern aesthetic patterns and his indifference to contemporary challenges. For him, the arrival of sound technology had misconstrued cinema's proper expression by enhancing its artless "realistic disposition" and by creating hybrids that alternated spoken dialogues and mute scenes. Their different tempos showed that music had the rhythm words lacked. Often citing Nietzsche, Wagner, Caravaggio, Debussy, and the tradition of melodrama, Luciani granted music an absolute stylistic prominence. His solution was to allow music to "escort" sotto voce all dialogues and erase all decorative and "realistic" noises. The *fonogenia* (phonogeny) of

S. A. LUCIANI

L'ANTITEATRO

IL CINEMATOGRAFO COME ARTE

CON 14 INCISIONI E UNA NOVELLA COMPLETAMENTE SCENEGGIATA

LA VOCE
EDITRICE
ROMA

7. Sebastiano Arturo
Luciani, *L'antiteatro. Il
cinematografo come arte*
(Rome: La Voce, 1928).

sound elements, including silence, had to dominate the *fotogenia* (photogeny) of the visual score, especially through post-synchronization.

Luciani did not devote much space to the linguistic features of the spoken dialogues. He was not interested in the problematics of the rapport between the quality of the utterance and the social or cultural status of the speaking characters, that is, in the "realism" of the representation.[56] In fact, the audiovisual tactics and ideals of a realist cinema, *en plein air,* were utterly discouraged.

> What matters is that music should be the connective tissue of a
> film, which would be like an organism enlivened by a rigorous
> rhythm, not by an amorphous series of dialogues and noises:
> transfiguration, as in every art work, not reproduction of reality.[57]

Displaying a formalist disregard for cinema's cultural and industrial dimensions, Luciani long remained faithful to his anti-mimetic idealism. In the early 1940s, the Italian critic was not simply refurbishing an obsolete and old-fashioned conception of the film spectacle. His attitude toward the medium was not utterly erased by the confusedly realist en-

8. S. A. Luciani, *Il cinema e le arti* (Siena: Ticci Editore, 1942).

deavors of the 1930s. Instead, it resurfaced here and there in the Italian film culture not engaged in praising naturalistic vocations for movies. Film historian Roberto Paolella, whom I will discuss below, displayed deep affinities with Luciani's audiovisual theorizations.

Contemporary and analogous to Luciani's earliest anti-realism was Futurism's fascination with the multisensorial and anti-mimetic expressivity of the new medium. Although cinema came quite late among the professed interests of the Italian avant-garde—especially due to Marinetti's prejudices against photography—the movement consistently displayed a keen attraction for the musicality of words, images, and colors. In 1916, seven years after the first publication of *Il manifesto futurista,* Filippo Tommaso Marinetti (together with Arnaldo Ginna, Bruno Corra, Emilio Settimelli, Giacomo Balla, and Remo Chiti) published *Il primo manifesto per la cinematografia futurista.*[58] In the cinema, symptomatically defined as *teatro senza parole* (theater without words), they envisioned a new kind of art that was very distant from current film dramatizations inspired by traditional theater or literature, which was, in their opinion, both passé and anti-modern. Futurists felt that cinema should serve the prismatic talent of the authentic modern artist by performing *polyexpressive symphonies* through all sorts of tools and sources: real life, colors, "Words-In-Freedom," the chromatic and plastic music of silent images, and even chaos. That year, the same Futurist group starred and directed in the first Futurist feature film, titled *Vita futurista*.[59]

Praising fantastic transfigurations of reality, Futurists endorsed rhythmical and metaphorical editing, asynchronous musical (and noise) accompaniments, and abstract and unreal representations of the world and of the human body: "We will set in motion words-in-freedom which will break the borders of literature, we will be marching toward painting, music, and the art of noise and will be laying a wonderful bridge between words and the real objects."[60] Unlike what happened in 1920s French and German film culture, though, Futurist film manifestos and their (rare) avant-garde productions did not initiate in Italy a consistent cinematic practice—although since the mid-1920s Marinetti had been claiming that "abstract cinema" was an Italian or, better, a Futurist invention. The incapacity or unwillingness of Futurists to cope with the industrial structure of cinema or with the popular appeal of narrative films led not just to their isolation but also to the dismissal of their poetics, since their scattered attempts did not demonstrate viable alternatives to traditional cinematic practices.[61]

The only author in tune with Futurists' idea of cinema, but working both on the threshold of the Italian avant-garde movement and within the established industrial cinema apparatus, was Anton Giulio Bragaglia, a multi-talented artist and critic whose interests spanned from archeology to photography, cinema, art, and theater. Like the Futurists, his contribution to sound film was more consistent and influential on a speculative level than on a practical one.[62]

In 1929, Bragaglia published a study on sound film, *Il film sonoro*, in which he expressed his reservations on the cinema's latest technological novelty and discussed silent film's "inherent" artistic possibilities. Like his predecessors, Bragaglia did not address the ultimate problematics of sound cinema and Italian language: his analysis reproduced a most typical abstract aesthetic stance. In his opinion, if the theater had the advantage and the curse of the word, cinema had the aesthetic prerogative of *visually* reproducing music and songs—not just plain dialogues. For him, the adding of sound inevitably erased the *artistry* of film, that is, the musicality of its optical score, the uniqueness of its pantomimic acting style, and its dreamlike allure. Sound cinema's "gross immediacy" contrasted with the speechless magic of silent movies. Furthermore, the aesthetic novelty of merging images and dialogues dramatically prevented cinema from remaining the Esperanto of modern times, forcing the medium into Babelian divisions.[63]

Bragaglia also touched upon the technical difficulties of sound re-

9. Anton Giulio
Bragaglia, *Il film sonoro*
(Milan: Edizioni
Corbaccio, 1929).

cording. He discussed the problematic interchangeability of sound systems, the necessity of live mixers ("because what is true is not per se artistic"), the need to shoot in a studio (artificial light versus natural light), and the need to arrange the mise-en-scène on the basis of recording necessities. Yet a "fully spoken" film would have been—in his words —"unbearable."[64] To save its original mark of modernity or its fast rhythm, cinema was not to imitate the stage, especially with verbose and silly dialogues; instead, it had to focus on what it could do best. To reproduce the quick pace of modern times through songs and music gave movies their peculiarly direct and universal form of communication. Quoting Luciani and Pirandello, Bragaglia insisted on a conception of cinema as the "universal language of pantomime and appearances" whose pure tongue, he claimed, was music. In one of his most logophobic and condescending pages, he wrote:

> One needs to take cinema away from literature and bring it closer to music, since cinema must be the visual language of music. Music talks to everybody, and everybody, by listening to it, is able to imagine something related to music's own rhythm: images which

are delicate, vague, painful, joyful, three-dimensional, dreamlike, or related to dance and flight. One does not need any other vision or music. The two senses par excellence, sight and hearing, lead us into our subconscious; whereas literature stems from our consciousness and carries out, with its words, a judgment which is not for everybody to understand.[65]

Bragaglia never spoke of any particular spectator; his reference was always sociologically undetermined. Still, in his opinion, the transition to sound was driving the cinema toward the communicative crisis and poetic inconsistencies already experienced by theater and literature. Silent cinema had been an art, but sound cinema was just a new technique—and one that was still impure and primitive.

An aesthetically more complex contribution came from Luigi Pirandello, who had been consistently interested in the communicative power and limits of language, but whose attitude toward the cinema displayed some remarkable adjustments. In his 1915 novel *Si gira . . .* (aka *Quaderni di Serafino Gubbio operatore* [*Shoot!*]), he narrated the life and the daily struggles of a film cameraman and discussed the cinema's technological dangers in quite a dystopian manner. In the novel, the objective camera does not simply capture the outside reality *as it is* but also depersonalizes characters (like cinema's famous *dive*), reducing them to an histrionic vacuity and an unsettling loss of corporeality.[66]

Yet, if in the mid-1910s, cinema's "silent" exhibitions were still regarded by Pirandello as performatively inadequate, since the only sound that could tame their deficiency was the mechanical *bruitage*, the flickering of the movie camera, the late 1920s technological novelties and the subsequent introduction of sound films deeply affected his attitude toward the film medium. Cinema's technological innovations enhanced his formulation of a unique film poetics that had been inconceivable to him a few years earlier.[67]

In his late 1920s writings, Pirandello lucidly and consistently distinguished between "sound cinema" (*film sonoro*) and "spoken cinema" (*film parlato*)—a separation which had already emerged in Luciani's and Bragaglia's speculations but was also commonly used among film periodicals. This distinction, which favored sound cinema over spoken cinema, was based on the claim that the new forms of synchronized sound cinema were simply a form of (unnatural) "canned theater" and that, as such, they could not harm theater's poetic preeminence. In particular, Pirandello's well-known objection to the "spoken cinema," published in several leading papers in the spring of 1929,[68] participated in a common defensive attitude which ascribed the "presence of the word" to the artistic realms of theater and literature, but not to moving pictures:

> The voice in sound films, even when it reaches a perfect quality, and we are quite distant from such perfection, is a machine voice; true voice stems from a living body, and here a living body is missing. Let's go even further. Film images are always distant, figures we observe as moving in far away locations: a house, a steamship, a forest, a mountain, a valley, a street; outside, then, the theater where the film is being projected; whereas the voice always sounds inside the theater, always present and thus unnatural and unbearable. Now, to give the cinema the spoken word in a mechanical way is no remedy for the fundamental error, because, instead of healing the sore, it makes it worse by burying the cinema deeper and deeper in literature. With the word mechanically engraved on the film, the cinema—which is the dumb expression of images and the language of appearances [loses] all illusion of reality.[69]

Pirandello thus claimed that "talking close-ups" sounded artificial, unrealistic, and detrimental to the original and authentic non-verbal vocation of the cinema.

> In order to patch up this fault a still greater fault has been committed, that of showing close-ups of the talking images. . . . The lips of those huge images in the foreground are moving in vain because the voice does not issue from their mouths, but comes out in a grotesque manner from the machine—a machine-made voice far from human, the vulgar muttering of ventriloquists accompanied by the buzzing, frizzling noises of phonographs. But even when technical improvements have eliminated this frizzling nuisance, and have obtained a perfect reproduction of the human voice, the ailment will still be there, for the obvious reason that images are images, and images cannot talk.[70]

Without ever erasing the aural predicament of the image, Pirandello emphasized cinema's mute visuality by rejecting any interference with verbal tropes (literary or theatrical, including songs) since they would have turned the most universal medium into a national form of theatrical melodrama. What did not work for him was the mixing of images, sound, and speech: the first two belonged to the screen, the last did not. Still, film images had to be "seen" and "heard" because of their striking musical resonance, which he termed *cinemelografia,* the "visual language of music."[71]

As a man of literature and theater, Pirandello defended the artistic

10. Luigi Pirandello,
"Pirandello Views the
'Talkies'," *The New York
Times Magazine*, Sunday,
28 July 1929, Section V,
p. 1.

specificity of his two most familiar media. That is why he never theorized or developed a full-fledged verbal dramatization for the cinema, nor did he ever write a true *film parlato*. Such a venture would have threatened the specific and original artistic configurations proper to stage and literature. Instead, his writings on film, and in particular his much-discussed contribution to the film event *Acciaio* (produced in 1933 by Cines, under Emilio Cecchi's "enlightened" supervision, and directed by Walter Ruttmann, with music composed by Gian Francesco Malipiero), consistently displayed his critical affinity with pre-sound Italian and European film poetics.[72]

Aside from the innumerable misunderstandings and accidents around the production of *Acciaio*, Pirandello's intentions were quite explicit.[73] Interviewed in 1932 by Enrico Roma for the periodical *Comoedia*, Pirandello explained:

> I composed a script that is a true musical score. In many scenes I took into account the effects to be achieved through sounds, just like a musician would do for the instrumental section of an opera.

The sound score will have a great role in the film. At a certain point, the rhythm of the machines will become human; a perfect synchronism between the mechanical movement and the vibration of human life will be reached.[74]

Cinematic expression was not paired with verbal articulation, but with music, rhythm, and pulsation. Thus the question about film's nature was more than Laocoontian (that is, connected to hierarchy of arts); it was also communicative. And yet, Pirandello did not apply to the medium of film the same linguistic mindfulness he so carefully displayed in his Italian prose. Like a modern hymn, cinema was to be popular but cryptic, direct but unspoken, eloquent but aphasic.

At this point, the understanding of the cinema as a musical performance was seemingly limited to critics or artists working in the field *before* or *during* the transition to sound. Although in the 1930s and 1940s, silent melodramas no longer amused or overwhelmed their audiences, the attachment to silent film poetics, as we have seen, did not die completely. It would resurface in the work of film historian Roberto Paolella, who in the mid-1960s was still approaching the medium through "older" tropes of pantomime, plasticity, and rhythm. Although this essay focuses on the aesthetic debates about cinema as they emerged before neorealism, Paolella's "tardy" contributions are symptomatic of a speculative continuity that sheds light on an unresolved question of Italian film discourse.

Author of both a silent and a sound film history as well as numerous articles on film history and aesthetics, Paolella has been all too often consulted as simply a source of references, hardly ever as an original critic.[75] His work, instead, is very unique for its time because it addresses the specificity of the cinematic expression mainly in terms of gestural language, or pantomime, and utterly ignores the political and ideological investments of other contemporary film critics. In two essays published in 1943 in the periodical *Cinema* and in a later, more elaborated, version printed as the introduction to his 1956 *Storia del cinema muto*, Paolella attempts to retrace the historical genealogy of the language of gesture and mimicry in contrast to verbal language and to the read the former as the truest aesthetic proficiency of the cinematic expression.

Employing concepts and tropes derived from the linguistic and anthropological investigations of Marcel Jousse of the mid-1920s and the ethnological work of Ernesto De Martino of the 1940s and 1950s, Paolella distinguishes among different forms of *mimicry*.[76] Identifying

them by degrees of complexity, he discusses three types: reactive, voluntary, and cutting/combining; the last one strikingly resembles film
language.[77]

In order to show the inherent centrality of mimicry for cinema, including sound films, Paolella distinguishes between oral and written
forms of verbal language (Italian linguist Giovanni Nencioni termed
these forms *parlato-parlato* and *parlato-scritto*).[78] He then claims that the
former is more elementary and spontaneous than the latter—whose syntax governs modern forms of communications—and thus conjoins the
immediacy and naturalness of orality with the language of gesture and
mimicry.[79] Against the predominant model of the Word and its written,
prosaic form, cinema is able to restore more authentic approaches to
knowledge and reality, and thus to perform, in Tom Gunning's expression, a better "gnostic mission."[80] Cinema, like symbolist poetry, brings
humanity to its ancestral age and rescues human communication from
the banality of everyday conversation. Citing Valéry, Mallarmé, and
Eleonora Duse, Paolella revives the gestural and lyrical intensity that
endowed silent cinema at its apex, but he complained about both operatic and verbal exchanges and useless "realistic" noises in sound films.[81]
In the mid-1950s, he alone argued that film theory and practice needed
a new start.

Ultimately, in his survey on sound cinema published in 1966, the
transition between silent films and talkies is "wishfully" described as an
expressive continuance. Accordingly, the claimed affinity between the
two periods is played out in a symbolist manner: literal significations are
in both cases transfigured by mute or musical intensities. With the technical developments of synthetic and electronic music, Paolella noted,
cinema might again abandon the realistic obligations of conventional
dubbing and assemble, through invention and selections, unheard and
fantastic sonorities. Citing Wagner, he envisioned a form of musical accompaniment that "would no longer make us blind while open-eyed" or
disturb the poetic unfolding of the images but would instead release
Baudelairean correspondences between light and sound.[82]

As one reads Paolella's contentions, which were written as late as the
mid-1960s, a few pressing questions inevitably arise. They are questions
that exceed the goals of this essay, but not the extent of the subject.
If one examines post-1945 Italian cinema, what are the relationships
among images, sound, and words? Was the solution of the neorealists
an irreversible one? Or was their arrangement a parenthesis? Did the
"realist vocation" of modern Italian cinema, understood as a granted
privilege to the visual score, tacitly prevent directors and screenwriters
from adopting silence, sounds, and words in a meaningful, inventive,

and imaginary manner? Had a politically engaged notion of cinema as "visual evidence" prevailed? What could then be said of Antonioni's logophobic cinema or some of Visconti's *mélo* films, such as *Death in Venice*, or the sound and verbal score in Pasolini's films?

"Now You See It, Now You Don't (Hear It)"; or, The Riddles of Realism

Silent cinema's fiction film practices did not attempt to document or narrate contemporary reality; their effort to create a "suitable past" or an "adventurous present" was performed by aiming at the characteristics of spectacularity, refinement, and artistic value. At the end of the 1920s, however, modern poetic requirements such as "realism" and "cultural nationality" assailed the post-Romantic and Crocean ideals of art as pure form (which had praised cinema as a multisensorial, synesthetic form of poetry) in the name of a much-needed and effective medium of mass communication.[83] Interestingly, Blasetti was among the pioneers of this cultural project for a new Italian cinema.

Throughout the 1930s, often under the influence of Soviet, German (*Neue Sachlichkeit*), and American new poetics, realism was a shared endeavor by Italian novelists, filmmakers, writers, and critics "to create a culture that would reflect the notion of fascism as a revolutionary 'third way' after liberalism and Marxism. . . . If Italian realism was to be 'revolutionary,' though, it was also clearly distinguishable from contemporary realist literature in Weimar Germany and Russia. Fascists claimed that while the materialistic mentality of leftist authors limited them to the mere reproduction or documentation of reality, the new Italian novelists were free to transfigure reality and produce works that would chronicle the present and yet bear the imprint of an individual creative and ethical sensibility."[84] The issue, of course, was whether a "national reality," or specifically, a reality (and a folklore) that would have symbolically appeared as "national," was *there* to be captured (visually and aurally) and even transfigured for artistic purposes or, instead, had to be somehow invented.

The cinema of the 1930s participated in the public circulation of an "invented," compromised, but still highly literary national tongue. Films were part of a larger arena of cultural and performative endeavors which included radio broadcasts (especially, but not only, of Mussolini's speeches), the theater and stage comedy's linguistic transformations (from the late *café-chantant* and *rivista* to early forms of *avanspettacolo*), mass journalism, the long-term nationalization of operas, and the rise of Italian modern *canzonette*.[85]

Popular melodies and songs became then an easy and necessary texture of film style. *Canzonette* and famous opera arias (or *contrafacta*) were in fact widely adopted as narrative devices and musical accompaniments. If Gennaro Righelli's *La canzone dell'amore* (1930), the first Italian sound film, mixed literary dialogues with serious and cheerful tunes[86] or Alessandro Blasetti's *Resurrectio* (1931) and *Terra madre* (1932) praised workers' and peasants' musical folklore as refreshing and uncontaminated, Mario Camerini's *Gli uomini, che mascalzoni!* (1932) launched Vittorio De Sica's career as a singer, notably with the hit song "Parlami d'amore, Mariù."[87] Other films that literally staged the effort to master a national linguistic articulation on different registers (informal or conventional) were Nunzio Malasomma's *La telefonista* (1932), which told a love story through phone conversations; Raffaello Matarazzo's *Treno popolare* (1933), which made a hit song out of a celebration of the Fascist uplifting programs of *dopolavoro;* Blasetti's *1860* (1934), whose storyline, based on the events of the *Risorgimento,* embodied the co-optation of a Sicilian peasant's actions, imagery, and dialect, occurring amid the echoing of other Italian dialects and foreign tongues; and Camerini's *Il grande appello* (1936), which narrativized the struggling relationship between language and national identity in an African outpost of trade and colonial battles.[88]

Still, the 1930s Italian film discourse on realism rehashed the expressive power of the senses in a very partisan manner: it gave vision the privileged task of direct aesthetic signification, and it warned that a highly coded or even mildly arranged use of sound would be inauthentic and manipulative. Most notably, Umberto Barbaro's sophisticated notion of cinematic realism, which was embedded with the theoretical densities of Soviet montage, or Luigi Chiarini's concept of *specifico filmico* (film specificity), tended to privilege vision as the cipher of cinema's rendering and structuring of reality at the expense of sound and words.[89] The critical disregard for the serious problems posed in Italy by the encounter between cinema and orality began in the 1930s and lasted longer than the Fascist regime. "Hearing" common people on screen speaking in Italian was still not as familiar as "seeing them speaking": their utterances struggled to resound verisimilar. After World War II, Italian leftist film critics and intellectuals correlated realism, Resistance, and national unity into neorealist master narratives, embedded with anti-Fascist political and cultural urgencies. Rossellini's *Paisan* (1946) played various Italian dialects, often opposing them to the foreign tongues of Germans and Americans. But the film's narrative and ideological structure intended to tie such differences to the nation's liberation, not to map linguistic and cultural isolations. Even Visconti's *La terra trema* (1948) took the anthropological difference of Sicilian fishermen and turned their everyday harsh fate into a political allegory. In the film, antique destitution and fatalism were narrativized as capitalist oppression and exploitation.

In the end, this study, while unearthing a very specific tradition of Italian film discourse and practice, may well be connected to wider concerns related to the ways in which in Italy the emergence of modern media impelled the "rendering and vocalization" of a national-popular culture. I believe that a discussion of how the tropes of aurality—understood as music, silence, and orality—affected postwar Italian cinema may reveal the endurance as well the reworkings of older aesthetic problematics.

During Fascism, cinematic (more than critical) efforts were the very sign of a fracture that, like a nonsynchronous dubbing, opposed the state's nationalistic rhetorics and the new modern media to the Italian society. Neorealist and postwar cultural critics acted in a contradictory manner: while denying that Italy's population had been effectively influenced by two decades of cultural life under Fascism, they still took the regime's nationalistic efforts for granted when presuming or, more precisely, never problematizing Italy's linguistic and cultural unity. By doing so, they demonstrated a very approximate or partisan reading of Gramsci's cultural and political analysis.[90]

After the war, apart from the "operatic" Visconti and Bertolucci,[91] the director most interested in (and endowed with) critical analysis of the audiovisual duality of Italian cinema was Pier Paolo Pasolini. At the end of his early film period (*Accattone*, 1961; *Mamma Roma*, 1962; and the segment of *La ricotta* in *Rogopag*, 1963), in which he attempted to literally voice the culturally dying breed of *borgatari* and their dialect, Pasolini wrote an important essay on cinema and oral language, written in the context of contemporary semiotic debates and published in *Cinema nuovo* in the fall of 1969.[92] Pasolini wrote:

> In cinema the word (with the exception of the least relevant instances of road signs and "credits") must be considered in its ORAL manifestation. . . . Now for centuries we have been used to making aesthetic evaluations based exclusively on the WRITTEN word. It alone seemed worthy to us of being not only poetic but also simply literary. Because in cinema instead the word is ORAL, it is naturally perceived as a product of little worth or actually despised.[93]

After turning to Paul Valéry (through the critical lens of Roman Jakobson) for a definition of poetry as a prolonged hesitation between meaning and sound, the director of *Teorema* denounced the scarcity of critical attention to the oral dimension of film images—a dimension he claimed was most crucial and revealing.[94] A dimension, we may add, that still has not borne its full historiographical fruit within Italian film studies.

Notes

I would like to thank Giovanni Cocconi, Pierluigi Ercole, and, in particular, Giuliana Muscio, all of whom provided or shared crucial material and information. I also would like to thank Jacqueline Reich and Piero Garofalo for their patient and astute readings: their comments clarified both my prose and my thought. I am of course solely responsible for remaining mistakes and imprecisions. Unless otherwise noted, all translations are my own. This is for Benedetta.

1. Alessandro Blasetti, "La musica nel film. Il parere del regista," *Bianco & Nero* 11, nos. 5–6 (May–June 1950), now in A. Blasetti, *Il Cinema che ho vissuto,* ed. Franco Prono (Bari: Dedalo, 1982), 163 (italics in the text).

2. The history of Italian film periodicals before and during World War II is crucial for an understanding of the poetic and ideological ambitions and failures of a national film discourse. Between 1937 and 1943, *Bianco & Nero*—as the periodical of the Rome-based Italian film school (Centro Sperimentale di Cinematografia)—constituted the main scholarly reference for Italian film culture. It was less polemical than its contemporary, *Cinema* (1936–1943), and, apart from a short interruption following the collapse of the regime, it was able to resume its publications in 1947. The story of *Cinema* is rather different. It was founded in 1936, and despite the fact that it was the official organ of the Federazione nazionale fascista degli industriali dello spettacolo since 1938, *Cinema* published the very radical opinions of leftist critics such as Mario Alicata, Giuseppe De Santis, Carlo Lizzani, and Massimo Mida, as well as the contributions of Luchino Visconti and a young Michelangelo Antonioni. For overviews and excerpts from *Bianco & Nero* (1937–1943), see *Antologia di Bianco & Nero: 1937–1943,* ed. Mario Verdone and Leonardo Autera, 5 vols. (Roma: Edizioni di Bianco e Nero, 1964); and for *Cinema* (1936–1943), see *Il lungo viaggio del cinema italiano. Antologia di* Cinema, *1936–1943,* ed. Orio Caldiron (Venezia: Marsilio 1965).

3. Although Bollati never mentions cinema or film poetics, his essays on photography and Italy's nineteenth- and twentieth-century culture have been a continuing source of inspiration for this essay. See his "L'Italiano," in *Storia d'Italia,* vol. 1: *I caratteri originali* (Torino: Einaudi, 1972), 951–1022, and "Il modo di vedere italiano (Note su fotografia e storia)," in *Storia d'Italia,* vol. 2: *Tomo I L'immagine fotografica, 1845–1945* (Torino: Einaudi, 1979), 3–55. Both essays are now included in *L'Italiano. Il carat-*

tere nazionale come storia e come invenzione, ed. G. Bollati (Torino: Einaudi, 1983), respectively, 34–123 and 124–178.

4. As late as the late 1920s, in fact, Italy was still a nation where the vast majority of the population mainly spoke local dialects. From the early 1930s, however, the government's linguistic policy made strenuous efforts to prohibit the uses of local idioms (from education to the press and radio, from literary productions to film titles and intertitles), since dialects were deemed to be signs of cultural backwardness and political resistance. As language historian Tullio De Mauro has argued, the literacy rate, which had reached an average of 80 percent by 1931, did not imply an actual use of the Italian language, only a potential capacity. Still, by the early 1930s, the southern regions had a rate of illiteracy of about 40 percent. See T. De Mauro, *Storia linguistica dell'Italia unita* (Roma-Bari: Laterza, 1963), 99 and 91. On the translation into Italian of film titles written in dialect, see Sergio Raffaelli, *La lingua filmata. Didascalie e dialoghi nel cinema italiano* (Firenze: Casa Editrice Le Lettere, 1992), 64–86.

5. On the problematization of the very existence of a "Fascist ideology" or a "Fascist culture," see Norberto Bobbio, "La cultura e il fascismo," in *Fascismo e società italiana,* ed. Guido Quazza (Torino: Einaudi, 1973), 211–246; and Alberto Asor Rosa, "La cultura," in *Storia d'Italia,* vol. 4: *Dall 'unità a oggi* (Torino: Einaudi, 1975), 1358ff. For a general discussion on the problematics of Fascism in Italian historiography into the mid-1980s, see Emilio Gentile, "Fascism in Italian Historiography: In Search of an Individual Historical Identity," *Journal of Contemporary History* 21 (1986): 179–208. For more recent revisionist references, see Giovanni Belardelli, Luciano Cafagna, Ernesto Galli della Loggia, and Giovanni Sabbatucci, *Miti e storia dell'Italia unita* (Bologna: Il Mulino, 1999).

6. Such critical hostility, which began in the early 1940s, doubled in ferocity for those films produced in the first half of the decade, especially the works of Alberto Lattuada, Ferdinando Maria Poggioli, Mario Soldati, and Mario Mattoli, all of whom were labeled "calligraphers" (*calligrafici*). They were accused of producing politically apathetic portrayals of bourgeois formality, decadent romance, and costume dramas. On this issue, see also several examples of Giuseppe De Santis's harsh criticism in his *Verso il neorealismo. Un critico cinematografico degli anni Quaranta,* ed. Callisto Cosulich (Roma: Bulzoni, 1982), 155–161; and Lino Miccichè's general discussion, "L'ideologia e la forma. Il gruppo 'Cinema' e il formalismo italiano," in *La bella forma. Poggioli, i calligrafici e dintorni,* ed. Andrea Martini (Venezia: Marsilio, 1992), 1–28.

7. Such a general investigation already exists, although it is quite isolated. See Sergio Raffaelli, *La lingua filmata;* Raffaelli, *Il cinema nella lingua di Pirandello* (Roma: Bulzoni, 1993); and, in a more systematic way, *Dialoghi di regime. La lingua del cinema degli anni trenta,* ed. Valentina Ruffin and Patrizia D'Agostino (Roma: Bulzoni, 1997). Other studies include Paola Micheli, *Il cinema di Blasetti parlò così . . . Un'analisi linguistica dei film*

(1929–1942) (Roma: Bulzoni, 1990), a case study of the use of language in Blasetti's films. See also Nicoletta Maraschio, "L'Italiano del doppiaggio" and Emanuela Cresti, "La lingua del cinema come fattore della trasformazione linguistica nazionale," both in Accademia della Crusca, *La lingua italiana in movimento* (Firenze: Presso l'Accademia, 1982), 137–158 and 277–322, respectively, on the transformations of the Italian language through foreign and dubbed films and through Italian films.

8. Departing from the fundamental work on Fascist cinema by Marcia Landy and James Hay, who have mainly concentrated on post-1930s cinema and film culture, I have chosen instead to focus my attention on the often-neglected silent film discourse of the 1910s and 1920s, which deeply affected Italian film culture of the following years. Elsewhere, I have begun to explore the communicative and linguistic problematics related to Italian cinema's transition to sound in light of Gramsci's cultural criticism, a historiographical problematic that Landy, in a recent and otherwise remarkable study on Gramsci's cultural theory and cinematic representations (Italian and non-Italian), has not addressed. See M. Landy, *Film, Politics, and Gramsci* (Minneapolis: University of Minnesota Press, 1994); and G. Bertellini, "The Tain of the Mirror: Gramsci, Italian Talkies, and La questione della lingua," unpublished paper presented at Italian Cultural Studies: A Symposium at Dartmouth College, 29–31 October 1999. For Landy's work on cinema during Fascism, see *Fascism in Film: The Italian Commercial Cinema 1930–1943* (Princeton, N.J.: Princeton University Press, 1986); *The Folklore of Consensus: Theatricality in the Italian Cinema, 1930–1943* (Albany, N.Y.: SUNY Press, 1998); and *Italian Cinema* (New York: Cambridge University Press, 2000), especially Chapters 2–4. For Hay's work, see *Popular Film Culture in Fascist Italy: The Passing of the Rex* (Bloomington: Indiana University Press, 1987).

9. Italian film discourse in the late 1920s and early 1930s rarely made any serious reference to Neapolitan regional productions, preferring to focus instead on domestic productions with a "national" appeal (i.e., Blasetti's *Sole* [1929] and *1860* [1933]; Camerini's *Rotaie* [1930], and Matarazzo's *Treno popolare* [1933]) or, more often, on foreign "universal" ideals filtered through Soviet realism and the cinema of Chaplin and Dreyer. Several very influential essays by critic Umberto Barbaro written in the late 1930s, aimed at recovering ex post facto early examples of popular and national realism, were remarkable exceptions. Barbaro critically "rescued" two films produced in the silent era, *Sperduti nel buio* (1914) and *Assunta Spina* (1915), first in a 1936 article published in the theatrical periodical *Scenario* ("Un film italiano di un quarto di secolo fa") and later in a lengthy and famous essay about film technique and realist poetics titled "Film: Soggetto e sceneggiatura," first published in *Bianco & Nero* in 1939. For Barbaro, the two films' regional features constituted a crucial prolepsis of Italy's most authentic film aesthetics, which was closer to Russian realist cinema. Later on, neorealist critics would make an identical critical gesture

by praising film adaptations of Verga's novels as Italy's quintessential realist output. Barbaro's two essays are now available respectively in U. Barbaro, *Servitù e grandezza del cinema* (Roma: Editori Riuniti, 1962), 142–
149 and, in an expanded version retitled "Soggetto e sceneggiatura," in
U. Barbaro, *Il film e il risarcimento marxista dell'arte*, ed. Lorenzo Quaglietti (Roma: Editori Riuniti, 1960), 55–176. On Barbaro's realism and
his attraction to Soviet cinema, see Gian Piero Brunetta, *Umberto Barbaro
e l'idea di neorealismo* (Padova: Liviana, 1969). On the critical debate around
Dreyer's cinema, see Orio Caldiron, *La paura del buio. Studi sulla cultura
cinematografica in Italia* (Roma: Bulzoni, 1980), 57–149; and on the critical
debate around Chaplin's cinema, see G. Viazzi, *Chaplin e la critica. Antologia di saggi, bibliografia ragionata, iconografia e filmografia* (Bari: Laterza,
1955); and Guido Oldrini, *Chapliniana. Chaplin e la critica* (Bari: Laterza,
1979).

10. In 1910, the average length of an Italian movie was about 200 meters (660
feet), two-thirds of a single 300-meter reel (1,000 feet). In 1914, this
measure had more than tripled to about two reels, precisely 620 meters (ca.
2,050 feet); and, by 1919, the average length had reached 1,473 meters (ca.
4,833 feet), almost five reels. For this data I am indebted to Aldo Bernardini, *Archivio del cinema italiano*, vol. 1, *Il cinema muto, 1905–1931*
(Roma: ANICA, 1991), 1112–1113, Tables 1 and 2. For a comparative
study of the development of Italian feature film within the world scene, see
Riccardo Redi, ed., *1911 . . . La nascita del lungometraggio* (Roma: CNC,
1992).

11. UCI was created from an alliance among the majority of Italy's most
prominent production companies (Caesar, Cines, Tiber, Itala, Incit, and
Pasquali). Financially supported by two leading banking institutions,
Banca Italiana di Sconto and Banca Commerciale Italiana, from the start
UCI acted as a national monopoly capable of fighting back the American
competition. Headed by manager Luigi Barattolo, UCI gathered the leading directors and actors of the time and produced as many as 150 films per
year during the 1919 and 1920 seasons. UCI developed unrealistic and extravagant plans of production without securing distribution and exhibition
outlets: it squandered resources on lavishly expensive costume films and on
exorbitant contracts to actors and actresses who were already becoming
unpopular. When its credit backup failed in 1922, the entire Italian film
industry collapsed. See G. P. Brunetta, *Storia del cinema italiano* (Roma:
Editori Riuniti; 1993 [1979]), 1: 238–259. As Giuliana Bruno emphasized,
the trust privileged the well-established Rome-Turin production axis, further marginalizing southern filmmaking centers and styles which had been
already chastised by domestic criticism and distribution. Needless to say, a
consistent disregard for regional productions long affected historiographical views about what Italian cinema had been before the 1930s. See
G. Bruno, *Streetwalking on a Ruined Map: Cultural Theory and the City Films
of Elvira Notari* (Princeton, N.J.: Princeton University Press, 1993), 18ff.

12. Throughout the 1920s, several of the most talented Italian directors (and former *dive*) who had found jobs abroad after the failure of UCI earlier in the decade continued to work outside of Italy. Among them, there were both young and experienced directors such as Nunzio Malasomma, Carmine Gallone, Mario Bonnard, Augusto Genina, and Guido Brignone, and prominent actresses such as Carmen Boni, Maria Jacobini, Marcella Albani, and Clara Galassi. For an informative overview, see Vittorio Martinelli, "I Gastarbeiter fra le due guerre," *Bianco & Nero* 39, no. 3 (1978), 3–93; and Martinelle, "Cineasti italiani in Germania tra le due guerre," and "Destinazione Parigi," in *Cinema italiano in Europa, 1907–1929*, ed. V. Martinelli (Roma: Associazione italiana per le ricerche di storia del cinema, 1992), 131–159 and 160–169.

13. Apart from the extraordinary worldwide successes of pre–World War I distribution, the postwar years witnessed a surprisingly minor interest in and effort to commercialize film, both domestically and internationally. The only figure of some expertise was a true manager, Stefano Pittalunga, who helped restructure and adjust Cines (together with other film companies) to the sound system. Unfortunately, he died soon afterward.

14. The vast majority of them (1,179) exceeded the length of 1,000 meters (3,281 feet). See Bernardini, *Archivio del cinema italiano*, vol. 1, 1112–1113. When compared to the distribution of French and American productions within the Italian market, the circulation of domestic productions was strikingly low from the mid-1920s to the late 1930s; it was consistently around or below 20 percent of the total number of films exhibited in Italy. Bernardini's systematic study slightly corrects, without changing the overall assessment, James Hay's charts. See J. Hay, *Popular Film Culture in Fascist Italy*, Appendix B, 252.

15. On Ghione's cinema, see Giovanni Calendoli, "L'amabile teschio di Za-lamort e il film a dispense," *Filmcritica* 2, no. 18 (1952): 139–142; and G. P. Brunetta, "Emilio Ghione," in *Catalogo della Mostra internazionale del cinema* (Venezia: La Biennale, 1979), 87–94. On "strong men" heroes, see, among others, Vittorio Martinelli and Mario Quargnolo, *Maciste & Co. I giganti buoni del muto italiano* (Gemona del Friuli: Edizioni Cinepopolare, 1981); Alberto Farassino and Tatti Sanguineti, eds., *Gli uomini forti* (Milano: Mazzotta, 1983); and Monica Dall'Asta, *Un Cinéma musclé* (Disnée: Yellow Now, 1992).

16. The major reference for data about and discussions on historical films during the Fascist regime is Gianfranco Gori, *Patria Diva. La storia d'Italia nei film del ventennio* (Firenze: La casa Usher, 1989). A few historical films were colossal productions, though they were rarely very successful: *La nave* (1921), directed by Gabriellino D'Annunzio; *Messalina* (1923), directed by Enrico Guazzoni (who had directed *Quo Vadis?* in 1913); and an umpteenth version of *Gli ultimi giorni di Pompei* (*Last Days of Pompeii*, 1926), directed by Carmine Gallone and Amleto Palermi, whose intertitles were written by Luigi Pirandello, Silvio d'Amico, and Alfredo Panzini, all of

whom had been members since 1920 of the Film Censorship Commission For Artistic and Literary Subjects. On Gallone and Palermi's film, see Riccardo Redi, with Pier Luigi Raffaelli, eds., *Gli ultimi giorni di Pompei* (Napoli: Electa, 1994).

17. The amount of literature on the "star system" of early Italian cinema is massive. For a thematic and bibliographic orientation, see Brunetta, *Storia del cinema italiano,* I: 71–91.

18. For a discussion of the representation of suburban space in Italian cinema, see Giorgio Bertellini and Saverio Giovacchini, "Ambiguous Sovereignties: Notes on the Suburbs in Italian Cinema," in *Suburban Discipline,* ed. Peter Lang and Tam Miller (New York: Princeton Architectural Press, 1997), especially 87–95.

19. The genre of *Vedute* ("views") was popular both in Italy and in the Americas; it was particularly successful among the numerous southern Italian immigrants. For a detailed account of Neapolitan cinema from its inception to the present, see *Napoletana: Images of a City,* ed. Adriano Aprà (New York/Milano: MoMA/Fabbri Editori, 1993). For a specific cultural investigation of one production company, Films Dora, headed by Elvira and Nicola Notari, see Giuliana Bruno, *Streetwalking on a Ruined Map,* especially Chapters 5 and 6. On the encounter of New York immigrants with Italian cinema, see G. Bertellini, "Italian Imageries, Historical Feature Films, and the Fabrication of Italy's Spectators in Early 1900s New York," in *American Movie Audiences: From the Turn of the Century to the Early Sound Era,* ed. Richard Maltby and Melvin Stokes (London: British Film Institute, 1999), 29–45; "Shipwrecked Spectators: Italy's Immigrants at the Movies in New York, 1906-1916," *The Velvet Light Trap* no. 44 (Fall 1999), 39–53 (special issue on "Beyond the Image: Race and Ethnicity in the Media").

20. For a discussion on *sceneggiate* in silent Neapolitan cinema, see Vittorio Paliotti and Enzo Grano, *Napoli nel cinema* (Napoli: Azienda Autonoma Turismo, 1969), especially 95–111; and Stefano Masi and Mario Franco, *Il mare, la luna, i coltelli: per una storia del cinema muto napoletano* (Napoli: Tullio Pironti Editore, 1988), especially 21–129. This film genre developed after the popular success of stage *sceneggiate,* which emerged during World War I, when ordinary singing in public became heavily taxed. Soon the genre perfected itself through a much-admired synchronization, a live dubbing between singer (who was often in front of the screen) and the moving picture.

21. Among the most renowned ones: *Fenesta che lucive* (1914, remade in 1925), based on a famous song long attributed to Rossini or Bellini; *A Marechiaro ce sta 'na fenesta* (1913, remade in 1924), based on the song "A Marechiare" by Francesco Paolo Tosti; *E' piccerella* (1922) and *L'Addio* (1924), based on Libero Bovio's compositions; and *Core furastiero* (1924), based on a song by di Melina and E. A. Mario. During premieres, the protagonists of the film

would sing live against the backdrop of their own film image, through an expected process of materialization and authentication, which connected the modern medium to cherished and shared musical tunes. For this data I am indebted to G. Bruno, *Streetwalking on a Ruined Map*, 92–97 and Chapter 10.

22. Ibid., 169. In particular, regarding Dora Film, Bruno notes: "Notari's cinema attempts, by narrativizing its sound and staging them live, to re-create the urban public drama. Cities have a distinct sound, and Naples, in particular, is a city of sounds, especially musical ones. The bustle, cries, and singing of its open-air public living are a loud presence in the cityscape. Performing these sounds is an important part of *sceneggiata*. The mode exhibits the 'silent' cinema's desire to immerse itself in the collective voices of the piazza, the sounds of Naples' popular neighborhoods, and the city's spectacles" (170).

23. Another case of technological and cultural repression must be made for those film productions with a close kinship to the Venetian vernacular stage tradition, which became quite renowned after Carlo Goldoni's eighteenth-century productions. Born in 1707, Goldoni had successfully reworked the commedia dell'arte conventions with a distinct Venetian accent and mood and had exported it—like the local Carnival—to the Comédie Italienne in Paris and all over Europe. Among these films, which, once again, were deeply imbricated with the gestures and idioms of a city theater, were *El moroso de la nona* (1927), *Il carnevale di Venezia* (1927), *Mia fia* (1928), *La locandiera* (1929), and *Il cantastorie di Venezia* (1929).

24. At times, such Neapolitan "realism" was also mixed with leftist concerns about social injustice and class conflict, as was the case for Ubaldo Maria Del Colle's *I figli di nessuno* (1920), adapted from a Zola-like novel by Roberto Rindi, a story about marble workers who refuse to continue risking their lives without safer work conditions and better salaries. See R. Redi, *Ti parlerò . . . d'amor. Cinema italiano fra muto e sonoro* (Torino: ERI, 1986), 40–41.

25. Later such poverty was presented as temporary and curable through the positive, progressive intervention of "enlightened" outsiders, as in Domenico Paolella's *Gli ultimi della strada* (1940), set in Naples, but actually a remake of the Soviet film *Putevka v zhizn'* (*The Path to Life*, 1931), directed by Nikolaj Ekk.

26. For a general discussion of the transition to sound, see the classic works by Harry M. Geduld, *The Birth of the Talkies: From Edison to Jolson* (Bloomington: Indiana University Press, 1975); Alexander Walker, *The Shattered Silents: How the Talkies Came to Stay* (London: Elm Tree Books, 1978); Mary Lea Bandy, ed., *The Dawn of Sound: American Moviemakers* (New York: MoMA, 1989); Christian Belaygue, ed., *Le Passage dumuet au parlant: Panorama mondial de la production cinématographique 1925–1935* (Toulouse: Cinémathèque de Toulouse/Editions Milan, 1988); Roger Icart, *La*

Révolution du parlant, vue par le presse française (Perpignan: Institut Jean Vigo, 1988); Alberto Boschi, *L'avvento del sonoro in Europa. Teoria e prassi del cinema negli anni della transizione* (Bologna: CLUEB, 1994); and Donald Crafton, *The Talkies: American Cinema's Transition to Sound, 1926–1931* (Berkeley and Los Angeles: University of California Press, 1997). The fundamental reference that collects historiographical and critical contributions on classical sound theory and practices (and extensive bibliographies) is the 1985 critical anthology edited by Elisabeth Weis and John Belton, *Film Sound: Theory and Practice* (New York: Columbia University Press, 1985).

27. This move was shared, with some important differences, but often independently, with Soviet (S. M. Eisenstein, V. I. Pudovkin, and G. V. Alexandrov), French (R. Clair and J. Epstein), British (B. Wright and B. V. Braun), German (S. Kracauer and R. Arnheim), and Hungarian (B. Balazs) film theorists. Several of the most important essays on this topic have been collected and rubricated as "Classical Sound Theory" in Weis and Belton, *Film Sound*, 75–144.

28. "That is why the cinegraphic poem—such as I conceive it and which tomorrow should represent the highest form of expression in the cinema—will be so close to the symphonic poem, the images being to the eye in the former what sounds are to the ear in the latter." Léon Moussinac, "Du rythme cinégraphique," *Le Crapouillot* (March 1923), 9–11, now in English as "On Cinegraphic Rhythm," in *French Film Theory and Criticism: A History/Anthology, 1907–1939*, vol. I, *1907–1929*, ed. Richard Abel (Princeton, N.J.: Princeton University Press, 1988), 282. Moussinac acknowledged analogous positions expressed several years earlier by film critic Emile Vuillermoz and music and literary historian René Dumensil. For a general discussion of 1920s French criticism, see R. Abel, "*Cinégraphie* and the Search for Specificity," in *French Film Theory*, 195–223.

29. If in the early 1920s, Vertov had theorized the capacity of the Camera-Eye (*Kinoki*) to achieve truthful knowledge, later in the decade he extended such proficiency to sound. Because sound played a fundamental role in his editing work, Vertov called it "the Radio-Ear." Aural connotations then accompanied his comments about his late silent films: for Vertov, *One Sixth of the World* (1926) was a film experimenting with "radio-thematic words," whereas *The Eleventh Year* (1928) was "a visible-audible film." His most famous work, *The Man with the Movie Camera* (1929), marked a transition from the "Cinema-Eye" to the "Radio-Eye"—a new poetic which combined visuality with the wireless musical variances of radio broadcasting—not exactly what later sound cinema happened to become. See Yuri Tsivian, "Dziga Vertov's Frozen Music: Cue Sheets and a Music Scenario for *The Man with the Movie Camera*," *Griffithiana* 18, no. 54 (1995), 93–95.

30. "The history of this [musical] analogy shows that, however imperfect it may be, it has functioned to break a tendency to think of cinema as an art of the real. Music has become a model of how formal unity can check,

control, and override representation. This depends, in turn, upon conceiving music as the art of pure pattern and process. It is not only that music
is nonreferential, as the purist avant-garde assumes. Music is useful as a
model because of its architectonic features." David Bordwell, "The Musical Analogy," in "Cinema/Sound," ed. Rick Altman, *Yale French Studies*,
no. 60 (1980): 142.

31. The most illustrative example of this kind of reaction is writer Maxim
Gorky's review of the Lumière program published in a Russian newspaper
in 1896: "Last night I was in the Kingdom of Shadows. If you only knew
how strange it is to be there. It is a world without sound, without color.
Everything there—the earth, the trees, the people, the water and the air—
is dipped in monotonous grey. Grey rays of the sun across the grey sky, grey
eyes in grey faces, and the leaves of the trees are ashen grey. It is not life
but its shadow, it is not motion but its soundless spectre." "I. M. Pacatus"
[M. Gorky], "A Review of the Lumière Program at the Nizhni-Novgorod
Fair," *Nizhegorodski listok*, 4 July 1896, trans. Leda Swan, now in Jay
Leyda, *Kino: A History of the Russian and Soviet Film* (Princeton, N.J.:
Princeton University Press, 1960), 407.

32. This perception made quite a lasting impact. Walter Benjamin in his most
celebrated 1936 essay, "The Work of Art in the Age of Mechanical Reproduction," wrote: "Even the most perfect reproduction of a work of art is
lacking in one element: its presence in time and space, its unique existence
at the place where it happens to be." W. Benjamin, *Illuminations*, edited
and with an introduction by Hannah Arendt, trans. Harry Zohn (New
York: Schocken Books, 1969), 220.

33. "The technical development of the motion picture will soon carry the mechanical imitation of nature to an extreme. The addition of sound was the
first obvious step in this direction. The introduction of sound film must be
considered as the imposition of a technical novelty that did not lie on the
path the best film artists were pursuing. . . . The introduction of sound
film smashed many of the forms that the film artists were using in favor of
the inartistic demand for the greatest possible "naturalness" (in the most
superficial sense of the word). . . . [Movie producers] do not see that film
is on its way to the victory of wax museum ideals over creative art." R.
Arnheim, "The Complete Film," in *Film as Art*, trans. L. M. Sieveking
and Ian F. D. Morrow (London: Faber and Faber, 1933; reprint, Berkeley
and Los Angeles: University of California Press, 1967), 154. Arnheim conceptualized this position during his stay in Rome where he was working in
the early 1930s as a contributor for the projected *Enciclopedia del Cinema*.

34. Quite interestingly, an initial "realist" response, similar to the one that
emerged with the mechanical reproduction of images, surfaced with the
arrival of the talkies. The perception of synchronized sound, apart from
some initial flaws and blatant distortions, postulated that the recording
rendered the original faithfully, in its full three-dimensionality. Once
again, artistic merits were denied. Recorded sound appeared to retain a

stubborn indexical relationship with its original source, entertaining with it a deep existential kinship. The new technical novelty seemed, at first, to push the cinematic medium toward an inescapable realism and thus to mortify any aesthetic intervention on behalf of the artist/director. Strangely enough, that occurred even when common experience had sensed that the industry of telephonic communication, phonograph records, and radio entertainment was busy at work trying to "enhance" "greater volume, presence, or intelligibility, while reducing unwanted characteristics." That "realist" response symptomatically displayed what Rick Altman has termed "reproductive fallacy": it ignored that "recordings do not reproduce sound, they represent sound." R. Altman, "Introduction: Four and a Half Film Fallacies," in *Sound Theory Sound Practice*, ed. R. Altman (New York: Routledge, 1992), 40ff.

35. Antonio Gramsci, *Selections from Cultural Writings*, ed. David Forgacs and Geoffrey Nowell-Smith (Cambridge, Mass.: Harvard University Press, 1985), 378.

36. A. Gramsci, *Selections from Cultural Writings*, 201.

37. Although as early as 1907 there were already as many as seven film periodicals, with a peak of thirteen in 1917 and a low of two in 1910, for quite some time Italian film discourse could not produce critical figures that were widely respected and impartial. Those publications, in fact, were mostly trade journals, and Italian film criticism long remained attached to the business necessities of the industries. For an overall approach to the relationships among newspaper, culture, and cinema before neorealism, see Lino Miccichè, "Le parole del muto. Nota introduttiva," in *Tra una Film e l'altra. Materiali sul cinema muto italiano, 1907-1920*, ed. Mostra Internazionale del Nuovo Cinema (Venezia: Marsilio Editori, 1980), 7-25; and G. P. Brunetta, *Storia del cinema italiano*, 1: 107-129 and 295-312. The fundamental guide to Italian film periodicals is Riccardo Redi, ed., *Cinema Scritto: Il catalogo delle riviste italiane di cinema, 1907-1944* (Roma: Associazione italiana per le ricerche di storia del cinema, 1992), an updated version of Davide Turconi, ed., *Il cinema nelle riviste italiane dalle origini ad oggi* (Roma: Associazione italiana per le ricerche di storia del cinema, 1972).

38. On the subject of cinema and Italian literature and writers, see Sara Zappulla-Muscarà, "Contributi per una storia dei rapporti tra letteratura e cinema muto (Verga, De Roberto, Capuana, Martoglio e la Settima Arte)," *Rassegna della Letteratura italiana* 86, no. 3 (September-December 1982): 501-560.

39. The establishment in 1909 of a production company called Società Italiana per la Film d'Arte (following the example of the French Film d'Art) meant the adoption of more narratively elaborate standards and the tendency to adapt distinguished literary and historical dramas for the screen—from Shakespeare to Dante, from the epics of Risorgimento to religious novels

such as *Quo Vadis?* Furthermore, to better compete with the grand and acclaimed theater representations, cinema extended its length from one-reelers to multi-reelers in the early 1910s. Those years witnessed also the emergence of the film review, the most legitimate art discourse format.

40. *Cabiria*'s artistic fame relied not only on the learned intertitles written by D'Annunzio (on the narrative blueprint director Pastrone prepared for him) but also on the musical score, in particular on *La sinfonia del fuoco*, an original composition written by Pizzetti specifically for the film. Any of the several municipal premieres of *Cabiria* where a full orchestra had been arranged became a unique literary and musical event. Interestingly, after that experience, Pizzetti decided not to work on a film soundtrack for more than two decades. However, his solemn style was co-opted again for Carmine Gallone's *Scipione l'Africano* (1937).

41. Still, these were the conclusions of an inquiry published in *Il Nuovo Giornale di Firenze* on 13 November 1913, with contributions by several well-known writers such as Nino Martoglio, Roberto Gracco, and Giovanni Prezzolini. For a detailed discussion, see Peter Del Monte, "Le teoriche del film in Italia dalle origini al sonoro," *Bianco & Nero* nos. 5/6 (1969): 23ff.

42. In a provocative manner, D'Annunzio himself had answered these questions in an interview published in *Il Corriere della Sera* on 28 February 1914, less than two months before *Cabiria*'s premiere (18 April 1914). In the interview, he presented himself as the visionary creator of *Cabiria*, and cinema, as the realm of magnificent wonders and free transformations, had finally replaced theater's weary and inarticulate lines.

43. The essay titled "Del cinematografo considerato come uno strumento di liberazione e come arte di trasfigurazione" is now preserved at La Fondazione del Vittoriale (Gardone Riviera, Italy); it is composed of twelve sheets which clearly show D'Annunzio's ex post facto insertions to the text of the interview he gave to *Corriere della Sera* on 28 February 1914. The essay's subtitle, "Quasi prefazione a Cabiria," is evidently an attempt to surreptitiously advance the period of its elaboration before the production of Pastrone's film. The essay is now included in *Giovanni Pastrone. Gli anni d'oro del cinema a Torino*, ed. Paolo Cherchi Usai (Torino: UTET, 1986), 115–122. For bibliographic notes and riddles, see, in particular, 25–26.

44. "Recently, the filmmaking industry . . . has aspired to renew the ancient art of Pantomime and, perhaps, could even give birth to a new aesthetic of movement. Let us consider the cinema an instrument of liberation. Couldn't it also become a silent art, deep and musical like silence?" or "Cinema's truest and most singular virtue is that of transfiguration; and I state that Ovid is its poet. Sooner or later the poetry of Metamorphosis will enchant the crowds that today enjoys pranks so vulgar." G. D'Annunzio, "Del cinematografo considerato," now in Usai, *Giovanni Pastrone*, 115–116 and 122.

45. In 1915, journalists Antonio Scarfoglio and Francesco Bufi founded a film periodical called *L'Arte muta;* and, a year later, the advertising brochure of Eduardo Bencivenga's film *La figlia di Jorio* (a play written by D'Annunzio in 1904) bore the same title. In *La lingua filmata*, Raffaelli tried to register the earliest occurrences of respectively *teatro muto*, *dramma muto*, and *scena muta*. He found these occurrences in L. Marroco, "Il teatro muto" in *Il Cinema Teatro*, 1 September 1912, especially p. 3; Pier Antonio Gariazzo's theoretical work *Il teatro muto* (Torino: Lattes, 1919); A. Montanarello's "Dal dramma musicale al cinedramma musicato," *Apollon* (1 April 1916): 8; and U. Modugno's "La scena muta ed Edoardo Boutet," *Apollon* (1 May 1916): 21. See Sergio Raffaelli, *La lingua filmata*, Chapter 4.

46. In his 1919 treatise on film language, titled *Il teatro muto*, theater historian Piero Antonio Gariazzo was quite explicit in this sense. In Chapter 6, which is entirely devoted to pantomime and stage representations, Gariazzo insists on the universality of mimic gestures, their anthropological primacy, and the musicality of human emotions: "Sensation is like a musical wave hitting our nervous centers; its major or minor resonance determine[s] a correspondent reaction or exterior signification; without resonance there is no signification." Gariazzo, *Il teatro muto*, 261–262.

47. Canudo was born in Bari in 1877 (not in 1879, as most accounts report), but lived in Paris from 1902; he developed his cultural refinement in France, where his reputation quickly grew among artistic and musical circuits. A close friend of Apollinaire and D'Annunzio, the Italian émigré published novels; books on painting, literature, and music (*Psychologie Musicale des Civilisations*, 1908); and he edited an art journal, *Montjoie!* (1913–1914). Only after his death, however, were his film writings collected and published by a friend, Fernand Divoire, as *L'usine aux images* (1927). Canudo developed a film aesthetic quite similar to, although more elaborate than, D'Annunzio's; they were consistently inspired by comparison with the theater and deeply influenced by Wagnerian theories of "total and synthetic art." *L'usine aux images* contains Canudo's famous essay "L'Esthétique du septième art," which was first published in 1911 as "La naissance d'un sixième Art. Essai sur le Cinématographe" in *Les Entretiens idéalistes*, 15 October 1911, reprinted as "L'Esthétique du septième art," in R. Canudo, *L'usine aux images*, ed. Fernand Divoire (Paris: Etienne Chiron, 1927), 13–26. It was translated by Ben Gibson, Don Ranvaud, Sergio Sokota, and Deborah Young as "The Birth of the Sixth Art," *Framework* (Autumn 1980), 3–7, and is now in Abel, *French Film Theory*, 58–66. In Italian film criticism, Canudo has always been highly regarded, but oftentimes in a very superficial manner. He is acknowledged as the first theorist of cinema as art—or as "total art"—but no further specifications are generally offered as to what that entailed. Not by chance, *L'usine aux images* was not translated into Italian until 1966, although it had been reviewed thirty years earlier in the first issue of *Bianco & Nero* (1937) and briefly excerpted in the section on theoretical contributions by Italians in the an-

thology *Problemi del film*, ed. Luigi Chiarini and Umberto Barbaro (Roma: Edizioni di Bianco & Nero, 1939), 47–59. For a theoretical assessment of Canudo's position, albeit limited to the European debates of the time, see Giovanna Grignaffini, *Sapere e teorie del cinema. Il periodo del muto* (Bologna: CLUEB, 1989), 59–65 and 105–136. Useful contributions, especially with regards to exact dates of Canudo's publications, are *Ricciotto Canudo, 1877–1977 Atti del Congresso Internazionale nel centenario della nascita*, ed. Giovanni Dotoli (Fasano: Grafischena, 1978); and G. Dotoli, *Lo scrittore totale (Saggi su Ricciotto Canudo)* (Fasano: Schena, 1986). On the relationship between Canudo and the avant-garde in Europe, see Sergio Miceli, *La musica nel film. Arte e artigianato* (Fiesole, Firenze: Discanto Edizioni, 1982), 84–104.

48. Canudo, "The Birth of the Sixth Art," 59 and 61 (Canudo's italics).

49. Together with other critics, Luciani took part in the "anti-naturalistic crusade" initiated by *Apollon* (1916–1921), one of the most sophisticated periodicals in the Italian critical scene; it was known (and respected) for its various theoretical contributions aimed at establishing cinema as "an art, among other arts." For a discussion of some of these important (yet fairly neglected) *Apollon* essays, see Del Monte, "Le teoriche del film in Italia dalle origini al sonoro," 31–33; and Brunetta, *Storia del cinema italiano*, 1: 126ff. For a study of Luciani's general contribution, see Vito Attolini, *Sebastiano Arturo Luciani teorico del film* (Bari: Ed. Centro Librario, 1971).

50. This necessity was later voiced in a typical symbolist style; "the expressive vagueness of the silent gesture can only find an equivalent in a wordless music." S. A. Luciani, "La musica al cinematografo," *Il primato* (1919). The same sentence reappears in Luciani, *L'Antiteatro. Il Cinematografo come arte* (Roma: La Voce Editrice, 1928), 56. All of Luciani's articles discussed in this essay—apart from the one published in *Il Marzocco*—are included in *Tra una film e l'altra*. See also *Verso una nuova arte. Il Cinematografo* (Roma: Casa Editrice Ausonia, 1921 [actually 1920]). To my knowledge, the only article by Luciani translated into English is "The Future of Sound-film," *The New Review* (Paris) 1 (Winter 1931–32): 300–303 (translated by Samuel Putnam).

51. Luciani, *L'Antiteatro*, 21.

52. In 1942, Luciani returned to this point in his *Il Cinema e le Arti* (Siena: Ticci Editore, 1942). Referring to the efforts of painters to capture on canvas the dynamism of objects and emotions, he brought as examples the mysterious fascination with Leonardo da Vinci's female portraits, which rested on the incipient vibration of their smile. Luciani argues that if painting can merely suggest the beginning of an emotional release, the cinema is uniquely able to render its full dynamics, *musically*, "as we have never learned to see and hear" (16–17). Interestingly, D'Annunzio himself elaborated on the tension between vision and aurality in a short story about

da Vinci's *Mona Lisa* written in 1920 explicitly for the cinema but never adapted into a movie. Titled "L'uomo che rubò la Gioconda," the story was first published that year in the Paris daily *Excelsior* and in 1932 in the French periodical *Ambassade;* it is now included in Mario Verdone, *Poemi e scenari cinematografici d'avanguardia* (Roma: Officina Edizioni, 1975), 64–85. I have discussed this D'Annunzio "script" in relation to 1910s Italian film aesthetics in Bertellini, "Mute Visuality: Notes About D'Annunzio and the Eloquent Bodies of Italian 'Hysterical' Cinema," presented at the *Rutgers University Italian Film Conference,* October 18, 1996; at the 17th *Annual American Association of Italian Studies Conference,* Winston-Salem, N.C., February 22, 1997; *Writing Italia Conference,* Columbia University, New York, April 5, 1997; *SCS Conference* (Society for Cinema Studies), Ottawa (Canada), May 16, 1997; and at the University of California, Davis, Humanities Institute, June 2, 1998.

53. Luciani was among the first Italian film theorists (together with Porzio and Masi) to explicitly recognize the aesthetic value of artificial light, which enabled the director-artist to fully create his own version of the world—in the tradition of painters such as Rembrandt and Caravaggio. In contrast, he hailed realism as the opposite of true art, since it opposed, at least rhetorically, the use of fiction, allusions, and artifacts. Luciani, *L'Antiteatro,* 39ff., especially 42–43.

54. These films were the most notable ones in which a synthesis of images and music had been attempted in Italy. See Luciani, *L'Antiteatro,* Chapter 7; and *Il Cinema e le Arti,* Chapter 4. Sergei Diaghilev (1872–1929) was a Russian ballet impresario.

55. Luciani, *Il Cinema e le Arti,* 40.

56. Luciani claimed that even characters' dialogue was to be turned into a highly suggestive musical performance. When he blamed the average stage actors for their standard and unnatural diction, he did not do so in the name of a "poetic of authenticity." On the contrary, by insisting that characters' voice should be adjusted to the kind of environment—for example, their social rank but also the photographic illumination—he simply wanted to capitalize on the different musicality of characters' distinct inflections. If that distinctness could be preserved, he claimed, silent and sound sequences would integrate well with each other in a highly poetic consonance of rhythm—something that would not necessarily occur in a naturalistic rendering of a social setting.

57. Luciani, *Il Cinema e le Arti,* 63. Luciani brought as authorial examples of his critical orientation the aestheticism of Walter Pater, the intuitions on music by Giacomo Leopardi, and the provocative aesthetic theories of Oscar Wilde's *Intentions*—quoted in the first pages of *Il cinema e la Arti*—according to whom nature mimics art, and reality exists only in our perception.

58. Now in Chiarini and Barbaro, eds., *Problemi del film*, 21–25: and Mario Verdone, ed., "Cinema e letteratura del futurismo (Ginna e Corra)," *Bianco & Nero* 28, nos. 10–12 (October–December 1967): 230–234.

59. *Vita futurista* was divided into episodes that combined daily gestures performed *à la futuriste* with social and political satire. On the film, see Verdone, *Cinema e letteratura del futurismo*, 105ff. Ginna and Corra had already experimented with the new medium in a few shorts they called *astratti* (abstract), in which they attempted to perform *sinfonie cromatiche* (chromatic symphonies) by correlating colors and musical rhythms; among them were *Accordi di colore, Arcobaleno, Les fleurs*, and *La danza*. For a discussion on these experiments, see Bruno Corra, *Il pastore, il gregge e la zampogna* (Bologna: Beltrami, 1912), excerpted in Verdone, "Cinema e letteratura del futurismo," 242–250.

60. Verdone, "Cinema e letteratura del futurismo," 232.

61. Marinetti's emphatic contention about the influence of Italian film theory and practice on European experimental cinema ("La cinematografia astratta è un'invenzione italiana") was first published in *L'Impero* on 1 December 1926. In 1938, almost a decade after the introduction in Italy of sound cinema, Marinetti (with Ginna) published another film manifesto in *La Gazzetta del Popolo*. The piece advanced no theoretical novelties in terms of artistic or political uses of the language uttered by characters on screen, for instance. It simply restated previous modernist strategies such as "asynchronous sound editing" or "musical dissonances." See Verdone and Autera, *Antologia di Bianco & Nero*, 461–462.

62. Born in 1890, he became famous in 1910 for his photographic experiments called *Fotodinamismo* (which were inspired by the *Manifesto of Futurist Painters* and produced with the help of his brother Arturo) aimed at exploring the different phases of human gesture as they were recorded on a photographic plate. On a single photo, Bragaglia would reproduce the blurred trajectory of a movement; thus, he did not isolate its distinct moments (as E.-J. Marey did by breaking the action's duration into subsequent but discrete images), nor did he recompose the entire dynamics (as moving pictures did). The end result was the absolutely non-naturalistic and yet poetic rendering of the continuum of a human action. This rendering style was for him "the expression and the vibration of modern life." Later in the decade, influenced by German and French avant-garde and Expressionist cinema, he directed two of the most stylized early Italian films, *Thaïs* (1917) and *Perfido incanto* (1917), both starring *diva* Thais Galitzky. Impressively active throughout the 1920s and 1930s, Bragaglia wrote, directed, and choreographed innumerable plays, translated European playwrights, and made unique contributions as a critic and art exhibitor; his work brought the latest European work in art, film, and theater to Italy.

63. A. G. Bragaglia, *Il film sonoro* (Milano: Edizioni Corbaccio, 1929), 54ff.

64. Ibid., 99. "Sound film seems to me the antithesis of mute art, since film

characters, performing on screen with their mouth open, with their voice coming from I-don't-know-where, appear like tense and disoriented ventriloquists" (129).

65. Ibid., 151–152.

66. "[Film actors] feel as if they were sent to exile—exiled not only from the stage, but almost from themselves as well. Because their action, the *animated* action of their *animated* body does not exist anymore, there, on the screens of the cinematographs; there appears only *their image*, caught in motion, busy in a gesture, in an expression which sparks and disappears. Confused and with a vague feeling of discomfort, they sense an inexplicable emptiness: their bodies are almost stripped, deprived of their reality, breath, voice, and any of the noises they produce in their gestures, just to become a flickering mute image, appeared for a moment on a screen, later silently disappeared." Luigi Pirandello, *Shoot! (Si gira): The Notebooks of Serafino Gubbio, Cinematograph Operator*, trans. C. K. Scott Moncrieff (New York: Dutton, 1926; reprint, New York: Howard Fertig, 1975), 64 (Pirandello's italics). Pirandello's novel had been published in book form as *Si gira . . .* (Milano: Treves, 1916), but it had already appeared a year before, between 1 June and 16 August 1915, in the literary periodical *Nuova Antologia*. For a discussion of the significance of Pirandello's novel for film theory, see Gavriel Moses, "'Gubbio in Gabbia': Pirandello's Cameraman and the Entrapments of Film Vision," *MLN* 94, no. 1 (1979): 36–60; and "Film Theory as Literary Genre in Pirandello and the Film Novel," in *Annali d'Italianistica* 6 (1988): 38–68 (special issue on "New Perspectives on Italian Films and Literature," edited by John Welle).

67. Interestingly, in the Ur-text of contemporary critical (and cinema) studies, Walter Benjamin's 1936 essay "The Work of Art in the Age of Mechanical Reproduction," the German critic quotes *Si gira* (citing it from an essay by Léon Pierre-Quint) for its remarks about the metamorphosis of film actors before the camera. Although Benjamin was aware that Pirandello was referring only to the silent film period, his critical emphasis on the mechanical recording of the performance and on the loss of the artwork's physical aura illegitimately extends Pirandello's claims by pairing silent and sound cinema together. He wrote, "For in this respect, the sound film did not change anything essential. What matters is that the part is acted not for an audience, but for a mechanical contrivance—in the case of the sound film, for two of them" (229). The position of the Italian playwright, as we shall see, was more complex, because he differentiated between the two film forms of silent cinema and sound cinema.

68. The first contribution was an interview done in London (where he had been invited by the British International Pictures to view some "talkies") that was published in *Corriere della Sera* on 19 April 1929—coincidentally, the very day *The Jazz Singer* premiered in Rome. Pirandello's influential intervention later appeared in a more systematic fashion in an essay published in *Corriere della Sera* on 16 June 1929 that was titled "Se il film

parlante abolirà il teatro." The essay was quickly translated into English and published that same month as "Pirandello Views the 'Talkies'," in the *Anglo-American Newspaper Service* (London-New York) and in *The New York Times Magazine* on 28 July (Section V, 1–2). Here I am using the *New York Times* translation. The original Italian version of "Se il film parlante abolirà il teatro" is now included in Francesco Càllari, ed., *Pirandello e il Cinema. Con una raccolta completa degli scritti teorici e creativi* (Venezia: Marsilio Editori, 1991), 118–120.

69. Pirandello, "Pirandello Views the 'Talkies'," 2.

70. Ibid.

71.   The Cinema must free itself from literature in order to find its real expression. Literature is not its element: its real element is music. Let the cinema free itself altogether from literature and plunge into music—but not that type of music which accompanies singing; singing is uttering words, and words, even when sung, cannot belong to an image. And the image, as it cannot speak, so it cannot sing. . . . The music I mean is that music which speaks to everybody without words, the music that expresses itself with sound and of which the cinema could be the visible language. In other words, pure music and pure vision. . . . "Cinemelography" should be the name of the revolution —the visible language of music. Any music, from the popular kind, the genuine expression of sentiment, to that of Bach or of Scarlatti, of Beethoven or of Chopin. (Ibid.)

Hypotheses about the origins of the name and concept of "cinemelography" range from Wagner's aesthetic of "verbal associations" or French impressionists' theories of cinema's visual rhythm to a possible connection with Pasquale Pagliej, inventor in 1906 of a very popular talking cinema apparatus. See Raffaelli, *Il cinema nella lingua di Pirandello*, 116–117.

72. *Acciaio*'s director, Walter Ruttmann, had been known for his experiments with geometrical images and musical rhythms since the early 1920s. Before his famous city film, *Berlin, Die Symphonie einer Großstadt* (1927) and his *Melodie der Welt* (1929), Ruttmann had made experimental shorts such as *Die tönnende Welle* (a sound film without images, only tones) and *Opus I, Opus II,* and *Opus III* (1922, 1923, and 1924). Malipiero, one of the most original composers of his generation, was fairly unknown abroad but extremely appreciated at home for his operas and his editorial works on the complete editions of Monteverdi and Vivaldi. Despite his great knowledge of older music, his musical taste and technique, which privileged great rhythmic freedom and modal harmony as opposed to more traditional counterpoint or thematic developments, was recognized as highly modern. *Acciaio*'s "Symphony of the Machines" was said to unequivocally cite *Steel Foundry* (1928), a futurist musical poem by Soviet composer Aleksander Mossolov.

73.   The film's high artistic ambitions generated continuous friction on and off

the set. On the complex negotiations made by Cines's director Emilio Cecchi to tame the conflicts between Pirandello, Ruttmann, Mario Soldati (screenwriter), and Gian Francesco Malipiero (music composer), see Claudio Camerini, ed., *Acciaio. Un film degli anni Trenta. Pagine inedite di una storia italiana* (Torino: CSC/Nuova ERI, 1990), 11–63 and 237–265. In the end, under Pirandello's request, the film's opening title became: "Free interpretation of a story by Luigi Pirandello" (*Libera interpretazione di una trama di Luigi Pirandello*).

74. Enrico Roma, "Pirandello e il cinema," *Comoedia* no. 7 (15 July–15 August 1932), quoted in Gian Carlo Bertolina, "La Musica," in Camerini, *Acciaio*, 175ff. Bertolina claims that, regardless of the isolation in which both Ruttmann and Malipiero happened to work, *Acciaio* represents a unique example within Italian sound cinema of an effective coupling of visual and musical scores.

75. I will be referring here to several essays and monographs by Roberto Paolella, "Origine e senso dell'espressione cinematografica," *Cinema* 8, no. 157 (10 January 1943): 10–12; "Origine e senso dell'espressione cinematografica: dal muto al parlato," *Cinema* 8, no. 161 (10 March 1943): 140–142; *Storia del cinema muto* (Napoli: Giannini, 1956); and *Storia del cinema sonoro (1926–1939)* (Napoli: Giannini, 1966). Surprisingly, Redi does not mention Paolella's crucial essays in his review of the critical literature published in *Cinema* (1937–1943). See Redi, *Cinema Scritto*.

76. Marcel Jousse (1886–1961) was a renowned scholar in orality-literacy studies, whose work circulated widely in continental Europe in the 1920s and 1930s. He became famous after the publication of "Le Style oral rythmique et mnémotechnique chez les verbo-moteurs" in a 1924 issue of *Archives de philosophie* that was reprinted a year later as a monograph by Gabriel Beauchesne. Among his later works are *Du Mimisme à la Musique chez l'enfant* (1935); *Manducation de la Parole* (1950); *L'Anthropologie du geste* (1974); and *Le Parlant, la Parole et le Souffle* (published posthumously, 1978). From 1932 to 1950 Jousse held a chair of Linguistic Anthropology at the Ecole d'Anthropologie. Ernesto De Martino (1908–1965) was an Italian anthropologist, author of various works on Italy's southern religious rituals and magical practices. Among his works are *Il mondo magico. Prolegomeni ad una storia del magismo* (1948) and *Sud e Magia* (1960).

77. The first one, called "reactive mimicry," is instinctual, biologically defined, and quite visible with surprisingly universal similarity among children, indigenous peoples, and deaf-mutes. The second one, termed "voluntary mimicry," is an act of intelligent consciousness; it is culturally defined and pertains to the social life of individuals (e.g., conventional reactions such as showing attention, sorrow, etc.). The third one, which Paolella calls "cutting and combining mimicry" (*mimica abbreviatrice e combinatrice*) is a full-fledged language which cinema employs at its best. It is "cutting" in the sense that gestures are not fully performed to convey their meaning: the most suggestive expression is "shortened" to its essential core. It is

"combining" because cinema, like the rhythm of our life, edits several of these emotional heights in one fluent continuum. Paolella explicates the comparison by speaking of *stacco*, when an image is suddenly interrupted (*funzione abbreviatrice*), and of *attacco*, when a new one makes its appearance (*funzione combinatrice*). Paolella, *Storia del cinema muto*, 5ff. The similarities to "fade in/fade out" and "cut" are obvious.

78. Nencioni's categories are actually three: *parlato-parlato, parlato-scritto*, and *parlato-recitato*. Hence, they cover characters' spoken, performed, and written exchanges. See G. Nencioni, "Parlato-parlato, parlato-scritto, parlato-recitato," *Strumenti critici* 10 no. 29 (1976), now in G. Nencioni, *Di scritto e di parlato. Discorsi linguistici* (Bologna: Zanichelli, 1983), 127–179.

79. The fact that orality is closer to mimicry and gesturing than verbality is does not imply that orality equals pantomime; orality, in fact, holds for Paolella an inferior aesthetic efficacy in expressing emotional depth and truth. He supports this view by resorting to Croce's *Estetica*, the anthropological findings of Theodule A. Ribot and Lucien Lévy-Bruhl, and the linguistic theories of Léon Verriest.

80. Tom Gunning, "In Your Face: Gnostic Mission of Early Film," *Modernism/Modernity* 4, no. 1 (1997): 1–29.

81. As he best summarized, if silent films should be regarded as "talking images without the words" (*immagini parlanti senza la parola*), sound films should be described as "spoken images, regardless of the word" (*immagini parlate, malgrado la parola*). Paolella, *Storia del cinema muto*, 10.

82. Ibid., 37.

83. In this direction, the most interesting contributions were Blasetti's early writings and the articles published in the daily *Il Tevere* or in periodicals such as *Il Cinematografo, Il mondo e lo schermo, Lo schermo*, and *Lo spettacolo d'Italia* since the late 1920s. See Blasetti, *Il Cinema che ho vissuto;* and Adriano Aprà, ed., *Scritti sul cinema* (Venezia: Marsilio, 1982).

84. Ruth Ben-Ghiat, "Fascism, Writing, and Memory: The Realist Aesthetic in Italy, 1930–1950," *Journal of Modern History* 67 (September 1995): 631. For a detailed study of realism in Italian literary and film culture, see R. Ben Ghiat, "The Formation of a Fascist Culture: The Realist Movement in Italy, 1930–1943" (Ph.D. dissertation, Brandeis University, 1991), 71–152. For an overview of early inceptions of neorealist film criticism in the 1930s, read Brunetta, *Storia del cinema italiano*, 1: 197–230.

85. For an analysis of the language spoken in radio programs, especially comedies, dramas, cultural and religious education, and news, see Gianni Isola, *Abbassa la tua radio, perfavore. Storia dell'ascolto radiofonico nell'Italia fascista* (Firenze: La Nuova Italia, 1990). An excellent analysis of Mussolini's phonic-rhythmic language (which was often utterly de-semanticized) is in Ermanno Leso, Michele A. Cortellazzo, Ivano Paccagnella, and Fabio Foresti, *La lingua italiana e il fascismo* (Bologna: Consorzio Provinciale Pubblica Lettura, 1978), 15–62. For the evolution of Italian theater, see

Stefano DeMatteis, Martina Lombardi, and Marilea Somaré, eds., *Follie del Varietà. Vicende, memorie personaggi, 1890-1970* (Milano: Feltrinelli, 1980). On the visual and musical rhetorics of the regime's journalism, see Mario Isnenghi, *Intellettuali militanti e intellettuali funzionari. Appunti sulla cultura fascista* (Torino: Einaudi, 1979), 175-185. On the nationalistic instrumentality of opera and on the immense popularity of songs between the wars, see respectively Giovanni Morelli, "L'opera" and Emilio Franzina, "Inni e canzoni," in *I luoghi della memoria. Simboli e miti dell'Italia Unita*, ed. Mario Isnenghi (Roma-Bari: Laterza, 1996), 43-113 and 115-162.

86. The film was an adaptation of a Pirandello's novella *In silenzio* and became famous for the film's leitmotif, the song *Solo per te Lucia*.

87. From the late 1930s on, a musical autarchy revitalized the tradition of *bel canto*, as opposed to popular and regional songs, and opera singers once again returned to the movie scene as successful presences. A few examples would include Tito Schipa in *Tre uomini in frack* (1933) and *Vivere!* (1937), Giacomo Lauri Volpi in *La canzone del sole* (1933), Beniamino Gigli in *Mamma* (1940) and *Torna piccina* (1955), and Carlo Buti in *Se vuoi godere la vita* (1945).

88. The film presents a vast and disorienting panoply of languages—Italian, French, Spanish, and various Italian dialects. Still, it may be surprising to note that it was not an isolated case, but was actually in line with several Italian military films that presented multiple languages and dialects. See *Scarpe al sole* (1935), *Il piccolo alpino* (1940), *La nave bianca* (1941), *Bengasi, Giarabub, I tre aquilotti*, and *Alfa tau* (all made in 1942), and *Quelli della montagna, Marinai senza stelle*, and *Gente dell'aria* (all made in 1943). Interestingly, it is on the front or during military emergencies that dialects acquire an aura of Italianness, authenticity, and realism. See Ruffin and D'Agostino, eds., *Dialoghi di regime*, 106ff. I have discussed in more detail the linguistic fabric of this Camerini film in "Whitened Heroes, Auditory Rhetorics, and National Identity in Interwar Italian Cinema," in *A Place in the Sun: Africa in Italian Colonial Culture*, ed. Patrizia Palumbo (Berkeley and Los Angeles: University of California Press, forthcoming).

89. Symptomatically, Barbaro and Chiarini discarded Luciani's discussion as passé or as limited to films of another historical period. See their *Problemi del Film*, 31; or Luciani's obituary, authored by Barbaro, "Ricordo di S. A. Luciani," first published in *Filmcritica*, no. 2 (January 1951), now in Barbaro, *Servitù e grandezza del cinema*, 99-105.

90. Leading intellectual sponsors such as Lizzani, but also De Santis or Aristarco, often expressed distaste or hostility for *feuilletons* and *letteratura popolare* and did not grant any positive legitimacy to the "heretical" but quite successful comedies and melodramas made in the 1950s in a somewhat neorealist style. Such an attitude distanced them from Gramsci, whom they read late and in very limited terms (*Gli intellettuali e l'organizzazione della cultura, Il Risorgimento*, and *Letteratura e vita nazionale* were

first published only between 1947 and 1951), while their emphasis on the unambiguous singleness of the artistic realm made their positions akin to those of Croce. For instance, Mario Alicata's and Giuseppe De Santis's articles on Verga and Italian cinema published in *Cinema* in the fall of 1941 quietly disregard the dazzling contradictions of merging ambitions of high art with an overt populism. For a general discussion of these discrepancies, see Alberto Asor Rosa, "La resistenza e il gramscianesimo: apogeo e crisi del populismo," in Asor Rosa, *Scrittori e popolo. Il populismo nella letteratura italiana contemporanea* (Roma: Savelli, 1965), 153–280; and Alberto Abruzzese, "Gramsci contro il neorealismo," in Abruzzese, *Verso una sociologia del lavoro intellettuale. Materiali per una sociologia del lavoro intellettuale negli apparati dell'informazione* (Napoli: Liguori, 1979), 59–110.

91. I have examined the relationship between the visual and the aural in Visconti in G. Bertellini, "A Battle *d'Arrière Garde:* Notes on Decadence in Luchino Visconti's *Death in Venice,*" *Film Quarterly* 50, no. 4 (Summer 1997): 11–19.

92. Pier Paolo Pasolini, "Cinema and Oral Language," in *Heretical Empiricism,* ed. Lousie K. Barnett, trans. Ben Lawton and Louise K. Barnett (Bloomington: Indiana University Press, 1988), 264–266.

93. Ibid. (Pasolini's capitalization)

94. "Every poem is metalinguistic, because every poetic word is an incomplete choice between its phonic value and its semantic value. . . . Now music applied to words is simply the extreme example of what I have said. Music destroys the 'sound' of the word, it then takes care of effecting the 'semantic expansion' of the word, and what a semantic expansion we have in the words of *Traviata!* . . . Words are therefore not all ancillary in melodrama; they are extremely important and essential." Pasolini, "Cinema and Oral Language," 265.

3

Intimations of Neorealism in the Fascist *Ventennio*

Ennio Di Nolfo

> For anything so o'erdone is from the purpose of playing,
> whose end, both at the first and now, was and is, to hold
> as 'twere the mirror up to nature: to show virtue her fea-
> ture, scorn her own image, and the very age and body of
> the time his form and pressure.
> —William Shakespeare, *Hamlet,* III.2

Since its inception, many critics have regarded Italian cinematic neo-realism as a splendid and sumptuous flower that bloomed miraculously, almost by chance, among the ruins of a country ravaged by war. How-ever, it would be more accurate to say that, despite the postwar devasta-tion, Italian filmmakers' ingenuity allowed them to recover the cine-matic thread that had been severed by the war and, in representing the country's recent tragedy, to permit this flower to display its final colors before quickly withering. Indeed, this neophyte innocence of the critics has for several decades ceded space to a more attentive study of neo-realism's sources. Many avenues, even the most bizarre, have been pur-sued in this research. Nevertheless, with a little diligence, it has not been difficult to trace the origins of neorealism. As Peter Bondanella mischievously recalls, Umberto Barbaro and George Sadoul (two lead-ing Marxist critics and historians of cinema) situated Nino Martoglio's silent film *Sperduti nel buio* (*Lost in the Dark,* 1914) "in the artistic tra-ditions leading to *Rome, Open City*."[1] Unfortunately, no extant copies remain following the film's destruction by the Germans during World War II. Others have traced the inspiration of neorealist cinema to none other than one of the founders of the Italian Communist Party, Antonio Gramsci,[2] ignoring the not-insignificant matter of Gramsci's incarcera-tion by the Fascists in 1926 and his subsequent death in 1937. Although his *Notebooks,* which were preserved and published between 1948 and 1951, had a profound influence on Italian culture, it appears unlikely that they could have influenced cinematic neorealism, which, in 1948, had already reached its peak and was starting to decline. These varied explanations demonstrate that one can say almost anything when the research methodology for the origins of a cultural phenomenon depends upon the point of departure. That holds true whether one wants to understand the ontological nature of neorealism or wants only to delineate its technical or defining characteristics.

Nonetheless, it is difficult to ignore some points of fact that are placed in the background (or in the foreground, for that matter) for anyone confronting this issue. Neorealism's theorists were, almost without exception, the same individuals who had opened the general debate on the trends in Italian cinema after the second half of the 1930s. Luigi Chiarini, founder of the Centro Sperimentale di Cinematografia (CSC, 1935); Umberto Barbaro, faculty member at the CSC (both he and Chiarini had been writing about cinema since the early 1930s); Luchino Visconti; Mario Alicata; Giuseppe De Santis; Massimo Mida; Michelangelo Antonioni; Carlo Lizzani; Cesare Zavattini; and Gianni Puccini all gained experience as critics (and some also as directors) in the same period. The directors, from Vittorio De Sica to Francesco De Robertis, from Roberto Rossellini to Luchino Visconti, were already on the brink of neorealism in 1941–1943, as were Alessandro Blasetti, Mario Camerini, Ferdinando Maria Poggioli, and many others. Among the actors, De Sica could justly be considered one of the most popular in Italy, along with Amedeo Nazzari, Clara Calamai, Alida Valli, and Aldo Fabrizi. The scriptwriters, the photographers, and the musical score composers (already Nino Rota stood out) were also well established. In short, the people who constituted the neorealist cinema community were the same ones who had constituted the cinema community in the decade preceding the fall of Fascism. Men made new by the new times? Perhaps there was a different chemistry, derived from building on pre-existing ideas that were evident during Fascism? Was it then the age itself that made the difference? In other words, with the fall of Fascism, did the neorealist potentialities finally have the possibility to manifest themselves, and did the fertile ground in which they had incubated yield its fruits? Indeed, the neorealist films were more anti-German than anti-Fascist; thus, the chemistry would acquire a national temper, tied more to the Resistance movement against the Germans than to militant anti-Fascism. Moreover, it could be said that there was not a substantial homogeneity of political or technical inspiration among the well-known neorealist films of the Golden Age. And it could even be added that some Fascist films of the waning months of the war (although there is a tendency not to discuss them) follow more closely certain tenets of theorized realism than the neorealist films of the Golden Age.

To understand this transitional period better, it is necessary to return to neorealism's underlying themes. Among the infinite variants, there are some extreme definitions that, by contradicting each other, cancel each other. Cesare Zavattini, in the footsteps of Dziga Vertov, theorized the "cinema-truth." "I am the eye of the film. I am a mechanical eye; I am the camera that shows the world as it sees it," was the maxim-manifesto of the author of *Man with a Movie Camera* (1929).[3] Later, Cesare Zavattini (who wavered in praxis from one extreme to another) theorized an analogous approach. In his view, life had to be captured in its everyday aspects. Today, one could say that the director should wander about the streets with a steadycam and his film would be complete. "Our cinema," Zavattini used to say, "would like to make erupt on the screen, as a supreme act of faith, ninety consecutive minutes of a man's life. Each one of these shots will be equally intense and revealing and will no longer be just a bridge to the next shot, but will vibrate within itself like a microcosm."[4] It was the subjective artistic illusion of knowing how to capture the truth through the camera. It is worth remembering when encountering this way of thinking that, since 1915, Luigi Pirandello's *Shoot!* (published in installments in *Nuova Antologia* and in definitive form in 1925 as *The Notebooks of Serafino Gubbio Camera-Man*) had pointed out bluntly the deformation implicit in the cinematographic fact—a valid observation for every type of language.

In the end, the position of the prewar realists, who were drawing from Giovanni Verga and Luigi Capuana (that is to say, from the Italian literary tradition of late nineteenth-century *verismo*), was not very far from that of Vertov or of Zavattini. In the November 1941 issue of *Cinema*, the journal edited by Vittorio Mussolini, Mario Alicata and Giuseppe De Santis exploit this literary precedent. Invoking Verga and Capuana, they declaim:

> We want to bring our movie camera in the streets, in the fields, in the ports, in the factories of this country; we are also convinced that one day we will make our most beautiful film following the slow, tired step of the worker returning to his home, narrating the essential poetry of a new and pure life that contains within itself the secret of its aristocratic beauty.[5]

From the end of the 1930s until 1943, the debate that these and other authors initiated in the pages of *Cinema* illustrated the progressive surfacing of the need for a break from traditionalism. Some translated this need covertly into underlying political stances, while others considered it to be completely compatible with a reformatory vision of Fascism. Thus, Fascism remained an incidental fact with respect to the dominant critical current, which was concerned, instead, with the idea of cinema. Not by chance, when one examines neorealism, one finds that one of its "founding fathers," Luigi Chiarini, gave very clear-cut definitions: "The soul of neorealism was . . . the social reality, the human condition of the Italian people, during the German occupation, the Allied one, in the chaos immediately following the war. . . . Every other interpretation is arbitrary and tendentious. In the neorealist films . . . it is the facts that speak . . . in their social historical meaning." However, according to Chiarini, this view of neorealism was acquired during the war and was a concept to which no precedents could be linked precisely because it was a breach that was situated between two extremes: "two dates [1945 and 1948] between which is enclosed the beginning and the end of a period." After 1948, neorealism was finished. "The chrysalis," a dejected Chiarini admitted, "did not become a butterfly."[6] Thus, Chiarini alluded to breaches, but he emphasized the war and the postwar period, Nazism and the Allied occupation, over the Fascist period. Not by chance, the Fascist experience was excluded from the extremist definition. The "war," the "Germans," the "Allies"—not Fascism—became the dominant motif, the clear line that traced the boundaries between realism in the "anthropomorphic" sense (to use Luchino Visconti's definition) or in the "Verghian" sense and the cinematic neorealism of the postwar period. But by speaking of breaches, Chiarini contradicts himself, imputing the solution of continuity to traumatic events beyond Italian control, events that were influencing a journey already under way. The contradiction was Chiarini's, not neorealism's, nor of those who instead were theorizing continuity, affirming that neorealism's importance could be understood only by "starting from the cinema of the '30s."[7]

Bazin, one of the most resolute apologists of neorealist poetics, wrote:

> Some components of the new Italian school existed before the Liberation: personnel, techniques, aesthetic trends. But it was their historical, social, and economic combination that suddenly created a synthesis in which new elements also made themselves manifest. . . . In Italy the Liberation did not signify a return to the old and recent freedom; it meant political revolution, Allied occupation, economic and social upheaval.

In fact, in Italy, Bazin noted in 1948:

> The Liberation came slowly, through endless months. . . . When Rossellini made *Paisà*, his script was concerned with things actu-

ally happening at the time. . . . Italian cinema was noted for its concern with actual day-to-day events. . . . Even when the central scene of the script is not concerned with an actual occurrence, Italian films are first and foremost reconstituted reportage. . . . The recent Italian films are at least prerevolutionary. They all reject implicitly or explicitly, with humor, satire or poetry, the reality they are using.[8]

In such a way, tortuous though it may be, the elements compose themselves: the breach is a rhetorical artifice, or the result of the grandiloquent sense of Italy's history. To understand this, one must look back to the 1930s, or, in the opposite sense, one must discover if there exists an autonomous neorealist aesthetic with respect to party politics after 1948. Also, one must show where, how, when, and with what technical language the new cinema asserts itself. Alternatively, the equation acquires an almost subversive simplicity with respect to the commonplace: neorealism is one of those strains of Italian cinema (the most important one aesthetically and poetically, even if not the most economically remunerative) that was born from the evolution of a debate begun years before and developed at a time in which the historical circumstances imposed contact with the immediate reality. If for no other reason than the unavailability of the studio complex at Cinecittà, Italian filmmakers, whose numbers had increased dramatically, had to find places and ways to carry out their work. Ironically, this limitation gave them greater freedom to develop both their aesthetic propensity and to escape mannered and adulterated comedies through a more direct language, one that was better suited to expressing less arbitrary metaphors that were, instead, inspired by daily experiences.

Perhaps the traits of neorealism are more easily grasped by trying to identify them retrospectively rather than relying on either the theoretical or the sociopolitical speculations of its protagonists. From the outside, that is, in a pragmatic manner, it is easy to see that there are several common traits in the neorealist filmography: the intention to treat relevant themes; the desire to immerse oneself in everyday matters; the desire to show things "as they are," or, rather, "as they appear" to the author of the film; the desire to express in a direct, immediate, and sincere manner the drama that Italians lived during the war, or even the very drama of daily life in every period of time; the propensity to film on location; the search for non-professional actors; the will to follow a narrative structure tied less to formalist tradition, a narrative that is more free, more capable of expressing in an explicit manner, almost screaming, at times too loud (and thus artificial), its own ideas.[9] These traits cannot be separated from the war experience; therefore, they tend to enclose neorealism in a brief arc of time, occupied by a few directors and a few works. However, perhaps the question becomes clearer if one observes the state of Italian cinema during the passage from Fascism to liberation. Only by looking closely at that transition is it possible to become aware of the elements of both continuity and discontinuity in their specific limits.

From the beginning of the war to mid-1943, the "four musketeers" of Italian neorealism, Francesco De Robertis, Roberto Rossellini, Vittorio De Sica, and Luchino Visconti, were all engaged (with one exception) in their first films and projects suggestive of neorealism. Other directors were also active, but their cases need to be considered separately, because in their works the discontinuity is less startling than in the above cases (with one exception: that of Luchino Visconti, who was working on his first film and therefore lacked terms of comparison other than the theoretical purposes which inspired him).

De Robertis, usually considered to be Rossellini's mentor, was in charge of the Centro Cinematografico del Ministero della Marina. In 1941, he directed *Uomini sul fondo* (*SOS Submarine*), the rescue story of sailors trapped in a submarine. The lack of professional actors, the dry and documentary style, the forsaking of military and Fascist rhetoric in cogent moments gave the war film the feel of a rough, proto-realist documentary. In 1942, De Robertis directed another film set in the navy, *Alfa Tau*. Also bare and without protagonists, *Alfa Tau* showed the exploits of the Italian submarine *Toti*, the ramming of a British cruiser, and the daily lives of the sailors on board.

In 1941, De Robertis offered Roberto Rossellini his first opportunity to direct a feature-length film. Until then Rossellini had produced three documentaries and had been assistant director to Goffredo Alessandrini on a film of military and Fascist propaganda, *Luciano Serra, pilota* (*Luciano Serra, Pilot*, 1938). During the war, he completed three works. Even the first one contains certain recognizable characteristics of Rossellini's future cinematic trademarks. *La nave bianca* (*Hospital Ship*, 1941) is the story of Italian sailors recovering from an enemy attack and being cared for on a Red Cross ship. Rossellini's use of weak plots and basic stylistic elements gives his films a similar feel to those of De Robertis, although Rossellini tended to maintain a propensity for the (melo)dramatic. As Rossellini's biographer writes: "The strength . . . of the film, in its best moments, is the stamp of an impressive authorial personality who knows how to probe that lesson of 'integral realism' in contact with other human and social situations, which are just as tragic and desperate."[10] Indeed, it presents an apologia for the Fascist war,

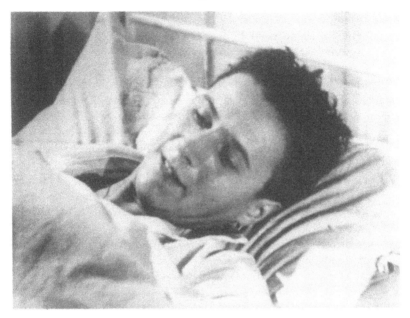

11. *La nave bianca* (Roberto Rossellini, 1941).
Courtesy of the Museum of Modern Art Film Stills Archive

filmed soberly and without concessions to rhetoric. In 1942, Rossellini abandoned both the purely documentary genre and the navy in favor of the air force. Using the screenplay written by Vittorio Mussolini, Michelangelo Antonioni, and Massimo Mida, he directed *Un pilota ritorna* (*A Pilot Returns*), which had professional actors. The dry, sober style likely contributed to the film's first-place award in 1942 at the international film competition sponsored by the GIL (Gioventù Italiana del Littorio, the youth organization of the Fascist Party).[11] These early efforts revealed Rossellini to be something more than just a promising director. Their technical confidence and sensitivity to human vicissitudes demonstrated an incisive personality. The opportunities followed one after the other. In 1942, Rossellini was again at work on a more demanding film, *L'uomo della croce* (*Man of the Cross*). This was the apologia for the two Rossellinian ideals: love for the Fascist fatherland and religious sensibility. In fact, *L'uomo della croce* tells the story of an Italian chaplain on the Russian front. Captured by the Soviets while aiding a wounded soldier, the chaplain is able to escape and to hide while always managing to care for both his fellow Italians and the Russian peasants, who are devastated by the war. When he is killed by the Soviets while trying to aid a Russian soldier, his martyrdom is complete. The combination of elements could not have been more explicitly propagandistic. Asvero Gravelli, one of the scriptwriters and a Fascist extremist, devised the figure of the protagonist, inspired by the story of Father Reginaldo Giuliani, another chaplain of Fascist martyrology; he was the recipient of the Gold Medal posthumously after being killed during the war in Ethiopia. The need to update the subject led to the change in both setting and character, but the sequence of shots depicting Ladispoli (the location where the film was partly shot) shows huts that are as indigenous to the Russian steppes as they are to the Denakil Plain. The film premiered in June 1943. Giuseppe De Santis recognized in it "a pure documentary vein," too often imbued, however, with an "intimate vein," to the point of giving the impression that "two different hands" had "presided over the making of the film." However, this objection did not prevent the critic and future director from appreciating the rhythm of many dramatic scenes that avoided the temptation of heavy-handed rhetoric.[12] Despite these concessions to style, even in Rossellini's texts it was difficult to find a markedly anti-Fascist realism: while Mussolini's Italy was crumbling around him, the propaganda of his films still attempted to maintain a moderately high level of patriotic morale.

De Sica had no need to make a name for himself. He had debuted with *Rose scarlatte* (*Scarlet Roses*, 1940), which was followed by the more realist bent of *Teresa Venerdì* (1941). Alongside the latter, his two works that best reflect the changes in progress were *Un garibaldino al convento* (*A Garibaldian at the Monastery*, 1942) and *I bambini ci guardano* (*The Children Are Watching Us*, 1943). Although Giuseppe De Santis liked *Un garibaldino al convento*, noticing traces of René Clair and even distant reminiscences of Jacques Feyder's *La Kermesse Héroique* (*Carnival in Flanders*, 1935), it was not well received by the anti-conformist critics. De Santis appreciated "the quick-paced and excited rhythm" and the acute psychological observations that the director had ably infused in the choral construction of the film.[13] However, he failed to recognize the political significance of De Sica's clever identification of female adolescence in bloom (the young boarders in the convent) with volunteerism that is sacrificed for the national cause. What eluded the critic was the fact that the film, more or less consciously, was an apologia of Fascist volunteerism against the enemy—the Bourbon officials followed by the Anglo-American invaders. Finding the genesis of neorealism in the sentimental sketches of De Sica's comedies seems to be a rather reckless operation, just as it is reckless to read too much into the facts that *I bambini ci guardano* marked the beginning of the fruitful collaboration between De Sica as director and Cesare Zavattini as screenwriter and

12. *L'uomo della croce* (**Roberto Rossellini, 1942**).
Courtesy of the Museum of Modern Art Film Stills Archive

that its representation of bourgeois tragedy can somehow be characterized as an expression of anti-Fascist realism. The fact that the adultery
and suicide of the betrayed husband are seen from the visual perspective
of a child certainly anticipates the director's sensitivities toward both
family problems and the emotive potentials offered to cinema by the
gaze of the child. However, the critique of the bourgeois family was
certainly neither new nor inherently anti-Fascist, since it dated back,
first in the theatrical tradition and then in the filmic one, to the very
origins of the bourgeoisie. This critique spans from Goldoni to Pirandello and includes Mussolini's voluminous speeches aimed toward de-
molishing the bourgeois lifestyle's softness in order to create both a
militant and a military spirit in Italians. Thus, paradoxically, one could
say that this film was in line with Fascist criticism, although not with
Catholic mentality.

Italian cinema's turning point under Fascism would then be the one
film that actually does anticipate neorealism: Luchino Visconti's *Ossessione* (*Obsession*), shot in 1942 and screened in 1943. There is little
doubt that Visconti's first film, prepared after years of theoretical reflection and collaboration with French directors such as Jean Renoir, repre-

13. *I bambini ci guardano* (Vittorio De Sica, 1943).
Courtesy of the Museum of Modern Art Film Stills Archive

sents an aesthetic watershed for Italian cinema. *Ossessione* shattered the traditional canons of the elegant Italian comedies of more or less realist inspiration. The film confronted the complex realities which, not by chance, and despite the formal limitations of the text from which Visconti drew his inspiration (James Cain's *The Postman Always Rings Twice*), would then influence so many directors. However, since *Ossessione* was made when the fall of Fascism was still far off, expressions of anti-Fascism could be made only through a codified language. Even if such covert subversiveness were enough to give the film a precise political connotation, is it enough to bestow upon *Ossessione* the definition of "neorealist"? Despite the difficulties of finding a conventional definition of neorealism, it seems rather difficult to classify it as an expression of immediacy, a representation of the real, because it is being perceived, in a direct, sincere way, without artificial constructions that give the product a "calligraphic" character. In those same years, another young director, Renato Castellani, completed his first film, *Un colpo di pistola* (*A Pistol Shot*, 1942), which was reviewed as charming and well constructed but was criticized by the writers of *Cinema* (the breeding ground of realism and proto-neorealism) for being "a film in which everything [was] calculated and therefore . . . lacking any energy."[14] However, was there a film in Italy during those years that was more calculated, more conceptualized, more prepared, and consequently less spontaneous and less realist than *Ossessione*?

In his study of the sociology of cinema, Pierre Sorlin dedicates to *Ossessione* over forty pages, in which he analyzes the film's structure. He seeks to demonstrate that its construction is perfectly symmetrical on the basis of 490 shots. In these, he identifies such a clear-cut division that the central shot, number 248, in his view can be considered an "axis of symmetry" that would permit "the folding of the two halves of the film, one on the other." For Sorlin, this effect brings to light "obvious relations" that lead him to the conclusion that "*Ossessione* appears from the beginning like a film with a rigid structure."[15] As far as the anti-Fascist apologist chorus implicit in Visconti's film,[16] Sorlin contrasts the usual interpretation with a more objective one:

> It would be humorous to search for traces of Fascism in *Ossessione:* the producers highlighted their disapproval by avoiding the immediacy of the present and instead presenting an unusual and atemporal Italy, dusty and ignorant of politics and war. And yet, without having to imagine direct influences, it is difficult to ignore that which is not a simple coincidence: the film illustrates, at least partially, a view of social relations that the Mussolini regime had no reason to condemn.[17]

In a less articulate and subtle manner than Sorlin, Massimo Girotti also revealed the calculated and structured characteristics of the film when, in 1989, he related the following anecdote. The actor recalled that Visconti made him repeat the final sequence of the film more than forty times. Finally, on the last take, Girotti appealed to the mercy of the director in order to spare himself a dramatic effort that he was no longer capable of sustaining. Visconti answered that indeed this last take had provided that type of expressive reality for which he had been searching for so long.[18] Thus, the anecdote relates an "unusual and atemporal" reality, a valiant search for the most suitable formal solutions with the desired aesthetic result. But was this neorealism? Or even, as Father Felix Morlion, one of Rossellini's sources of inspiration, wrote a few years later, "perhaps the most accomplished and complex work of Italian realism?"[19] Only by overlooking the many paradoxes and manipulating history is it possible to answer in the affirmative.

So the "four musketeers" of neorealism lived in a phase of preparation. How was it possible that, despite everything, they achieved such different goals? Perhaps all the histories of Italian cinema that examine the years from 1944 to 1948 slight the name of De Robertis. Unlike the majority of directors, De Robertis did not interrupt his work after the armistice on 8 September 1943, when Italy was divided in two. As the Allies slowly advanced up the peninsula, entrusting the south to a "free" government, De Robertis fled north, which was occupied by the Germans, under whose auspices Mussolini's Social Republic was formed. Here, the Republic waged constant battle against the armed Resistance that aggressively pursued the new enemy in the cities and in the mountains. Despite what was happening around him, De Robertis continued with his artistic itinerary and prepared, in full stylistic continuity, the first neorealist film shot in Italy: *La vita semplice* (*The Simple Life*). He filmed in Venice in 1944, using the facilities that Luigi Freddi had built on the Lido for those few actors and directors that preferred to work under the Republic of Salò rather than align themselves immediately with anti-Fascism or prudently wait to see where the events would lead.

Although copies of *La vita semplice* in circulation (it was screened in Italy in 1947) are extremely rare, those who are able to view it cannot ignore the evidence. Certainly it is a transitional film, adapted to the presumed needs of the new postwar public. It grafts a silly sentimental tale to a robust trunk of pure neorealism to explain the happy ending. The entire first half of the film anticipates neorealist forms. Of course the characters' basic needs were represented in terms of a providential apologia and of a willful poverty as a premise for happiness. Also, the social denunciation, implicit or explicit in mature neorealism, is clearly absent. However, the entire first half of the film is filled with neorealistic elements: the on-location shooting of the work sites of the *squeri* (the gondola carpenters), the use of Venetian dialect as a functional language and not as a quaint or odd artifice, the representation of the exhaustion of working in poverty, the depiction of the daily hunger of the poor worker, the denunciation of financial capitalism as an element of corruption, and the petition for justice and work. Nor does it lack the figure of the tiny foundling—Mao is a runaway who is spontaneously good, a dreamer, and innocent. Already a tested stereotype through other representations of youth, he is also a direct precursor of Rossellini's and De Sica's children—a connection made even more striking by the physical similarities they all share. What is there to say about such a movie in those historical conditions? Was it De Robertis's style? But is not such a simplistic response too limiting? How could De Robertis make that type of cinema under the Nazi-Fascist regime of the Republic of Salò and without having undergone the anti-Fascist experience? Was the war experience enough? Does this mean that the conflation of "anti-Fascism" and "war," generally viewed as essential to neorealism's development, is unnecessary? In other words, is anti-Fascism but a chance political addition, when the war itself might suffice to explain neorealism?

As it is easy to see, these are fundamental questions that re-propose in full the issue of whether there is continuity or rupture between Fascism's realist cinema and post-Fascist neorealist cinema. However, perhaps the answer to this question is not as difficult as first appearances might lead one to believe. The first neorealist film to appear after the war (although it was shot in liberated Rome while the war still raged in northern Italy) was *Roma città aperta (Rome, Open City)*, screened at the Quirino Theater in Rome on 24 September 1945. The second film of this new type was *Sciuscià (Shoeshine)*, released on 27 April 1946. In December 1946 (after its presentation in Venice in September), *Paisà*, also by Rossellini, appeared on the screens. In 1948, De Sica's *Ladri di biciclette (The Bicycle Thief)*, Visconti's *La terra trema (The Earth Trembles)*, and Rossellini's *Germania anno zero (Germany, Year Zero)* came out. Alongside these, some lesser-known directors were making films inspired by the same subjects but with less public recognition. In practice, neorealism's Golden Age alludes only to the above-mentioned films. It is a stretch to include the later works of De Sica such as *Miracolo a Milano (Miracle in Milan*, 1951) or *Umberto D.* (1952), or Visconti's *Bellissima* (1951). *Riso Amaro (Bitter Rice*, 1948) by Giuseppe De Santis represents a separate case: a work, which, despite the external trappings, can be considered a true neorealist film rather than an actively committed political film only through rationalization.

Except in friendly environments, the great neorealist films did not receive a warm reception from Italian critics. As far as the public went, with the exception of *Roma città aperta*, which stayed in the theaters for forty-eight days, they all lasted less than twenty days. *La terra trema* showed for eight days in Rome and in Milan for only six.[20] In general, even taking into account the subsequent screenings at the second-run theaters, the neorealist films did not enjoy great public success and registered at the bottom of box-office receipts—especially when compared to escapist films or the American films that had recently returned to the Italian market. Among Italian films, the great successes were *Come persi la guerra (How I Lost the War)*, which boasted the highest revenue for 1946 thanks to the simplistic comedy of Erminio Macario, and the heroic-comic parody of neorealism, *Vivere in pace (To Live in Peace*, 1947), by Luigi Zampa. However, the new Italian films received an enthusiastic reception abroad. In 1946, *Roma città aperta* was awarded the grand prize at Cannes. In 1947, De Sica won an Oscar for *Sciuscià*, and then in 1949 he took home another for *Ladri di biciclette*. In Italy, the only public recognition was the Golden Medal given to *Paisà* in 1946 at the Venice Film Festival. In New York, *Roma città aperta* showed in the same theater for over a year and recorded receipts of 1 to 3 million dollars, while it only took in 61 million lire in Italy in 1945.[21] In other words, "neorealism" was a foreign discovery rather than an Italian one. In France, André Bazin provided neorealism with an apologia, bending it to his own interpretation but also elevating it to the height of cinematic art.[22] This success abroad made even Italians understand the force of the new cinema and made them believe in it. Like a returning wave that was imbued with provincialism, neorealism became important for Italians, too. Elevated to the status of something important and completely new, it became the cinema of a free and democratic Italy. In its representations of the war, anti-Fascism, the Resistance, and the Liberation, it signaled a break with the past.

These are the concepts that need to be examined. While it is not possible to analyze briefly the works of the "three musketeers" (deprived of De Robertis's guidance, who, for unknown personal reasons assumed a marginal role after 1944 and fell into relative obscurity to the point that no one recognized the pioneer value of *La vita semplice* when it was shown in 1947), even a cursory glance demonstrates the profound diversity of their inspirations and methods. With *Roma città aperta*, Rossellini remained faithful to himself. As in *L'uomo della croce*, the image of the priest was at the heart of the story. In 1943, it was a chaplain in the Fascist war effort; in 1945, it was Don Pietro Morosini, a priest moved by anti-Fascist pietas. However, the entire film projected a sense of harsh and painful bitterness that was tied to themes of the Nazi occupation. In a practical sense, it represented a kind of moral stand for the Catholic–Christian Democrat Rossellini against the horrors that the regime, which he had so recently served, had inflicted at the hands of the German torturers. *Paisà* too was a melancholy sequence of apologues—almost a canticle on the conditions in an Italy overrun by war and occupied by the Allies. The film addressed neither anti-Fascism nor social issues; it represented only shock and pain in the efforts to confront daily life. In the same way, *Germania anno zero*'s fulcrum is the dramatic image of childhood lacerated by the miseries of the postwar era. Enemies, Fascists, and society were all relatively absent; in the forefront were the dramas of moral and civil conscience.

With De Sica, the social commitment becomes explicit. However, in *Sciuscià*, a film orchestrated to the most minute details, the miserable reality of Neapolitan youth is transfigured into the dream of possessing something mythical: a horse for the two young protagonists. More composite and more complex, *Ladri di biciclette*, hinging on the drama of a father-son relationship in a climate of poverty made even more desperate by unemployment, broached directly the harshness of social relations. However, to reduce it to this dimension betrays the diverse interpretations to which the film lends itself. At any rate, as a preliminary conclusion, between Rossellini and De Sica there existed a political and cultural abyss. A similar abyss existed between each of them and Luchino Visconti. *La terra trema* is a formal and substantial model for a cinema of denunciation and represents neorealism tinged by Communist propaganda and dominated by a Zhdanovian aesthetic—it was partially financed by the Italian Communist Party.[23] Today both the film's inspiration and its neorealist designation seem debatable. Robert J. Flaherty's 1934 film *Man of Aran* developed an analogous theme to Visconti's, although some critics have refuted the idea, preferring to emphasize the differences rather than the similarities which are instead difficult to ignore.[24] Perhaps it is true that Flaherty's intentions were more mythical, poetic, or anthropological than social; however, after fifty years, it seems reasonable to question Visconti's realism. Certainly Visconti selected real fishermen as actors and had them act, or, more precisely, filmed them while they went about their daily routines. On this he imposed an entirely personal aim, a laborious and detailed script, and the use of human material that was called upon to speak in dialect but then dubbed to make the film comprehensible to its spectators. These actions raise the question of whether he manipulated reality rather than the question of whether he actually captured the real. Thus, despite the profoundly distinct styles of Rossellini, De Sica, and Visconti, the works of the three filmmakers continue to be subsumed under a monolithic neorealism.

On the basis of these differences, is it still possible to talk about one voice or one school that was inspired by the same project although lived and filtered through distinct personalities? Is it really possible to think that a handful of films, which are different by nature and inspiration but all tied to the biographies of their directors, formed a miraculous new cinema? Or is it not perhaps more reasonable to imagine a colossal error to which these directors gladly lent their support because they gained fame and prestige from its propagation? In this respect, if one considers neorealism to have been an American invention, then what are the underlying premises that led American critics to this erroneous conclusion? While Giovanni Pastrone's *Cabiria* (1914) and a few other silent films had achieved international success, Italian talkies remained practically unknown to the American public. This lack of familiarity was compounded by the relatively late development of sound film in Italy and the government-decreed protectionist regulations in 1938 to shield

Italian film production from foreign competition.[25] These actions meant that after the removal of trade barriers, postwar Italian films erupted onto a virgin market and appeared as a novelty when in actuality they were nothing but an evolutionary phase of an industrial sector that was searching for an identity after the war.

It is necessary, at this point, to take a step back. Italian cinema enjoyed a degree of success abroad during the silent era. *Cabiria* is just the most famous example of that success. In the United States, Griffith looked to Pastrone's film as a model for *The Birth of a Nation*. After 1923, the fortunes of Italian cinema underwent a severe crisis. Production dropped to an average of some twenty films a year, many of which were part of the *Maciste* series (a kind and generous strongman, not unlike certain American prototypes). The advent of sound and the economic crisis of 1929–1932 dealt a fatal blow to Italian producers. An industry that during the golden years was able to produce over 150 films a year found itself in 1930, for example, able to produce only seven.[26]

The state intervened in response to the crisis. Fascist leaders were too aware of the issues of consensus to ignore cinema, which had emerged as the most formidable means of manipulation/education of the masses. Moreover, the general thrust that this intervention impressed on the economy found its confirmation in the field of cinema. The law of 18 June 1931 reorganized film financing in the industry. The law, which was influenced by Cines magnate Stefano Pittaluga, went into effect after his death and expanded the financing options that would eventually bear fruit. Following this preliminary interest in cinema, in the context of reorganizing the press and propaganda sectors (that would lead in 1935 to the birth of the Minister of Popular Culture, or Minculpop), the Direzione Generale per la Cinematografia was established under the directorship of the dynamic Luigi Freddi. His task was both to obtain increased and more reliable financing for production and to guarantee "moderate" political control. The result was that production increased to thirty-five films in 1935.

Furthermore, the Venice International Film Festival had been established in 1932. It was both a showcase for Italian cinema and a sign of a global political engagement. Politically controlled, first through Mussolini's offices, then, after 1935, under the direction of the Minculpop, the Italian film industry enjoyed, until the eve of the war, a series of administrative measures designed to give it financial and contractual strength. A special section for cinema accounts was created at the Banca Nazionale del Lavoro, the construction of the Cinecittà complex was initiated, the Ente Nazionale Industrie Cinematografiche (ENIC) was established, and the Centro Sperimentale di Cinematografia was founded.

In 1938 1939, over seventy films were produced—a complete reversal with respect to the crisis.[27]

The increased production was not enough to saturate the demand of the Italian market. On 4 September 1938, when "autarchy" reigned, and with the need to prevent the transfer of currency to the United States, Mussolini's government approved a decree which was to go into effect on 1 January 1939. From that date forward, all problems related to the film industry were assigned to the ENIC, a move that actually translated into a series of restrictive measures regarding the importation of films (in particular, American films). This action led American producers, coordinated by the Motion Picture Association, to abandon the Italian market. However, even before war hostilities broke out, a trade war had erupted between Cinecittà and Hollywood that for over five years would prevent contact between the two cinemas.[28] That was the real disaster for Italian cinema: its film production, after the economic revival of 1931, remained unknown in the most important market in the world, and the Italian market remained closed to American films, with few, circumscribed, exceptions.

Sheltered behind that solid protectionism, the Italian film industry was reborn. It built functional facilities, trained qualified operators, developed quality actors, and nurtured directors who were concerned about the quality of cinema. It is in those years that the more modern and more passionate Italian film criticism emerged. It was born under the protective wings of Fascism, but Fascism did not succeed in controlling this emergent critical culture. From 1931 until the war, Italian cinema chose its own particular paths: comic, adventurous, national/ Fascist, regional, and realist. Legend has it that in those years, Italian cinema was dominated by witty comedies, the so-called white telephones, to use a phrase that has become almost axiomatic. In truth, as has now been recognized, very few white telephones were seen on Italian screens.[29] However, the genre did have its successes.

In this nuance-filled era, the pre-realist or pre-neorealist films are situated. Now for the fundamental question: Were realist films before 1943 exceptions, felicitous exceptions, that together formed a school that had been tested by the critics and was prepared to display, at the opportune moment, the fruits of its labor? When leafing through histories of Italian cinema covering the Fascist period or looking at lists of Italian films of the era, one cannot help but be struck by the frequency with which certain works are isolated from the rest, considered chance exceptions which anticipate neorealism.

In 1933, Raffaello Matarazzo directed *Treno popolare* (*Popular Train*), which some self-righteous critics judged to be propaganda for the Fascist *dopolavoro* (an institution that organized the leisure-time activities of workers), but which has elicited recently the following opinion: "At the time . . . it was not understood (in many ways it anticipated, at least in the filmic practice, the concept of neorealism)."[30] The case of Matarazzo (who directed another realist film in 1942, *Giorno di nozze [Wedding Day]*) was hardly isolated. The term *"popolare"* in the title of his first film bestowed upon him instant realist accreditation (or made him suspect of populist Fascism). However, in the case of a master such as Alessandro Blasetti, it is difficult to affirm definitively that his works which came before the "chivalric" cycle and were directed between 1929 and 1934 do not belong to the realist tradition. His first film, *Sole* (*Sun*, 1929), was an apologia for film that reflects reality; in *Terra madre* (*Mother Earth*, 1931) and in *Resurrectio* (*Resurrection*, 1931), Blasetti remained faithful to that initial inspiration. In *1860* (1934), one of Blasetti's masterpieces, the epos of the Thousand of Garibaldi was represented from the point of view of a poor Sicilian peasant. "*1860*," as Liehm writes, "is remarkable for its use of Sicilian locations and nonprofessional actors. . . . Faces of Sicilian women clad in black often appear against the white backdrop of the countryside, foreshadowing the images of the neorealist films set in Sicily (e.g., *The Path of Hope*, *La terra trema*)."[31] Not only Flaherty but also the domestic Blasetti had paved the road for Visconti. With *Vecchia guardia* (*The Old Guard*, 1935), an openly Fascist film depicting the preparations for Mussolini's "March on Rome" in October 1922, Blasetti worked according to criteria that suggested to one American historian of Italian cinema that "Blasetti's realistic portrayal of this dramatic moment in Italian history employs a documentary style that would later find favor during the postwar period."[32]

In those same years, and with a chronological progression that cannot be considered coincidental, other directors followed Blasetti's example. Mario Camerini, to whom some have referred in a disparaging sense as "calligraphic," directed a series of films that anthologies describe in similar terms to those of Blasetti: *Rotaie* (*Rails*, 1930), *Darò un milione* (*I'll Give a Million*, 1935), *Grandi magazzini* (*Department Store*, 1939), and *Batticuore* (*Heartbeat*, 1939). In 1939, Carlo Campogalliani directed *Montevergine*, also known as *La grande luce* (*The Big Light*), which experimented with a linguistic mélange, the use of dialect, and social explanations for the mass emigration; however, "unlike other films of the period, the inciting incident of injustice is set in Italy."[33] Between 1940 and 1942, Ferdinando Maria Poggioli, with *Addio giovinezza* (*Good-bye Youth*, 1940), *Sissignora* (*Yes, Ma'am*, 1940), and *Gelosia* (*Jealousy*, 1942), follows the path of realism. Other directors, considered "minor" after the war, contributed forcefully to this turning point. For example, Gianni Franciolini's *Fari nella nebbia* (*Beacons in the Fog,* 1942) has been characterized thus: "A frank film, and instinctive for its time . . . immersed in a popular atmosphere that is turbid, sensual, and aggressive, and usually not tolerated by the regime. [It was] the sign that something was really changing in Italian cinema."[34] Aldo Fabrizi's and Anna Magnani's talents were showcased in Mario Bonnard's films *Avanti c'è posto* (*Move Forward, There's Room,* 1942) and *Campo de' fiori* (*Peddler and the Lady,* 1943), two popular comedies that already obeyed the tenets of neorealism.

This partial listing suffices to show that the realism of the "four musketeers" did not arise out of nowhere but was the result of over a decade of intense activity. The realist current in the Italian film industry grew stronger and more variegated, gradually producing higher-quality works. In the waning years of the war, it had already developed into a mature realism, and the fact that a film such as Blasetti's *Vecchia guardia* is part of that formation demonstrates how the Fascist/anti-Fascist element was but an extenuating accessory to the cinematic discourse.

Realist cinema was the product of the rebirth of Italian cinema after the crisis of 1923–1931. It grew as the result of the government's intention to use film for propagandistic purposes; but these interventions allowed sufficient space for the formation of realist currents that were not in contradiction with certain aspects of Fascist politics with respect to the masses. This infusion provided a fertile source of directors, scriptwriters, actors, producers, and technicians that, between 1942 and 1943, yielded results worthy of note. Then from these, there emerged, on the historiographic level, the films tied to the names of Rossellini, De Sica, and Visconti, since they were the "heroes" of neorealism. However, the voices of the chorus were far more numerous. Neorealism's success came after the fast of late 1943 to 1944 (a fast broken only by those directors who worked in Venice with Luigi Freddi under the Italian Social Republic—not that this meant that they were automatically philo-Fascists), which ended when the Allies allowed production to resume. At first, the ramifications of what had been accomplished were not understood in Italy because the two salient characteristics of neorealism (on-site filming and the use of non-professional actors), although now used to greater effect, had already been in use. The only revolutionary technical innovation tied to neorealism was its photographic style, which abandoned diffused lighting or back-lighting in favor of direct lighting made up of sharp cuts and sharp back-lighting. However, this innovation was due to circumstances not intrinsic to neorealist cinema: first, the directors had to use low-sensitivity film stock (because higher-quality film was not available on the Italian market) to shoot outside, which resulted in more strongly lit takes; second, there was the influence of the cinematographer Aldo R. Graziati, whose previous work in photography directed his sense of lighting.[35]

Outside Italy, the achievements made at Cinecittà prior to the war remained (for the aforementioned reasons) virtually unknown. From this lack of familiarity arose the sense of surprise at films which seemed to come from nowhere but were really a meditation of years of experience, representing to the world in explicit frankness and with enviable immediacy what had happened in Europe during the war. British cinema was well known, French cinema was struggling to find its own path, and German cinema would be forced into a prudent silence for several years. All that remained were the Italians. Rossellini's and De Sica's images amazed viewers who did not know the historical background. This astonishment had a rebound effect in Italy. Thus, realism, which until 1943 had been linked to the Fascist experience, was re-baptized and called "neorealism," but its roots were deeply embedded in the Italian film industry's development dating back to 1931. After the war, filmic realism continued to evolve, blending with both the bitter socio-political debates of the immediate postwar period and the years of the "economic miracle." The "musketeers" of neorealism were not the only ones in the vanguard. They had followers, friends, imitators, and successors who for over two decades animated Italian cinema with realism.

Notes

This essay was translated from the Italian by Piero Garofalo.

1. Peter Bondanella, *Italian Cinema: From Realism to the Present* (New York: Continuum, 1983), 8–9. The writings to which Bondanella refers first appeared in Umberto Barbaro, "Un film italiano di un quarto di secolo fa," *Scenario*, November 1936, now found in Massimo Mida and Lorenzo Quaglietti, eds., *Dai telefoni bianchi al neorealismo* (Bari: Laterza, 1980), 137–138; and Georges Sadoul, *Dizionario dei film*, Italian edition (Firenze: Sansoni, 1990), 360.

2. For example, Mira Liehm, *Passion and Defiance: Film in Italy from 1942 to the Present* (Berkeley: University of California Press, 1984), 43.

3. See Neya Zorkaya, *The Illustrated History of the Soviet Cinema* (New York: Hippocrene Books, 1989), 55. For Italian criticism of Vertov (the pseudo-

nym of D. Arkadievic Kaufman), see Glauco Viazzi, "Dziga Vertov e la ten-
denza documentarista," *Ferrania* (August–September 1957), now in Glauco
Viazzi, *Scritti di cinema. 1940–1958* (Milano: Longanesi, 1979), 141–158.
Vertov was accused of "Futurism," "technical fetishism," and individual-
ism in his filmic work, which led to his marginalization in the Soviet
Union and his ostracization from the circle of Marxist criticism.

4. Cesare Zavattini, *Neorealismo ecc.*, ed. Mino Argentieri (Milano: Bompiani,
   1979), 64.

5. Mario Alicata and Giuseppe De Santis, "Ancora di Verga e del cinema
   italiano," *Cinema* (10 November 1941), now in Mida and Quaglietti, *Dai
   telefoni bianchi al neorealismo*, 209–212. Alicata would use similar terms in
   "Ambiente e società nel cinema italiano," *Cinema* (10 February 1942), now
   in *Dai telefoni bianchi al neorealismo*, 152–153. Moreover, Alicata and De
   Santis were taking up a topic that they had already dealt with a month
   earlier (10 October 1941) with another article, also in *Cinema*, titled
   "Verità e poesia: Verga e il cinema italiano," now in Mida and Quaglietti,
   Dai telefoni bianchi al neorealismo, 201–205. See also Fernaldo Di Giam-
   matteo, *Lo sguardo inquieto. Storia del cinema italiano (1940–1990)*
   (Firenze: La Nuova Italia, 1994), 48–49.

6. Luigi Chiarini, "Discorso sul neorealism," *Bianco e Nero*, July 1951 (from
   a conference held in Bari on 11 April 1951).

7. Lino Miccichè, "Per una verifica del neorealismo," *Il neorealismo cinematografico italiano* (Venezia: Marsilio, 1978), 11–13.

8. André Bazin, *What Is Cinema?* (Berkeley: University of California Press,
   1971), II: 17–19.

9. In this sense, see Bondanella, *Italian Cinema*, 31–37; and Di Giammatteo,
   Lo sguardo inquieto, 76–80.

10. Gianni Rondolino, *Roberto Rossellini* (Torino: UTET, 1989), 53. On De
    Robertis's and Rossellini's works before *La nave bianca*, see 23–53.

11. Ibid., 53–59.

12. Giuseppe De Santis, "L'uomo della croce," *Cinema* (25 June 1943), now in
    Mida and Quaglietti, *Dai telefoni bianchi al neorealismo*, 263–266.

13. Giuseppe De Santis, "Un garibaldino al convento," *Cinema* (10 April 1942),
    now in Mida and Quaglietti, *Dai telefoni bianchi al neorealismo*, 254–256.

14. F. Pasinetti, "I film della Mostra di Venezia. I primi 5 giorni," *Cinema* (10
    September 1942), cited in Gian Piero Brunetta, *Storia del cinema italiano
    1895–1945* (Roma: Riuniti, 1979), 503.

15. Pierre Sorlin, *Sociologia del cinema* (Milano: Garzanti, 1979), 163–206,
    esp. 164–166.

16. See Liehm, *Passion and Defiance*, 46–51; Di Giammatteo, *Lo sguardo in-
    quieto*, 52–63; Brunetta, *Storia del cinema italiano*, 512–513; Gianni Ron-
    dolino, *Luchino Visconti* (Torino: UTET, 1981), 124–143. ("The work,"

writes Brunetta, "becomes the highest model for a generation of young cinema intellectuals and its exit signals the official moment of [the] birth . . . of a new way of conceiving cinema and of making cinema in Italy.")

17. Sorlin, *Sociologia del cinema*, 189.

18. This anecdote, which I had heard, was confirmed to me directly by Girotti himself.

19. Felix A. Morlion, "Crisi e prospettive del realismo cinematografico," in *Bianco e nero* (June 1949), page 9 of the extract.

20. This data is neatly summarized in a synoptic chart in P. Lughi, "Il neorealismo in sala. Anteprime di gala e teniture di massa," in *Neorealismo. Cinema italiano, 1945–1949*, ed. Alberto Farassino (Torino: EDT, 1989), 60.

21. Liehm, *Passion and Defiance*, 329 n. 12.

22. Bazin, *What Is Cinema?* I: 37–38 and II: 16–60.

23. Rondolino, *Visconti*, 197.

24. See, for example, Liehm, *Passion and Defiance*, 333 n. 57.

25. See Brunetta, *Storia del cinema italiano*, 295–298.

26. Lorenzo Quaglietti, *Storia economico-politica del cinema italiano. 1945–1980* (Roma: Riuniti, 1980), 245.

27. See Valerio Castronovo, *Storia di una banca. La Banca Nazionale del Lavoro e lo sviluppo economico italiano. 1913–1983* (Torino: Einaudi, 1983), 151–154; Quaglietti, *Storia economico-politica del cinema italiano*, 255; and Brunetta, *Storia del cinema italiano*, 286–289, 290–296, 307–309, and 311–319.

28. See Ennio Di Nolfo, "La diplomazia del cinema americano in Europa nel secondo dopoguerra," in *Hollywood in Europa: Industria, politica, pubblico del cinema 1945–1960*, ed. David W. Ellwood and Gian Piero Brunetta (Firenze: Casa Usher, 1991), 32–33, and the sources cited therein.

29. Liehm, *Passion and Defiance*, 322 n. 56.

30. See Paolo Mereghetti, ed., *Dizionario del film* (Milano: Baldini & Castoldi, 1996), 1564.

31. Liehm, *Passion and Defiance*, 23.

32. Bondanella, *Italian Cinema*, 15.

33. See Mereghetti, *Dizionario del film*, 696.

34. Ibid., 555.

35. Stefano Masi, "L'Hardware del neorealismo. Ferri del mestiere e strategia della tecnica," in Farassino, *Neorealismo. Cinema italiano, 1945–1949*, 49–51.

4

Placing Cinema, Fascism, and the Nation in a Diagram of Italian Modernity

James Hay

The Mattering of Fascism and Cinema in a New Diagram of the Nation

Accounts of modern Italy frequently have drawn a sharp distinction between pre- and post–World War II Italy. In the Cold War era, historians in Britain and the United States often described modern Italian history as a nation in slow progress toward a democracy and away from the perils of "totalitarianism" represented by Italy's Fascist legacy.[1] In part, these histories have been prone to divide up Italian modernity this way because they see geography, history, culture, and an array of social practices as epiphenomena of national state government and, to a certain extent, economic conditions or because they emphasize only the synergism among multiple mechanisms upon which the nation-state depends. In this way, they can speak in generalized terms about a "Fascist culture" or a "Fascist nation" (or the coextensiveness of culture, Fascism, and nation, or, worse, the undifferentiated roles of these factors in producing uniformity) displaced by successive governments and political "movements." To the extent that accounts of Italian Fascism have tended to view state power as the primary, most influential apparatus for governing, Italian Fascism often has functioned historiographically as an allegory of state control—of how the state intervened directly into all spheres of life and thus how the Fascist state was replaced by democratic and liberal forms of government.

Unlike histories organized around a succession of state government and/or economic conditions, cultural histories of Italian modernity primarily have negotiated aesthetic canons (e.g., Futurism, Modernism, Rationalism, neorealism), one of the most conspicuous exceptions to this trend being work about "Fascist culture." To the extent that a cultural history understands culture to be primarily about the production of meanings, identities, and representations, it explains Italian modernity largely in terms of aesthetic conventions, signification, and textual practice.[2] Furthermore, cultural histories have tended to concentrate on a particular cultural form, often leaving the impression that cultural forms have relatively discrete histories or that culture is a separate sphere of practice (i.e., one that acts upon or is controlled by the state, the economy, or some other discrete set of practices). Despite their differences, many cultural histories of Italian modernity implicitly have reproduced the organizing tropes of these other histories, more or less accepting the historiographical distinction between pre- and postwar Italy.

This essay begins from a different position and with a different perspective: one that does not assume state power (or a collectivity of industrial interests administering state programs) to be *necessarily* or *always* the primary, most influential apparatus of governing (either during Fascism or thereafter) and does not understand culture as a separate sphere of social practice (culture being one of many sites and kinds of technologies that has organized national life). Instead, it proposes that Italian modernity has occurred through the gradual *arrangement* (agreement/configuration) and interdependence (not unified or unifying) of a variety of assemblages that organize and govern through particular sites and social spaces. Focusing upon these developments leads me to a version—a map/diagram—of Italian modernity that has been relatively ignored by the kind of historical accounts that I have cited above.[3]

As a way of discussing the relationship of Italian cinema to Italian modernity during the 1920s, 1930s, and early 1940s, I want to focus on a particular term and formation: the nation, particularly as it developed and came to be governed through interdependent technologies of power, as a concept, an assemblage of spatial representations, a social arrangement, and a territory. Cinema's mattering in nation-formation is not something that can be well addressed simply by considering cinema as a distinctive and/or discrete cultural form or as interchangeable with any other technology/institution of power. By "mattering," I mean how cinema became instrumental and acquired value in nation-formation—a process that pertains less to cinema as a separate form, technology, or social sphere than to the cinematic as a process of assembling and of historical and spatialized interdependencies.[4] Understanding the "mattering" of cinema in the formation of Italy as a modern nation(-state) necessarily involves considering how the cinematic has been articulated (linked and, in its linkages, made to matter) to and through other technologies/assemblages of power; it involves considering cinema in terms of its dependencies—as integral to and shaped by the production of social space and distributions across territory. Because film histories and cinema studies tend primarily to be interpretations that focus on film form, ideology, and the distinctiveness of a corpus of texts (i.e., filmic representations of the nation or nationhood rather than cinema's implication in organizing the nation as environment and territory), they often have ignored cinema's relationship to other technologies of power as well as cinema's place within a network of power. I argue, here and elsewhere, that cinema has mattered in nation-formation through its imbrication in, reliance upon, and continual conversion of other technologies that shape/govern the nation as an assemblage of representations of places/landscapes, as a socio-spatial arrangement, and as a territory (a space of inclusions and exclusions).[5]

In order to consider the nation's formation and governance as dispersed through spheres and technologies beyond direct state control, in order to consider Italian modernity as a diagram/geography of power, and in order to consider cinema's mattering to both, I have chosen to discuss cinema's relation to telephony and telecommunications. Many of the technologies and assemblages (such as cinema and telephony) upon which the Fascist state depended before 1945 not only remained relatively intact but became more indispensable to postwar forms of organizing and governing social life in Italy. Cinema, in conjunction with telecommunications and broadcasting, perpetuated and in some ways strengthened a diagram (map/arrangement) through which the prewar nation-state had emerged. This diagram gradually took shape over the late nineteenth and early twentieth centuries, but it established itself most forcefully during the period of Italian Fascism and remained relatively intact until the mid-1980s, when a new model of the nation emerged.

Rather than moving directly to the period from the 1920s to the early 1940s, I want to consider briefly several of the recent discourses in Italy about the nation and their relevance to both the early and late modern formations of power. Given that histories (here, of Italian cinema and Italian Fascism) are conducted from within a set of conditions in the present, proceeding this way allows me to demonstrate why it is necessary to rethink some of the ways that Fascism and Italian cinema have been linked in earlier studies. *Cinema and the state now matter differently in the formation of the nation precisely because of the current discourses about nationhood in Italy and elsewhere.* Understanding how much Fascism and cinema matter within the contemporary discourses about the nation involves recognizing the long *durée* of an early modern model of the nation, its unraveling, and its residual implications within an emerging diagram of power.

So let me begin by identifying four discourses that over the 1990s have come to designate new coordinates within which the nation has been instated and its established meaning and status thrown into question or crisis: Federalism (a new governmental rationality about regionalism), Padania (a discourse of secession), *extra-comunitari* (a discourse of immigration), and "*il* Far West" (a discourse of Americanization, "free-market" capitalism, and globalized networking through electronic technologies). The list that I address is partial, in part because I want to avoid suggesting that they constitute an overview of the nation as a coherent and stable space or referent. These coordinates are only part of a process of nation formation.[6] I have chosen these, however, in order to emphasize the geographic or spatial terms—the topological lexicon—of governing the nation and maintaining its sovereignty. This lexicon underscores that national identity, governing, and sovereignty all are predicated upon spatial frames of reference and territorializing practices (which include the claim made upon a place through the circulation of discourses). Descriptions of these new coordinates in nation formation also outline a few ways that these practices and frames of references contrast with, though they also are predicated upon and grow out of, a spatial definition of the nation that developed during the 1920s and 1930s.

Federalism

To a certain extent during the 1980s, but particularly by the 1990s, the autonomy of cities and regions became an issue central to governmental policy and in other discourses about the status and future of the nation-state. These discourses began to occur amid a significantly changed set of geographic relations, particularly those engendered by commercial flows that transformed certain regions and cities into global centers of particular industries and trade. Northeastern cities and regions became increasingly less dependent upon a state economy that was increasingly in conflict with Rome as the center of the early modern nation-state and more constitutive of an "industrial district" of small and medium industry supported by local institutions and imbricated in a system of global production and distribution.[7] While some of the tensions and conflicts that have fueled current movements toward the realignment and autonomy of cities and regions are centuries old, their connection to the issue of federalism is a modern one (which has marked Italian modernity) to the extent that they have accompanied the formation of Italy as a nation(-state).

Italian modernity, marked by the formation of the nation(-state), was a historical process of realigning—of spatially redefining—the relationship among regions and of those regions collectively to an "outside," to territories (other nations) beyond its border. While "unification" in the mid-nineteenth century and the subsequent formation of the Italian nation(-state) may have signaled a new manner of governing (and a new disposition of regions to be governed this way), this spatial and governmental arrangement involved a different set of regional tensions and, occasionally, conflict. Distinctions between northern and southern Italy, for instance, came to be as much a judgment about modernization and being modern (the "backwardness" of the south) as they are about geographic indeterminacy (where exactly the south "begins").[8]

Given these circumstances, it would be inaccurate to claim that federalism is an issue in Italy that has suddenly irrupted in the 1990s. Furthermore, federalism has never signified a single idea—one that percolated for decades and finally came to fruition in the 1990s.[9] Instead, it has been historically articulated to and through various discourses about the nation, inasmuch as the national has depended upon the disposition of regional cultures, economies, and governments toward the programs and infrastructure of the nation-state.

A discourse on federalism in the 1990s, however, pertains to a new socio-spatial arrangement and a way of mapping the nation during most of the twentieth century. From the 1920s through the early 1940s, during what had become the most centralized model of the Italian nation-state, federalism marked the antipode of Fascism (by both Fascists and anti-Fascists). Even after the demise of the Fascist government, however, federalism never became a widespread discourse or one central to national or local policy. Even though Italy's postwar constitution gave a legal status to regional governments, regionalism continued to pertain to a model of the nation that developed during the prewar years and remained relatively intact for decades thereafter, supported by a broad array of practices that sustained concrete and abstract (spatial) relations and flows that constituted the nation as a territory.

Padania—the Invisible Nation

Over the 1990s, the meaning of federalism in Italy was articulated most often and most widely to and through the formation of the Northern

League—the most recognized separatist movement in contemporary Italy and one whose implication in the federalist discourse heretofore has most threatened or called into question the sovereignty of the nation-state and the way to designate and spatially define the nation as territory. That the Northern League cannot easily be disarticulated from federalism (or vice versa), or that discourses about the one have emerged through the other, makes it necessary to weigh their historical convergence and association.

One of the most significant features of the Northern League, particularly within Italian modernity, is its (albeit vague and contradictory) conception of the nation, of territorial sovereignty, and of identity. If the nation has been a sort of supra-formation, produced out of—replacing but always referring back to—traditional, premodern forms of community, then Padania pertains to a very late modern set of conditions. The Northern League, for instance, has invoked "ancient" (premodern) origins in order to claim sovereignty over certain territories and to forge a territorial identity: Padania. Such claims consign a premodern bond of a people to the land (*terra*, or soil/earth), so that the myth of a people's organic "rootedness" to land becomes the basis for a claim to (and thus a politics of) territory. Significantly, however, the Northern League relies upon references to a pre-urban bond with the land in order to establish an identity for and its territorial imperative over the most urban and commercially developed area in contemporary Italy.

The Northern League furthermore has attempted to disarticulate the nation from the state. Its efforts have largely been directed against the centralized power of the state, while they offer scant indication of what form of power and governing would be implemented in a northern regional alliance—a vaguely defined territory presumably constituting a nation but not a state.[10] The ambiguity and contradiction of designating this formation (as a positive or negative term/space) reside in its challenging a formation that has been relatively intact since the 1920s and 1930s while rearticulating earlier connotations of national.

For instance, a northern nation is not based upon a distinct language or culture. To claim this would be to ignore the polyglot linguistic and cultural practices in this area before Italian modernity and the transregional and transnational circulation of media/cultural forms in Italian modernity. But in the midst of these latter flows, it has attempted to base its identity upon its difference from the south (which it designates as less modern) and from the early modern conception of the Italian nation-state (which it deems an anachronism). As stated above, it relies upon the premodern, Latinate and early Italianate ("organic") association of *natio/nationes*, both to a subject's affiliation with a community and to a place of birth. It perpetuates a utopian model of the nation (and national culture), a "national-popular" ideal, and a transcendent (nostalgic) identity of Italy as *patria* that is similar to those that took shape in early Italian modernity during the Fascist regime.[11] In addition to these premodern and early modern associations, the League imagines a nation engaged with the European Community—a flexible nation for a region that rapidly has come to be located within (and to see and envisage itself within) a global economy.

Extra-comunitari

Between 1992 and 1997, the number of documented immigrants living in Italy grew from roughly 500,000 to a million. Over this same period, the number of "undocumented" immigrants living in Italy is estimated to have risen from roughly 200,000 to anywhere between 300,000 and 800,000.[12] Though the percentage of immigrants in Italy has remained extremely small (particularly in comparison with percentages of immigrants in other western European countries), the pattern of immigration and the issue of representing immigrants have been significant factors in the changing spatial definition—the material and cultural geography —of the nation over the 1990s.[13]

Numerous factors distinguish this trend, however, from earlier migration patterns. One is that the preponderance of these immigrants come from outside western Europe, particularly from Africa, Eastern Europe, and the Philippines. Another is the state's reluctance to define the status of immigrants as citizens and its difficulty in monitoring and regulating the movements of immigrants it has been slow to recognize and "count."[14]

The impermanence of these immigrants (for various economic and governmental factors) has had the effect of producing a kind of "negative community," that is, a community marked by its "illegality," "irregularity," "secretness," subversiveness, and invisibility. Their otherness is most emphatically designated through the common expression *extra-comunitari*—literally, "outside the community." This designation pertains particularly to the new diagram of late modern Italy because the "community" to which they do not belong is both the early modern Italian nation-state *and* the new European Community. The *extra-comunitari* therefore affirm Italy's Western pedigree, its belonging to a community of European nation-states whose confederation increasingly depends upon the labor of the *extra-comunitari*. Like Padania (a reference point that has become conjoined to this abstract community of recent immigrants), they constitute a "phantom nation" in and for Italy and contribute to a new cartography that departs from an early modern spatial definition of the nation-state. Within the framework and borders of the early modern model, these recent immigrants are another example of a nation without a state, recognized by the Italian state more as seasonal laborers than as Italian citizens or, for that matter, as the responsibility of any state. Unlike Padania, they are an invisible nation by default—their "statelessness" a condition of their mobility rather than their rootedness. And while the path of the African immigrants could be described as "postcolonial" in that their path both reinscribes and inverts the Italian colonialist geography under Fascism, these immigrants have yet to define themselves (as Algerian "nationalists" have in France) as subjects of a postcolonial, transnational ethnic formation.

As *extra-comunitari*, the new immigrants constitute an identity abstracted (i.e., *extra*cted) from the nation. But their separateness, in this sense, serves also to anchor, reify, and reinstate the abstractness of the "community" from which they are separated. As such, this designation underscores the fragility and, simultaneously, the tenacious persistence of the early modern conception of the nation whose wholeness was achieved as abstract/imagined community. The fragility lies in the state's task of somehow locating them within the nation, even though the *extra-comunitari* reaffirm the early modern definition of the nation which had rearticulated premodern models of community through a map about the coherent and coterminous relation among cultures, identities, and places in a single, abstract territory.

The "Far West"

The Far West became a common trope for describing various aspects of Italian government and business practices during the early 1990s. In part, the Far West (an imaginary place) came to describe (and often suggested great apprehension about) a new context marked by the relatively rapid deregulation of earlier national economies—a transformation that had come to alter the conditions upon which the nation-state had been organized for decades. Generally, therefore, the Far West expresses the intensity of flux and instability in an environment marked by the three coordinates discussed above. The expression (always in English—"*il* Far West") clearly conjures the kind of frontier zone mythologized in the classical Hollywood western, wherein governing and legislating occurred through mob rule and rugged individualism, beyond the direct rule of the state.

While the expression circulated before the 1990s through a discourse in Italy about the American West and the western, it assumed a specific inflection and currency in the early 1990s amid the electoral and commercial triumphs of media mogul-cum-politician Silvio Berlusconi. Whether connected specifically or not to Berlusconi, the Far West refers to a more general uncertainty about how to maintain sovereignty and identity, about the parameters of jurisdiction and governing, in the wake of an emerging economy wherein ownership is multinational and the flow of capital, commodities, images, and so forth are transnational. To the extent that industries in this emerging economy have been or have come to depend upon media industries (broadcasting, telecommunications, telematics), regulating (media) borders and the reterritorialization that accompanies the flow of these media has become an increasingly central issue for the survival of an early modern model of the nation-state. In its connection to the erosion of boundaries accompanying deregulation and these media flows, the Far West also has become consonant with Jean Baudrillard's invocation of the American West as a borderless hyperspace—a utopia desired by Europeans but endemic to the United States' sense of its own international dominion, its belief that it can exercise its freedom anywhere.[15] In this sense, the Far West does express and mediate an ambivalence about national identity—about the erasure of national difference and the new identities being formed amid multinational and transnational (media) flows. The Far West is not about Italy becoming America (or America devouring Italy) but about the challenge of regulating flows and governing within a space of flows that is no longer organized as national territories.

The Far West is less an internal, invisible nation than a correlative for an unstable position just beyond the boundaries upon which the nation has thus far been instantiated. It is a territory or zone that is therefore imagined to be both premodern and postmodern—an emerging *state* of the nation lacking the rationalist diagram of the early modern nation(-state) but based upon an early modern chronotope (the Western frontier) so crucial to the formation and expansionism of European and North American nations. The Far West in Italy may indeed be about the erosion of spaces such as the nation that defined Italian modernity. And it may seem that it ironically and nostalgically rearticulates an early modern (Hollywood) chronotope about premodernity in a discourse about the future of a re-networked society. But the Far West, and its relationship to the other coordinates that I have addressed above, is not simply about the erasure of boundaries or about a world everywhere marked by virtual vectors and virtual boundaries. Instead it is part of a recent way of framing a discourse about the nation that is bound to the institutional realignment and flows accompanying a new commercial/cultural economy and practice of governing at a distance. And it is a recent discourse that affirms the tenacious persistence of the early modern chronotopes upon which the nation was formed.

* * *

The discourse in the 1990s about the nation presumes a new diagram—one emerging on top of, superimposed upon, an older definition of the nation(-state). Whereas the early modern (spatial) definition of the nation(-state) was predicated upon a rationalist design that idealized the coordination of dispersed localities around a center of power (i.e., Rome), this new diagram no longer assumes the feasibility or the necessity of coordinating localities in that way. The above terms/coordinates thus make the early modern conception of the nation-(state) untenable. Still, the nation persists as a point of reference disarticulated from the early modern state and rearticulated through a new space of flows and new technologies for governing. These new conditions have done more than just persist; they have deepened an essentialist conception of the nation (Padania, or the notion of community implied by *extra-comunitari*) while they have simultaneously fostered a more "flexible" model of the nation than the rationalist project enacted and embodied since the 1920s and 1930s. The early modern model of the Italian nation, as abstract community through rationalist map, was essentialist; it aspired to monumentality rather than to flexibility. It was certainly consonant with objectives of Fascist state government and developed most rapidly during the 1920s and 1930s but involved assemblages that were not controlled directly by the state and that persisted—more or less intact—until the late 1980s.[16]

The coordinates that I have addressed above do not constitute a complete map, not because they signal the dissipation or break-up of the nation but because the nation never was a single, essential point of reference or an immutable set of geographic relations. For this reason, the nation needs to be deconstructed. But deconstruction only demonstrates the slide or instability of definition rather than how the circulation of statements and other flows occur within, perpetuate, and transform a particular (spatial) arrangement of power and governance. These coordinates and their correspondence to one another over the 1990s are evidence of (part of) an "abstract assemblage" of coordinates through which the nation is being (spatially) redefined.[17] The nation is contingent upon the relationships that constitute the diagram but are not synonymous with it. The diagram may change but only very gradually, as has been the case in Italy with what I am loosely referring to as the early modern diagram. I am reluctant to argue that the new diagram has made the nation or the nation-state anachronisms; in any case, addressing this question involves recognizing that nation-formation and governance occur up through "concrete assemblages" that collectively comprise and are instrumental to an arrangement (a diagram) of power.

Cinema as a Concrete Assemblage and a Technology of Power in the Early Modern Diagram: The White Telephone and the Utopian

The terms/coordinates that pertain to the new lexicon/geography of the nation rely upon and rearticulate an earlier model of the nation that has been organized through assemblages such as cinema. Whereas the preceding section indicates how Fascism and early models of the nation(-state) are imbricated in (however residually) the new lexicon/coordinates and the new assemblage(s) of power in Italy, this section begins with the 1920s and 1930s in order to locate cinema's implication in the formation of a diagram that remained relatively intact until the 1980s. In so doing, this section locates the recent terms within a broader historical context, fleshing out the transformation that the first section sketches. Like the preceding section, this part of the paper considers *the nation as concept, spatial representation, social arrangement, and territory,* specifically considering cinema as a technology/assemblage that (in relation to other technologies/assemblages of power) contributed to the formation of the nation.

In order to consider how power was exercised through a diagram that brought the Fascist state, the nation, and particular social spheres and sites of cultural production into a historical relationship with one another (and to continue an argument that I have advanced elsewhere about the importance of a "spatial materialism" in cinema studies), this section of the essay revisits and rethinks a term that, still and for many, sums up the relationship between film and Fascism: the "white telephone."[18] "White telephone" suggested several interconnected qualities of Italian films during the 1930s. It designated an aesthetic regime which, it wrongly implied, was dominated by and could be explained by reference to romantic comedy and romantic melodrama. As a formal, iconic feature of Italian films during the 1930s, the white telephone was said to have displayed the opulence, monochromatic luminescence, and social privilege of modern, bourgeois settings/characters/dialogue. As such, it was also perceived as a powerful and pervasive sign of the "escapism" of these films; white telephones were at the center of a utopia that "captivated," "distracted," and "concealed from" the audiences of the films. It became therefore a synecdoche used by postwar critics, intellectuals, and historians to generalize and condemn the form and ideology of these films and to contrast them with neorealism, whose "dominance" after the war was believed to be an indication of a break from a prewar "Fascist" aesthetic, culture, ideology, and mode of governing. Aside from the expression's adoption by critics and historians, it became part of a vernacular, circulating in a nation whose identity was being distinguished from the prewar period but whose environment continued to be organized through concrete assemblages and a diagram that had emerged during the 1920s and 1930s.

Among film critics and historians, the expression has had mostly to do with film aesthetics, film ideology, and film history (understanding ideology and history through film form), but little of substance has ever been said about the telephonic. For most critics, the telephone was just another instance of how these films fetishized leisure and the modern—filmic utopia as false consciousness. Film was the subject of formalist analysis (even in the generalizations about film form implicit in the term white telephone); the telephone was understood instead as a "mode of communication." Thus, whereas film was assumed to be an aesthetic issue, telephones pertained to a sphere of practice separate from aesthetics (and, for a culture understood through formalist analysis, separate from culture). As a result of distinctions such as these, the historical relationship between "the cinematic" and "the telephonic" has not been emphasized either in film studies or histories about Italian Fascism, and generally little attention has been paid to this relationship. Contemporaneously, however, they constituted two important formations or concrete assemblages through which "the national" came to be conceived, organized, and regulated as a territory.

In referring to each as a formation or a concrete assemblage, I mean to emphasize several things. First, the term complicates the assumption that film is primarily an aesthetic practice and that telephony is purely a mode of communication. Second, it suggests their historical contingency and interdependency in an abstract assemblage. In this way, one might ask how the one (as a set of practices that have had a particular connection to particular sites) might be understood through the other. Third, "assemblages" emphasizes their ontological status as dispersions, connections, and flows among sites, as sets of relations that organize and are organized spatially. As assemblages, cinema and telephony cannot be understood as closed, self-perpetuating systems—something particularly common in film criticism—but rather as imbricated, articulated, extroverted, porous, and territorializing systems. As an assemblage, cinema is not only or primarily a textual practice but also the circulation of texts and the adherence of texts and social subjects to particular places where they are imbricated in other practices. Thinking about the cinematic through the telephonic—the linking of sites by a line (a cable, circuitry, sound waves, electronic current)—also offers a strategic way to get outside film criticism's preoccupation with the internal machinations of screen space or what goes on inside a movie theater or inside a film spectator. It accentuates cinema's and telephony's mutual production as assemblages and networks.

Precisely through the relationships and flows constituting these formations, the cinematic and the telephonic have organized and been organized through an environment. This is to reiterate that their sociality and effectivity can only be understood in terms of their relationships to other sites, flows, and formations constituting their environment. But "environment" also calls attention to their materiality. As concrete assemblages, neither cinema nor telephony can be understood only as aesthetic, textual, or discursive; rather, they condition and are conditioned by material environments. In fact what is useful and challenging in thinking about the one through the other is not in comparing the cinema or the telephone as separate systems or in examining them (for predictable results) as twin apparatuses in the same configuration of control, but as a strategic and partial way of considering how each has found places in social relations organized spatially as an environment.

While one might accomplish this by considering their dispersal among, convergence in, or connection of any number of sites or spaces, I particularly want to return to their historical relationship to the nation, assuming that the nation has also been (spatially) defined through a diagram constituted in part by cinematic and telephonic sites and flows. The national has been articulated through a relationship between the cinematic and the telephonic, while these latter two assemblages have organized the national spatially. Here allow me two brief clarifications about terminology. First, the adjective "national" (after the cinematic and the telephonic) may be more useful than the noun to underscore that the nation has been rearticulated. But (second), its rearticulation has been both discursive and non-discursive; and as concrete assemblages, the cinematic and the telephonic have organized the nation as both map and territory. The process of mapping an environment or territory through cinema or telephony occurs through their particular ways of placing, channeling, organizing, and thus managing discourse. How they map and represent an environment, by establishing coordinates (of the nation, of everyday life), therefore cannot be readily extricated from their territorializing function, that is, their location (within buildings or cities), their material linking of these locations, or social subjects' differential access to them locally and within particular domains of everyday life.

Understanding cinema and telephony as (part of) a "regulated dispersion" also is not to suggest that they are controlled ("regulated") by the state or are merely instruments of state control. In Italy, even during the 1920s and 1930s, cinema and telephony were certainly not controlled directly by the state, nor were they merely apparatuses of state power. The formation of the modern state, as Foucault and others have noted, refined procedures for governing at a distance—upon the dispersal of power and management of resources and populations across different institutions, through different technologies, and over increasingly extensive territory.[19] This involved organizing social subjects across dispersed sites and bringing different spheres of sociality into a relationship with one another in a manner that could most effectively sustain a whole field of social management, though never through a single institution or technology. Although Fascist state government actively developed, sponsored, and maintained numerous programs for shaping citizens of the nation (across the nation and in diverse spheres of everyday life), the effectivity of state programs was dependent upon the rapid development of mechanisms, such as cinema and telephony, for overcoming distance, for defining the extensions of national territory/empire, and for coordinating movement among places—and doing so in a way that made Rome central to the map/network of nation and empire.

I therefore want to outline some of the convergences that, for Italy, shaped (spatially defined and articulated) the nation(-state), the cinematic, and the telephonic during the late 1920s and 1930s—a period when they first achieved their coherence as mutually dependent formations. Before the late 1920s, cinema and telephony's relationship to places did not constitute a regulated dispersion for and within the national, and the national had not yet come to be organized in a way that facilitated or required their coherence. Before the late 1920s, cinema and telephony were primarily part of urban environments (though urban environments had not yet begun to be organized in conspicuous ways around either of them), and their production and distribution were at best regional; films made in Italy before World War I had an international circulation that was more lucrative than their national distribution. From the late 1920s through the 1930s, the number of films, movie spectators, and theaters in Italy escalated as sharply as the number of telephones and telephone customers. By 1925 (forty years after the commercial availability of telephones), there were only 131,00 private customers and 190,000 telephones in Italy. This number climbed to (by some estimates) 512,000 customers and 700,000 telephones by 1940—roughly tripling over fifteen years. The state's role in the formation of both the cinematic and the telephonic became more pronounced over the 1920s, though in both cases the state was involved in very particular kinds of intervention and regulation rather than in wholesale efforts to direct.

In regulating the use of telephones during the 1920s, the fledgling Fascist government delegated the formation of urban telephone services to private, regional companies while becoming involved in interurban services. Thus from the 1920s, and definitively by 1933—with the formation of STET (Società Torinese Esercizi Telefonici) as a national regulatory agency—the state's role became one of encouraging interurban, transregional alliances among semi-privately run services that collectively formed the basis for a national network. Still, in the formation of a national network in the 1920s and 1930s, telephone use remained concentrated largely in urban and northern Italy—STET was formed from the three most lucrative regional companies in northern Italy.

During the 1920s and 1930s, the state's interest and investment in defining and governing the nation as a space/territory occurred through an emerging relationship between cinema and telephony. Significantly, this was a period when the state sponsored numerous initiatives designed to stimulate and protect national film production (efforts that encouraged a centralization of national production and training and that increasingly involved protectionist policies against the influx of Hollywood films). Other state-sponsored initiatives attempted to enhance national distribution, including a program for an unprecedented national distribution of newsreels, quotas guaranteeing national distribution of films produced in Italy, and a program of traveling cinema caravans that brought movies to provincial Italy. Aside from its involvement in newsreels, the state however did not and could not directly control film production and distribution[20] or the telephone system. Still, nation-formation was an objective as much of the Fascist state as of film production/distribution and the rapid development of a telephone system, and in this sense the cinematic, the telephonic, and the nation (-state) were interdependent assemblages—each shaping the others' formation.

To see the formation of a "national-popular" space (or to see the "national-popular" in spatial terms) points to a kind of utopianism underpinning the administration of power during those years—utopia not as a fetishization and distraction through film form (what has been at stake for film critics and historians who have seen the white telephone as a marker of Fascist ideology), but rather utopia as the elimination of distance and difference among places (in the archaic sense, an "every-place" or "no place"). The nation as utopia was predicated upon the cinematic and the telephonic as means of technologically mediating cities (and cities to rural areas) during a period when there was a rapid influx of people from the provinces to the cities, when new areas of existing Italian cities were being redesigned to regulate the greater number of inhabitants, when new "model" cities (città rurali, città minieri) were being planned to alleviate urban overcrowding, and when the highway and railway systems also were being redesigned and rapidly elaborated to open up and accelerate travel in and between Italian cities.

Significantly, this is a moment when Rome emerges as a center around which a utopian model of the nation takes shape. The planning and construction of Cinecittà (Cinema City) on the outskirts of Rome after 1934 was a project that had just as much to do with Rome's emergence as a center of filmmaking as it did with the city's rapidly solidified position as hub of an emerging national political and cultural economy. Cinema City was also integral to a new map and network that was extending Rome's purview; for instance, Cinema City's construction on Rome's outskirts was a concrete part of new programs for reclaiming the land around Rome, mythologized already through Blasetti's 1929 Sole (Sun).[21] In this regard, Cinema City pertained to a program of planning and constructing "model" cities in the provinces and of redesigning Italian cities (and the "ancient city"), making them more suited to the national space of distribution.

The contemporaneous institution of cinema and telephony as national projects/programs during the 1930s (the substantial increase in the production and distribution of Italian films, the formation of a "national" telephone network) became integral to governing through a new socio-spatial arrangement and became dependent upon managing resources and population through a new space of distribution, a new political economy, and a cultural economy and through a new regime that valued technologies of transport (e.g., the rapid development of the rail and highway system). By the 1930s, the nation had become an objective of telephony and cinema (as map and site/network); the formation and governance of the nation as utopia in turn relied upon the assemblage of networks, upon rearticulating various scales of social space—regional, urban, domestic space—and defining new relationships between public and private, civic and leisure spheres. In that the circulation of films relied on technologies of transport (trucks, trains, roads, rails), the apparatus of transportation came to be shaped through technologies of communication such as telegraphy and (by the 1920s) telephony, just as telephony most quickly became established in areas with the most elaborated transportation grids—initially (as in the case of telegraphy) following routes of travel. Whereas telephony refined links between the places that were most important to—had the most value for—a national space of distribution, cinema rapidly became a means of displaying the disposition of places to the national space wherein films circulated. The simultaneity of telephone conversation among private residences, the proliferation of public and private telephones, the semi-public nature of the movie theater, the practice of open-air evening screenings in piazzas (some of which were part of the national traveling cinema caravans) all redefined and reorganized social space, making any space more disposed and relevant to the national as a space of distribution and governing. Cinema and telephony also became contemporaneous mechanisms for bringing the rural and the urban into new relationships with one another. Not only were films such as *Sole* (1929), *Terra madre* (*Mother Earth*, 1931), *Treno popolare* (*Popular Train*, 1933), and scores of newsreels and documentaries visual narratives about a new bond between urban and rural spheres but, in their distribution, they became technologies of an emerging circulatory system that, along with telephonic grids, made the "modernization" of a still largely rural and provincial Italy into a national project. And as a technology of national extension and of governing over greater distance, cinema and telephony became technologies of empire—not simply of constructing modern cities in previously remote provincial areas inside national borders (as new points and displays of a connection between city and country, north and south) but of maintaining settlements beyond the national border.

Replacing the Rationalist Diagram: From the White Telephone to the *Telefonino*

The utopian ideal informed Italian film narrative during the 1930s, though reconstructing how this occurred involves considering cinema as a site/distribution and utopia as a spatial model/arrangement, rather than using utopia to describe "popular film" as a form of escapism, fetishism, and false consciousness. This latter usage of utopia is particularly consonant with Fredric Jameson's call to decipher "the Utopian impulse of . . . ideological cultural texts." For Jameson, utopia is a generalized conception of an equally generalizable formation: "the collective" and "the culture."[22] He argues that the task of criticism should be to read all texts as an (ideological) expression and desire of the collective/culture for transcendent unity. Utopia, in this sense, is an identity produced through the formal properties of texts (i.e., "culture") and fulfilling/managing the desire of social subjects to imagine their wholeness within the social. Jameson understands this desire/expression to be endemic to modern "mass culture," symptomatic of all nationalisms, and vital to the functioning of any state. He thus uses utopia to describe the form, the referent, and the goal of expression in modern culture.

By arguing that modern culture is essentially utopian and that utopia is the (textual/psychic) process of imaging and imagining social unity, Jameson fails to acknowledge that this process is always contingent upon specific arrangements (of populations, institutions, resources over territory), specific distributions or networks through which power is exercised.[23] Or one could say that he presupposes an essential diagram for all modern societies.[24]

As concrete assemblages, cinema and telephony were part of an abstract assemblage and a material environment that they worked to map. Whatever might be said about film narrative as utopian, therefore, involves coming to terms with cinema's role in reproducing a diagram and in continually renegotiating its relation to that diagram. In Italy during the late 1920s and 1930s, the "design" of the diagram followed and was embodied in Rationalism—a term that had referred generally to the introduction of calculation, geometry, and mechanics into the organization of modern societies but that in Italy referred to a design practice and ideal that came to dominate architecture.[25] As a design concept and practice, a Rationalist architectonics became arguably the most ubiquitous and vivid way of displaying the most modern sites of social interaction. Rationalist design emphasized a new, "anti-decorative" symmetry based upon the repetition of concrete blocks and cells. Rationalism was considered the "architecture of the state," since it defined many of the government buildings erected by the Fascist state, but it also figured prominently in most newly constructed public buildings or spaces, for example, stations, post offices, apartment buildings, and movie theaters. The Fascist doctrine of "corporativism"—a model of a new economic and social order—was enacted and interpreted through a Rationalist architectonic whereby the nation could be "coordinated" as a Rationalist city whose social subjects adhered to particular social spaces that cumulatively (and through a geometric symmetry) adhered to one another. Overall, then, an Italian Rationalist architectonics was the abstract "design" ideal and the concrete embodiment in everyday life of Italy's early modern utopian diagram.

Recognizing the Rationalist orientation of the early modern diagram in Italy is useful in discussing Italian cinema during the 1930s (and its relation to telephony) for several reasons. Rationalism describes a historical organization of social space and the material environment that

14. Telephony as cinematic assemblage: *La telefonista*, 1932.
From the author's private collection

was appropriated by the Fascist state but not confined to state programs. It thus connected the state to other spaces while affirming that the state did not control (and did not need to control) every domain in everyday life. Furthermore, it was a design principle that continued in Italy at least through the 1970s—a point to which I return below—and thus cannot be equated with the era of the Fascist state. Given that it was a principle organizing concrete assemblages such as cinema and telephony, it also was instrumental in how cinema mapped its own relationship to the diagram and its environment. And one way of examining this process is to consider briefly Italian cinema's discourse about telephony during the 1930s and how filmic references to telephony served as a strategy in narratives redefining social relations and the nation "geographically."

La telefonista (*The Telephone Operator*, 1932), is undoubtedly the most overt statement about telephony in Italian films during the 1930s. The title refers specifically to telephone operators but also more generally to the professional and bureaucratic organization of telephony, that is, that using the telephone required certain technical skills (of being a *telefonist*) and that its use was thus part of a new specialization of labor around a technology rapidly being imbricated into the everyday. Because the film was one of the earliest Italian sound films and part of a renewed

15. *La telefonista,* 1932.
From the author's private collection

productivity of Italian cinema, the film's use of the telephone is about a modern cinema's relationship to sound technologies and an environment that was being reorganized through them.[26] In the film, the telephone serves as a way of dramatizing links between different places and spheres of activity. For instance, the film casts telephony as both an occupation and a recreation, defining a connection between work space (particularly the telephone switching station) and leisure space (seemingly anything outside it). It also involves distinctions between public and domestic space that are being transformed through telephony as a new form of social interaction (a new form of publicness and privateness that cinema-going had also transformed).[27]

One of the most well-known vignettes in the film is a musical number. In many respects, this scene is the closest that Italian filmmaking during the 1930s came to the "mass" choreographies of Hollywood cinema.[28] The scene follows a concatenation of telephone calls to operators at a switching station. Although the calls are presumably being made simultaneously, both the calls and the operators' responses are organized sequentially as a song. The operators and the callers (and their dispersed locations) therefore are linked together diegetically through the telephone apparatus—with its central switching station—and diachronically by the film/sound editing. The chorus of operators sing (literally the song's refrain) in unison as if offering an identical response to the various questions and requests from the callers. Through the editing and "spacing" of this scene, the film thus choreographs a Rationalist regimen of social interaction figured spatially. Significantly, this set of relations is represented on the wall of the station director's office, where a formal diagram of a system of points connected by lines—a pattern of unified, increasingly concentrated hubs and spokes—hangs conspicuously.

In one respect, this scene bears out Siegfried Kracauer's observation about the Rationalist organization of German society in the late 1920s through popular spectacle.[29] In another respect, however, the scene acknowledges and lightly lampoons the unregulated features of telephony in everyday life: many of the callers display an uneasiness about playfully singing operators (and female "professionals"), questioning their implication in the operators' performance. Singing telephone operators and uneasy callers, however, are less an indication of resistance to this system than of a faith in freedom of flows and movement within the diagram. Because telephony and cinema are not directly controlled by the state, they rely upon practices of "mapping" such as this to display a mobility heightened through a choreography of telephony and cinema. Here the telephone customers and telephone workers' song outlines a program of flow and movement that governs the telephonic and cinematic "assemblage," making direct control or references to the state unnecessary. As a cinematic mapping of an environment organized and disorganized telephonically, *La telefonista* thus affirms the flows and the spatial regime of the Rationalist diagram rather than the authority of the Fascist state.

This film exhibits many of the qualities of white-telephone films. But to see it as mapping an environment being reterritorialized through the cinematic and the telephonic is different from arguing that cinema (or telephony, for that matter) functions as a form of escapism in a repressive, "totalitarian" society whose unity is never in doubt or whose subjects can only find brief moments of distraction from uniformity. This is also different from conceiving of film as a form of false consciousness or cinema as an apparatus for interpellating subjects through their identification with an image, a voice, or a narrative. It proposes instead that social subjects produce maps of and navigate their environment through sites, technologies, and concrete assemblages such as cinema and telephony. *In this way, cinema and telephony can be said to govern subjects through their mobility, that is, through their coming and going to, from, and through sites/spaces where they momentarily are engaged with the technology of cinema or telephony.*

Over the 1930s, Italian films did not reference telephony in a uniform way. But this lack of uniformity is not simply an issue of film style or of telephony's meaning and identity. It attests to cinema's and telephony's gradually changing relationship to one another, to other concrete assemblages, and to a changing set of geographic relations through which the nation was being reterritorialized. *Squadrone bianco* (*White Squadron*, dir. Augusto Genina, 1936), for instance, begins with a telephone conversation between two lovers—a male character whose jealousy and suspicion prompt him to phone, and a duplicitous femme fatale who uses the phone to put him off. This scene involves one of the very few *white* telephones in Italian cinema during the 1930s, and the telephone does fetishize both female sexuality and her upper-class privilege, imaged in the opulence of her boudoir. But the film goes on to condemn her modern environment, where relationships (like the one between the central couple) are formed and individuals are distanced (the man deceived) through telephone conversations. The sphere of the telephonic gets contrasted in this film with the North African desert, an utterly empty environment, devoid of telephones, where relationships get formed more directly but where the lack of reliable communicative and navigational technology becomes as formidable an enemy as African "rebels." As a colonial film that works to map Italy's new "empire," *Squadrone bianco*'s discourse about the parameters of telephonic space is also a discourse about the most contested zones of national sovereignty.

The cinematic representations of telephony during the 1930s were never as abundant as in northern European and Hollywood films. In fact, *La telefonista* was a remake of a German film, and *Squadrone bianco* a filmic adaptation of a French novel. The abundance of foreign (particularly Hollywood) depictions of telegraphically and telephonically structured environments were significant because the percentage of Hollywood films continued to outnumber Italian films and because in Italy the use of the telephone (while escalating quite rapidly) was still 0.5 percent—the lowest in Europe—and by 1940, 1,300 provincial Italian towns still lacked telephone service altogether. In this respect, foreign cinema's mapping of telephonic space is part of a process of spatially defining nations and their sovereignty. And after the 1930s, state policy in Italy concerning telecommunications and broadcasting became an exercise in "nationalizing" services, of marking national boundaries through their networks, and of insulating national territory from the intrusion of other national networks.

At the end of World War II, the reconstruction of the national telephone system—which was devastated during the war—occurred alongside a restabilization and rapid growth of Italian film production. As I have noted above, however, the national remained intact after the Fascist regime and roughly through the 1970s in part through broadcasting and telephony. During this period, the Radiotelevisione italiana (RAI) remained a centralized model of broadcasting whose networking and programming perpetuated a Rationalist program for the administration of a national culture.[30] And in a manner virtually unique among national broadcast companies, the RAI television news service for decades used a prominently displayed telephone in every news broadcast to enable news commentators to speak with the news director during the broadcast—a practice that wedded the narrative and material structure of national news broadcasting with telephony and that came to mark broadcasting and telephony's central place (and increasingly their pedigree, their authority) for "administering" to the nation and for organizing everyday life. So even though the myth of the white telephone functioned in the postwar years to distance the nation (and the center-Right, Christian Democrat government) from Fascist culture, the telephonic was rearticulated as an important point of reference to a centralized system of administering national culture (and, on a daily basis, in the national news).

Since the 1990s, cinema, "public" broadcasting, and telephony's effectivity have been largely residual formations. For cinema, this occurred sooner (during the 1980s), through its increasing convergence with and reliance upon the televisual and subsequently all of its increasingly varied telecommunication and computer technologies that have furthered its dispersion. By the 1990s, more films were watched in Italy (and elsewhere) via television and the VCR than at movie theaters.[31] Cinema, public broadcasting, and telephony's collective reconfiguration in the 1990s, consequently, has had a dramatic impact on the fate of the early modern diagram. One of the most everyday indices of this transformation was the practice throughout the 1990s (most notably by RAI-3's *Blob*) of lampooning gaffes by RAI television's use of the telephone in its news broadcasts, wherein the telephone appears as a trite remnant of the RAI's authoritative position as broker of "national news."

While telephony in Italy continues to be an important way that the nation is spatially defined, telephonic practices and institutions no longer sustain the early modern diagram. Over the 1990s, the Italian government and Telecom (the national state monopoly) have gradually had to abandon a system of telephony that had been in place since the late 1920s. This change has occurred particularly in response to three circumstances: the rapid convergence of telephony and broadcast media with the Internet and telematics, the multinational reorganization of the telecommunication industry, and the proliferation, particularly in Italy, of portable telephones (*telefonini*).

By 1996, the per-capita number of portable telephones and the number of mobile telephone transponders per acre was greater in Italy than in any country in the world.[32] Between 1994 and 1997, the number of telephones sold in Italy grew by almost 50 percent, compared to an average growth rate of 3.6 percent in the rest of the world. During this same period, the widespread use of portable telephones in Italy had occurred as the Italian government and Telecom were pressed to allow competition in the mobile telephone market with a second, privately owned telecommunication company, Omnitel. And by 1998, negotiations began for a third privately owned competitor for the mobile telephone market. This realignment has also entailed mergers between telecommunication corporations that were at one time restricted to particular national markets; Telecom entered into a pact with AT&T, and the third mobile telephone company became a multinational consortium. This has meant that telecommunication in Italy involves multinational business ventures and that multinational telecommunication companies (whether formerly parastate ones such as Telecom or private ones such as the one that will own the third mobile telephone service) have reterritorialized other nations through the efforts of these companies to expand their markets.[33]

It may be tempting to argue that the *telefonino* is becoming the white telephone for Italy in the 1990s. The traditional distinction between public and private space that underpinned public and private telephone use in Italy for decades has rapidly been redefined through telecommuting. And it is certainly no longer uncommon in Italy to hear the ringing of *telefonini* in movie theaters or to have telephone conversations mix with the long-standing practice in Italy of talking at a theater during a film. In Italian cinema the portable telephone and its user-subject have become as prominent a cultural stereotype as was the white telephone. Most often, as in *Chiedi la luna* (*Ask for the Moon*, dir. Giuseppe Piccioni, 1991), *Io ballo da sola* (*Stealing Beauty*, dir. Bernardo Bertolucci, 1996), and *Ferie d'agosto* (*August Holidays*, dir. Paolo Virzì, 1996), films deploy the portable telephone as one of the most devastatingly recognizable signs of a malaise and neurosis associated with yuppieness (particularly yuppie masculinity). And, as in the 1930s films, these films often exhibit a nostalgia for forms of sociality "uncontaminated" by recent media technologies.[34] But the construction of this figure and its landscape bespeaks Italian cinema's emerging strategies for mapping an environment and for a nation that is being spatially reorganized through telecommunication networks, spaces, access, and flows (and for mapping its own relation to this environment). In *Chiedi la luna*, the male protagonist's trek from Milan into the provinces and his regular use of his *telefonino* to remain in touch with the city become about the transformation of the urban/rural chronotope and of the impossibility of any longer "escaping" the urban. In *Io ballo da sola*, the *telefonino* is used to re-map the Tuscan countryside's relation to the "outside" (of locality to global flows) and to resituate that landscape as cultural chronotope. That these narrative strategies occur through the film's discourse about the production, rootedness, and circulation of cultural forms (the landscape sculpture and the Walkman) ties the film's mapping of locality to Italian cinema's struggle to define its own position (even as a residual formation) within these current flows and geographic realignments.

These films constitute a discourse about landscape and environment, mobility and access, locality and globalization, and the nation across a new set of spatial relations. To understand this discourse, however, requires more than simply recognizing narrative conventions. It involves trying to understand what kind of concrete assemblage "the cinematic" (or "the telephonic") constitutes and defines any longer. Particularly within the current tendency to understand the space, vectors, and sociality of "new media" only as "virtual," it becomes more incumbent on cinema and cultural studies to be attentive to the institutional embodiments, locations, arrangements, and interdependencies of the cinematic and other cultural practices. Locating cinema and the cinematic also entails considering how its current status is conditioned by and a condition of the emergence of the new cartography of the nation that was discussed in the first section and considering what remains of the early modern diagram that cinema and telephony shaped and sustained.[35] Whereas the aura of the white telephone (its place in 1930s film and its rarity in Italian homes) represented the intersection between cinema and telephony and between Hollywood and Cinecittà, the *telefonino* is an instrument of a new regime of mobility and of governing at those places and along those paths where the Far West (globalized networking through electronic technologies) intersects with other new coordinates of national life.

Notes

The author is grateful for suggestions from Flavia Martinelli, Franco Minganti, and Piero Borghi.

1. Typical examples of this tendency were Serge Hughes's *Fall and Rise of Modern Italy* (New York: Macmillan, 1967) and Margaret Carlyle's *Modern Italy* (New York: Praeger, 1965), wherein Italian modernity begins in 1945 as a "rebirth" or "recovery" from the Fascist period. Even some of the

most recent and renowned treatments of modern Italy, however, are organized this way, perpetuating a myth about recovery and transformation after Italian Fascism. See, for instance, Denis Mack Smith's *Modern Italy: A Political History* (Ann Arbor: University of Michigan Press, 1997); Donald Sassoon's *Contemporary Italy: Politics, Economy, and Society since 1945* (New York: Longman, 1997); and Martin Clark's *Modern Italy, 1871–1995* (London and New York: Longman, 1996). Ernesto Galli della Loggia discusses this tendency in Italy, noting the persistence of Croce's reasoning in 1948 that Fascism was a development with a clear beginning and ending (he argues that "that which chronologically pertained to Fascism pertained only to Fascism"). Della Loggia thus sees the dismantling of the Fascist state as the defining historiographic moment in Italian accounts of modern Italy. See Ernesto Galli della Loggia, "La morte della patria: la crisi dell'idea di nazione dopo la seconda guerra mondiale," in *Nazione e nazionalità in Italia,* ed. Giovanni Spadolini (Roma-Bari: Laterza, 1994), 131.

Some histories of modern Italy rightly consider the persistence after World War II of "public administration" and "public institutions" (or the practice of private ownership of "public" entities) that developed mostly through the Fascist state. See, for instance, *Storia del capitalismo italiano: dal dopoguerra a oggi,* ed. Fabrizio Barca (Roma: Donzelli Editore, 1997). In certain respects, this essay supports that account while addressing two other concerns: that the organization of state government, financial institutions, and industry cannot sufficiently account for formations of power, for the nation as a socio-spatial arrangement/map, or for how a nation is governed; and that accounts which emphasize these institutions seldom consider the limits of their purview in nation formation and governance. Italian cinema cannot be explained either as a program of the state or as a practice that had nothing to do with the objectives of state government.

This essay therefore is less interested in producing a history of modern Italy as a nation-state (wherein the state is the primary or only way of explaining nation formation and governance) and more interested in an account that considers the formation and governance of the "national" as a way of understanding Italian modernity. This distinction rests upon two different conceptions of power—the former, which attributes power primarily to state government, financial institutions, and industry (often in a way that ignores the limits of their authority), and the latter, which sees power as assembled and re-assembled out of (and up through) a multitude of diverse institutions, programs, and spheres and which sees space as productive and not simply as an epiphenomenon of a single force.

2. These trends are addressed in this book's introduction, but my point here particularly concerns the "historico-*geographic*" problematic of Italian modernity and cinema's *place* in Italian modernity. Since the 1980s, some studies about Italy between the two world wars have devoted considerable attention to particular cultural forms and practices. Most of this work has focused on literature and film, but some has dealt with theater, opera, and

advertising. Despite the importance of this body of work in correcting the longstanding tendency in histories of Fascism to devalue culture or the complexities of culture as a sphere of social formation and transformation, this work has tended to demonstrate cultural complexity through a *particular* cultural form or sphere of cultural production. In part, this was a consequence of having to do the kind of carefully descriptive analysis that was lacking in histories that overemphasized state control. It was also however a consequence of the equally long-established tendency in literary and film criticism to devalue the organization and materiality of the *environment* where these forms were produced, where they were consumed and circulated, and where they could be said to have social effects. From the perspective of such studies, "culture" was a sphere best analyzed through close analysis of the ways in which meaning, identity, ideology were produced through these forms and "their subjects." To have taken more seriously the materiality of the social *field* in which literature and film circulated would have required these studies to consider issues that are not as easily or typically understood through textual analysis of literature and film. Doing so would also have entailed working harder at explaining the literary or the cinematic as distinct social spheres and sites *imbricated* within other spheres of sociality and other sites of power—in short, of recognizing that the specificity of the literary or the cinematic is not just a formal issue but rather concerns their *location* and the ways they matter within the organization of populations and social relations through/as a material environment. What was lacking, in other words, was a keen sense of the literary or the cinematic as concrete assemblages and technologies of power whose possible uses and effects were contingent upon the relational status of the assemblages within a diagram (discussed in the next note).

3. I adopt the term "diagram" to emphasize several issues about the relationships between cinema, the nation, and Italian modernity. First, this essay is interested in thinking about the nation as a historico-geographic designation/formation. The nation is a way of defining and representing (from within a context) the relationship between a territory and the arrangement of a population (the socio-spatial relations of a society) to a history. In that sense, the nation has operated as a *chronotope*—formed and circulating through particular mechanisms such as cinema. The nation is not only a concept/identity that has been produced through film narrative but is also a social arrangement and a territory that the distribution of films has facilitated and (over time and in conjunction with other networks) transformed.

Second, to see the nation as formed, instated, through a diagram builds upon Gilles Deleuze's view that power (as relations of force) is administered through and relies upon multiple assemblages that separately but interdependently facilitate the circulation of power. In his book on Michel Foucault, Deleuze describes Foucault as a "new cartographer" who conceives of modern societies in their spatial arrangements and who sees power as dispersed (rather than as vertically structured), emanating from and operating through distributions and arrangements (Gilles Deleuze, *Foucault* [Minneapolis: University of Minnesota Press, 1988]). In this sense, according to Deleuze, Foucault views power as a "diagram"—a map that is coextensive with the entire social field but that is non-unifying even as it organizes and limits social forces and social subjects. From this perspective, things happen in a particular society not because of any single force—not "from above" and not as a result of a direct cause and effect—but because of the historical and spatial relation and convergence of forces. As a non-unifying immanent cause, the diagram is neither an ideological superstructure nor an economic base—terms that have been central to classical Marxist theories of power. Unlike these binary categories, "diagram" emphasizes the more loosely coordinated array of "assemblages" that are singularly specific and concrete while operating interdependently. In Foucault's work, these would include schools, hospitals, courts—the institutional mechanisms that carry out the organizing of modern societies, that independently yet collectively administer the diagram.

This essay is particularly interested in the dismantling of an early modern, "rationalist" diagram that has taken place since the 1980s. I adopt the term "rationalist" to link the dominant architectural and design style in Italy during the 1920s and 1930s with a broad social arrangement—or "diagram"—on which Italian modernity depended. By considering how the Italian nation(-state) was organized and represented through multiple mechanisms and assemblages (to use Deleuze's terms), many of which were beyond direct state control, this essay seeks to understand the relationship between technologies of power in Italian modernity and recent developments that have contributed to advanced or neo-liberalized forms of governing.

I have used the term "early modern" to describe the gradual interdependence (over the late nineteenth and early twentieth centuries) among a variety of mechanisms shaping and governing the nation as social arrangement and territory and as an *assemblage* of spatial representations whose diffusion, through mechanisms such as cinema, helped establish the nation as territory—particularly over the 1930s. "Early modern," however, is a relative term, since Italian modernity—to the extent that it involved the formation of Italy as a nation-state—occurred in the late nineteenth century, later than other European nations and modernities. There was certainly a discourse of the *nazione* and *patria* in Italy before the 1860s (e.g., Leopardi and the early nineteenth-century historical novel), which imagines the formation of a sovereign territory in the future, though typically through classical and medieval allegory and with a circulation limited to those who could read. Furthermore, as Silvana Patriarca has demonstrated, even the governmental rationality of the fledgling Italian nation-state during the late nineteenth century relied upon apparatuses of control such as population accounting that still pertained to a regionalism and the territories of empire from before the 1870s. See Silvana Patriarca, *Numbers and Nationhood: Writing Statistics in Nineteenth-Century Italy* (New York: Cambridge University Press, 1996).

4. For more on this distinction, see James Hay, "Piecing Together What Remains of the Cinematic City," in *The Cinematic City*, ed. Dave Clarke (London and New York: Routledge, 1997).

5. Thinking about nation formation and governance as a spatial problematic allows me to decenter cinema (accentuating its interdependencies), to emphasize the site and territory (purview) of the cinematic, and to consider cinema as an apparatus for defining the nation (as map) through representations of places and landscapes *and* as an apparatus of transport and distribution, as a site (anchoring other sites and thus organizing environments), and as a circuit of reception. Proceeding this way also allows me to discuss how cinema mattered in articulating nation (as concept, but also as an assemblage of spatial representation, as social arrangement, and as territory), how the state's articulation to the nation occurred through cinema's imbrication in other technologies, and how cinema and the Fascist state relied upon one another, accomplishing interdependent tasks that partially and strategically contributed to a particular formation of the nation.

6. For many reasons, including pressures to keep the length of the essay reasonable for publication, I am not able to offer a fuller account of these discourses and have had to shorten my description of some the terms included in this section. I do not, for example, consider the very important discourse about Italy's relationship to the European Economic Community. That discourse is certainly crucial to understanding the terms that I do consider in this section. I want to thank Flavia Martinelli in particular for her suggestions pertaining to the following discussion about "coordinates" of the nation in contemporary Italy.

7. Supported by local government and part of a global economy, these regions and cities thus developed relationships with sites/flows outside Italy that were as important as relationships within it. The financial success in an area of loosely connected light, global industry also exacerbated the disparity in economic development between northern and southern Italy, though one could argue that the kind of "underground economy" from which the new industry in the northeast emerged remained "underground" and "global" in the south.

8. Distinctions between the north and the south also took shape through conflicts about the cultural difference, political autonomy, or separatist movements of "border" and "island" regions—of Sicily, Sardegna, and regions along Italy's northern border whose inhabitants have maintained strong cultural bonds with France, Switzerland, Germany, Austria, or Croatia. In this respect, the north/south distinction (as an "internal" distinction) could

not be bracketed easily from the place of "border" cultures in the formation of a nation-state nor, more generally, could they be bracketed from
Italy's formation "under" and "against" territories outside its borders.

9. See Raimondo Strassoldo, "Ethnic Regionalism vs. the State: The Case of
Italy's Northern Leagues," in *Borders, Nations, and States: Frontiers of
Sovereignty in the New Europe,* ed. Liam O'Dowd and Thomas M. Wilson
(Aldershot, U.K.: Avebury, 1996).

10. The closest that the Northern League has come to identifying a suitable
formation of state has been its aspiration for a collectivity of (both "global"
and medievalesque) city-states. When I state above that the Northern
League "relies upon references to a pre-Urban bond with the Land," I
recognize that its mythologizing of Land is articulated to/through a plan
to justify the medieval city-state as a model of governing in the late twentieth century.

11. Umberto Bossi, the leader of the Northern League, is careful, however, not
to associate the League with Fascism; instead, he has likened the imagined
community to the Scotland of the film *Braveheart* (and has likened his own
role less to that of Mussolini than to that of the film's director and star,
Mel Gibson). Various references to Bossi's statement appeared in Italian
newspapers during the spring of 1996.

12. *La Repubblica,* 15 August 1997.

13. Over 50 percent of these immigrants have settled in northern Italy, where
they have "resettled" outlying zones and towns of cities. In some respects,
immigration has been as significant a factor in the spatial redefinition of
the nation during the 1990s as was the migration from the southern regions
of Italy to northern Italian cities and northern European countries during
the 1950s and 1960s, or as significant a factor in the early modern formation of the nation as was migration from the provinces to cities, the pre-
cipitous decline in emigration, and Fascist colonialism during the 1920s
and 1930s.

14. The exact number of immigrants cannot be determined because the state
government has never recognized immigrants as citizens. A government
report from 2000 (http://www.governo.it/sez_dossier/immigrazione/pre-
sentazione.html), however, states that between 1993 and 1995, the number
of immigrants repatriated was 19,107; between 1996 and 1998, 106,851
immigrants were recorded (17 percent of which were repatriated); and between July 1998 to 2000, 293,302 immigrants were recorded (of which 58
percent were repatriated).

In 1990, the Martelli Law made it lawful for immigrants who had not
registered with the state to remain in Italy legally, though without citizenship rights. The Dini decree of 1997 updated the Martelli Law, though as
of 1997 the Italian government still refused to confer full citizenship
status and rights upon immigrants working (legally or illegally) in Italy
since 1990. In March 1998, the "Napolitano-Turco" Law (Legge 6, no. 40,

"Disciplina dell'immigrazione e norme sulla condizione dello straniero") formalized the Italian immigration policy that continued through 2001. This law accepts the designation *extra-comunitari* by distinguishing between "foreigners" (*stranieri*) and immigrants/visitors who are not citizens of European Union nations. The law acknowledges the human and civil/ juridical rights of everyone within the Italian borders, but it devotes most of its attention to defining what constitutes illegal entry or residence and to the procedures for removing and expatriating foreigners who have entered or who reside in Italy illegally.

The liminal status of immigrants was exacerbated in 1996 when the government decided to allow those found without a visa for two weeks to leave on their own accord—a policy that had the effect of neither forcing their expatriation nor attributing a legal status to them. Even after the 1998 law, the "impermanence" of these immigrants—both in terms of their ambiguous state status and their relative mobility as a "flexible" labor pool for the recent industries and commercial economies of Italy and western Europe—has been a significant factor, therefore challenging some of the state's traditional roles, that of administering immigration law, or providing social services, and, by complicating definitions of citizenship, of governing the entire population. Over the 1990s, one of the most notable revisions of immigration laws, decrees, and policy (in addition to the ones mentioned above) has been that surveillance and regulation of immigrants, as well as meager programs to assist them, have been delegated to local/regional governments.

15. Jean Baudrillard, *America*, trans. Chris Turner (London/New York: Verso, 1988).

16. This is an important point because it counters the facile dichotomy between Fascism as total control by the state (the "totalitarian" thesis) and "neo-liberal" modes of governing as total lack of reliance upon state government. State government in Italy during the 1920s and 1930s relied upon assemblages not controlled directly by the state, just as advanced liberal government in Italy (represented through the discourses considered in this section) relies upon assemblages that are producing a new model of the nation-state.

17. Deleuze uses the term "abstract assemblage" to explain how Foucault describes and emphasizes the interdependence of specific, "concrete" assemblages:

> It is as if the abstract and the concrete assemblages constituted two extremes, and we moved from one to the other imperceptibly. Sometimes the assemblages are distributed in hard, compact segments which are sharply separated . . . (such as school, army, workshop, and ultimately prison, and as soon as you're in the army, they tell you 'You're not at school any more'). Sometimes, on the other hand, they communicate with the abstract machine which confers on them

a supple and diffuse microsegmentarity, so that they all resemble one
another and prison extends throughout the rest . . . (school, bar-
racks, and the workshop are already prisons). (Deleuze, *Foucault*, 40)

18. As recently as 1991, historian Doug Thompson accepted this term, arguing not only that "cinema remained outside the mainstream of Italian culture" and that "little of any lasting value emerged from it," but that almost
every film was a "fascist film" and included a white telephone. *State Control
in Fascist Italy* (Manchester: Manchester University Press, 1991), 121–122.

19. See Michel Foucault, "Governmentality," in *The Foucault Effect: Studies in
Governmentality,* ed. Graham Burchell, Colin Gordon, and Peter Miller
(Chicago: University of Chicago Press, 1991).

20. See James Hay, *Popular Film Culture in Fascist Italy* (Bloomington: Indiana
University Press, 1987).

21. As a center of film training and production, the district around Cinecittà,
a studio compound directly adjacent to the Centro sperimentale and the
LUCE Institute, became a cornerstone to a program linking land reclamation, the expansion of Rome's purview, and a new national territory of distribution. As a film about land reclamation and as a film widely proclaimed
to be the harbinger of a new ("reborn") national cinema, *Sole* is a vivid
example of these intersecting projects.

22. Fredric Jameson, *The Political Unconscious* (Ithaca, N.Y.: Cornell University Press, 1981), 296.

23. This is a point that Tony Bennett has made about Jameson in *Outside Literature* (London and New York: Routledge, 1990).

24. Interestingly, in order to explain the utopian as a principle of unity, Jameson cites a passage from Marx's *Grundrisse* about "Asiatic" land-forms but
then turns it into an analogy about interpellation rather than considering
how the formation of social relations therein involves a spatial and environ-
mental arrangement. Deleuze and Guattari (and in the very reference that
Jameson acknowledges in a footnote) do introduce this spatial problematic
into their discussion of "Asiatic production" as a territorializing machine.
Jameson is more interested in literature's textuality than in theorizing the
practices that situate the literary as a concrete assemblage.

25. Italian Rationalism is most associated with the Gruppo 7, a circle of young
Milanese architects who described and displayed the objectives of this
style in the First Italian Exposition of Rational Architecture, Rome 1928.
Their design style developed out of *Novecento* ("modern") Italian architecture. See particularly the controversy surrounding the design of the Corso
Cinema in Rome in 1918 described in Richard Etlin, *Modernism in Italian
Architecture* (New York: MIT Press, 1991). Rationalism, however, became
the first architectonics in twentieth-century Italy to emphasize a new relationship between architectural design and machines (e.g., the house as machine and the distribution of interdependent parts, each serving a precise

purpose). As G. Terragni (a member of the Gruppo 7) wrote: "Nothing useless or superfluous must be there because, as with machines, this would end up hindering [its] operation," unpaginated manuscript, 1928, cited in Etlin, *Modernism in Italian Architecture*, 632.

26. Although film montage is a narrative technology that facilitated the kind of spatial ellipses necessary to represent simultaneity of sound from different places (cross-cutting among talking/singing characters), I am more interested in cinema and telephony as twin technologies for producing social space.

27. *Canzone dell'amore* (*Song of Love*, dir. Gennaro Righelli, 1930) does somewhat the same thing with radio and phonography.

28. Two other contemporaneous films, *Rubacuori* (*The Charmer*, dir. Guido Brignone, 1931) and *La segretaria privata* (*Private Secretary*, dir. Goffredo Alessandrini, 1931) are similar in this respect.

29. Kracauer, "The Mass Ornament," in *The Mass Ornament: Weimer Essays*, trans. Thomas Levin (Cambridge, Mass.: Harvard University Press, 1995).

30. During the late 1950s and early 1960s, the TV program *Campanile sera*, for instance, weekly reproduced the nation by broadcasting telephonic conversations between the central broadcasting studio and various localities around Italy.

31. For an account of this tendency among Italian youth, see "I giovani amano il cinema ma non sullo grande schermo," *La Repubblica*, 4 June 1997; or "I film di cassetta," *Il Manifesto*, 4 June 1997.

32. *La Repubblica*, 27 May 1997.

33. The Telecom-AT&T company has attempted to become the dominant provider of telecommunication services in Latin America.

34. This tendency has been particularly evident in *Vito e gli altri* (*Vito and the Others*, dir. Antonio Capuano, 1991) and *Caro diario* (*Dear Diary*, dir. Nanni Moretti, 1993).

35. Post-scriptum on the place where cinema and telephony converge: My thinking about the relationship between Italian cinema and telephony was prompted in part by a paper that I was asked to present on the subject at a conference (about film representations of the telephone) sponsored by Italia Telecom at the University of Rome in June 1996. I mention this event not only to acknowledge my gratitude to its hosts and participants but to gesture, in closing, to an occasion that serves as a way to think about "what remains of the early modern diagram that cinema and telephony shaped and sustained": among other things, a retrospective by the old public monopoly on the importance of telephony in twentieth-century Italian culture.

PART II
Fascism, Cinema, and Sexuality

5

Sex in the Cinema

Regulation and Transgression in

Italian Films, 1930–1943

David Forgacs

I

One of the received ideas about the popular films made in Italy under the Fascist regime is that there was not much sex in them. When they did deal with sex, it is claimed, they did so indirectly or evasively, displacing attention outward to its superficial areas and social rituals: courtship, flirtation, schoolgirl crushes, modest kisses, the seduction routine. Francesco Bolzoni, writing about what he calls the *commedia all'ungherese* (a category which overlaps with what have become known as white-telephone films), claims that for clerico-Fascist Italy this type of film supplied an acceptable alternative to the French vaudeville plot based on marital infidelity because "although it is full of courtship and amorous rebuttals it puts sex in brackets. It changes it into a society game, a respectable parlour entertainment." Ernesto Lauro approvingly reproduces this statement in another article on the same comedies.[1] Gianfranco Casadio lists forty-one films made between 1939 and 1945, mainly Italian adaptations or remakes of German and Hungarian films or stage plays, and argues that "while not spurning sex," they were quite different from contemporary French comedies: whereas the latter had marriages breaking up and risqué "erotic situations," in the former sex was "merely suggested"; "the whole thing was conducted as in an innocent and carefree game."[2] The practice of putting sex "in brackets," turning it into a "game," is attributed to the combined effects of Catholic and state censorship on the one hand and a conformist film industry on the other. This idea fits neatly with the view of the entertainment cinema

141

of the Fascist period as a mainly apolitical, morally bland, and conformist *cinema di evasione:* a cinema of "distraction," to use Claudio Carabba's words, or, in Adorno and Horkheimer's more sinister expression, "mass deception" (*Massenbetrug*).[3]

These descriptions seem to me inaccurate in every respect: in the way they talk about sex, in the assumptions they make about the film industry and censorship under Fascism, in their implied judgement of why audiences went to the cinema and what happened to them when they watched popular films, and as accounts of the films themselves. The notion of *evasione* itself is a legacy of the politically driven history of the Italian cinema which was first developed by anti-Fascist critics in the late 1940s; it was reproduced in standard textbooks and is still widely accepted as the truth. In giving priority to whatever traveled along the high road of social realism toward neorealism and finding it under Fascism in a handful of films or even just in certain sequences and techniques—for instance the location shoots and tracking shots of *Gli uomini, che mascalzoni!* (*What Rascals Men Are!*, dir. Mario Camerini, 1932) or the non-professional actors, regional speech, and natural lighting of *1860* (dir. Alessandro Blasetti, 1934)—this account pushed to the wayside all those films with romantic intrigues, glamorous costumes, stars, and studio sets and whole genres such as comedy and melodrama, including the much-derided white-telephone films, which made up the bulk of domestic production in the second half of the 1930s. Many of these films invited a strong identification with female characters and love stories, and their critical downgrading in favor of social realism can be seen as yet another instance of legitimate cultural history elevating the public sphere, politics, and seriousness over the private sphere, domesticity, and pleasure, which in addition to being feminized is now tainted by being associated with Fascism. For Bruno Torri in 1976, white-telephone films were "escapist films which uphold the ethic of the family and religion, concealing exploitation and the class struggle." Guido Aristarco, speaking in 1989 not just about Italian white-telephone films but also their Hungarian, Czech, and Polish counterparts of 1935-1940, said, "There is no doubt in my mind that these films—all of them, without exception, until 1939—had and still have a subtle fascist ideology." Casadio in 1991 called white-telephone films "indirect propaganda."[4] The very notion of cinema as *evasione* defines films by what they do not deal with, what they fail to show—working-class life, social conflict, "reality," sex—rather than what they do show. As a consequence, those people who remember watching the Italian popular films of the Fascist period and the postwar generations who have seen them subsequently at festival screenings, in film courses, or on television and video have been taught to look at them as a series of absences and erasures; in other words, not to look and to feel guilty about their "feminine" pleasures of identification with "Fascist" pictures.

If the notion that these films put "sex in brackets" sounds familiar, it is because it is the same as the notion frequently found in descriptions of American films made from the mid-1930s to the late 1950s under the Production Code Administration (PCA). "For more than two decades sexuality was replaced by coyness, and controversy by blandness," writes John Izod of these films. For James Skinner "a curious prudishness reigned supreme."[5] These statements, like those by Bolzoni and Casadio, do not merely say that there are various *aspects* of sexuality which the cinema, given the prevailing codes of propriety, did not represent. They go farther and claim that sexuality *as a whole* was excluded from representation, that it was transmuted into something else—something bland, coy, prudish, and respectable—for fear of falling foul of the censor. But there is a double fallacy here: first, in the idea that there is a reality or truth of sexuality which exists prior to representations; and second, in the notion that censorship acts as a repressive brake on the free expression of this reality. Against the first idea we may invoke Foucault's arguments that there is in human societies no "real" sexuality outside the circuits of discourse in which sex is spoken about and that to approach sexuality historically means to look at how different regimes of "power-knowledge-pleasure" have variously put sex into discourse.[6] Against the second notion I would argue that films on sexual themes (as the "Hungarian comedies" invariably were) always produce particular accounts of sexuality and of sex-gender relations, whether they depict physical contact or not. All films are made in accordance with, or in resistance to, codes of censorship which are generally visible to the scriptwriters, director, and producer, as well as unwritten but generally understood codes of propriety and good taste. These codes become internal to their narrative construction, and in this respect censorship becomes an active, productive force in the making of films. Only less frequently does it intervene externally and subsequently upon films through repression or excision.[7] Even when it does, the boards of censors do not act alone but interpret and transmit the values of a set of institutions—the Church, the police, the magistrature, schools, the press, and the family—which collectively mold a discourse of reality and sexual normality.[8] This discourse draws the line between on the one hand the normal, the acceptable, the representable and on the other the deviant, the unacceptable, the unrepresentable, thereby producing the very boundary between the permitted and the prohibited which institutional censorship then polices.

Thus, even if one were to concede that these films were "asexual," they would still belong by virtue of this asexuality to a discourse about sexuality. But I want to claim that these films are in fact replete with sexual signs, that their very modesty generates a plethora of erotic suggestions. We need to learn to look at the blush, the pass, the adolescent infatuation, the display of naked flesh on the back or thigh, the double entendre as themselves part of a truth and substance of sex, as belonging to a historically located system of erotic signs. This system includes the sexual codes of other films, both domestic and imported, and a variety of extracinematic codes that circulated in Italian society. All these codes already incorporated censorship because they had developed in an environment where certain forms of overt sexual display were forbidden, but proscription had created over time, in addition to absences or elisions, a whole array of positive transferred erotic meanings.

The main theoretical supports of my argument here, in addition to Foucault on sexuality, are Simmel's essays on the sense of shame (1901) and on flirtation (first published in 1909 and later revised). If Foucault's work has helped us think of sexuality not as a timeless continuum of bodily practices but as a set of historically variable discourses and forms of experience, Simmel's essays suggest ways of analyzing the public manifestations of sexual behavior as involving modesty and embarrassment, a structured switching between the offering and withdrawal of the body (his definition of *Koketterie* or flirtation), and a channeling of erotic attention toward particular parts of the body or toward clothes or "extraneous objects." The modes of displaying sexuality in films of the 1930s and 1940s are part of this elaborate economy of social transactions. In this respect, one of Simmel's arguments about flirtation, namely that it disperses and prolongs pleasure across all stages of the "erotic sequence," may be applied also to these films:

> The meaning of pleasure extends to moments of the erotic domain which are all the more remote, allusive, and symbolic as the personality is more refined and cultivated. This process of psychic retreat can go so far that, for example, a young man in love draws more bliss from the first secret clasp of the hand than from any subsequent unconditional concession; and for many delicate and sensitive natures—who are by no means necessarily frigid or chaste—the kiss, or even the mere consciousness of the return of love, surpasses what might be called the more substantial erotic delights.[9]

This ties in well with more recent arguments about the diversity of forms of sexuality and intimacy, from Adrienne Rich's notion of a "lesbian continuum" ranging from female friendships to physical sex to

Martha Vicinus's work on schoolgirl crushes in late nineteenth- and early twentieth-century England:

> Bodily self-control became a means of knowing oneself; self-realization subsumed the fulfilment of physical desire. Love itself was not displaced, but focused on a distant object, while nonfulfilment—sacrifice—became the source of personal satisfaction. . . . Distance was a means of deepening a pleasure, which was expressed as the more fulfilling because nonsexual.[10]

This description is also appropriate for the Italian popular films of the Fascist period, though I do not agree with Vicinus's classification of "nonfulfilment" as "nonsexual."

II

Two innovative discussions of sexuality in Fascist Italy have suggested that the period was crisscrossed by tensions between repression and modernization, regulation, and transgression. For Bruno Wanrooij, in *Storia del pudore,* the terms are *"rigore"* and *"liberalizzazione,"* whereas Victoria de Grazia, in her chapters on "Growing Up" and "Going Out," in *How Fascism Ruled Women,* uses a variety of expressions: "conservative," "conventional," and "official culture" on the one hand; "modern," "secular," and "commercial culture" on the other.[11] A central plank of de Grazia's argument—and this is consistent with the pioneering work she has done elsewhere on the commercialization of popular leisure, advertising, "Americanization," and the growth of consumer culture in the interwar period in Italy—is that civil society under Fascism was an arena in which different forces sometimes conflicted and sometimes meshed or found mutual accommodation. These forces included, on the one hand, the institutions and agencies of the state—the Fascist Party (PNF) and the Church—and on the other, particularly in cities, the expanding area of commercial culture and leisure—films and fashion magazines, department stores, domestic consumer durables, advertising, radio, and cinema.

Both these analyses have added important details to the picture sketched by other historians of the Fascist period as one of "repressive modernization," that is to say, one in which certain forms of adaptation to "mass society" were carried forward—mass production and rationalization of the labor process in large industrial firms, the creation of the mass party and other mass associations, state welfare programs, and the development of modern communications media—but unevenly, with a simultaneous bolstering of ruralism, tradition, and the cult of antiquity and under conditions of political repression: withdrawal of liberal and democratic rights and freedoms, intensification of policing and surveillance, restrictions on movement, and tightening of censorship and the penal code. Just as in the civil and political sphere the tensions between these two tendencies caused conflicts and fuelled aspirations that could not be fulfilled, so in the sexual and personal sphere the tensions between repression and liberalization caused conflicts within families, between generations, and within individuals, which were either externalized and worked through as rebellion against prevailing norms or became internalized in the form of anxiety, doubt, and guilt.

Two findings of this body of research are of particular interest for the question of sex in the cinema. The first is the evidence it provides to show that the Fascists were as internally divided over modernization in the sexual sphere as they were in other spheres and that there was never a simple alignment between Fascist ideology and Catholic traditionalism. This certainly helps account for the fact both that the Catholic board of censors, the Centro Cattolico Cinematografico (CCC), instituted in 1934, classed as "excluded to all" or "excluded to minors" a number of films to which the state censorship body, the Commissione di Revisione Cinematografica, had granted a *nulla osta,* and that in different provinces Fascist prefects (who were empowered to sequestrate films) sometimes supported and sometimes overrode local Catholic opposition to the screening of a particular film. In Wanrooij's terms, the line between *rigore* and *liberalizzazione* ran not just between Catholics and Fascists but between Fascists themselves, some of whom sided with the Church while others took a modernizing line, whether for pronatalist reasons or because they espoused an ideology of sexual health and physical fitness against the allegedly unhealthy effects of prolonged chastity and sexual repression (onanism, nervous disorders, etc.). One example of the internal conflict in Fascism was the reaction by Fascist moralists to the law of 1927 which obliged the ONMI (Opera Nazionale Maternità e Infanzia) to pay cash benefits to unmarried mothers. They opposed this on the grounds that it made public and tacitly sanctioned the unmarried woman's dishonor, and they pointed out that over 27,000 single mothers had received benefits under the law in 1928–1929 while many equally needy married mothers got nothing.[12] Another case is that of Rinaldo Pellegrini, director of the Istituto di Medicina Legale at the University of Padua, who was suspended from his teaching duties by the rector in 1934 for having assigned to one of his students a survey-based *tesi di laurea* on the sexual behavior of young people. The suspension followed a letter of protest sent by the bishop of Padua to PNF secretary Achille Starace, who had then asked the rector to intervene. Pelle-

grini appealed, defending his actions to the rector, and thus by implication to Starace and the Party, on the grounds that they were furthering
the aims of Fascism: scientific research into sexual behavior was a contribution "to the continuous development of the Fascist fatherland,"
and the state's task, as he understood it, was to "keep watch over the
sexual morality and sexual life of its young people" and where necessary
to "correct and modify it independently of traditional and clerical education whose aims do not always coincide with its own." He opposed the
"hypocritical modesty" (*pudore ipocrita*) of the traditionalists—in other
words, their promotion of chastity and coyness—because it conflicted
with the interests of the Fascist demographic campaign.[13]

The second interesting finding is the evidence of just how rapidly
new attitudes toward sexuality and traditional gender roles pervaded
parts of Italian society under the regime. Both Wanrooij and de Grazia
cite a 1937 survey of 1,000 female school students aged 14–18 in *scuole
professionali* and *istituti magistrali* in Rome. The replies suggest that the
Fascist and Catholic promulgation of a sexual ethos directed toward
subservient feminine roles and large families had largely failed among
this social group (young urban middle-class women). Only 10 percent
expressed an interest in housework and 27 percent were negative about
it; the majority were uninterested in knitting and sewing. More of them
preferred "to command rather than to obey," valued self-confidence
over tractability, and said they were studying in order to get a job and
did not expect their husbands to support them. Very few said they liked
looking after children and only a few aspired to become mothers of
large families. Their favorite pastime was going to the cinema.[14]

It is clear from these and other sources that the cinema played a big
part in the sexual development of adolescents, exposing them, particularly through imported films, to more liberal sexual attitudes and serving as a space of fantasy and erotic identification. Italo Calvino, born in
1923, recalled in an essay of 1974 the sensual pleasures of his solitary
film-going in San Remo in the period 1936–1942 as well as his different
perception of French and American female stars: "French cinema was
as heavy with smells as American cinema smelt of Palmolive, of shiny,
sterile places. The women had a carnal presence which fixed them in
your memory as both living women and erotic spirits . . . whereas in the
Hollywood stars the eroticism was sublimated, stylized, idealized."[15]
The cinema was also a place where young people went as groups of
friends and where courting couples could experiment sexually away
from the gaze of their parents. Gino Gentilezza, born in 1920, was living in the late 1930s with his anti-Fascist parents in an apartment on
the side of the cinema. "When I went to the cinema with a girl to be

honest I didn't watch the film. I'm not a hypocrite like so many other people. . . . It was dark, a good place because I couldn't go to a hotel, they would have arrested me because I was an anti-Fascist and I didn't have any money, so we sometimes went to the cinema. It was in the dark, we did something a bit more."[16] This meaning of "sex in the cinema" was widely acknowledged. A British popular song of the period exhorted:

> Take your lessons at the movies
> And have love scenes of your own.
> When the picture's over and it's time to leave,
> Don't forget to brush the powder off your sleeve;
> Take your girlie to the movies
> If you can't make love at home.[17]

The increased visibility of intimacy in cinemas and other public places had been noted with alarm by Catholics since the 1920s. Giovanni Agnese, writing in 1929, deplored the behavior of couples "who make a spectacle of their amorous intimacy in every public place, sit indecently close together in cafés and embrace in theatres and public parks." He proposed that screen kisses be prohibited, that public meeting places be closed at midnight, that no girls under nineteen be allowed to dance in public, that short dresses be banned, that overcrowding on trams be prevented ("so that indecent contact, voluntary or otherwise, may be avoided and the sensitivity of the flesh may not be pointlessly exercised"), that beauty contests be stopped, and that the woods be patrolled by *carabinieri* and *guardie forestali* to root out lovers. At bathing resorts, women and men should be separated by "a thick and impenetrable palisade going down from the beach where the sand begins and continuing into the sea to where the water is at least two metres deep at low tide"; women's bathing costumes should include a knee-length skirt and men's costumes should cover the chest and back.[18] These prescriptions may have been extreme, but they indicate both the depth of anxiety in traditional circles about the changes in sexual behavior and the public places on which that anxiety was particularly focused: beaches, woods, parks, trams, cafés, dance halls, theatres, and cinemas. The notion that the cinema was a place of danger, particularly for youth and working-class audiences, appeared also in Pius XI's encyclical of 1936 to the American bishops, *Vigilanti cura:*

> Cinematic images are shown to people sitting in a dark theatre, whose physical faculties, and often also their spiritual faculties, are relaxed. One does not have to go far to find these theatres; they are

next to the houses, churches and schools of the people, bringing the cinema to the very centre of popular life.

Moreover, the actions shown in the cinema are performed by men and women chosen for their art, for all those natural endowments and for the use of those expedients which can also become an instrument of seduction, especially for young people.

The cinema also has at its service the luxury of the building, the pleasure of the music, the vigour of realism and every form of extravagant caprice. For that very reason its fascination is exerted with a particular power of attraction on youth, adolescents and children.[19]

The encyclical gave papal endorsement to views already formulated by American Catholics: the proposal drafted in 1930 by the Jesuit Father Daniel Lord and the lay Catholic Martin Quigley and adopted in March 1931 as the Production Code or Hays Code had voiced similar anxieties about the greater susceptibility to films of "immature" audiences—in this case, this meant not just the young but also the "rude" and "criminal" classes.[20] By the time of *Vigilanti cura*, the PCA had been set up (1934) by the Motion Picture Producers and Distributors of America (MPPDA) to give the Code teeth against recalcitrant producers. The whole purpose of the MPPDA's involvement, however, was to promote "self-regulation" by the industry and, as case studies of particular interventions have demonstrated, this created a push-pull between producers and the PCA over specific areas and boundaries of decency, and this in turn generated a peculiarly quantitative discourse of the erotic.[21] Sex in the movies became a matter of carefully calibrated measurements—length of skirt, height of neckline, duration of kiss—as the studios increasingly drove themselves to see how "far" they could go and were matched at every notch by PCA strictures. In Italy self-regulation was not institutionalized and codified in the same way and there was not, as there was in the United States, an oligopolistic studio system driven by competitive risk-taking and the search for innovation and product differentiation. It was this difference, rather than the conservative Catholic-Fascist axis in official public morality, which emerged from the Lateran Pacts (1929),[22] or the operations of censorship through the law and the *commissioni di revisione*, that explains, I believe, the absence of a similarly quantitative discourse of the sexual and the relatively greater restraint in Italian cinema of the period. If conservative public morality or legal restrictions were the main factor, then it would be impossible to explain why more sexually "risky" films emerged in Italy around 1940 or why, as I discuss below, naked breasts began to appear in 1941, when there had been no change in either official morality or censorship codes.

III

The opposition between sexual regulation and transgression may be approximately mapped onto Simmel's explanation of the sense of shame as the product of a conflict between "affirmation and negation of the self." According to this definition, we experience feelings of shame or modesty (*Scham*) when we are made the center of others' attention (affirmation of self) and when at the same time our ideal of who we are suddenly fails or collapses (negation of self). It is this basic mechanism which, for Simmel, links such apparently unrelated emotions as those we might experience when our nakedness is exposed, when we are singled out for applause or public praise, when a minor transgression we have committed is discovered, and when we are subjected to another person's unrelenting sexual attention. Simmel himself was insistent that *Scham* should not be seen as exclusively or fundamentally sexual. Indeed, he criticized Havelock Ellis's explanation of shame as a result of the sense of disgust that the "focal points of physical attraction and repulsion" are located close together in the body on the grounds that it did not adequately explain these other social manifestations of shame or modesty.[23] However, what Simmel's explanation does indirectly account for, despite his declared intention of generalizing modesty beyond the sexual realm, is the fact that certain specific discourses do associate the term strongly with its sexual meanings. In Catholic doctrine, notably, the woman's modesty or sense of shame (in Latin, *pudicitia* and *pudor*), whether exemplified in the exaltation of the Virgin Mary as *aula pudoris* (hall of chastity) or in the cult of a secular figure such as Maria Goretti, the young Italian woman who was held up by the Church as a "martyr of purity"[24] (she was murdered in 1902 while resisting a rapist), is in its very essence defined sexually as the preservation of the intact hymen until marriage (hence the term "*pudenda*" for the female genitals, also called "*die Scham*" in German, namely those parts of which the woman should be ashamed and which modesty requires her to hide from view) so as to guarantee procreation for reproducing an approved bloodline.[25] At the same time, the woman's modesty must be manifested to the public gaze in a whole series of prescribed social behaviors, from the wearing of suitable dress at appropriate times and places to gestures (lowered eyes, hands clasped in lap) to the observation of silence and deference in speech. The transgression of any one of these social rules is, by association, construed as a sexual transgression as well.

It is because of this expansion of the sexual into other manifestations of modesty that the terms "modesty," "decency" and "chastity" historically acquired, as Simmel deploringly noted, a "prevalently sexual connotation." And it is just these kinds of associations between modesty and sexuality that we find in films where embarrassment and a sense of shame are central both to plot and to bodily performance. For example, the plot tangle of *Maddalena—zero in condotta* (*Maddalena—Zero in Conduct,* dir. Vittorio De Sica, 1940) involves an unsigned love letter written as a private fantasy by the pretty but shy young Miss Malgari (Vera Bergman), who teaches commercial letter-writing at an expensive girls' school in Rome. The school's custom, we learn, is to address its sample business letters to the family firm of Alfredo Hartman in Vienna, and it is to this name that Miss Malgari has addressed her love letter. The letter is stolen by Maddalena (Carla Del Poggio) who, to avoid being discovered, passes it to her classmate, the *contessina* (Irasema Dilian), who, being naïve and new to the school, innocently posts it. The letter is received in Vienna by the youngest bearer of the Hartman name (played by De Sica) who, moved by the anonymous expression of love, travels to Rome with the letter in his pocket to find his Cinderella, whom he assumes to be one of the students at the school. The love letter risks exposing Miss Malgari, who has already been threatened with dismissal for failing to keep discipline in her class. In order to protect her, Maddalena claims she wrote it herself. The plot thus plays repeatedly on embarrassment through a series of actual or threatened exposures. Maddalena is embarrassed when she reads the letter, but at the same time it makes her feel close to and protective of her teacher. Miss Malgari's fear of being exposed is compounded by her subservient and precarious position in the school hierarchy and her inferior social status to the girls she teaches. She is embarrassed when the well-heeled Maddalena comes to visit her in the apartment she shares with her mother and finds her in an apron drying the dishes. The culmination of Miss Malgari's embarrassment comes when the compromising letter is passed round in a staff meeting that has been called to decide on Maddalena's punishment and Malgari reads her own words, which are described by one of her elder female colleagues as "precocious perversity" (*precoce perversità*). This reinforces the point that the embarrassment has a sexual core, even as the film dwells on the play of surfaces: the feints, denials, and near-discoveries. Maddalena ultimately fixes everything, like the resourceful maid in a Marivaux play, by arranging a meeting between Hartman and Malgari, who fall in love, while she gets Hartman's Italian cousin Armani (Roberto Villa) for herself.

In this and other comedies set in girls' schools or orphanages, including *Seconda B* (dir. Goffredo Alessandrini, 1934; the title is the name of a class), *Ore 9, lezione di chimica* (9 *A.M.: Chemistry Class,* dir. Mario Mattoli, 1941), and *Teresa Venerdì* (dir. Vittorio De Sica, 1941), there is an opposition between disciplinary rigor, represented by the old-guard teachers, and liberalization, an opposition sometimes negotiated by a kind and tolerant teacher, as the apparently stuffy *direttrice* in each of the two De Sica films turns out to be.[26] Both sides of this opposition are invested with sexual meanings through dress and body codes: the stern older women wear suits and tightly tied-back hair; the older male teachers usually have some combination of pince-nez, goatee beard, and starched collar; and the adolescent girls sometimes wear pinafores, neckties, or bows, sometimes casual clothes, but they always mix girlish rowdiness with an interest in men. Teresa Venerdì (Adriana Benetti) writes in her diary after her first meeting with the orphanage's new health inspector, Pietro Vignali (De Sica): "He is younger than Doctor Paoloni and better-looking too. But he said 'Hello, little girl' to me (*'Ciao, ragazzina'*). I'm not a little girl, though. Maybe it's because I acted silly." She and her friend Giuseppina subsequently perform a love scene from *Romeo and Juliet* clandestinely in front of the other girls. The stern *istitutrice* (Sandra Adari), tipped off by the spy Alice (Zaira La Fratta), catches them in the act. She punishes Teresa by removing her from the infirmary where she had been Vignali's assistant and putting her on kitchen duty instead. Unbowed, she continues to tell Giuseppina romantic stories. When Vignali asks Alice why Teresa has been punished, she replies that according to the *direttrice* "She gave a display of immodesty" (*"dava spettacolo di impudicizia"*).

This definition of Teresa's transgression is evidently a caricature of conservative sexual mores; however, it serves, like the definition of Maddalena's supposed transgression as *precoce perversità,* as a marker against which the more liberal positions sanctioned in the film can be measured. Like most sexual comedies and farces, these films create situations in which certain consensually agreed-upon boundaries of sexual propriety are crossed, stretched, or broken down, and new boundaries are established at the end. Vignali, who at the end of this film will propose to Teresa, is initially unsuitable for her because he is sexually experienced and in a relationship with another woman, the showgirl Loletta (Anna Magnani). Like the other characters played by De Sica during this phase of his career as a romantic male lead (whether they were lower class like the drivers in *I Grandi Magazzini* and *Gli uomini, che mascalzoni!* or wealthy like the heir to a family fortune in *Maddalena—zero in condotta*), Vignali is seductive, charming but an idler. Creditors call to see him: it is apparent that his impecuniousness is both because he rarely makes himself available to see patients and because Loletta has expensive tastes. To raise money to pay his debts, he arranges to sell his villa to the wealthy Passalacquas, who are going to buy it for their spoiled daughter Lilli (Irasema Dilian). He arrives at their house, finds Lilli sweeping the path, mistakes her for a maid and is free with her: he touches her on the face and arm and kisses her on the mouth just as her parents come to the door. Vignali is taken by the parents for Lilli's fiancé, she does not object to the sudden match, and Vignali finds himself stuck in an unwanted engagement. Just as Teresa needs to grow from girlhood to young womanhood to become a suitable future wife for Vignali, so Vignali needs to make a transition to maturity by giving up philandering, getting a secure income, and settling down. The implication at the end of the film is that his forthcoming marriage to Teresa, who has proved herself loyal, loving, and resourceful (she pays off Vignali's creditors and sends her two rivals, Loletta and Lilli, packing), will bring this about. The ending is additionally sentimentalized in that marriage will provide the orphan Teresa with a real home and she will trade in her foundling name "Friday" for Vignali's name.

Along the way to this sexually regulated ending are some transgressive moments which are central to the comedy. Vignali may be irresponsible but he is not particularly young (De Sica was forty when the film was released) and his sexual knowledge makes him a potential danger in the girls' orphanage. There is a brief sequence near the end which encapsulates the erotic dynamics of the film. Vignali is in the back of the orphanage limousine, being driven to his apartment to fetch Teresa, who has run away and spent the night on his divan. With him are the *direttrice* (Elvira Betrone), a young female teacher, a group of little girls, and an older girl of about sixteen.

> *Vignali* (to the *direttrice*): Put yourself in my shoes, madam. Imagine finding a girl in your house at midnight . . .
> *Direttrice:* Doctor, please, that's enough for now (*glances at the little girls*). You can explain later.
> *Vignali* (*silenced, looks down, then turns to the older girl seated next to him*): What's your name, little one (*piccina*)?
> *Teacher:* Maria, come here. (*The girl gets up and the teacher seats her next to herself, safely out of Vignali's reach*).

The basic situation of the schoolgirl comedy is that of a world of female friendships and solidarity into which a man's sexual desire intrudes. He can be safely flirted with (both invited and refused) because he can always be outnumbered and his desire kept in check. The De Sica character, at once seductive and clumsy, perfectly embodies this containable sexual threat. For women in the films, and also in the audience, the friendships may become implicitly eroticized, although the stories explicitly disavow any suggestion of lesbian desire by directing the burgeoning sexual longing onto a male third party: the way in which Maddalena resolves to draw out her teacher's secret desires by arranging her encounters with Hartman is a good example of this erotic triangle. For men, the narcissistic fantasy which mirrors this triangle—like that classic topos of male pornography, the "lesbian number"—is one of voyeuristic penetration into an all-female space in which the man disrupts its self-sufficiency and imagines himself becoming the center of attention and the focus of desire. For both male and female audiences, the girls' school functions nostalgically as a lost threshold between childhood and adulthood in which the line between girlish innocence and sexual self-awareness is not clearly drawn and thus not yet traversed.

To apply Simmel's analysis of female flirtation as a controlled switching by the woman between the offering and withdrawal of her body, for female spectators the narratives are about controlling the movement into sexual adulthood and for male spectators about transgressive intrusion into female space. In this liminal world on the edge of adulthood, it is not clear whether the girl's apparent offering of herself is intentionally sexual; in other words, whether it is conscious flirtation or simply a child's desire to please the paternal figure. The narrative of *Seconda B* turns on this ambiguity and the transgressive desire to which it gives rise. The middle-aged natural history teacher, Professor Monti (Sergio Tofano), has been gingerly courting the plain unmarried gym teacher, Miss Vanni (Dina Perbellini), but he becomes infatuated with the coquettish rich girl Marta Renzi (Maria Denis). Marta leads him to believe that she reciprocates the desire, but this turns out to be a practical joke for the amusement of Marta and her friends, who spy on her and Monti through a window. Miss Vanni, who has meanwhile been driven to quiet desperation by Monti's neglect, overhears Marta and her friends laughing about Monti, and she subsequently slaps her in class. Marta tells her father, a local politician and friend of the principal's, and he protests: Vanni is dismissed, Monti resigns too, and the suitable couple, of the same age and class, are thus ultimately reunited. In *Teresa Venerdì*, the transgressive situation is regularized by the "*ragazzina*" herself becoming a consenting adult. It is interesting to compare *La signora di tutti* (*Everyone's Lady*, dir. Max Ophuls, 1934), which is tangentially related to this genre (its inner narrative, framed by a flashback, starts in a girls' school), since it offers a variation on the transgressive fantasy which is not safely closed off. Here the adolescent Gaby (Isa Miranda), who seems unconscious of the sexual power she has over men, is accused of causing the suicide of a teacher who had fallen for her to the point of destroying his own marriage and leaving the country. The episode is the first in a series of deaths—it is followed by that of Leonardo Nanni's wife Alma (Tatiana Pavlova), then that of Nanni (Memo Benassi), and ultimately by her own suicide—which appear to result directly or otherwise from Gaby's fatal attractiveness to men. The film is stylistically very different from others made in Italy in the early 1930s—for instance, in its lighting design and its use of multiple embedded narratives—but it still works within a sexual economy of the unstated, the suggested, the struggle against passion, and a sense of guilt about desire. In this respect, it is very different from the source text by Salvator Gotta, a novel in the sub-d'Annunzio vein in which the Gaby character, Chicchi, consciously desires her adulterous affair with Leonardo and justifies it to herself in terms of a kind of moral exceptionalism.

The fact that the schoolgirl films are located in unspecified places or earlier times or in aristocratic or upper middle-class milieus replete with objects of conspicuous consumption—Lilli speaks on a white telephone, Marta's father in *Seconda B* (set in 1911–1912) throws a lavish party in his palatial apartment, Maddalena and the *contessina* eat cream puffs in expensive tea rooms—has often been remarked upon as an index of their escapism, of fantasy in the negative sense of distraction from reality, and thus as evidence of their complicity with Fascism's hegemonic project. But this argument overlooks a number of important considerations. The first is that fantasy in the cinema may offer pleasures which are not instrumental to the interests of a nation's rulers; the righteous condemnation of "escapism" ignores this possibility because it neglects the complexity of psychic experience and what audiences do with films. The second is that the use of exotic or historical locations and symbols of unattainable social status are some of the standard conditions that enable spectatorial fantasy to operate and were just as much a characteristic of contemporary American films, such as *Anthony Adverse, The Scarlet Pimpernel,* or *Gone with the Wind,* which may be considered reactionary as historical fictions but which are not generally accused in the same way of escapism as a political ruse. The third is that these films were often adaptations or remakes of Hungarian, Austrian, or German originals; indeed, this was one of the reasons for their exoticism to Italian audiences, their appearance of taking place in unspecific environments, and thus their appeal as fantasies. Both of De Sica's schoolgirl films were remakes of Hungarian films: *Maddalena—zero in condotta* was closely based on László Vajda's 1936 film of László Kádár's original play; *Teresa Venerdì* was based on Emil Martonffy's script for the 1938 film *Péntek Rézi (Rézi Friday,* the name of the resourceful orphan girl) from a novel by Rezsö Török. They belonged, in other words, to a European circuit of production, distribution, and exchange of narratives. This is not the least of reasons why it is procedurally questionable to identify the ultimate political meanings of their narratives with the specific ideological aims of the Fascist regime in Italy. At most one can talk, if one so wishes, about a common conservative or Fascist axis in these European countries.

IV

The tension between *rigore* and *liberalizzazione* was as central to melodrama as it was to comedy, since in melodrama the dramatic situation of the main female character is typically founded on a conflict between duty and desire. Melodrama also frequently embodies the conflict between ideal self-image and negation of self which, in Simmel's analysis, underlies feelings of shame and inadequacy. In *La peccatrice* (*The Sinful Woman,* dir. Amleto Palermi, 1940) the conflict for Maria Ferrante (Paola Barbara) is between her sense of her own worth and her internalization of others' condemnation. She becomes pregnant by Alberto (Gino Cervi), who promises to marry her but then abandons her. The baby dies in infancy. Maria has meanwhile agreed to wet-nurse the child of a peasant whose wife, Adele, is unable to feed him herself. The grateful couple subsequently invites Maria to stay in their house, but she leaves after Adele's brother Salvatore (Fosco Giachetti) bursts into her room drunk one night and threatens to rape her. She then falls in successively with two men who are unsuitable in different ways. Pietro (Vittorio De Sica) entices her with a promise of material well-being that he cannot sustain and is imprisoned for debt. The rich Ottavio beats her and forces her to work as a prostitute. At the end she escapes from the city, successively takes her leave of all the men in her life, and returns to her mother in the country, who embraces her tearfully.

The woman's "immodesty" and "sin" are made explicitly central to the film, from the title onward, but its point, I think, is to open up these notions to critical scrutiny. *La peccatrice* is certainly a schematic and sentimental film, particularly in its contrast between the corrupt city and the honest country, its mawkish ending, and in the way it dwells on Maria's basic goodness, religiosity, and sense of shame when she thinks of her mother. It is also remarkable for its series of critical representations of men—Alberto, who leaves Maria in the lurch; Salvatore, who feels free to assault her when he learns of her irregular sexual past; the feckless Pietro; and the coercive Ottavio—and for its portrayal of Maria as a victim of callous men who ultimately regains control of her life and respect for herself. In the scene with Salvatore, the dialogue lays bare the man's assumptions that the woman who has transgressed the accepted codes of female modesty (through loss of virginity and unmarried motherhood) is at once contemptible and sexually available. As he puts it, Maria is not, as he had believed, "a girl"; he can therefore switch to addressing her as "*tu*" and treat her body as his possession, as "others" have done before him.

Maria: Salvatore—what's wrong with you?
Salvatore: What do you think's wrong? Nothing. Here I am in your room [*in camera vostra*]. Oh, I know, men aren't supposed to go into girls' rooms, specially not at night. But you are not a girl [*tu non sei una ragazza*]. And I really believed you were. I even thought I shouldn't raise my eyes to you, to look at your mouth and the rest (*he looks down at her body*) because it was a sin. But now it's different; now (*he seizes her and pulls her to him*) you'll do it with me too, won't you?
Maria: You're crazy. Listen, Salvatore, I respect you because you're Adele's brother and I think you've just had too much to drink and you feel like fooling around.
Salvatore: Fooling around? Me? I'd like to. But it takes two to do it. Because otherwise, you see, we'd have to get serious, and I don't know what I'd do to you then, I'd have to . . .
Maria: Salvatore (*she pushes him away*), listen, I'm telling you again that maybe you've had too much to drink, but if you don't go right away I'll call Adele.
Salvatore: You send me away, that's easy, you call Adele. But if it hadn't been for her I'd still be here like a fool thinking you were what I thought you were. But when she saw how desperate your indifference made me she thought she would try to help, poor girl, so she told me everything. It was like taking away the air I breathed. But then I said to myself "What's wrong with you?" I can do like the others have done, can't I? And why shouldn't I? Tell me, why shouldn't I?

When Salvatore meets Maria again some years afterward he apologizes for his behavior, and he subsequently warns Pietro, who has followed her into the country, to leave her alone because she is "*una ragazza buona come il pane*": "as good as bread." Through these and other scenes, the latter part of the film carefully underlines Maria's heightened moral stature. As she walks past a restaurant window, she spots Alberto, whom she has not seen for several years. She goes in, orders a coffee, and sits at another table looking at him as he sits alone finishing his meal. The scene is played almost entirely without dialogue and Cervi builds the character of the fastidious and self-important Alberto out of just a few gestures. The waiter brings him a plate of cheese: he carefully cuts off the rind. The waiter brings coffee and he lets it slowly drip into the cup before removing the filter and raising it to his lips. At no point does he notice Maria, who sits watching him with pure hatred. Finally, as he leaves and walks past her, he sees her. "What are you doing here?" "I'm watching you." (*"Cosa fai qui?" "Ti guardo"*).

The treatment of unmarried sex and pregnancy in *La peccatrice* is also more radical than in the later *Quattro passi tra le nuvole* (*Walking in the Clouds,* dir. Alessandro Blasetti, 1942, from a story by Cesare Zavattini and Piero Tellini), a social comedy which has the same resolution— the daughter's transgression is forgiven by her family—but without the critical representation of male behavior and societal double standards or the narrative of the woman's growth toward autonomy and control. On the contrary, the resolution in the film is brought about by a transaction between men; the modern city-dweller, the traveling salesman Paolo (Gino Cervi), upbraids the traditional peasant father for proposing to cast out his pregnant daughter and the father relents and accepts her. The young woman herself remains the passive object of this male transaction.

What really drives the story of this film is, again, the play of modesty and the fantasy of a sexual transgression. The film begins and ends with Paolo making coffee in the kitchen of his Rome apartment as part of a stale daily routine; we hear, but do not see, his wife in a bad temper, and we learn that they have one or more children. This sets up his journey as a possible occasion for an adulterous encounter. He kindly helps out Maria (Adriana Benetti), and when she starts to cry she explains that she is pregnant by a man who has abandoned her. She is going home to her parents, honest *"gente di campagna,"* to whom she will have to reveal the truth. She persuades Paolo to go with her, pretend he is her husband, and then say he has to go away for his work. This will enable her to disclose the pregnancy and pretend the baby is legitimate while allowing Paolo to disappear. The plan begins to work, but Paolo misses the last bus back and has to stay the night. Maria's parents put them in a room together: there is no divan, no armchair, only hard chairs and just one double mattress, so it looks as if they will have to share the bed. Paolo solves the problem by leaving the room and staying awake. But this only serves to focus the audience's attention on the missed opportunity. The comedy plays, therefore, on the simultaneous possibility and impossibility of an adulterous transgression taking place, and this is fed on the one hand by Maria's insistent gratitude for Paolo's kindness and on the other by Paolo's enforced self-restraint. When they touch hands at the end it is as if the adultery is almost consummated and this, to recall Simmel's description of the erotically charged clasp of the hand, is because of the mutual desire it at once alludes to and represses. When adultery is impossible, as it is in the cinema of this period, adulterous desire must either be wistful, as it is here, or tragic, as in *I bambini ci guardano* (*The Children Are Watching Us*, dir. Vittorio De Sica, 1943, co-scripted with Zavattini). In the latter film, the married woman's conflict between the desire to escape with her lover and to stay in her unhappy marriage for the sake of her son is finally resolved in favor of the adultery, but at an unbearably heavy cost. Her husband puts the boy, Pricò (Luciano De Ambrosis), in a boarding school and shoots himself. When she comes to see Pricò at the school, he refuses to kiss her. His withholding of the kiss echoes an earlier scene: on the night the mother first ran away, she kissed Pricò good night and, in a gesture heavy with symbolism, covered his pet bird's cage with a piece of dark cloth. In the morning the father, alerted to her departure by the maid, entered the room, removed the cloth, and opened the curtains on the boy, who asked where his mother was.

V

La cena delle beffe (*The Jester's Banquet*, dir. Alessandro Blasetti, 1941), based on the 1909 play by Sem Benelli set in early Renaissance Florence, is remembered as the first Italian film made under Fascism to show a woman's naked breasts. It would be more accurate to say that it was the first to show a white woman's breasts—it was shortly to be followed by *Carmela* (1942), starring Doris Duranti—since the breasts of women in Italy's African colonies had been freely photographed and shown, with the usual pseudo-ethnographic justification, in newsreels and documentary films and in a feature film set in Ethiopia, *Sotto la croce del sud* (*Under the Southern Cross*, dir. Guido Brignone, 1938), the third reel of which begins with the Italian settlers watching a fertility dance.[27] Indeed, it was the naked breast's function as a signifier of "native" sexuality that presupposed its exclusion from representations of white sexuality, and it was against this background that the shot in *La cena delle beffe*, which lasted only about a second, was seen as transgressive. The breasts were those of Clara Calamai, an actress whose reputation for playing sexually forward women had been established in earlier films such as *Ettore Fieramosca* (dir. Alessandro Blasetti, 1938; a film based on a novel by Massimo d'Azeglio about a historical figure of this name) and *Addio, giovinezza!* (*Farewell to Youth!*, dir. Ferdinando Maria

Poggioli, 1940). Here she played Ginevra, the object of desire and rivalry of three young men: the two Chiaramantesi brothers, Neri (Amedeo Nazzari) and Gabriello (Alfredo Varelli), and their enemy Giannetto Malespini (Osvaldo Valenti). The film, like Benelli's play, is notable mainly for the unremitting sadism of the revenge plot, but the brief scene of Calamai's "nudity" generated huge publicity. Blasetti told Francesco Savio in an interview in 1974 that it caused "great consternation and a national scandal." He explained the scene to Savio by saying "I always had within me the need to display my open liking for the fact of sex (*il fatto sessuale*)."[28] The Catholic censors classified the film as prohibited to all. The case shows how, as in Hollywood with the PCA, the conflict between the drive to transgress sexual boundaries and the drive to uphold morality became channeled into a conflict over specific areas of the female body, which became identified tout court with "*il fatto sessuale.*" In both cases, censorship produced an account of sexuality as a matter of concealing and revealing parts of the body. The main difference was that Hollywood ruled out the full naked breast but allowed the low-cut dress (in other words, it admitted the exposure of half the breast above the nipple), whereas in Italy there was a polarization between a repressive Catholic tradition, which condemned as indecent any exposure of the woman's shoulders, upper arm, and breasts,[29] and the influence of a liberalizing tradition in European cinema (from Gustav Machaty's scandalous *Ecstasy* of 1933 to the French films of Max Ophuls), where breasts were more freely displayed. This polarization was coded within the films: for instance, in *Addio, giovinezza!*, set in pre–World War I Turin, the demure and loyal shopgirl Dorina (Maria Denis) wears a white lace blouse buttoned up the neck, whereas her rival, the lascivious Elena (Calamai), is dressed in a spangly black décolletage and plumed hat.

Calamai's function in *La cena delle beffe*, and the collective memory of her role in it, was effectively reduced to that glimpse of her breasts. The better-endowed Paola Barbara had refused to audition for the part, despite the encouragement of the producer, Peppino Amato; she told Savio "I was ashamed, I'm telling the truth." Valentina Cortese, who played Elisabetta, the young woman in love with Neri who releases him from his chains, recalled that Calamai "had wonderful breasts. I remember that scene made an incredible stir." Cortese herself had to have her breasts tightly bound inside her dress so as to appear like "a very pure and slender little girl" ("*una ragazzina molto pura e magrina*"). According to Blasetti, Calamai agreed to do the scene "absolutely without reservations."[30] Her own recollection was different:

The business of the naked breasts was not in the script. Blasetti put it in, but he had to work hard to convince me. I was forced to give in. At that time actors had no protection; there were no unions to look after their interests. He decided that my breasts had to be seen so my breasts were seen. To overcome my resistance he made a promise: "Clara," he said, "I'll clear everyone off the set: there will just be me, the cameraman and Nazzari." So we shot the scene, I don't remember if we did one or two takes. The next day I found out that a whole load of people had been watching, perched on the barriers behind the lights. I was blinded by the lights and couldn't see anything.[31]

"Don't talk to me about *La cena delle beffe*!" Calamai told Savio when he went to interview her in 1974.[32] The coercion of the actress to reveal her breasts mirrors the coercion of the character Ginevra within the story. She functions solely as the object of the rival men's desires and the body on whom their rivalry is played out. The film tells how Giannetto, injured and humiliated by the Chiaramantesi brothers, plots and exacts his revenge on them. At the beginning, Neri tears off Ginevra's dress (the nude scene) in order to humiliate Giannetto, who is held by Neri's comrades and forced to watch. After Giannetto has tricked Neri and had him captured, he has sex with Ginevra, not only to satisfy his desire but also to punish Neri by taking "his" woman. Now it is Neri's turn to be restrained by guards; he screams at Giannetto: "You've had her! You've had my woman!" ("*L'hai goduta! Me l'hai goduta!*"). Finally, Giannetto arranges for Gabriello, Neri's brother, who also desires Ginevra, to have sex with her, knowing that Neri, believing it to be the hated Giannetto in Ginevra's bed, will burst in and run his sword through his own brother. The woman functions in this story as a token in a transaction between men. This is a film of male sodality or, to use the terms of Eve Kosofsky Sedgwick's analysis, of male homosocial desire: the woman is locked in a triangular structure of desire that flows between men over and through her body.[33]

VI

Ossessione (dir. Luchino Visconti, 1943) has always been treated as an exception in the cinema of the Fascist period, as marking a break and a transition to postwar cinema. I do not wish to dispute this characterization. Nor do I wish to dispute the reason that has usually been invoked to explain the film's innovativeness: the fact that Visconti and his

co-writers were young anti-Fascists critical of mainstream Italian cinema who had absorbed heterodox influences, from the French Popular
Front directors to Verga to American hardboiled fiction. But I should
like to draw attention to a peculiarity of its critical reception which has
led to a political interpretation of its sexual content and to a cloaking of
the reactionary elements in its sexual ideology.

Criticism of the film from the early reviews onward has concentrated
overwhelmingly on two aspects: its difficulties with the censors because
of its alleged immorality, and its nature as the film which threw out the
"corpses" of Fascist genre cinema and ushered in neorealism. The fact
that it was censored and sequestrated for its sexual "explicitness" or
"directness" was thus indissolubly linked by critics to the anti-Fascist
credentials of its director and scriptwriters. Consider, for example, the
following passage from Gino Avorio's satirical column "*Schedario segreto*," published in the Rome journal *Star* on 9 September 1944, reporting a meeting in spring 1943 between the writers of *Ossessione* and the
minister of popular culture at the time, Gaetano Polverelli:

> They explained in vain that if a people cannot be left alone with
> reality for five minutes they are not adults: his Excellency persisted
> in deploring the shots where Clara Calamai nibbles greedily on
> Massimo Girotti's bare chest and said: "I have thought carefully
> about this and I think I've got you with your backs to the wall.
> Answer one question: when the man and the woman in your film
> are on the bed together and Calamai's lips are feeding on Girotti's
> unshaven face, is the door open or closed?" "Closed," they said.
> "Apart from the couple who else is in the room?" the Minister
> went on triumphantly. "No one," the amazed artists replied; then
> they waited, shuddering. "Well then," Polverelli concluded, with a
> note of jubilation in his voice, "why should the public have to see
> what happens? It seems to me that apart from anything else you
> are contravening logic here."[34]

According to this account, the first bedroom scene with Gino and
Giovanna is an aspect of reality that an adult people should be allowed
to watch; the Fascists wanted to keep the people infantilized, so Polverelli invoked his "logic" of verisimilitude to justify an act of paternal-
istic censorship. It does not matter how true the anecdote is. What is
significant are the equivalences Avorio establishes between, on the one
hand, sexual explicitness, realism, and anti-Fascism and, on the other,
evasiveness, Fascism, and a censored or falsified reality. At work here is
that powerful critical orthodoxy to which I referred at the start of this
chapter which identifies codes of sexual restraint with a project of Fas-

cist and Catholic hegemony and a breaking of those codes with anti-Fascism. What I would dispute is not whether Visconti's film *appeared* to be more sexually transgressive, or even more realistic, to contemporary audiences than other Italian films or American films. Almost certainly it did, though it is worth reminding ourselves that transgressions are always a relative matter: what the film shows and what Polverelli wanted kept behind closed doors is not a "sex scene" in the manner of post-1960s cinema but two lovers together on a bed after sex has taken place. Nor would I dissent from the view that Catholic and Fascist censorship had made such transgressions political. The debatable point is whether the transgressiveness was in fact ideologically progressive and whether "evasiveness" was, by the same argument, reactionary.

Consider two interconnected aspects of the film: the representation of Giovanna (Clara Calamai) as femme fatale and the male bond that develops between Gino (Massimo Girotti) and "the Spaniard" (Elio Marcuzzo). Giovanna gives off ambivalent signs throughout the film. In her opening encounter with Gino she is alternately enticing (singing a siren song, swinging her legs, painting her nails) and submissive to his sexual power ("You've got shoulders like a horse"). After they have had sex the first time, she grabs his hair to pull his head down onto hers, rubs her cheeks against his, and kisses him hard on the mouth; but when he sits up in bed, she nestles her head on his chest. The big eyes she repeatedly makes in the film suggest sexual longing, malicious intent, and childlike helplessness. This combination of the woman's assertiveness and dependency is presented as deadly for the man. Giovanna at first appears incapable of purposeful action, but she turns out to be decisive and controlling. It is she who spurs Gino on to kill Bragana (Juan de Landa), both initially and again just before the murder. In the sequence in Ferrara after the murder, Giovanna, enraged by Gino's flirtation with the dancer-prostitute Anita (Dhia Cristiani), threatens to betray him to the police. Gino, by contrast, acts like an *ingénu* who has learned the routines of heterosexual seduction but does not really know what he wants from women. Once he has had sex with Giovanna, he becomes passive, and she begins to realize how he can help her escape from her oppressive situation. The story began with him on the road, a vagabond getting a ride on the back of a truck, living from hand to mouth, and at various points after that he leaves again to continue the journey: he takes the train to Ancona saying he may go to sea; he picks up and has sex with Anita on the visit to Ferrara and subsequently confesses the murder to her as if to unload his burden of guilt; and, finally, he leaves in the car with Giovanna. Interior space (the roadside restaurant, the kitchen, Giovanna's bedroom, or Anita's bedroom) quickly becomes established as woman's space and Gino resists it and is only able to occupy it temporarily. Exterior space (the open road, ports, town squares) is space he can move through and dominate and in which he can feel liberated. This opposition is emphasized early on when Gino, after having had sex with Giovanna, picks up a seashell and puts it puckishly to his ear while she sits, head hanging and arms draped wearily between her legs, telling him how unhappy she is in her marriage to Bragana. In the final sequence before the car crash, for Giovanna to feel alive is to feel her pregnant body; for Gino it is to get back on the road: "Yes, this is life, at last, away from that house."

The film's overt narrative is that of the man's journey interrupted, deflected, and arrested by the encounter with the fatal woman, and it fits closely with the pattern of masculine narratives of ego formation (presented by the man as a journey of self-discovery or self-realization) by means of separation from the mother and the feminine in a fantasy of phallic autonomy. In these narratives, it is the bond with another male, in which homosexuality is disavowed, that secures the separation from the feminine. This narrative pattern was recurrent both in American popular culture (including cinema: war films, westerns) and in the American literary tradition, and during the war years and the Resistance it became strongly associated by male Italian intellectuals with anti-Fascism because it was a narrative of emancipation and mythic rebirth into open space. It recurs many times in the writers of the early postwar period, from Elio Vittorini to Italo Calvino to Cesare Pavese to Beppe Fenoglio, and Visconti's collaborators on the script of *Ossessione* —Mario Alicata, Gianni Puccini, and Giuseppe De Santis, all members of the clandestine Communist Party—clearly wanted to inflect the story in this direction, too.

In their politicized version of the narrative of male autonomy, the character of the Spaniard, who has no counterpart either in James M. Cain's original novel (1934) or in Pierre Chenal's earlier film version of it, *Le Dernier tournant* (*The Last Curve*, 1939), is central because he articulates the twin theme of separation from the woman and existential freedom. Gino encounters him at the point when he is caught between his attempt to run away to sea and the pull of his fatal attraction to Giovanna, and the Spaniard urges him to leave. "If you stay with me I'll teach you that you don't travel around just to court women. . . . Take my advice: go to sea. The sea air will clear your head of all these ideas. You'll feel free again." "Free, free," Gino repeats wistfully. Some accounts of the film describe the Spaniard as "a homosexual" attracted to Gino, and some suggest that the attraction is reciprocal. Gianni Rondolino maintains that Visconti, as a gay director less dogmatically politicized than his collaborators, imposed this suggestion of erotic intimacy, mainly through his directing of the actors and his control over the camera and editing, on straight scriptwriters for whom the Spaniard's primary meaning was political: to represent in a coded way, one that could pass the censors, the socialist values of fraternal solidarity, altruism, and independence from the bourgeois family.[35] The problem with this positing of a gay storyline in *Ossessione*, as with other films of this period, is that it remains so well closeted that it is at best a submerged "subtext" which can only be made to emerge by a knowing, "productive" reading of looks, gestures, and innuendoes. What does come across overtly in the narrative is not so much sexual attraction between the two characters but the collusive "homosociality" expressed in the Spaniard's invitation to Gino to abjure the feminine. In an account in the 1960s, Alicata was anxious to repudiate the "tainted" interpretation and reaffirm the political meaning:

> When I saw *Ossessione* again I realized it is not clear who the Spaniard is. He sometimes has the appearance of a very equivocal character, whereas he was meant to be the critical conscience of the film. When the Spaniard tries to drag the protagonist out of this morbid, or at any rate intense, passion, it turns out that he looks as though he is driven by a feeling of affection, of a friendship which is not without a murky streak ["*non esente da torbide venature*"], rather than by the conviction that one should not lose one's way with women and that there are other things to be done at this time.[36]

In stressing the film's conformity to the narrative stereotypes of the fatal woman, masculine separation, and the homosocial bond, I am not suggesting that it precludes all identification with Giovanna's subjectivity or sympathy with her position. On the contrary, the oppressiveness of Giovanna's situation is strongly conveyed, particularly in the scenes where Bragana makes her massage his fat torso and tells Gino that these are the joys of marriage and when she becomes desperate on a hot night as the cats howl outside. The film also shows the oppression continuing after the murder, when she makes a success of the restaurant while Gino, racked by guilt, turns to drink. After a busy evening, the customers leave, Gino goes upstairs to bed, and Giovanna enters a kitchen piled high with dirty dishes. She ladles herself a bowl of soup and starts to eat, propping up the newspaper to read; too exhausted to go on, she puts down the soup and falls asleep in the chair. Yet this sympathetic portrait does not alter the facts that she is the main agent of Bragana's death and that it was she who entrapped Gino in her plot.

166

She is contrasted as a feminine type with the good prostitute Anita, and her death and Gino's arrest are a fulfillment of retributive justice and yet another narrative regularization (under the authority of the police) after a woman's transgression. Just as this nemesis is about to be fulfilled, Giovanna squeezes her breasts and tells Gino they will soon be growing.[37] In doing so, she draws attention both to her maternal self-sufficiency and to her entrapment of Gino, since it is her pregnancy that has drawn him back to her and turned him finally away from his fantasy of separation from the feminine.

I am not trying to undermine the widely accepted judgement of *Ossessione* as an exceptional film but to show that, in common with many of the French and American films noir of the 1940s which it resembles, its narrative centers on a fatal desire for a powerful woman which leads to both the man's downfall and the death of the woman, and that *as a narrative* there is nothing intrinsically anti-Fascist about this. We need to kick the critical habit of assigning films to the Fascist or anti-Fascist camp on the basis of judgments about their presumed "indirectness" or "directness" about sex. To couch the argument in these terms is, let me finally repeat, to miss the central points about all of these films: they all contain discourses about sexuality and gender, they all in their different ways connect with the audience's experiences and fantasies, and they all open up a space of transgressive desire, albeit in different ways according to differences of genre and style, a space which is always necessarily closed off at the end.

Notes

1. Francesco Bolzoni, "La commedia all'ungherese nel cinema italiano," *Bianco e Nero* 49, no. 3 (1988): 15; Ernesto G. Laura, "Il mito di Budapest e i modelli ungheresi," in *Telefoni bianchi. Realtà e finzione nella società e nel cinema degli anni Quaranta*, ed. Gianfranco Casadio, Ernesto G. Laura, and Filippo Cristiano (Ravenna: Longo, 1991), 48.

2. Gianfranco Casadio, "Il cinema dei telefoni bianchi," in Casadio, Laura, and Cristiano, *Telefoni bianchi*, 29.

3. Claudio Carabba, "Pubbliche virtù e vizi segreti del cinema fascista," *Paese sera*, 11 October 1976, quoted in Casadio, "Il cinema dei telefoni bianchi," 12; Theodor W. Adorno and Max Horkheimer, "Kulturindustrie: Aufklärung als Massenbetrug," in *Dialektik der Aufklärung* (1944; Frankfurt am Main: Fischer, 1969).

4. Bruno Torri in "Seminario internazionale di studi sul cinema italiano,

1929-1943," *Ancona*, 5-11 October 1976, quoted in Casadio, "Il cinema dei telefoni bianchi," 11; Guido Aristarco in *L'Europe des téléphones blancs 1935-1940. Compte rendu du symposium historique à Rapallo à l'occasion du 37ème Congrès de la FIAF* (4-9 May 1989) (typescript), 71; Gianfranco Casadio, "Premessa," in Casadio, Laura, and Cristiano, *Telefoni bianchi*, 7.

5. John Izod, *Hollywood and the Box Office, 1895-1986* (New York: Columbia University Press, 1988), 108; James M. Skinner, *The Cross and the Cinema: The Legion of Decency and the National Catholic Office for Motion Pictures, 1933-1970* (Westport, Conn. and London: Praeger, 1993), xiii.

6. Michel Foucault, *Histoire de la sexualité*, vol. 1, *La Volonté de savoir* (Paris: Gallimard, 1976), 19: "il s'agit de déterminer, dans son fonctionnement et dans ses raisons d'être, le régime de pouvoir-savoir-plaisir qui soutient chez nous le discours sur la sexualité humaine." For a good elaboration of Foucault's approach, see Jeffrey Weeks, *Sexuality* (London and New York: Tavistock, 1986).

7. The best discussion of censorship along these lines remains that by Annette Kuhn, *Cinema, Censorship and Sexuality, 1909-1925* (London: Routledge, 1986). For a perceptive treatment of Hollywood censorship as a series of negotiated arrangements, see Lea Jacobs, *The Wages of Sin: Censorship and the Fallen Woman Film, 1928-1942* (Madison: University of Wisconsin Press, 1991).

8. The composition of the state censorship committees for cinema, the *commissioni di revisione*, was precisely stipulated in a series of laws from 1920 to 1931: as well as representatives of the state, the commissions had to include, according to Regio Decreto 109 of 8 May 1920, a magistrate, a journalist, a mother ("madre di famiglia"), a "member to be chosen from the teaching profession and the representatives of humanitarian associations for the moral protection of the people and of young people in particular," and a "person competent in artistic and literary matters." After a number of reshuffles, this composition was altered by Law 857 of 18 June 1931, which remained in force till the end of the regime. The teachers and artistic and literary experts were removed, the "madre di famiglia" remained, and the number of Fascist Party and state representatives was increased. For details of the relevant legislation, see Giacomo Gambetti, *Cinema e censura in Italia* (Rome: Edizioni di Bianco e Nero, 1972), 23-30.

9. "Flirtation," in *Georg Simmel: On Women, Sexuality, and Love*, trans. Guy Oakes (New Haven, Conn.: Yale University Press, 1984), 142; from "Die Koketterie," *Philosophische Kultur: Gesammelte Essais*, 3rd ed. (Leipzig: Kröner, 1923).

10. Martha Vicinus, "Distance and Desire in English Boarding School Friendships, 1870-1920," in *Hidden from History: Reclaiming the Gay and Lesbian Past*, ed. Martin Bauml Duberman, Martha Vicinus, and George Chauncey, Jr. (London: Penguin, 1991), 215-216.

David Forgacs

11. Bruno P. F. Wanrooij, *Storia del pudore. La questione sessuale in Italia 1860–1940* (Venice: Marsilio, 1990); and Victoria de Grazia, *How Fascism Ruled Women: Italy, 1922–1945* (Berkeley: University of California Press, 1992).

12. A. Lo Monaco-Aprile, in *Archivio Fascista di Medicina Politica* (1930), quoted in Wanrooij, *Storia del pudore*, 118.

13. Wanrooij, *Storia del pudore*, 110–112.

14. Ibid., 215; de Grazia, *How Fascism Ruled Women*, 119–120.

15. Italo Calvino, "Autobiografia di uno spettatore," preface to Federico Fellini, *Quattro film* (Turin: Einaudi, 1974), xiv.

16. Oral testimony collected in 1991 by Marcella Filippa and David Forgacs as part of the research project "Cultural Industries, Governments and the Public in Italy, 1938–1954," funded with a grant from the Economic and Social Research Council of the U.K. The results of the research will appear in David Forgacs, Stephen Gundle, and Marcella Filippa, *Stolen Bicycles: Mass Culture and Politics in Italy 1938–1954* (Berkeley and Los Angeles: University of California Press, forthcoming).

17. A recording of the song was used in "1927: Great Escape," part of the television series "People's Century," BBC2, London, 30 October 1995.

18. Giovanni Agnese, *Con quale mezzo vedo possibile il risanamento dei costumi e il progresso morale di una moderna nazione. Proposta di un codice dei costumi* (Turin: Botta, 1929), 13–16, 21. I am indebted to Bruno Wanrooij's work for the reference to this pamphlet.

19. "Vigilanti cura. Lettera enciclica di Pio XI," *Sequenze. Quaderni di Cinema* 2, no. 7 (1950): 5.

20. The Lord-Quigley code proposal is reproduced in Gregory D. Black, *Hollywood Censored: Morality Codes, Catholics and the Movies* (Cambridge: Cambridge University Press, 1994) 302–308; the text of the Production Code and the Resolution for Uniform Interpretation is reproduced in Harold J. Leff and Jerold L. Simmons, *The Dame in the Kimono: Hollywood, Censorship and the Production Code from the 1920s to the 1960s* (London: Weidenfeld and Nicolson, 1990), 283–292.

21. See the accounts in Leff and Simmons, *The Dame in the Kimono;* Black, *Hollywood Censored;* and Jacobs, *The Wages of Sin.*

22. The Lateran Pacts (*patti lateranensi*, also known as the Conciliation) between the papacy and the Italian state were signed by Mussolini and Cardinal Gasparri in February 29. They formally settled the conflict between the state and the Catholic Church which had opened at the time of unification (1861). The pacts had three main parts: a diplomatic treaty, in which the Italian government and the papacy recognized each other's sovereignty respectively over the kingdom of Italy and the Vatican City; a financial settlement, by which the Church was retrospectively compensated for its loss of sovereignty over the former Papal States; and a concordat specifying the respective spheres of competence of Church and state in

society. The concordat protected the Church's influence in the education system (permitting religious instruction in state schools) and its jurisdiction in matrimonial causes, confirming the impossibility of divorce.

23. Georg Simmel, "Sulla psicologia del pudore," trans. Marco Sordini and Vittorio Cotesta, in Simmel, *Sull'intimità*, ed. Vittorio Cotesta (Rome: Armando, 1996), 64 (original German text: "Zur Psychologie der Scham" [1901], *Schriften zur Soziologie*, ed. H.-J. Dahme and O. Rammstedt [Frankfurt am Main: Suhrkamp, 1983]).

24. The expression is from the title of a book published in 1931 by the Gioventù femminile cattolica italiana, *Maria Goretti martire della purità. La santa Agnese del secolo XX*; see the discussion in Wanrooij, *Storia del pudore*, 118–119.

25. This was part of Tertullian's definition of *pudicitia* in the third century: "Pudicitia, flos morum, honor corporum, decor sexuum, integritas sanguinis, fides generis, fundamentum sanctitatis, praeiudicium omnibus bonae mentis" ("Modesty, flower of virtue, honour of bodies, adornment of the two sexes, safeguard of the blood, guarantee of the race, foundation of sanctity, sign to all of a worthy spirit"), *La Pudicité (De pudicitia)*, trans. Charles Munier (Paris: Editions du Cerf, 1993), 144. The association between chastity and other types of purity was also fundamental to Saint Ambrose, the fourth-century bishop of Milan: the "cloying, labile mixture of male seed and female blood associated with the moment of conception struck him as a microcosm of the many smudged areas that weakened mankind in its present fallen condition." Peter Brown, *The Body and Society: Men, Women and Sexual Renunciation in Early Christianity* (London: Faber and Faber, 1990), 354.

26. In a pioneering analysis of the Italian schoolgirl film as genre, Jacqueline Reich has drawn attention to the contradiction running through the genre between the narrative of female autonomy and rebellion and the generally conservative plot resolution (marriage and female subordination): "Reading, Writing and Rebellion: Collectivity, Specularity and Sexuality in the Italian Schoolgirl Comedy, 1934–43," in *Mothers of Invention: Women, Italian Fascism and Culture*, ed. Robin Pickering-Iazzi (Minneapolis: University of Minnesota Press, 1995).

27. For a good discussion of this sequence, and the film as a whole, see Ruth Ben-Ghiat, "Envisioning Modernity: Desire and Discipline in the Italian Fascist Film," *Critical Inquiry* 23, no. 1 (Autumn 1996): 109–144; the dance footage "asserts the fascists' ability to probe and master the Ethiopians by placing them onstage to perform what to Western audiences would be coded as an extremely private and erotic act" (140).

28. Francesco Savio, *Cinecittà anni trenta. Parlano 116 protagonisti del secondo cinema italiano (1930–1943)*, 3 vols. (Rome: Bulzoni, 1979), 1: 150.

29. Catholic definitions of "nudity" or "nakedness" were affected to some extent by changing secular norms of costume and propriety but otherwise

David Forgacs

remained remarkably stable over time. In the seventeenth century, the neck, shoulders, and upper breasts were thought of as constituting a single area (in French "la gorge"), the public exposure of any part of which was considered indecent (see, for instance, the tract attributed to Jacques Boileau, *De l'abus des nudités de gorge,* English trans. *A Just and Seasonable Reprehension of Naked Breasts and Shoulders, Written by a Grave and Learned Papist* [London: Jonathan Edwin, 1678]). Until recently, the term "nudity" was used in Catholic publications to designate the exposure of men's bare chests and women's shoulders and legs. In addition to the prescriptions by Giovanni Agnese on men's bathing costumes mentioned above (1929), one may cite as examples some of the classifications of the Centro Cattolico Cinematografico, from its condemnations of the "nudity" of Tarzan films to its ruling that Carlo Campogalliani's sport film *Stadio* was "not to be recommended to young people" because of "the excessive nudity of the athletes." Gian Piero Brunetta, "La censura ecclesiastica," in his *Cinema italiano tra le due guerre. Fascismo e politica cinematografica* (Milan: Mursia, 1975), 64. In the early 1950s, Catholic activists in Rimini wrote to Minister of the Interior Mario Scelba to complain about the "nudity" of foreign tourists who walked about the town in bathing costumes. Here, as in other instances, the definition was also determined by where the person was: what was a scanty costume on the beach became nudity anywhere else. One may recall the scene in *Treno popolare* (dir. Raffaello Matarazzo, 1933), where Carlo (Carlo Petrangeli) and Lina (Lina Gennari), who have met only that day on a state-subsidized excursion from Rome to Orvieto, capsize in a rowing boat in the country and come ashore soaked. He tells her she needs to take off her clothes to dry them in the sun: "But you don't understand," she says. "How can I do it?" "What do you mean?" he replies. "Pretend we're at the seaside. It's easy." The resulting sequence when they undress behind separate trees produces a mild sexual *frisson* for the spectator and cements the couple's intimacy: after it Carlo switches from "lei" to "tu" in addressing Lina.

30. The statements by Barbara, Cortese, and Blasetti are in Savio, *Cinecittà anni trenta,* 1: 81, 376, 150.

31. The statement, from an interview with Piero Palumbo in *Gente* (14 December 1973), is reproduced in Franca Faldini and Goffredo Fofi, eds., *L'avventurosa storia del cinema italiano raccontata dai suoi protagonisti. 1935-1959* (Milan: Feltrinelli, 1979), 30.

32. Savio, *Cinecittà anni trenta,* 1: 203.

33. Eve Kosofsky Sedgwick, *Between Men: English Literature and Male Homosocial Desire* (New York: Columbia University Press, 1985).

34. Gino Avorio, "Schedario segreto," *Star* 1, no. 5 (9 Sept. 1944): 10.

35. Gianni Rondolino, *Luchino Visconti* (Turin: UTET, 1981), 132. Rondolino claims that Gino is "attracted at the same time by both sexes and by the models of life and relationships they represent." Peter Bondanella writes

similarly that "Visconti introduces into the plot a very ambiguous character, a homosexual nicknamed 'Lo Spagnolo' ('The Spaniard'), who will function as an alternative to Gino's sensual obsession with Giovanna." *Italian Cinema: From Neorealism to the Present* (New York: Frederick Ungar, 1983), 28.

36. Mario Alicata in Giorgio Tinazzi, ed., *Cinema italiano dal fascismo all'antifascismo* (Padua: Marsilio, 1966) (this extract is also reproduced in Faldini and Fofi, *L'avventurosa storia del cinema italiano*, 65–66).

37. The dialogue here, as at other points in the script, parallels Cain's text where the corresponding dialogue takes place as Frank and Cora bathe in the ocean before the fatal car crash: "A big one raised us up, and she put her hand to her breasts, to show how it lifted them. 'I love it. Are they big, Frank?' 'I'll tell you tonight.' 'They feel big. I didn't tell you about that. It's not only knowing you're going to make another life. It's what it does to you. My breasts feel so big, and I want you to kiss them. Pretty soon my belly is going to get big, and I'll love that, and want everybody to see it. It's life. I can feel it in me. It's a new life for us both, Frank.'" *The Postman Always Rings Twice: The Five Great Novels of James M. Cain* (London: Pan, 1988), 81.

6

Luchino Visconti's (Homosexual) *Ossessione*

William Van Watson

In his article "Anthropomorphic Cinema," Luchino Visconti disdained the term "vocation" in relationship to his profession as film director, calling it "a romantic notion far removed from our contemporary reality, an abstract term coined for the artists' convenience, to distinguish their own privileged activity from that of other men. . . . To choose a profession does not mean to seal oneself off in it, as many artists do."[1] Visconti used the term "anthropomorphic" as a euphemism for the "humanism" associated with French cinema of the period, particularly with the cinema of Jean Renoir, with whom Visconti had worked as an assistant. Visconti called for an *engagé* cinema that eschewed the "artificial superimpositions" of the calligraphers and established genres of Fascist-era cinema. Instead, he aspired to "tell the stories of living human beings, men living in the middle of things." As opposed to the calligraphers' emphasis on mise-en-scène, Visconti asserted that "the weight of the human being, his presence, is the only *thing* that fills up the motion picture frame. . . . The real problem is to find what is concrete and original in [his] personality." His stress on the iconic presence of the human being prompts Visconti to advocate the use of "non-actors who . . . have more authentic and healthier instincts" than professional actors who inhabited a rarefied environment both off-screen and on. Partly because of this expressed interest in an engaged, humanist cinema and his declared support for the use of non-professionals, Visconti's first film, *Ossessione* (1942), an adaptation of James Cain's *The Postman Always Rings Twice* (1934), has often been viewed as a precursor of the neorealist cinema which would later blossom in postwar Italy. The film's empa-

172

thy for the disenfranchised, its predominance of medium shots that prioritize human interaction, the rawness of its footage, its bleak conclusion, the dense and detailed texture of its social sequences, and its use of location shooting, especially the expanse of the murky Padana region that would reappear in Roberto Rossellini's *Paisan* (1946), all argue for *Ossessione* as a neorealist prototype. In opposition to Mussolini's Fascism, neorealism leaned toward the left from its inception, so that Visconti's longtime association with the Italian Communist Party (PCI) and his active participation in the partisan cause during the Nazi occupation of Rome served to provide retroactive confirmation of *Ossessione*'s proto-neorealist pedigree.

In contrast to neorealist theorists' attempts to reclaim *Ossessione* as a neorealist, and therefore, objective film, it is largely an example of auteurist, and therefore, subjective cinema. Despite his protests to the contrary, much of Visconti's work is bathed in "romantic notion[s] far removed from our contemporary reality," and the arc of his filmography reveals an artist increasingly "sealed off" in the sort of aesthetic hermeticism he disdained in the Fascist-era calligraphers. To be fair, though, Roberto Campari is perhaps most accurate in his assessment of Visconti as the "grand synthesis" of the dual and dueling Italian cinematic traditions of overt aestheticism and critical social engagement.[2] During his search for the "concrete and original" in the human being in *Ossessione*, Visconti employed calligraphism in a viably integrated manner. He recreates the work of painter Renato Guttuso when Giovanna sits down amid a mass of dirty bottles and dishes in the kitchen after a busy day at the *trattoria*. Another scene shows her slouched in an isolated chair in an homage to Vincent Van Gogh, while the very figure of Giovanna herself was consciously modeled after women in the paintings of the artist Amedeo Modigliani. One of Visconti's identifying characteristics as film auteur would become his meticulous and brilliant deployment of mise-en-scène, so much so that he is sometimes pejoratively dismissed as a mere "*metteur-en-scène.*"

Visconti's pessimism further distinguishes his filmography as a whole, and *Ossessione* in particular, from neorealist cinema. Millicent Marcus has sensitively recounted neorealism's provocative nature, its preference for proactive prescription over passive description, and its goal of inciting change with its agitational endings.[3] *Ossessione*'s bleak ending differs from those of the neorealist works of Rossellini and Vittorio De Sica, in that the death of Giovanna and the arrest of Gino inspire no call to arms, nor do they reverberate with echoes of social ills to be cured. Rather than looking forward to the Marxist utopian prescriptions of neorealism proper, *Ossessione* looks back to the fatalism of the Sicilian verist writer Giovanni Verga, whose "L'amante di Grami-gna" (in *Vita dei campi,* 1880) Visconti had originally hoped to make his first film project. Traditional Marxist discourses, such as those associ-ated with neorealist cinema, have concerned themselves solely with the body as site of labor rather than leisure, with the libido as font of work rather than pleasure. As a result, transgressive passion such as that of Giovanna and Gino finds little or no place in films such as *Paisan* (1946), *The Bicycle Thief* (1948), or *Umberto D* (1952). Without recourse to a social solution, the personal dilemma of Giovanna and Gino con-cludes with the sense of futility that characterizes much of Visconti's cinema and separates it from its more incendiary neorealist counter-parts.

Critic Gianni Menon has called *Ossessione* Visconti's "vehicle for lib-erating his own personal obsessions."[4] While auteurism, as it was later theorized in France in the late 1950s, championed the personal vision of the director as the primary artist of the cinema, Visconti's essay "An-thropomorphic Cinema" stressed the collaborative nature of the me-dium. He claimed, "Cinema attracted me because it brings together and coordinates the desires and needs of many people."[5] Despite his protests to the contrary, the wealthy aristocrat Visconti asserted the "privileged activity" of his role as director "as many artists do" by financing his film production through the sale of his family jewels. Such self-produc-tion imbued him with the clout to confound the "desires and needs" of his collaborators, particularly with regard to his use of the character of the Spagnolo (as discussed below) and his ability to assert his personal auteurist voice. Visconti's proto-auteurism subverts both the Marxist as-pects of neorealist filmography and the Fascism of Mussolini's Italy by emphasizing the importance of the individual over the mass. Visconti definitively authorizes *Ossessione* as his personal expression by drawing a parallel between his own birth and that of his cinema when he opens his first film with Bragana singing Germont's "Andante" from Giuseppe Verdi's *La Traviata.* This musical birth of Visconti's cinema should be read within the context of his self-mythologizing: "I was born Novem-ber 2, 1906, at eight o'clock in the evening. They told me that an hour later the curtains raised at the Scala for the premiere of *La Traviata.*"[6] Both *Ossessione* and this autobiographical account enact Visconti's pro-pensity for fiction-making, as the 1906–1907 opera season at La Scala actually opened with a December production of *Carmen.* In any case, the extensive use of operatic music and melodramatic scoring through-out the soundtrack of *Ossessione* established a precedent for the oddly intrusive scores of neorealist cinema proper.

While neorealist critics have addressed Visconti's Marxist, class, and historical concerns, and auteurist critics have addressed his aesthetic, familial, Romantic, pictorial, and operatic sensibilities, both groups have neglected or marginalized the homosexual component of his work, collapsing it into the non-specific category of "decadence." With the exception of Laurence Schifano, most of his biographers also avoid his sexual life and sensibility, reducing their discussions of his affairs with Donague Woolworth and Umberto Monaldi to a paucity of obscure sentences. More reprehensible still, in their efforts to heterosexualize him, these writers have devoted entire chapters to Visconti's aborted engagement to Irma Windisch-Grätz, a liaison which lasted only a few months. At the same time, they virtually ignore his more enduring relationships with the photographer Horst, the director Franco Zeffirelli, and the actor Helmut Berger, all of which lasted several years. Given the intimate connection between *Ossessione* and its director, heterocentrist readings of the film have been remiss in failing to take into account the homosexual nature of the director's personal obsession that Menon and others have seen as integral to the work. Lino Miccichè has even called homosexuality "the key . . . that dominates from the beginning to the end, the entire sequence of the narrative."[7] This key has not heretofore been used to open the closet of the film. A recuperative homosexual reading of *Ossessione* reveals that both the ostensibly universal concerns of Visconti's cinema, such as the conflict between reason and transgressive passion, and the ostensibly neorealist concerns of this film, such as social alienation and disenfranchisement, may actually have specifically homosexual causes. Visconti's propensity to adapt novels does not mitigate his role as auteur; rather, his mutations of these preexistent source materials highlight his authorship.

Visconti came of age amid the socially sanctioned gender normativity of Mussolini's Italy, wherein males succumbed to Fascist machismo posturings and women, depending on their class, were rewarded as gestational devices that produced a series of "Primos" and "Secondos." The intense homosocial male bonding promoted by Fascism risked the homoerotic. State-sponsored displays of machismo, such as Fascist parades and other saber-rattling events, ironically attempted to (over)compensate for this homoerotic threat, but a symptomatic homophobia remained. Not surprisingly then, Visconti's homosexuality retreated first to the closet (or rather the family stables, to be more accurately biographical) and then to France. As evidenced by the lives and careers of Jean Cocteau, André Gide, and others, attitudes toward homosexuality in France in the 1930s were more tolerant, allowing Visconti to confront his sexual inclinations in a more direct manner. His closeted nature was not merely a matter of generational or social context but a question of personal temperament as well. Characterizing Visconti as a lover, Horst noted: "He was never forthcoming, did not smile easily, and seemed continually to put the brakes on his Italian temperament. . . . For me, homosexuality was nothing but fun, but for him it was otherwise."[8] Gay critic Boze Hadleigh reports that "[Visconti] reminded me that he'd speak with me on the condition that I not probe into his private life."[9] Instead, Visconti derailed Hadleigh's interview into a discussion of Johann Joachim Winckelmann, an eighteenth-century German scholar of classical Greece, who, like Pier Paolo Pasolini, died at the hands of a young male prostitute whose services he had engaged. Such deflection of his own homosexuality onto that of a third person or character marks Visconti's cinema. Throughout the Hadleigh interview, Visconti evaded addressing his sexuality by responding with a coy but silent smile. While film directors of subsequent generations, such as Rainer Werner Fassbinder, John Waters, Derek Jarman, and Pedro Almodóvar discarded the closet as obsolete, Visconti remained at best on its threshold.[10] His homosexual sensibility in *Ossessione* both manifests itself and seeks refuge in a variety of closets: in the structuring of the narrative, in the deployment of the camera and gaze, in the use of visual metaphors such as closed doors and actual closets, and, finally, in the exercise of a verbal double entendre which permits both heterocentrist and homosexual readings.

Cain's original novel addressed the vast numbers who were economically disenfranchised in the United States by the Great Depression of the 1930s, but in Italy to assert that anyone was loose from the state-sponsored weave of the Fascist social fabric would have constituted a subversive act. Italian writer Vitaliano Brancati has described Fascism as "the joy of the herded animal: the joy of being in accord with millions of people."[11] Neither Visconti, as isolated homosexual, nor his cinematic characters, as bearers of equally transgressive desires, ever experienced this Fascist joy. With the notable exception of Bragana, virtually all Visconti's major characters—Gino, the Spagnolo, Anita, and Giovanna prior to her marriage—at best dangle from the Fascist social fabric by a thread, a fact which may explain some of the difficulties the film had with the censors. The original screenplay passed, but only with great reservation, as Visconti explains:

> They breathed down my neck all the time I was shooting; they insisted on seeing the rushes as I sent them off to be developed and they came back to me in Ferrara with orders to cut certain passages. According to them I should have cut everything. I turned a deaf ear, edited my film the way I wanted, and organized a show-

ing in Rome. The effect on the audience was explosive. They couldn't believe they were seeing such a film.[12]

Film director Alessandro Blasetti had edited an earlier version, which Visconti had thrown out as a violation of his auteurist privilege. An audience accustomed to the more antiseptic offerings of genre film, slick studio production, and Fascist (semi-)documentaries revolted at the perceived vulgarity of Visconti's disenfranchised world. In the town of Salsamaggiore, bishops even exorcised a cinema in which the film had been shown.[13] After a limited run in a few theatres, Visconti's version was withdrawn from distribution. Members of the journal *Cinema*, with Vittorio Mussolini as editor-in-chief, intervened and arranged a showing for Benito Mussolini, who agreed to approve the film with a few cuts, eventually absconding with a copy of the film to Salò when his Fascist government fled north. Throughout these vicissitudes Visconti kept a print of his own original, self-edited version. Distribution of this version remained limited after the war as well, due to Visconti's violation of Cain's copyright, as only the failure of Fascist Italy to recognize international copyright law had enabled the director to make the film in the first place.

In *Ossessione*, Visconti transposes his own illicit homosexual love into the illicit adulterous heterosexual love of the characters. The heterosexual narrative disguises the sensibility of the director, allowing him to light, costume, and film Massimo Girotti in a manner that (homo)eroticizes him. Visconti structures the film in a manner that permits him to use a male of inferior class standing, Gino, as an object of desire from the point of view of a female of superior class standing, Giovanna. The apparition of the young male incites the female protagonist to an action more than merely sexually transgressive. As an embodiment of the proprietary class, Bragana appears sexually and aesthetically undesirable. The third male character in the film, the Spagnolo, functions as a representative of desired but unrealized solidarity. Angela Dalle Vacche has noted, "The diva was linked to a struggle among social classes in . . . Italy, for she would often seduce a wealthy nobleman and lead him into bankruptcy."[14] As Gino seduces the comparatively wealthier Giovanna, he inadvertently negotiates for himself a place in the proprietary class and thereby enacts the *diva* role. While Giovanna might be viewed as a *diva* figure vis-à-vis Bragana, Visconti conceived of her as "a woman of the common people." The first thing Visconti did was remove Clara Calamai's makeup, muss up her hair, and deglamorize her, rendering her almost unrecognizable from her earlier filmography. The attractive sophistication of her screen persona as previously established in comedies and white-telephone films had discouraged Visconti from casting her in the role even after Anna Magnani's pregnancy had disqualified her. While Visconti fetishized Calamai's swinging legs to evoke Giovanna as a *diva*-like seductress, he reserved a much more elaborate visual tease to introduce Gino. Gino first appears in the rear of a supply truck posed like an Ingres odalisque with the curve of his back to the camera. Unless Visconti's sexual preference is taken into account, the erotic connotations of such a harem figure are strikingly incongruous. As Gino gets up, the camera repositions itself to avoid his face while the men talk to him. The camera then takes a high overhead shot from behind him as he walks toward the *trattoria*. When he enters, a low shot tracks his worn shoes as he crosses the floor. It then accompanies him to the kitchen door, where we even hear his voice before we see his face. Visconti reveals Gino's face only after cutting to a close-up of Giovanna, as if his face existed only in and for her eyes, as little more than a visualized projection of her desire. Visconti even punctuates the moment with Calamai's double take of Gino as object, her desire for him pulling the camera into a close-up of his features.

The subjective shot sutures our vision to hers. In a reversal of the male-biased heterocentric gender paradigm outlined by Laura Mulvey in her article "Visual Pleasure and Narrative Cinema," Visconti establishes Giovanna as bearer of the desire-laden gaze and Gino as its recipient.[15] Giovanna is subject and Gino is object. This dynamic also reverses the male-biased heterocentric gender positioning of both Cain's novel and Tay Garnett's 1946 homonymous American film version. In contrast to Visconti, Garnett quickly establishes John Garfield as Frank as bearer of the gaze and Lana Turner as Cora as object. Garfield's Frank even spies on her through a window. Hair bleached blonde, make-up perfect, dressed in halter top and high heels, Turner's Cora is the very icon of screen glamour that Calamai's Giovanna is not. In opposition to Giovanna's habitual black, Hollywood costumer Irene incongruously outfits Turner's Cora in white, despite her position working at the counter of a diner. As Visconti teases with his introduction of Girotti as Gino, so does Garnett tease with his introduction of Turner as Cora. A symbol of her status as phallicized female, her lipstick is first heard rolling across the floor toward Frank even before her character is ever seen. Sutured to Frank's gaze, Garnett's subjective camera follows the rolling lipstick back to its source, slowly and provocatively panning up Turner's legs to her exposed midriff and pert ample breasts. Garnett punctuates this apparition with an obligatory Hollywood softly lit close-up of the woman's face with pouting, parted lips. Aware of her role as object of the gaze, Turner's Cora meticulously retouches her make-up after

Frank's kiss and carries her lipstick with her at all times. The sound of this lipstick rolling from her dead hand after the final car accident condemns her appropriation of the phallus in accordance with the male-biased heterocentric paradigms of Hollywood.[16] The femme fatale must be *fatale* to herself.

In both Garnett's film and Cain's novel, Frank's first-person narration guarantees identification with his subjectivity. The novel also translates this subjectivity into the dynamics of the gaze, as Frank specifies: "Then *I* saw *her*."[17] As bearer of the gaze, it is also Cain's Frank, rather than Cora, who is the primary bearer of desire: "I wanted that woman so bad I couldn't even keep anything on my stomach."[18] In contrast, Visconti's Giovanna cannot keep from cooking. From the first meeting of Gino and Giovanna, Visconti deploys a sequence of shots that establish Giovanna as subject and Gino as object of the gaze. He then repeats this strategy with almost programmatic regularity. Such a shot sequence occurs when Gino and Giovanna talk during Bragana's singing competition in Ancona and later in the same scene during their celebratory toast. Visconti again uses this pattern of shots when the couple goes to the garage to retrieve Bragana's car and share a brief moment alone. Much later, in the streets of Ferrara, even when Gino seems actively to confront and strike her, this same shot formation reduces him to a passive object. Giovanna's actions have simply provoked his responsive fit of temper.

Ossessione reveals Visconti's auteurist displacement of the (homo)erotic into the equine, a metaphoric substitution that canters throughout his cinema and reaches full gallop in *Ludwig* (1973). When Gino and Giovanna meet in the kitchen, she watches as Gino turns away from the camera and takes off his jacket to reveal his back and shoulders. Visconti provides a close-up of Giovanna's emphatic reaction: "You've got the shoulders of a horse!"[19] Visconti exploits Cora's original and solitary offhand comment about "how nice and hard [Frank's] shoulders are" as a rationale to fetishize Gino's shoulders in an obsessive manner far beyond that found in Cain's novel.[20] Girotti's hirsute shoulders both animalize and eroticize his character, as excessive body hair has been considered a sign of hypersexuality in Mediterranean societies since ancient Athens and the myth of the satyrs. The comparison between Gino and horse relates not only to Visconti's public experience as passionate equestrian and horse breeder but also to his more private homosexual experience; his first encounters occurred with stable boys in his employ, much as Gino is in the temporary employ of Giovanna's husband.[21] In 1942, prior to making the film, Visconti had published a short story in *Corriere Padano* entitled "The Straw Hat." The tale recounts the am-

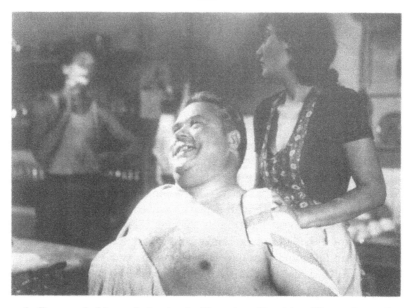

16. Bragana's bloated obesity in *Ossessione* (Luchino Visconti, 1942).
Courtesy of the Museum of Modern Art Film Stills Archive

bivalent tensions of a male friendship that escalates to love and also establishes connections between the homoerotic, the equine, and the pas-
toral as a characteristic of Visconti's auteurist sensibility. In *Ossessione*,
when Giovanna and Bragana call Gino to dinner, it is noteworthy that
he is lying in the hay, and even the Spagnolo's habit of holding straw
between his teeth functions suggestively within this paradigm.

Working within Hollywood's male-biased heterocentrist conventions, Garnett demurs from showing Garfield's body, fully dressing
Frank in shirt and jacket for most of the film. In the beach scenes, his
camera retreats to modest long shots, avoiding any homoeroticization.
In stark contrast, Visconti costumes Gino in a sleeveless undershirt during the first part of his film to accommodate his fetishization of Girotti's
"equine" shoulders. Visconti also lowers the diegetically functional over-
the-shoulder shot to include Girotti's shoulders as an element of the
composition in their own right. Visconti opens the first bedroom scene
with a close-up shot of a shirtless Gino and a fully dressed Giovanna
distanced in a mirror shot. Throughout the scene, Visconti foregrounds
Girotti's chest and shoulders, even when Giovanna undresses down to
her slip. Visconti keeps the potentially provocative imagery of female
sexuality in the background in a manner that contrasts with Garnett's

male heterosexual direction. Later, when Giovanna wipes the sweat off Bragana's naked torso, Visconti juxtaposes the invasive proximity of Bragana's bloated obesity with Gino's tempting but inaccessible lean body in the background, the camera empathetically approximating Giovanna's point of view as subject. In Ancona, when the Spagnolo lights the match in his room with Gino, he holds it over Gino's back, extending the shoulder fetish beyond Giovanna's subjectivity to the film as a whole and positing it within a homosexual narrative context. Visconti prefers Girotti's left shoulder in particular as fetish object, so that the injury to this arm from Bragana's murder constitutes, from a purely visual perspective, a sort of symbolic castration. When a shirtless Gino confronts Giovanna in a bedroom scene after the murder, he throws her onto the bed and himself on top of her, untying his bandaged arm in symbolic refusal of such castration. The visual presentation of this heterosexual aggression again homoerotically privileges Gino's back and shoulders, which are stretched out over and covering Giovanna's body. At the end of the film, Visconti concludes this shoulder motif on a nurturing rather than aggressive note, when Gino tells Giovanna to rest her head on his shoulders as they drive away from the *trattoria*.

Lino Miccichè has painstakingly recounted how, contrary to popular belief, Visconti's film does not merely use Cain's novel as a point of departure but rather constitutes a genuine adaptation, as the film appropriates not only its plot but at times also its actual dialogue from the book. Insofar as Visconti's invention of the character of the Spagnolo deviates from Cain's original text, this breach of fidelity stands out as a sore auteurist thumbprint, prompting much critical speculation. Fernaldo Di Giammatteo sees him as "Gino's alter ego." Schifano dubs him "the ironic and disenchanted conscience of the film." Screenwriter Mario Alicata laments that "he was supposed to be the positive character in the film," but that he ended up "a highly equivocal figure." Giulio Cesare Castello calls him "a nebulous symbol of a particular sexual rapport." Miccichè reports that "the adjective most often used by Italian critics to describe the Spagnolo is 'ambiguous.'" Perhaps because he is not Italian, Geoffrey Nowell-Smith could be more blunt: "The Spagnolo is a homosexual."[22] Visconti closets this homosexuality in the carefully crafted double entendre of the exchanges between the Spagnolo and Gino in order to accommodate heterocentrist readings. The Spagnolo asserts that "in two you can do many things." He tells Gino that "if you stay with me, I'll teach you that life on the road doesn't involve only making love to women."[23] He retorts to the landlady, "We won't spoil your honeymoon sheets!" He exclaims to Gino, "Let's go to Genoa, where you can walk along the port in the evening and make lots of new friends." Such dialogue subtextually alludes to a homosexual relationship between him and Gino while never overtly breaking the heterocentric bonds of the surface text. When Gino hits him, the Spagnolo's declaration that "you used to only threaten me. . . . I can see you've gotten more courageous" raises the question of what previously might have provoked such a passionate display on Gino's part. Throughout the film the Spagnolo deploys the term "wanderer" as a virtual code word for "homosexual," allowing Visconti to hover on the threshold of his closet. Finally, and far more definitively, the Spagnolo's jealous betrayal of Gino to the authorities near the end of the film retroactively argues for a sexualized dimension to their relationship.

This double entendre strategy also operates in the actions of the characters and in Visconti's visual presentation of them. The Spagnolo's offer to pay Gino's train fare accommodates Marxist heterocentricity as an act of solidarity exemplifying the Spagnolo's declared philosophy that "money has legs and was meant to walk." However, as Nowell-Smith and others have noted, the incident is essentially a pick-up.[24] The Spagnolo's decision to shack up with Gino in Ancona instead of continuing on to Trieste as he had intended hints at homosexual motivation. When the Spagnolo and Gino enter their room to share a matrimonial bed, Gino sits slouching slump-shouldered with his legs apart on the edge of the bed, recreating Giovanna's body position in their earlier bedroom scene. This calculated repetition and transfer of imagery prompts a reading of similarity between the two relationships, specifically that they are both sexual in nature. From a literal and heterocentric perspective, the Spagnolo's turning off the lamp only to light a match to illuminate Gino's body seems totally illogical, but this otherwise contrived moment does express the furtive and the clandestine nature of his homosexual gaze. Miccichè has noted the homoerotically romantic connotations of the Spagnolo and Gino "sitting together on the panoramic town walls like a couple of lovers" as they contemplate the sea from Piazzale San Ciriaco in Ancona.[25] Similar imagery recurs when the two look out at the river from the riverbank by Bragana's *trattoria*.

In this latter scene, Visconti's cinematic syntax as he presents the images as well as the images themselves invite a homosexual reading. The scene opens with an excited Gino discovering the Spagnolo in the crowd below and running down to meet him.[26] Once together, the camera encircles and caresses them in a manner usually reserved for a couple on the verge of a film kiss. Later in the scene, Visconti tracks the two in a shared close-up, providing a sense of the intimacy between the characters, and indeed the two are within kissing proximity throughout

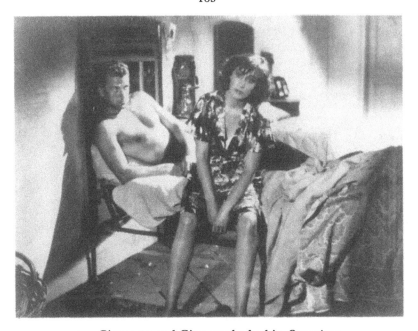

17. Giovanna and Gino on the bed in *Ossessione.*
Courtesy of the Museum of Modern Art Film Stills Archive

much of the scene. Such visual intimacy contributes to the intensity of
Gino's passion as he grabs the Spagnolo by the shirt, pulling his face
even closer to his own. The cinematic syntax anticipates a kiss, but Visconti favors his heterocentric text (and audience) over his homosexual
subtext (and personal life), just as Gino closets his passion in violence
and punches the Spagnolo instead. In contrast to Visconti's use of the
extended shared close-up, cinematic punching scenes have traditionally
employed rapid shot-countershot sequences which divide the characters
oppositionally in order to establish their bond as one of competition
rather than intimacy. As a visual coup de grace, Visconti concludes his
presentation of the incident with the Spagnolo's reaction shot, much as
male-biased heterocentrist filmmaking prefers the reaction shot of the
woman after she has been kissed. Visconti then returns inside the *trattoria,* where among the dancers are two men, a shorter one in a hat leading a taller one in an undershirt, their outward appearance and interpersonal dynamic recalling those of the Spagnolo and Gino.

Ossessione has long been viewed as a precursor not only of Italian
neorealism but also of American film noir. During his time in France in
the 1930s, Visconti saw Pierre Chenal's film version of the Cain novel,

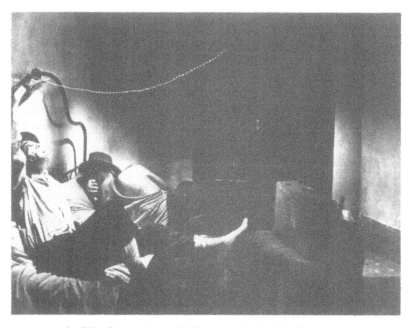

18. The Spagnolo and Gino on the bed in *Ossessione.*
Courtesy of the Museum of Modern Art Film Stills Archive

entitled *Le dernier tournant* (English: *The Last Turning Point,* 1939), and Renoir gave Visconti a copy of the book and suggested an Italian adaptation. When Visconti met with the young producer Giuseppe De Santis to discuss possible film projects, De Santis's enthusiasm for American literature guaranteed the selection. Visconti's dim lighting, resulting from the exigencies of using train batteries for indoor scenes that were shot in a Ferrara theatre, would become a staple of American film noir. His use of hatched lighting, derived from window shutters, most notably in Anita's apartment, found its American counterpart in the blinds of southern California homes, another hallmark of the film noir genre. However, the grittiness of Visconti's adaptation more closely approximates the depression-era squalor of Cain's original than do the sleek surfaces and visually antiseptic treatment in Garnett's MGM version. Perhaps more than aesthetically, Visconti's film serves psychologically and ideologically as a corollary of American film noir, as both *Ossessione* and the Hollywood film genre addressed the gender dynamics of male subjectivity under siege. Although *Ossessione* follows Gino throughout almost every scene, his subjectivity is under siege from a variety of characters, namely Bragana, Giovanna, the Spagnolo, and

Anita, who all make assumptions about Gino and project identities upon him as a sort of tabula rasa of their desires. At one point, Gino experiences a virtual identity crisis, squirming in bed, caught between Giovanna hosting the *trattoria* below and the Spagnolo awaiting him outside. With his subjectivity under siege, Gino is more acted upon than active. For instance, Giovanna precedes her ordering of Bragana's murder in the Ancona garage by putting her arm around Gino's neck and forcefully pulling him into a kiss. Only with Anita does Gino recuperate his traditional male privilege of sexual assertion; he initiates their encounter, but only after refusing her earlier advances. He then dispatches her to divert the police, even as Giovanna had dispatched him to kill Bragana.

In the Ferrara sequence, Visconti extends Gino's desirability not only to the various characters of the narrative, namely Giovanna, Anita, and the Spagnolo, but also to his cinematic world as a whole. During Gino's meeting with Anita, an affluently dressed man stares obsessively at Gino, as if wanting to pick him up. After her departure, the man approaches Gino and offers him a freshly lit cigarette, in a symbolic sharing of the phallus. The moment is replete with homoerotic undertones, as the sexual connotations of a lit cigarette were established in the first bedroom scene between Gino and Giovanna, much as they also are between Garnett's Frank and Cora. Visconti extends the older man's illicit (homo)sexuality into an even more illicit pederasty, texturing the squalor of his film in a manner that foreshadows the pederast who tempts Bruno with a bicycle bell in De Sica's *The Bicycle Thief.* As Gino and the man sit on the park bench, both Anita and a group of schoolboys pass by. The man tells Gino that if he likes them, he knows where they will be and where to find better ones. The incident marks perhaps Visconti's most coy deployment of his strategy of using double entendre in dialogue, because the remark accommodates both heterocentrist and homosexual readings, depending on its ambiguous referent.

Most pervasively, Gino's subjectivity is under siege from Visconti's homoerotic sensibility, which insists on objectifying him. As auteurist cinema, *Ossessione* expresses the subjectivity of the director more than that of its leading male character. The relationships of Visconti's characters to Gino replicate his own extracinematic relationship to Massimo Girotti. Visconti's first task was to reduce this latter-day D'Annunzian *übermensch* hero of Blasetti's *Crown of Iron* (1941) to the modest human dimensions of his disenfranchised Gino. In terms which again evoke Gino-Girotti as horse, Calamai described how Visconti molded the young actor: "Massimo was transformed, as little by little we saw him broken in."[27] According to Girotti's account, Visconti had been interested in him since their work together in the 1941 film version of *Tosca*, which Jean Renoir had filmed in Italy but could not complete for political reasons, and for which Visconti had served as his assistant.[28] Menon has described Girotti's Gino as a version of the Jean Gabin figure that fuses French poetic realism with Padana naturalism. However, in profile and in three-quarter shots, and especially in his more meticulously groomed appearances during the second part of the film, the blond Girotti more closely resembles the actor Jean Marais, Cocteau's erstwhile lover, whom Visconti met and got to know in 1937 during his sojourn in France. Marais's 10-year age difference from Visconti paralleled that between the director and Girotti, and Visconti's use of Girotti in *Ossessione* approximates Cocteau's use of Marais, whom Cocteau homoerotically presents as object-of-desire in his filmography. Visconti himself later used Marais as the dream lover in *White Nights* (1957). For *Ossessione*, fellow screenwriter Giuseppe De Santis had deemed Girotti "a boy not nearly mature enough" for the role.[29] However, Girotti's youth facilitated his dual function as tabula rasa and object of desire for both Visconti and his cinematic characters.

Calamai's Giovanna, along with Alida Valli's Livia in *Senso* (1954) and Magnani's Maddalena in *Bellissima* (1957), must be classified as one of Visconti's early active female protagonists. Such fuller character types oppose themselves to the moving statuary of Silvana Mangano, Ingrid Thulin, and Claudia Cardinale, who serve as decoy objects of desire in Visconti's later filmography. Much feminist film criticism has argued that female characters created by male directors are essentially male projections, constructions of an other, a sort of sexualized bogeyman. However, male homosexual directors tend not so much to project onto their female characters as they project into these characters. Specifically, they project into their female characters the sort of vulnerability, sensitivity, and (sometimes hysterical) emotionalism that characterizes the effeminacy with which they themselves have at times been inaccurately tainted by a patriarchal, homophobic, and heterocentrist hegemonic culture. For male homosexual artists, female characters are often not so much sexual objects as they are surrogate subjects. Such characters are not the other, but the closeted secondary self. This dynamic has operated in the filmography of a variety of closeted homosexual screenwriters and directors, most of whom have either gravitated to or vacillated from melodrama, the genre traditionally devoted to the feminine or "effeminate" qualities described. These artists include such film directors as George Cukor, Rainer Werner Fassbinder, and Pedro Almodóvar, as well as playwrights from Euripides to Tennessee Williams, the latter of whom provided the dialogue for Visconti's film *Senso*

(1954). Visconti confirmed his own awareness of this dynamic of surrogacy by nicknaming Williams "Blanche" in reference to the libidinally unbalanced protagonist of his play *A Streetcar Named Desire*. Schifano has assessed Visconti's "tendency to identify with the American dramatist," so it is not surprising that he adopted the same strategy of displacement with Giovanna as Williams used with Blanche DuBois and his other sexually frustrated female protagonists.[30] Had Visconti received the cast for *Ossessione* he originally intended, with a 34-year-old Magnani playing opposite a 24-year-old Girotti, the female protagonist would have replicated his own age vis-à-vis his leading actor. As Visconti's surrogate, Giovanna is not the site of misogyny but rather of the director's own internalized homophobia. His condemnation of Giovanna's exercise of sexuality is a condemnation of his own.

Just as Marxism has traditionally ignored the body as site of libido rather than labor, so also communism has historically been as intolerant, if less punitive, of homosexuality as Fascism, and this was particularly true in Italy. The notoriousness of the PCI in this regard was best exemplified in the puritanical expulsion of the vociferously leftist Pasolini from the party in the late 1940s. Visconti's relationship to the party, like his cinematic relationship to neorealism, was problematic and ambivalent. Although he professed faith in the Marxist cause throughout his life, as a homosexual he never officially joined the Italian Communist Party, thereby avoiding the sort of scandal to which Pasolini had been exposed.[31] A sense of isolation from the fraternity proffered by communist solidarity permeates the entire arc of Visconti's filmography. In *Rocco and His Brothers* (1960), *Sandra* (1965), and *The Damned* (1969), fraternal relationships are fraught with danger. *The Stranger* (1967), *Death in Venice*, and *Ludwig* investigate the alternative of isolation which stems in these films from existential, aesthetic, and aristocratic elitism, respectively. Film editor Mario Serandrei reports that in Visconti's efforts to isolate his figures in long shots in *Ossessione* "he continually directed his camera at a distance of three hundred meters, which was the limit" for his lenses and film stock.[32] Visconti was not the only homosexual director working in Fascist Italy, however. Ferdinando Maria Poggioli, "a homosexual without complexes," had been making successful films since the early 1930s.[33] Poggioli's cinema has been described as "a refusal of Fascism . . . that passes more through psychoanalysis than through politics," and as such established a precedent for Visconti's *Ossessione*.[34] In a gesture of covert homosexual solidarity, the more experienced Poggioli offered assistance to the novice Visconti with his first cinematic venture. Although Visconti refused, with Calamai as Giovanna, Dhia Cristiani as Anita, and Elio Marcuzzo as the Spagnolo, he had already borrowed much of his cast from Poggioli's stable of actors. Visconti may also have acknowledged the kindness, if the Spagnolo's suggestion that he and Gino go to Genoa is read as an intertextual reference to Poggioli's *Sissignora* (1940), which was set in Genoa with Marcuzzo in the cast.[35]

Ossessione's sense of moral, emotional, temporal, and geographic isolation renders "politics . . . an off-screen voice."[36] Numerous critics have commented on the relative lack of political content and context in the film, the virtual absence of the war and Fascism, which was reduced to little more than the portrait of a missing sailor on Anita's bureau. Arguably, Visconti's disregard for politics subversively diminishes Fascism to an irrelevancy in the lives of his characters, but he also avoids any viable socialist alternative that might have provoked censors to preempt production. The screenwriter Mario Alicata explains the original conception of the Spagnolo as "a proletariat who returned to Italy, becoming a vagabond in order to disseminate propagandistic ideas about socialism, antifascism and communism."[37] In an exquisite move of sublime perversity, Visconti confounds the historic homophobia of the Italian Communist Party that ostracized him by conflating Marxism and homosexuality in the character of the Spagnolo. The Spagnolo's experience abroad, codified in his name and foreign appearance, reflects Visconti's experience abroad. The youthful Visconti had been nominally seduced by the spectacularity of Fascism because it offered him an Oedipally rebellious role opposing his father, who despised Mussolini's bullyish swaggering. Visconti's time as an expatriate in a more liberal France encouraged changes not only in (homo)sexual views because of his relationship with Horst but also changes in his political views because of his relationship with Renoir and the director's array of communist and socialist friends. As site of his sexual and political awakening, Visconti dubbed Paris his own personal "road to Damascus."[38] The Spagnolo's time in Spain both parallels and confuses this dual awakening. In contrast to the intentions of the screenwriters, Visconti exposes the Spagnolo's altruistic generosity to Gino in the train as little more than a self-interested sexual overture.[39] Far from being a champion of the masses, the Spagnolo exploits and dupes them with his fortune-telling during the *Ferragosto* festivities in Ancona. The most profound breach of the Spagnolo's professed solidarity occurs when this would-be Communist collaborates with the Fascist authorities by reporting Gino to the police. Visconti condemns this treachery by replicating the imagery that concluded Gino and Giovanna's confrontation with these same authorities. In both scenes, Visconti alludes to the guilt of the respective parties, first Gino and Giovanna and then the Spagnolo, by presenting them in silhouette behind the glass door which closes after them.

Insofar as the Marxist-sympathizing Visconti renders the lower-class male in *Ossessione* desirable, he also renders the superior-class male undesirable, most notably in his casting of the grotesquely obese Juan De Landa as Bragana. Bragana's disproportionate interest in a 10-pound eel marks him as one who ingests rather than uses the phallic. It is this interest which detours him from his appointed errands and enables Gino and Giovanna to begin their affair. Gino fixes the internal workings of Bragana's car engine and pump, whose mechanical dysfunction serves as an objective correlative for the sexual dysfunction in Bragana and Giovanna's marital relationship. Bragana is not so much a bearer of desire and a possessor of libido as he is a bearer of wealth and possessor of property. He buys his relationships with Gino and Giovanna, and his bloated body visually incarnates his interpersonal consumerism. Miccichè reads Bragana as a symbol of capital itself, an "obscene presence . . . that turns sexuality into a 'market,' personal relations into 'commerce,' marriage into an 'investment,' and coupling into 'business.'"[40] The character's self-important tendency to identify himself in the third person as *The* Bragana (in Italian: *Il* Bragana) indicates the degree to which he has suffered self-alienation through capital. Vaunting his fiscal potency after paying for the congratulatory toast made in honor of his own performance in the singing contest, he instructs Gino and Giovanna in the value of earning money: "What's important is to work to earn a lot of money." During his materialist pontification, Visconti's camera maintains a calculatedly alienated distance. In contrast to Bragana, the leaner Gino shrinks from capitalism, even after his change in material fortune from Bragana's death. He remains aloof from Giovanna's enterprising management of the *trattoria* and vehemently refuses any part of the insurance settlement. He physically struggles with Giovanna over Bragana's pocket watch, which Visconti exploits as a visual metaphor for class status throughout the film, and whose chain symbolically binds them to one another and ultimately to Bragana as well.

While *Ossessione* removes the patriarchal figure from the narrative, the residue of patriarchal privilege remains. Patriarchy enforces its reign throughout the film in a variety of ways. Cain's novel repeatedly refers to Cora as a "hellcat," and the death of a cat in an exploding fuse box foreshadows her own. Using such references as a point of departure, Visconti's film deflects the animality of desire between Gino and Giovanna into the sound of two howling cats mating outside when Bragana, Giovanna, and Gino sit down to dinner. Playing with double entendre on this metaphor, Giovanna complains of excessive heat, be-

19. The car as symbol
of sexual dysfunction in
Ossessione.
Courtesy of the
Museum of Modern Art
Film Stills Archive

comes particularly agitated, and prompts Bragana to go outside and kill
the cats in a gesture of overcompensatory phallicism. His gunfire punctuates a deliberately paced embrace between Gino and Giovanna, leaving a weighty silence on the soundtrack. In keeping with Visconti's
auteurial displacement of his transgressive homosexuality into their
transgressively adulterous heterosexuality, Gino and Giovanna continually closet their affair, symptomatically deferring to patriarchal authority. When Giovanna first lures Gino into the kitchen with her singing,
he closes the door behind him, only to have Bragana later disrupt their
interaction. Patriarchal privilege invades their furtively closeted privacy
in their first bedroom scene when a mirror shot of their heated embrace
gives (s)way to the symbolic presence of Bragana's suits as the door to
the armoire containing them swings open. Even after Bragana's death,
Giovanna's closed bedroom door does not prevent the child Elvira, as
envoy of innocence, from overhearing her incriminating conversation
with Gino. As the conscience of the film, Elvira is an equivocal presence
vis-à-vis patriarchal authority, at first absolving Gino of his guilt and
then dispatching the police to catch him and Giovanna on the road.
Ultimately, Visconti asserts patriarchal authority in *Ossessione* by exclud-

ing Bragana's murder as something visually unspeakable, only later to show the ostensibly poetic justice dealt Gino and Giovanna in a narratively parallel car accident in graphic detail. With a dead Giovanna lying alongside the road, Visconti effectively concludes his film with the punishment of his surrogate female character, and, by extension, his own homosexuality. The patriarchal voice of Bragana's Germont that opens the film still echoes at its conclusion.

Notes

1. Luchino Visconti, "Anthropomorphic Cinema," trans. Anne and Roger Meservey, in *The Fabulous Thirties: Italian Cinema 1929-1944* (Milano: Gruppo Editoriale Electa, 1979), 54. This very brief article constitutes Visconti's sole contribution to a theoretical discussion of cinema. All subsequent quotations in this paragraph are from this same article and same page.

2. Roberto Campari, *Il fantasma del bello: Iconologia del cinema italiano* (Venezia: Marsilio, 1994), 51-68.

3. Millicent Marcus, *Italian Film in the Light of Neorealism* (Princeton: Princeton University Press, 1986), 4-29.

4. Gianni Menon, "Note sul teatro di Luchino Visconti ma anche sul cinema e altre cose," in *La controversia Visconti*, ed. Fernaldo Di Giammatteo (Roma: Bianco e Nero, 1976), 115.

5. Visconti, "Anthropomorphic Cinema," 54.

6. Laurence Schifano, *I fuochi della passione: La vita di Luchino Visconti*, trans. Sergio Ferrero (Milano: Longanesi, 1988), 38.

7. Lino Miccichè, *Visconti e il neorealismo* (Venezia: Marsilio, 1990), 52.

8. Schifano, *I fuochi della passione*, 117-118.

9. Boze Hadleigh, *Conversations with My Elders* (New York: St. Martin's, 1986), 29.

10. In *I fuochi della passione*, 230, Schifano reports that at one point Visconti quite literally closeted his homosexuality by locking up his lover, the younger director Franco Zeffirelli, in an armoire! The parentheses in my title purposefully reflect Visconti's propensity for such closeting.

11. Mira Liehm, *Passion and Defiance: Film in Italy from 1942 to the Present* (Berkeley: University of California Press, 1984), 4.

12. Pierre Leprohon, *The Italian Cinema*, trans. Roger Greaves and Oliver Stallybrass (New York: Praeger, 1972), 87-88.

13. Bruno Villien, *Visconti*, trans. Salerio Esposito (Milano: Garzanti, 1987), 35.

14. Angela Della Vacche, *The Body in the Mirror: Shapes of History in Italian Cinema* (Princeton: Princeton University Press, 1992), 149.

15. Laura Mulvey, "Visual Pleasure and Narrative Cinema," in *Film Theory and Criticism*, ed. Gerald Mast and Marshall Cohen (New York: Oxford University Press, 1985), 803–816. Mulvey's argument that the male is the bearer of the gaze and the woman is its object presupposes a heterosexual male vision. Visconti uses Calamai to reverse this dynamic. An older Calamai in the role of prostitute would later again function as bearer of the gaze upon the younger Marcello Mastroianni as Mario in Visconti's *White Nights*, her intrusive stare disrupting an intimate moment between him and the character Natalia.

16. Turner's Cora, who prompts her husband's death and usurps his socio-economic status and power, may appropriate the phallus, but she has difficulty wielding it, at least when it comes to its metaphoric presence as a cigarette. Playing upon the psychosexual shorthand of the Hays Code era, Garnett presents Cora as incapable of lighting a match, so that she must accept the offer of a light from a man, Frank, in order to get her cigarette burning! So much for female self-sufficiency.

17. James Cain, *The Postman Always Rings Twice* (New York: Grosset and Dunlap, 1934), 5. Italics are mine.

18. Ibid., 11–12.

19. Unfortunately for my purposes, the English-subtitled version of the film inaccurately translates her exclamation as "You've got the shoulders of an ox!"

20. Cain, *The Postman Always Rings Twice*, 22.

21. Robert Aldrich, *The Seduction of the Mediterranean: Writing, Art and Homosexual Fantasy* (New York: Routledge, 1993), 5.

22. Di Giammatteo, *La controversia Visconti*, 11; Schifano, *I fuochi della passione*, 154; Gianni Rondolino, *Luchino Visconti* (Torino: UTET, 1981), 129; Menon, "Note sul teatro di Luchino Visconti," 114; Miccichè, *Visconti e il neorealismo*, 52; Geoffrey Nowell-Smith, *Luchino Visconti* (London: Secker & Warburg, 1967), 22–23.

23. The English-subtitled version compromises the gender specificity of this quote by translating the Italian phrase "making love to women" as simply "looking for love."

24. Nowell-Smith, *Luchino Visconti*, 22.

25. Miccichè, *Visconti e il neorealismo*, 53.

26. From his window above the *trattoria*, Gino eagerly watches the Spagnolo down below. The image functions as an auteurist prototype for Aschenbach's surveillance from his hotel-room window of Tadzio down at the beach in *Death in Venice* (1971).

27. In *I fuochi della passione*, 151, Schifano reports, "The actor, accustomed to an entirely different treatment from Blasetti, suffered full-fledged emotional breakdowns twice under Visconti's direction." In this same passage, Calamai uses the Italian term *domato* to describe the process, which has the

same equine connotations of domesticating and taming as the English "to be broken."

28. Villien, *Visconti*, 35.

29. Ibid.

30. Schifano, *I fuochi della passione*, 215.

31. Ibid., 168.

32. Villien, *Visconti*, 35.

33. Adriano Aprà and Patrizia Pistagnesi, eds., *The Fabulous Thirties: Italian Cinema, 1929-1944* (Milano: Gruppo Editoriale Electa, 1979), 105.

34. Ibid., 106.

35. Unfortunately for both Italian cinema and homosexual cultural history, Poggioli died in a gas accident in February 1945.

36. Di Giammatteo, *La controversia Visconti*, 83.

37. Rondolino, *Luchino Visconti*, 129.

38. Schifano, *I fuochi della passione*, 127.

39. In *Luchino Visconti*, 129, Rondolino records Visconti's eschewal of the intentions of his fellow screenwriters Giuseppe De Santis, Gianni Puccini, and Mario Alicata regarding the Spagnolo. Alicata has been particularly vociferous about Visconti's defiance of their original ideas. In Micciché, *Visconti e il neorealismo*, 52, Alicata relates, "In the treatment and the screenplay the Spagnolo was supposed to be something completely different from what Luchino ended up creating in the film." In Rondolino, *Luchino Visconti*, 129-130, Alicata further elaborates, "What was the character of the Spagnolo supposed to mean according to our rather naive intentions? He was of the proletariat, and had fought in the Spanish revolution on the just side, and not for the Fascists. . . . He was supposed to be the positive figure in the film, and the fact that he was not was not only due to government censorship. . . . He became, all of a sudden, someone of highly questionable characteristics, instead of the critical conscience of the film."

40. Micciché, *Visconti e il neorealismo*, 59.

7

Ways of Looking in Black and White

Female Spectatorship and

the Miscege-national Body in

Sotto la croce del sud

Robin Pickering-Iazzi

Enticing readers to look at what lies within, the cover created for the July 1936 issue of the Italian journal *Cinema* strikes the eye with a captivating photographic image that prompts intriguing questions about the female body, race, and the cinematic apparatus in colonial discourses produced in commercial film culture of the 1930s.[1] In the center foreground a white male, clean-cut, sporting stylish trousers and shoes visible below a white lab coat, which lends an air of technical precision to the scene, intently shoots a jet of dark paint from an electric spray gun onto the body of a young woman. This act of body-painting appears to complete a "native look," since familiar adornments already plentifully encode the feminine figure as "exotic other." A cluster of lush flowers blooms amid her dark tresses, two bands of seashells grace the woman's limbs, one on her left wrist and the other around her right ankle, and a halter top and skirt of palm-like fronds complete the ensemble of island native wear, though some paler skin on the upper thigh peeks through two leaves, belying the illusion this racialized image seems intended to sustain. As the camera shot catches particles of paint suspended in the air, it intriguingly exposes for Italian readers what is generally off-screen: the arts of technology applied to a white woman in the process of being "made up" as native for a colonial gaze, both in the sense of preparing her appearance with color, cosmetics, and costume and in the sense of invention, for she becomes a product of non-native fantasies, desires, and stereotypical notions.

But what I find particularly interesting is the way the photograph frames a crucial moment in the fabrication of the feminine exotic; it

marks the translocation of woman at the intersection of power systems
that constituted the colonial enterprise, thereby showing the necessity
of considering racial as well as gender differences. If we read the scene
symbolically and in the context of European patriarchal relations, the
white female occupies a subordinate position as passive object, quite literally a blank canvas for the male, who is represented as an agent of
culture and technology. The iconography of the tropical flora and shells
on the feminine figure, linked with the backdrop of jungle scenery, further anchors the woman as part of nature. At the same time, I propose,
viewing this representation through the critical category of race casts
its potential meanings in a different light. After all, the primitive ornaments and body paint applied to the white female body prepare her to
"perform" the native other. What does this kind of cinematic aestheti-
cization and appropriation of the black body say about the white woman's positionality in the relations between colonizer and colonized?
How, if at all, might this form of drag, a look designed from and for a
Western imperialist eye, affect the discursive naturalization of the racial
other, who is frequently associated with a primitive landscape, a territory to be conquered and cultivated? In other words, could the white
woman's native "act" possibly draw attention to its performative status
as artificial construction, thereby also working against the myth of the
"natural" indigene? And is it possible that Italian female spectators, by
virtue of their own positioning as other in patriarchal relations prior to
and during Fascism, negotiate the codes of gender and racial categories
in different ways?

I want to think through these speculative lines of inquiry with a
reading of the 1938 film *Sotto la croce del sud* (*Under the Southern Cross*)
by Guido Brignone, in many ways a model text of the colonial film genre
as it evolved in Italy during the 1930s, gaining special significance
with the foundation of the new Italian African Empire, which was proclaimed by the Fascist state pursuant to the conquest of Ethiopia in
May 1936. The narrative and images of the relations between Italians
and Africa, its landscapes, peoples, and cultures crafted in Brignone's
film, as in such other colonial texts as Mario Camerini's *Il grande appello* (*The Great Call*, 1936), Romolo Marcellini's *Sentinelle di bronzo*
(*Bronze Sentinels*, 1937), and Goffredo Alessandrini's *Abuna Messias*
(1939), clearly had a key role in casting black and white looks—ways of
seeing and being seen—that bore new meanings of empire for moviegoers in Italy. This genre of cinematic discourse thus offers a remarkable example of the cultural productivity of Fascism and, more specifically, of the regime's endeavors to construct a national colonial identity.[2]
But we must ask how the "bearings" structuring the systems of address

and representation that were produced respectively by the film industry and the Fascist State relate to each other. For instance, Ettore G. Mattia, a journalist in East Africa in the late 1930s, directly links the two discourses. Describing what he saw while Italian colonial films were shot on location, he recalls "the clear generic characterization that was given to blacks and whites; the former were docile as they served and the latter proud as they commanded, while, for the most part, the mulattos, in general guilty due to the mixing of races, had to be yoked with the role of scoundrels and unlucky individuals, people who despised Mendel's laws. For example, I remember Enrico Glori in the role of the evil mulatto in *Sotto la croce del sud*, a film constructed exactly on these elementary schemes."[3] Readers could take Mattia's eyewitness testimony about the equation between races and roles at face value. Brignone's film, which makes explicit reference to the war in Ethiopia and the "miraculous" creation of an empire, clearly invokes myths of the benevolent white Italian settler, the "good-natured" black natives, and the biracial villain that intersect with racialized images encoded in Fascist writings of the time.

However, ample cause also exists to question whether the representations of racial differences in the cinematic space of colonial narrative and mise-en-scène make up such a transparent system that unequivocally served the production of Fascist imperialist ideology. The studies on the Italian cinema during Fascism by Marcia Landy and James Hay provide important reassessments of the colonial film genre, among others, and suggest ways such texts, as complex signifying systems, may cooperate with official apparatuses of imperialist ideology and, at the same time, contest the borders of racial and gender differences.[4] More specifically for the purposes of this study, both scholars highlight the ambiguous positions inscribed by the female lead role of Mailù in *Sotto la croce del sud*. Bearing the markers of the feminine exotic, the biracial figure of Mailù is aligned with the primitive African landscape and, as Hay and Landy suggest, may be read as a seductive object of colonial desire, yet she also threatens to disrupt the harmonious new order of production the Italian men settlers seek to establish.

The following study takes this provocative line of inquiry in a relatively unexamined direction as it investigates problems concerning Italian female spectatorship and the differences gender and race possibly make in the ways racial identities are visualized and negotiated in colonial discourse.[5] In order to theorize some terms of female spectatorial positions in relationship to systems of representation in the Italian colonial film, this essay's field of inquiry includes writings on the Italian colonies published in the *Almanacco della donna italiana (Italian*

Woman's Almanac) during the 1930s. These articles, written by ethnographers, intellectuals, and Fascist colonial officials, are important for several reasons. They offer examples of colonial discourse addressed explicitly to women and delineate the special social and symbolic functions women were called upon to uphold in the formation of the national Fascist colonial identity. While indicating internal gendered differentiations articulated in colonialist ideology during the regime, these texts also employ diverse modes for soliciting potential women "settlers" and construct a variety of subject positions. They therefore force issues about the relativity of gender and race as terms of white female social identities and the power those identities had over indigenous men and women. Furthermore, the representations of the exotic, primitive lands of the Italian empire across the sea, the conditions and beliefs of African peoples, and the locations of Italian women in race relations enable one to construct a historically grounded critical frame for speculating about some of the interests, desires, and concerns "the Africas" elicited in the women of Italy. Of particular significance here are the ways depictions of the *meticci*, females and males of mixed Italian and indigenous races, change in the late 1930s, perhaps due to the pressures interracial relationships in the colonies brought to bear upon state institutions, laws, and policies that were developed to stave off the so-called threats miscegenation posed to the purported racial "purity and prestige" of Italy's imperial body.

While reading *Sotto la croce del sud* within this broader discursive system, I intend to examine the performativity of gender and race enacted by Mailù, which has unsettling overtones that explicitly engage with the lines of inquiry framed at the outset of this essay. For in fact, the biracial character Mailù was played by Doris Duranti, an Italian actress born in Livorno, who styled her particular movie-star mystique as the "black Orchid" both from her legendary, ravishing beauty and from the exotic looks she cast on the silver screen playing such roles as Dahabo, a Somalian woman in *Sentinelle di bronzo,* and Eliana in *Il cavaliere di Kruja* (*The Cavalryman from Kruja,* dir. Carlo Campogalliani, 1940), a film that treats the annexation of Albania to Italy.[6] We could reasonably expect that the biracial act delivered by Duranti, a purely artificial racialized image, would easily conform to the Fascist imperialist perspective on relations between Italian settlers and Ethiopian natives. Supporting this position, a 1938 review of Brignone's film, published in *Bianco & Nero* (*Black and White*), applauds the images of Italians who were working the land in Africa, which exhibited "a healthy Fascist ethic." However, the encoding of Mailù's racial origins and the crucial role she plays in the plot clearly trouble the reviewer, who complains "Her eyes are made up like a Manchurian. . . . Mailù is an 'Oriental' woman sick with spleen, and enthralls the Italian colonists, who make a horrible impression." As further support for his critique, the writer contends that Mailù represents a decadent model of the "vamp" that appears "out of place and wrong for the times."[7] This insight has useful applications for deciphering the highly equivocal meanings that drag images of the feminine miscegenational body possibly make available. On the one hand, within the historically and culturally specific context of the film's production, the visual registers Mailù bears stand for the transgression of the prohibition against miscegenation, an outpost signaling the boundaries between models of white and black looks and the dangers that lie in between. On the other hand, if the female body conventionally functions as seductive spectacle, a position many film scholars share, could the eroticized, beguiling artifice of the biracial femme fatale lure film viewers across the very boundaries she is designed to sustain? To avoid any misunderstanding, let me clarify that this study is not intended to propose that the white woman's performance of mulatto drag functions as a decolonizing strategy during Fascism. On the contrary, as the critical work by bell hooks has demonstrated, such filmic constructions support the architecture of the imperial gaze because they appropriate images of blackness, materially and symbolically colonizing black bodies. Yet, by looking closely at the iconographic markers inscribing Mailù's positions of enunciation and the spatialization of her relations to different settler and indigenous communities, this analysis aims to construct an introductory critical perspective on how Italian women figure as addressees and agents in the colonial politics of gender and race.

Expanding Horizons:
Italian Women and Colonial Discourses

Significantly, as *Sotto la croce del sud* begins, the opening shot gives viewers plenty of time to take in a spectacular panorama of the African landscape. Before our eyes, the plains land extends to the horizon, with a majestic tree situated in the foreground, its branches spreading, silhouetted against the sky. The musical score modulates the pitch of a rich spectrum of affective states associated with the land, ranging from a subdued tranquility to a heightened sense of power, drama, and foreboding as the last rays of sunshine filter through wisps of clouds and yield to nightfall's darkness. Dispelling any indeterminacy that could inhibit recognition of the geographic territory, the lands and skies are identified with the overlaid notice, "All outdoor scenes are shot on location in A.O.I." Thus, the visual composition of the shots beckons the audience into Italian East Africa, the distinct place and space of the New Roman Empire, even if only for a few hours. The opening panoramic shot works through a familiar convention in commercial colonial film, enabling spectators to feast their eyes on the visual pleasures of breathtaking cinematography that conjures foreign lands as the site of desire yet constitutes a politically and culturally specific outlook on the "natural" landscape as the ground for the production of Italian colonialist ideology. The performative model of landscape proposed by W. J. T. Mitchell elucidates how seemingly neutral landscape representations situate viewers in hierarchies of power. He explains, "Landscape as a cultural medium thus has a double role with respect to something like ideology: it naturalizes a cultural and social construction, representing an artificial world as if it were simply given and inevitable, and it also makes that representation operational by interpellating its beholder in some more or less determinate relation to its givenness as sight and site."[8] The filmic representations of such contrasting landscapes as the flat plains, the jungle thick with undergrowth, gigantic trees, and orderly rows of crops at the plantation thus invent the terms by which Italian viewers could create relationships, however imaginary, with the empire, appealing to more than the sense of adventure, dreams, and opportunities the land might awaken.

Fulfilling the promise of dramatic conflict foreshadowed at the film's outset, the lands of the Italian empire emerge as a contested space of ethical struggles that solicit spectators to take the high moral ground proclaimed by the Fascist model of colonization. The plot is fairly simple. The wizened, elder Marco, the handsome Paolo, and a group of Italian male settlers arrive at a large plantation in East Africa, of which Marco is the so-called legitimate owner, only to discover that "the *meticcio*" Simone has taken over the lands. Moreover, Simone breaks the laws that were established to structure relations between the races, beating the native laborers and paying them with whiskey. In order to stay on the plantation, Simone coercively enlists Mailù to cast her seductive wiles over Paolo. In fact, the young man succumbs but then discovers the subterfuge. Consequently, Simone steals the workers' pay, sets the plantation afire, and escapes. Yet as the native men track Simone down, he meets his demise and is swallowed by quicksand. Mailù leaves the plantation, and the Italian settlers begin to rebuild the plantation. Significantly, the struggle over the land is played out between white Italian settlers and the biracial Simone and his enigmatic companion Mailù, not black Ethiopian natives. The narrative thereby suppresses indigenous precolonial history and the violence of the war waged by Italy while focusing on attitudes toward miscegenation.

While Brignone's filmic re-creation of exotic panoramic space and movement addresses its Italian audience in terms of national and racial identity, this spectatorial mode may also have had a strong gendered appeal to women viewers in Italy, as suggested both by the history of Italian female spectatorship and by colonial writings published in the women's press. Giuliana Bruno's critical examination of the relations between gender and the mobile gaze is particularly helpful for theorizing the possible ways that colonial cinematic discourse solicits female spectators. Briefly, Bruno reconsiders the models of a mobile panoramic form of visuality produced by trains, cinema, and department stores as nineteenth-century technologies. She looks first at the work on travel by Wolfgang Schivelbusch and then at Mary Ann Doane's proposition that, given the parallels drawn between film and window-shopping, the prototypical "spectator-consumer" may be female.[9] Elaborating this premise in light of modern Italian sexual politics of space, Bruno elucidates the emancipatory avenues—material and symbolic—that cinema opened for women as it enabled them to transform excursions into the public sphere, previously viewed as illicit, into legitimate venturings. She acutely draws out the effects and implications such a process had for women as social spectatorial subjects:

> Mobilizing the gaze—the "panoramic" feature of cinematic language—implied the appropriation of territories and the freedom of "streetwalking." Textually and contextually, literally and figuratively, historically and fantasmatically, the female subject's encounter with the cinema constructs a new geography, gives license to venturing. In its embodiment of fantasy, female spectatorship maps out the spaces of the gaze as sites to traverse and trespass. . . . Female spectatorship triggers, and participates in, women's conquest of the sphere of spatial mobility as pleasure.[10]

Bruno's paradigm highlights the intimate relationship between female viewing pleasure and film's visual language and syntax of spatial movement, and thereby indicates, for our purposes, how the varied, unique terrain of exotic images of Africa might engage female spectators. At the same time, when applied to the colonial film genre, the terms and operations of the mobile female gaze appear highly problematic for the way they lend themselves to a Western imperialist spectatorial position. Certainly, as Mary Ann Doane cautions, it is necessary to remember that this position, as conceptualized in film theory, is not a "geographical but an epistemological position."[11] Yet we cannot ignore how in *Sotto la croce del sud*, among other colonial films, the look, authorized by white privilege, is constructed for the consumption of images of Italian East Africa and black races, promising a form of mastery. The gaze such films design therefore can be interpreted as symbolic domination that, however, has material effects on models of whiteness and blackness in social relations. Furthermore, in the field of interwar discourses that mapped the sexually embattled public sphere of Italian national life, culture, and society, Africa is envisioned as a different kind of space with profound implications for modern women. Although such Fascist organizations for girls and women as the Piccole italiane and the Fasci femminili staged events that put women into public review, conservative cultural commentators speaking under the auspices of Fascism and beyond[12] railed against women's growing incursions into Italian piazzas, claiming they formed a distracting, threatening presence marked by moral decline. In contrast, articles about the Italian colonies that explicitly addressed women readers authorized, indeed invited, them to occupy urban and frontier territories, depicted as land for free-ranging feminine desires. Such writings suggest a point of contiguity with colonial film culture; the verbal and visual representations promise the pleasure of spatial mobility.

During the publication run of the Florentine Italian woman's almanac (hereafter referred to as *Almanacco* [1920-1943]), the journal featured a variety of articles on the socio-cultural conditions of indigenous peoples in the colonies as well as the history and future of Italian women settlers. Representing a time span of more than twenty years, these texts inscribe the shifting, sometimes contradictory currents of colonialist thought and policy, which Angelo Del Boca and Karen Pinkus examine in their excellent studies.[13] Although the full range of colonial writings in the *Almanacco* provides invaluable information on the heterogeneity of positions on race relations during Fascism, I will focus on the articles published in the mid- and late 1930s, since they pertain directly to the period when *Sotto la croce del sud* was produced and viewed. To avoid generalizations about the ways female social subjects might negotiate colonialist ideology, it is important here to delineate the kinds of readers the *Almanacco* envisioned. Founded by Silvia Bemporad, the *Almanacco* addressed progressive housewives, "professional women and women who have neither the time nor means to devote themselves completely to their homes," according to a prefatory statement published in 1922.[14] The self-declared scope of the publication was to inform readers about topics as diverse as beauty and fashion trends, women's organizations and cultural, social, and political enterprises, and the accomplishments of female journalists, authors, and artists. Indeed, at the outset, the *Almanacco* promised to create a "mirror faithfully reflecting the gradual elevation of the female masses that are currently preparing themselves for broader horizons and wider ranges."[15] It would be reasonable to say that this women's publication attracted readers primarily from the middle classes in urban areas (including secretaries, teachers, nurses, and the like) with enough income to purchase magazines. Such a readership may have shared certain traits with the female film viewing audience, although Victoria de Grazia notes that going to the movies was perhaps more economically accessible and popular.[16]

The colonial writings published in the *Almanacco* suggest that women occupied a particularized position in what was represented as a distinctly Fascist system of colonization. They also illustrate the diversified, competing systems of address fashioned to mobilize Italian women settlers, which are aligned with three general models: the agent of moralization, the modern adventurer, and the professional woman. Yet what precise features and purposes did Fascist thinkers fashion to distinguish Italian imperialist expansion? How might the resultant codes and rhetorical strategies have enlisted the support of women of different ages who lived in their "home" towns, attended university, worked in the business sectors, or raised families? As Pinkus demonstrates, several key economic and political rationales (the need for natural resources, the alleviation of unemployment, and Italy's status as a great Western power, for example) were circulated in campaigns aimed at creating an Italian "colonial will."[17] Yet in the general discursive system and the *Almanacco* writings, a "moral" quintessence was presented as the definitive characteristic of the Italian colonial body, purportedly determining the uniqueness of its scope. Ciro Poggiali best exemplifies this position, maintaining that entire families were transferring to the East African colonies "because Italy deprecates and opposes that exotic brand of colonialism that sends a few melancholy, dominating people, either misogynist or destined to seek consolation in alcohol or in chocolate-coated distractions of gallantry."[18] While Poggiali privileges the Italian settler family as a micro-political site for the production of Fascist colonial values that explicitly condemn individualistic acts of race or gender oppression, as well as moral turpitude, Amadeo Fani, the president of the Fascist Colonial Institute, identifies women as the most important agents of colonialist moralization and the measure of its success.

In a manner not unlike Poggiali's, Fani opens his essay "La donna e l'impero" ("Woman and the Empire") by delineating the East African

empire, founded by Il Duce, as a populist enterprise that will not tolerate monopolistic exploitation. Instead, he invokes the colonial territory
under the name of "the Fascist Empire of the Great Proletariat" and
locates the proletarian body and African land in the genealogy of the
immortal Roman Empire. In this glorious lineage, Fani argues, women
have a greater importance than men do because female citizens "represent as a mass the picture of a particular nation in a particular historical
moment, its moral value."[19] Such a conceptualization of women bor-
rows from a broader discursive formation fabricated in the early years
of Fascism, which, as Mariolina Graziosi has demonstrated, interpel-
lated women as the protagonists in the sexual politics of moralization
launched on the Italian peninsula and islands.[20] In fact, Fani invokes
two female figures broadly diffused in such writings—Lucrezia and
Cornelia—to perform a slightly different twofold function: the models
exemplified by these historical women link the diverse epochs of the
Roman Empire, classical and Fascist, and symbolize "all the other obscure *matresfamilias*."[21] Yet Fani also re-crafts the female gender model
of moralizer as he forges a feminine system of codes and symbols to
articulate specific women's roles in the lands of East Africa, which is, in
his words, "a new Italy . . . bound to the Great Mother by political
ties."[22] While creating a history of colonial pursuits undertaken by Italian women, which incorporates such legendary pioneers as Maria Brighenti,[23] Fani calls on readers to fulfill distinct ethical duties in race relations between Italian male colonizers and native Ethiopian women. He
declares, "New duties are incumbent on our women who, in that Africa
where all promiscuity between races must be banished, will be the courageous companions of our brave colonists."[24] Elaborating further, Fani
invokes the ritual of the "Sacred Spring" as a trope to locate women's
reproductive function as part of a national labor to rebirth the Roman
Empire. This model implicitly draws upon familiar female roles as
sexual object and reproducer of the race. However, at the symbolic level
of signification, this representation simultaneously figures the woman
settler as an agent of the Fascist colonial mission that shall defend (not
be defended by) the national body politic from the threat of miscegenation. Moreover, in the texts cited, we see the deployment of the female
settler body as a sign registering the progress and superiority of Italy's
colonial expansion. Adopting the metaphor of maturation, which has
humanist social and phenomenological associations, Poggiali declares
"Today women are the most elect standard bearers of our maturity as
colonizers."[25] Similarly, the article "Attività dei Fasci Femminili" ("Activities of the Fasci Femminili"), which reports on the varied social programs Fascist women developed in colonial East Africa, touts the re-

gime's "perfect" inclusion of the female masses, which are described in militaristic terms as "an army of peace, of the greatest moral and social value,"[26] as a gauge of Italy's "supremacy" over other nations.

Although the thread of discourse examined thus far purportedly makes its appeal to female readers through purely ethical imperatives, it is significant that the very same texts also address modern Italian women as the subjects of desire, thereby creating a tension between personal affective and psychological drives and the notion of collective duty. This contradictory pull provides a central source of dramatic power in *Sotto la croce del sud*, though it is aroused through the male lead's unabashed romantic attraction to Mailù and is resolved by a conversion that restores his commitment to the common goals of the settler community. In contrast, the *Almanacco* articles written by cultural commentators and Fascist ideologues specifically address women as protagonists and represent new terms of identification that carry potentially emancipatory connotations. Fani provides an interesting example in the way he characterizes women teachers, who were generally perceived as a conservative sector of society during Fascism. Noting the high number of requests from female teachers for transfers to schools in Africa, Fani, somewhat ambivalently, attributes their motivation to a "desire for a new life . . . and the passion for that small taste of adventure that is always innate in the grandiose phenomenon of emigration."[27] We could also interpret such a trend as a response to general economic factors in Italy or the restrictions the Fascist State imposed on women's employment in higher education and advanced administrative positions. Yet Fani focuses solely on the component of desire. Moreover, he presents women educators as the most typical exponents "of the totality of Italian women,"[28] thereby identifying the desire for adventure and the opportunity to invent different forms of daily living as prominent elements of female subjectivities.

The essay by Poggiali crafts a similar image of feminine colonial desires;[29] the author claims that "today Italian women are pervaded by a provident thirst to know East Africa in person, and to settle in that land,"[30] though he notes that in 1939 under 10,000 Italian women had transferred to Italian East Africa, among whom 5,000 settled in the city of Addis Ababa. Indeed, perhaps as a means to mobilize potential women settlers, the National Fascist Party and the Fascist youth group Gioventù italiana del Littorio instituted a network of precolonial camps in 1937. An announcement published in the *Almanacco* (1939) advertises the program's courses while inviting women to enroll at sites located throughout Italy.[31] Preparing the female students for life in the colonies, the winter program offered courses on theoretical and practical subjects such as history, religion, problems of expansion and the defense of the race, home furnishings, crafts, cooking, and weapon training. In the summer, women could attend "precolonial camps" that simulated primitive colonial living conditions. Women's responses to the program appear far from negligible. As Silvana Palma reports, 100,000 female students took the courses in 1938.[32] The fascination with Africa was not merely academic. Poggiali, like Fani, recognizes the attraction the "unknown, risk, and romantic fantasies" of East Africa may have for women, yet he creates more provocative associations between female desire and the African landscape. Evoking the great expanses and the variety of the exotic land and fauna, he states that East Africa "can satisfy every kind of taste, fulfill all desires, yield to the needs of all temperaments."[33] Exemplifying the promise colonial life holds for Italian women, Poggiali's essay proceeds in the form of a travelogue with detailed descriptions of natural topography, resources, cities, and different racial and ethnic groups, organized according to such sub-headings as "How You Get There," "What You Find," "The Wild Lands," and, significantly, "Prestige of the Race."

Working in tandem with the general tendency to craft Africa into a floating signifier that could stand for whatever Italian women may desire is the representation of the new empire as a site for the fulfillment of women's entrepreneurial and professional aspirations.[34] Thus, Silvia Benedettini tells her reading audience, "Today a vast field of action is opening up for the Italian woman who will go to live in the colonies with her husband and children, or in order to practice a profession, an apostolate."[35] Benedettini charts the African territory as the land of female opportunities, outlining several areas for women's occupational expansion. These include fields generally sanctioned by the Fascist state, such as education, nursing, and social welfare (see Graziosi), as well as more groundbreaking positions as doctors and business developers. For example, Bianca Matteoda, the owner of a profitable coffee plantation, becomes an emblem of female entrepreneurial spirit, cited by Benedettini, among others. Benedettini's system of address to women operates in two key ways that concern us; it makes available multiple terms for professional settler identities and, at the same time, enables female subjects to see themselves in the Fascist model of national identity as builders, newly adapted to the so-called primitive colonial lands. Perhaps for fear that self-interest will win out, Benedettini reminds wives, mothers, and professional women that "this life must be undertaken with a dedicated, altruistic spirit, like a mission, a duty to fulfill, a contribution of valid, highly useful collaboration to offer."[36] Moreover, she claims explicit political functions for these roles and asserts that "with the light

of civilization," Italian settlers will provide material and moral assistance to the "unfortunate populations."[37] The range of gendered meanings attached to African lands and life in writings of the 1930s creates
a heterogeneous system that afforded diverse female subject positions in
complex figurations of the woman settler. This discursive field also suggests that cinematographic representations of the lands, life, and race
relations in colonial film may have been negotiated in a variety of ways
by women spectators.

"In Africa it is always necessary to remember that one is white, and, moreover, that one is Italian and Fascist"[38]

In the Italian colonial film genre, *Sotto la croce del sud* opens a unique
line of questioning due to the instrumental emphasis Brignone places
on the characters of mixed race, Simone and, especially, Mailù. They
serve as catalysts that provoke intrigue, conflict, and ethical dilemmas
which the Italian settlers must resolve as they and the native population
endeavor to reclaim the neglected plantation lands. By structuring the
conflict thusly, colonizers and colonized appear to share the same goal,
struggling side by side against the "evil" *meticcio* Simone. Mailù raises
problems of a different order through the plot of interracial romance. At
face value, the mulatto acts that are put on in the roles of Simone and
Mailù can be seen to function strategically as contrasting images to
whiteness—both a reminder to viewers of what it means to be white and
of the perils to the material and social body produced by any lapse into
forgetfulness allowing miscegenation, the interpenetration of bodily racial borders.[39] As a project designed to re-member the parts of the Italian imperial body, *Sotto la croce del sud* echoes the general concern over
the failure of racial laws instituted by the Fascist state to regulate distinct parameters for white and black bodies at the micro-political site of
daily colonial life. In fact, despite juridical prohibitions outlawing marriage and cohabitation between Italian and indigenous races,[40] Del Boca
reports that some 10,000 biracial children were born between 1936 and
1940 in East Africa alone.

However, the relationship between the racial images in Brignone's
text and their potential social meanings appears more problematic if
we look at the mulatto performance through the model of drag proposed
in different contexts by Wahneema Lubiano and Judith Butler.[41] In her
engaging analysis of race representation in film, Lubiano suggests the
ways in which the language, ideas, and behaviors associated with
"blackness" in black cultural nationalism are performatively enacted as

"a form of 'drag' assumed to construct masculinity for a straight, politically and economically powerful white male gaze."[42] This proposition is useful because it takes into consideration how race and gender figure in both the drag performance and the system of address. Yet, since the mulatto acts in *Sotto la croce del sud* are played by white actors, creating a dissonance between the race performed and the race of the performers, Butler's elaboration of the destabilizing effects drag has on gender constructions due to distinctions between gender performance, identity, and anatomical sex is also pertinent. Indeed, in this study, we could adapt the operations of drag Butler articulates in the following manner, indicated by the words I have added in brackets. Drag, Butler argues, "reveals the distinctness of those aspects of gendered [racialized] experience which are falsely naturalized as a unity through the regulatory fiction of heterosexual [racial] coherence. *In imitating gender [race], drag implicitly reveals the imitative structure of gender [race] itself—as well as its contingency.*"[43] This way of thinking about drag suggests how the cinematic performance of racial identity may work against the illusion of the real, natural quintessence it seeks to create and, as Butler concludes, it opens up such culturally constructed images to resignification. Therefore, I wish to speculate about how, in the process of retracing a "racial epidermal schema"[44] that might create a coherent relation between the visual racial signifier and the identity signified (incorporating a set of dispositions, behaviors, and values) in colonial power relations, the mulatto drag act performed by Doris Duranti and the mnemonic functions it is constructed to fulfill simultaneously expose a fault line, a space where codes and meanings become highly unstable, and raise questions that exceed the film's terms of representation.

At Mailù's first appearance, which is shot in a shadowy interior immediately after the landscape sequence, what struck this viewer was precisely the undecidability of visual codes ostensibly marking her as other in the bodily politics of race. The stylization of Doris Duranti's physical artifice features sleek black hair pulled back from her face, an olive-hued complexion, and dark brown eyes framed by severely plucked, arched eyebrows that undoubtedly suggest a somewhat threatening air of otherness. Yet the visualization of biracial feminine looks relies primarily on costume, which, however, resists clarification of the character's situatedness in race categories. The initial images of Mailù evoke associations with Africa: she wears a dress of material with a tropical visual motif, styled along the lines of a muumuu and belted around her slender waist, and her body is adorned with large hoop earrings and a long medallion necklace. However, we next see the female lead in an unbelted kimono with brightly colored dragons standing in stark contrast to the silky black material, projecting an Asian air as she assumes a pose veiled by feigned indifference for Paolo's eyes. The final example of a markedly different fashion statement pictures Mailù as she prepares to leave the plantation, wearing a black sheath dress with a necklace and bracelet that create a stylishly elegant look that might appeal to a Western European perspective. If we approach these costumes— an ensemble of racially and ethnically diverse codes—as markers of Mailù's positions of enunciation, the instability of the racially mixed feminine body as sign becomes evident.

The mixing of iconographic codes in Duranti's drag performance can surely operate in diverse ways. On the one hand, the mingling of signs in dress and ornaments conjuring African and Asian influences collapses distinctions, which are subsumed as non-Western, inscribing Mailù as exotic other. Yet a host of looks, gestures, and icons incorporated in Mailù's performance typify modern European style, thus blurring the boundary between Western and non-Western ways of looking. For example, Mailù is generally framed in poses constructed by established Western cinematic conventions. And she so frequently appears with a cigarette poised in hand or playing a phonograph record that croons the popular song "Sotto la croce del sud"—familiar trappings among female sets *alla moda* in Italy—that they are inseparable from her.[45] In significant ways, the undecidability of the racially mixed female as filmic image and meaning intersects with contradictory attitudes conveyed in writings of the 1930s. One of the fullest portrayals of the ideas and material practices that situated biracial sectors of the population in the Italian colonial hierarchy is provided in "La donna italiana e le nostre colonie" (The Italian Woman and Our Colonies), by Mercedes Astuto. This exposé first charts various points of diversity that distinguish indigenous populations in Eritrea, Somalia, and Libya. A subsequent shift in focus seems to signal a move from "native" peoples to the non-native. Astuto tells us:

The Italian woman has grafted her life onto this local picture taken as a whole, while little by little a new race was forming, the "*meticcia*," fruit of the cross between the indigenous female element and the European male element. The life of the *meticcia* woman, like that of the man, does not differ from the European woman's life. Educated in orphanages or schools run by nuns, when she is grown she works like a white woman. She is a secretary in offices, a clerk in stores, a seamstress, a maid, a babysitter, or a nurse in a hospital.[46]

Several points cannot fail to pique the reader's curiosity. For example, the model of race and gender in sexual relations that Astuto constructs to define the *meticcia* race raises questions about Italian women's desires for indigenous African men.[47] The use of the term *meticcia* also creates a source of confusion, though it is in tune with usage current in the 1930s. Literally, the word *meticcio* and its variants mean mestizo, indicating in Italian a person of mixed white and east Indian race.[48] Nonetheless, the word *meticcio*, and not *mulatto*, which existed as the precise racial term in Italian, was widely used to denote individuals with one parent of an African race and the other of European origin. Furthermore, as Astuto draws parallels between the life the biracial woman leads and that of a European woman, she mentions the educational role of orphanages as well as Catholic schools. Here, and in the description of institutions founded in Cheren and Asmara "for *meticci*, abandoned or boarded,"[49] the reader can glean the potential dislocation of persons of mixed race, who were placed in an institutionalized space separated perhaps from both their interracial family and from black and white communities. Clearly, biracial females and males were not entirely excluded from education and work in the colonies. In fact, according to Astuto, the seashore camp in Massau was set up for "poor, frail children, Italians and *meticci*."[50] However, the production and surveillance of such specific sites spatializes Italian colonial politics, thereby constructing the biracial body as "negating activity," to use Fanon's term. Although Astuto trains her eye on similarities between European and mulatto ways of daily living, six years later Law 822 (13 May 1940) was passed to define the status of the *meticci*, who, as Del Boca explains, "after a debate that lasted half a century to establish the race in which they must be aggregated, are definitively locked into the negro world."[51] Although this decision resolved juridical questions, it failed to solve the traumatic exile of biracial men and women from both white and black forms of affiliation and to allay the anxieties and threats to the imperial Italian body elicited by the *meticci*, who stood for what Guido Cortese characterized as "a politically and morally subversive nature."[52]

Similarly, Brignone's film inscribes both fears and desires attached to the *meticci*, invoked in debates as the "*piaga*," the sore or wound marring the ideal image of Italian colonial identity, while affording audiences with the opportunity to conquer such emotions. In the process, the narrative and visual constructions of biracial drag produce a gendered ideology of racial hybridity in which, as we might expect, the feminine exotic poses the most menacing threats to colonial consciousness. The transgressive performativity of the female *meticcia* act markedly contrasts to the functions fulfilled by the biracial male body. From the time Marco and Paolo first hear of Simone until the moment of his demise, he occupies a relatively stable position as the embodiment of evil[53] whose villainous acts serve as a constant reminder of the element against which the Italian settlers define themselves. As in Mailù's case, the visual language describing Simone's racial origins is not unambiguous. However, the dialogue nominatively classifies the racialized image of Simone and clarifies what he is intended to signify. Marco, for example, refers to Simone as "that *meticcio.*" In an important scene picturing the settler collective, one man declares that the *meticcio* is "a bastard race." From the perspective of native laborers, which is articulated by a worker whose broken Italian conveys his unique relationship to the language and power structure of the colonizers, Simone "is a very evil man," an idea repeated later in the film. The plot amply bears this out as Simone breaks the laws of the land and those of a higher order.

The feminine biracial performance functions in notably different ways, for Mailù's exotic looks heighten the seductiveness of her alluring surface, rendering the male settlers oblivious to the potential dangers hidden within. The opposition between mysterious beauty that invites visual pleasure and the threats concealed below also shapes the language of the femme fatale in Hollywood cinema. As Laura Mulvey contends in her examination of psychic and social structures that are projected onto the female body as sign, which she charts through film and the classical myth of Pandora, "The very attraction of the visible surface suggests an antimony, a 'dialectics of inside and outside,' a topography that reflects the attraction/anxiety ambivalence exerted by the iconography of femininity as mask."[54] Yet what effects does biracial drag have on the distinctions between outside and inside? Since femininity and race are floating signifiers, which connotations aim to anchor them discursively in the specific context of colonial space during Fascism? How does the dialectic between surface and interior, social fantasies and fears, affect the representation of the racially mixed body and the ways spectators may read it?

Shortly after Paolo sets eyes on Mailù, the tension between the exotic woman's captivating allure and her dangerous wiles comes into play, setting the terms of interracial romance and the broader problems it poses. Mailù displays an evocative spectrum of dispositions that range from brooding preoccupation to carefree abandon and romantic dreaminess, tinged with a smoldering sensuality and mystique. These features are unquestionably associated with the traditional femme fatale. However, through dialogue, certain characteristics become explicitly linked to feminine biracial identity as Mailù defines her notion of self. While the romance between Paolo and Mailù intensifies, in moments of intimacy she describes herself as a free-spirited soul and reveals "I like to lose myself dreaming. It's my race." Yet the desire she voices to Paolo, "to feel renewed," implies she may wish to shed the burden of guilt about deceiving Paolo as she plays her part in Simone's scheme. The mise-en-scène conjures the spatial dynamics of secrets, associated largely with the domestic plantation quarters—its windows, blinds, and doors—intensifying the desire and anxiety of discovery. Indeed, Simone spies on Mailù as she talks with Paolo. Unbeknown to Paolo, Mailù watches him from a window as he approaches. Later, she peers through a bamboo shade, gazing at Paolo as he walks off after overhearing Simone threaten to expose her.

Although many elements of the biracial drag act highlight the undecidability of Mailù's position, the representation of her relationships to diverse communities spatializes a bodily politics of race and gender as well as the boundaries transgressed by the trajectory of interracial desire. In contrast to the picture of similarities between European and biracial women drawn by Astuto, Mailù shares little, if anything, with the Italian women settlers who join their husbands once plantation lands have become domesticated, a process that is symbolized by the construction of homes. The three settler women seem to be cut from the same mold; they each have dark hair, full faces, and stolid bodies clothed in conservative rural dress. Moreover, the scenes picturing the white female settlers, which are admittedly brief, do not show them sharing social space with Mailù, though they gossip about the Italian men's infatuation with her and its divisive effects. Similarly, a world of differences separates Mailù from the indigenous black women. Footage of a tribal fertility ritual gives spectators the most sustained look at the young native women, who are lined in a row facing tribesmen. Distinctions between Mailù and the tribal women emerge through the rite defining the space of community affiliation, visual markers such as dress (the women are shot bare-breasted), and the composition of the shots, which are filmed in documentary fashion. Although a close-up catches one woman looking briefly into the camera, she and her fellow women appear impassive, in contrast to the Western poses struck by Mailù or, for example, those in ethnographic photos published in the *Almanacco*.[55] Significantly, Mailù does not appear among the Italian or native onlookers standing nearby to view the spectacle. Instead, intercuts capture the effects of the tribal music as she reclines on a chaise in the shade, her arms held back seductively cradling her head. Paolo, succumbing to the sensuality of Africa, joins Mailù under the canopy and, following a long look Mailù casts into the camera, time nearly stands still as they share a romantic kiss. We could say that such spatial relations and the structure of the gaze thus pose the problem of miscegenation from and for a Western imperialist eye. Although Simone spies upon Mailù, we see her primarily through the eyes of Paolo and the other Italian settlers who look longingly at her. The indigenous men have no access to the gaze. The power and dimensions of the attraction Mailù wields are made clear as the wise Marco tells Paolo, "Everyone's lost their head a little." Moreover, in some ways, the film symbolically associates the particular nature of Mailù's seductiveness with the African lands, which Marco bemoans for the way they slacken the men's will, making them vulnerable to the senses. In this respect, as Landy proposes, Mailù "seems, like the natives, to symbolize Africa, its seductiveness, sensuality, physical weakness, and emotional dependency, that aspect of native life that needs to be eliminated."[56]

From this perspective, the concluding scenes of the film that depict Paolo's conversion and Mailù's departure work within the parameters that structure Western colonialist vision. Once Mailù leaves the plantation, the threats miscegenation poses to racial distinctions disappear, making possible the restoration of the borders between the white settlers and natives, and therefore peace. I want to suggest, however, that upon closer scrutiny the feminine biracial drag performance operates in a more complex fashion, putting into question its terms of representation as well as more general stereotypes associated with women of color. As the scenes of intensifying conflicts between and among the racially mixed and white characters lead to a spectacular climax, viewers arguably see how Mailù's presence disrupts the spirit of collaborative labor, ethics, and the value of productivity, a material monument to "racial prestige." Thus, Marco tells Paolo that his involvement with Mailù "wasn't something worthy of you." However, Mailù also undergoes a conversion, which, in film criticism, is largely eclipsed by Paolo's renewed commitment to the colonial enterprise. Signs of Mailù's transformation come into view as raging flames engulf the plantation. The lens moves from panoramic shots of the fire profiled against the dark horizon to long shots picturing native and Italian men and women who pass buckets of water from one to another, each person working with the other, bound literally and symbolically by a single goal. While Simone makes his escape, we see a close-up of Mailù as she ministers to one of the injured Italian men, who looks up at her filled not with desire but with gratitude. This act of goodness, from which Mailù cannot benefit since she knows Paolo heard Simone's threats to expose her part in the scheme, aligns the racially mixed woman with the ethics of the social body, for she places another's welfare before self-interest.

As further demonstrated by the confession scene between Mailù and Paolo, the refashioning of the biracial drag act incorporates new codes, which resist stabilizing the feminine miscegenational body in the regulatory fiction spatializing the politics of race and gender that bind the Italian empire to the motherland. The dialogue and mise-en-scène alter the dialectic between beguiling surface and hidden deception because Mailù's unguileful revelations show a commitment to honesty and the order of production structuring the colonial settlement. Just before departing, Mailù declares her love to Paolo, and, most important of all, wants him to know her "motives are honest" and to remember her "without contempt." Indeed, she freely admits she deceived him. These disclosures suggest the purification of Mailù's love and the racialized image. The text therefore subverts the image of non-European women as always sexually available that circulated in Italy as well as other nations at the time.[57] Yet the final words Mailù speaks create the contradiction upon which Brignone's figuration of the racially mixed female rests. When Paolo suggests that Mailù could stay, she responds "There are good people here who have to work. My presence here is like a poison." The shot of the car taking her through the plantation gates testifies to Mailù's honesty, the purity of her motives, and the values of colonial settlement she appears to uphold through self-exile.

Yet as the biracial performance delivered by Duranti stirs interests, sympathies, and curiosity, it may engage female and male viewers in a process of decipherment that goes beyond the ending. In contrast to the plot line focusing on Paolo, which is neatly resolved as he and Marco resume their work, Mailù's story is open-ended. When Paolo wants to know where she will go, she replies "I don't know. Everyone has their own destiny." The opening of the plantation gates can suggest freedom and mobility. If Mailù returns to Italy, as Hay states, how will she fashion her identity? Do the final contradictory signs of Mailù's biracial looks create another racial mythology, similar to the model delineated by hooks as a "blending of black female savage tempered by those elements of whiteness that soften this image, giving it an aura of virtue and innocence"?[58] What symbolic implications might emerge as the biracial woman penetrates the motherland? We must also ask whether these questions and those raised explicitly within the film narrative pale because biracial feminine identity is represented through *meticcia* drag played by a white Italian actress. Donald Bogle examines a similar point in his study on black actors and the representation of race in American films. He argues that by casting white actors to play blacks, a common practice in the 1930s and 1940s which, he states, ensured both a larger audience at the box office and identification, an issue such as interracial romance "upset no one because, in actuality, it was no such thing at all."[59]

While keeping Bogle's proposition in consideration, we must also remember that Italy presents different political and cultural dynamics during Fascism. As Ben-Ghiat notes, commentators were deeply concerned that Brignone's film might incite forbidden interracial desires. Furthermore, I would like to open the possibility that spectators and, for the purposes of this study, Italian women spectators in particular might question features of biracial looks precisely because they were staged by the white female body and therefore did not slip into the illusion of a natural corporeality. If so, the representation of *meticcia* identity, interracial romance, attitudes toward miscegenation, and the system of colonial relations between Italians and indigenous African races may have engaged women among the viewing audience through their power as heated subjects of debate. The tastes and interests in the cinema expressed by women moviegoers in 1937 supports this speculation. In response to a contest promoted by the journal *Cinema*, a young woman from Milan wrote that she preferred "a film that poses a problem or has a thesis. Keeping in mind the social function of art, I find that this is a vital point for the film and the people who created it."[60] Similarly, a homemaker from Comense, who stated she went to the movies in search of an escape, proposed "If the cinema were defined as the visual book par excellence, then it has a real mission of its own to fulfill for humanity. And therefore, it must excite enthusiasm in the crowds and educate them, with works of art that debate the most current problems: psychological, human, moral, etc."[61] Although it would be unwise to claim paradigmatic value for these views, they suggestively introduce an alternative way to theorize positions of female viewing subjects and the ways they might be situated in relation to the colonial discourse constructed in *Sotto la croce del sud* and in the broader sphere of Italian popular film culture. Likewise, the materials examined here illustrate the need for a more critical frame of mind that looks at the roles played by both race and gender, among other terms of social identity, in the construction and negotiations of racialized images instantiating power relations. Such a project would ideally alter our perspective on the Italian colonial gaze that was designed during Fascism and on how it may or may not exceed the historical parameters of its invention in postwar cinema, as exemplified, for instance, by the unforgettable African tribal dance performed by Monica Vitti in full native drag, in Michelangelo Antonioni's 1962 film *Eclisse* (*Eclipse*).

Notes

I want to express my profound thanks to Fiovo Bitti for his work in Italian archives to locate the materials from the *Almanacco della donna italiana* on my behalf. I am also grateful for the award from the Consiglio Nazionale Delle Ricerche (1996), which made it possible for me to conduct research at the Library of Congress. Portions of this article were first presented at the 1998 AAIS Conference in Chicago. Unless otherwise indicated, all translations into English are my own.

1. *Cinema,* July 1936.

2. As I have suggested elsewhere, by the productivity of Fascism I mean the processes by which, as the regime stages, refashions, and distributes power and limits, it fosters productive engagements even among those texts that may refute Fascist positions. See Robin Pickering-Iazzi, *Politics of the Visible: Writing Women, Culture, and Fascism* (Minneapolis: University of Minnesota Press, 1997).

3. Ettore G. Mattia, "Testimonianza di Ettore G. Mattia," in *Pratiche basse e telefoni bianchi. Cinema italiano 1923–1943,* ed. Gianfranco Graziani (Pescara: Tracce, 1986), 54.

4. See Marcia Landy, *Fascism in Film: The Italian Commercial Cinema, 1931–1943* (Princeton, N.J.: Princeton University Press, 1986); and James Hay, *Popular Film Culture in Fascist Italy: The Passing of the Rex* (Bloomington: Indiana University Press, 1987).

5. Although the present study examines how white female viewers may be solicited by colonial discourses and how they may exert the power of racial oppression in the imbricating symbolic and material spheres, another pressing area of inquiry concerns black female spectatorship. For an important essay that examines the dangers of exposing Italian popular films to indigenous African peoples as well as the notions of so-called native spectatorship in the colonies, see "Cinema per gli indigeni," *Cinema* 64 (1939): 109.

6. In her informative study on Doris Duranti, Nunzia Messina underscores how the star came to epitomize the exotic, stating "The femme fatale of the Italian cinema of the 1930s was identified with the stirring, mysterious allure of Doris Duranti, the black Orchid." See Nunzia Messina, *Le donne del fascismo. Massaie rurali e dive del cinema nel ventennio* (Roma: Ellemme, 1987), 71. Also interesting are Duranti's own recollections of stardom during Fascism and its aftermath, presented from an apologist position in Doris Duranti, *Romanzo della mia vita* (Milano: Mondadori, 1987). I thank Jacqueline Reich for bringing this source to my attention.

7. Francesco Savio, *Ma l'amore no. Realismo, formalismo, propaganda e telefoni bianchi nel cinema italiano di regime (1930–1943)* (Milano: Sonzogno, 1975), 338.

8. W. J. T. Mitchell, "Introduction," in *Landscape and Power*, ed. W. J. T. Mitchell (Chicago: University of Chicago Press, 1994), 2.

9. See Wolfgang Schivelbusch, *The Railway Journey: Trains and Travel in the Nineteenth Century* (New York: Urizen Books, 1979); and Mary Ann Doane, *The Desire to Desire* (Bloomington: Indiana University Press, 1987).

10. Giuliana Bruno, *Streetwalking on a Ruined Map: Cultural Theory and the City Films of Elvira Notari* (Princeton, N.J.: Princeton University Press, 1993), 51.

11. Mary Ann Doane, "Misrecognition and Identity," in *Explorations in Film Theory: Selected Essays from Cine-Tracts*, ed. Ron Burnett (Bloomington: Indiana University Press, 1991), 19.

12. Texts exemplifying this tendency include Paolo Araldi, *La politica demografica di Mussolini* (Mantova: Mussolinia, 1929); Julius Evola, *Rivolta contro il mondo moderno* (1934; Roma: Mediterranea, 1969); and Alfredo Panzini, *Signorine* (Roma: Mondadori, 1921).

13. Angelo Del Boca, *Gli italiani in Africa Orientale. La caduta dell'Impero*, vol. 3 (Bari: Laterza, 1982); and Karen Pinkus, *Bodily Regimes: Italian Advertising under Fascism* (Minneapolis: University of Minnesota Press, 1995).

14. Elisabetta Mondello, *La nuova italiana. La donna nella stampa e nella cultura del ventennio* (Roma: Riuniti, 1987), 58.

15. Mondello, *La nuova italiana*, 165.

16. As de Grazia points out, levels of illiteracy, especially among women in southern agricultural zones, were still relatively high, and magazines were expensive in relationship to working-class earnings. Among girls and young women in urban centers, going to the movies became a popular pastime. For a more comprehensive treatment of female leisure-time practices, see Victoria de Grazia, *How Fascism Ruled Women: Italy, 1922–1945* (Berkeley: University of California Press, 1992), especially Chapters 5 and 7.

17. Pinkus, *Bodily Regimes*, 24–25.

18. Ciro Poggiali, "La donna italiana in A. O.," *Almanacco della donna italiana* (1939): 54.

19. Amadeo Fani, "La donna e l'impero," *Almanacco della donna italiana* (1937): 129.

20. Mariolina Graziosi, "Gender Struggle and the Social Manipulation and Ideological Use of Gender Identity in the Interwar Years," in *Mothers of Invention: Women, Italian Fascism, and Culture*, ed. Robin Pickering-Iazzi (Minneapolis: University of Minnesota Press, 1995).

21. Fani, "La donna e l'impero," 129.

22. Ibid., 130.

23. Several articles confer legendary status on Maria Brighenti (1872–1915), in whose name, according to Mercedes Astuto, "the Italian woman conse-

crated the new territories for the Motherland." See Mercedes Astuto, "La donna italiana e le nostre colonie," *Almanacco della donna italiana* (1934): 131. Astuto's representation is important for the image she fabricates for Brighenti, a woman of "charity and goodness" (132) and a "delicate, strong flower of Italian femininity" (133), who was killed in Tripolitania in 1915 as World War I incited rebel insurgence in the colonies. Fani's article and Silvia Benedettini's "La donna in Africa Orientale," *Almanacco della donna italiana* (1937): 399–402, invoke Brighenti in a similar fashion, as a heroic symbol of the Italian colonial pioneer woman.

24. Fani, "La donna e l'impero," 129.

25. Poggiali, "La donna italiana in A. O.," 73.

26. Mercedes Astuto, "Attività dei fasci femminili," *Almanacco della donna italiana* (1937): 391.

27. Fani, "La donna e l'impero," 130.

28. Ibid., 130.

29. Elsewhere, I further examine issues related to desire that were raised by exotic colonial fantasies crafted in writings published in the *Almanacco* and *Domus*. See Robin Pickering-Iazzi, "Structures of Feminine Fantasy and Italian Empire Building, 1930–1940," *Italica* 77, no. 3 (2000): 400–417.

30. Poggiali, "La donna italiana in A. O.," 73.

31. *Almanacco della donna italiana* (1939): 74–75.

32. Silvana Palma, *L'Italia coloniale* (Rome: Riuniti, 1999), 170.

33. Poggiali, "La donna italiana in A.O.," 56.

34. Among the articles detailing a range of sectors for women's employment in the colonies are Astuto's "La donna italiana e le nostre colonie," "Attività dei fasci femminili," and Benedettini's "La donna in Africa Orientale."

35. Benedettini, "La donna in Africa Orientale," 400.

36. Ibid., 400.

37. Ibid., 401. Mohamed Aden conducts a salient critique of the entrenched myth of the Italian colonist as a beneficent bearer of civilization and progress. See Mohamed Aden, "Italy: Cultural Identity and Spatial Opportunism from a Post-Colonial Perspective," in *Revisioning Italy: National Identity and Global Culture,* ed. Beverly Allen and Mary Russo (Minneapolis: University of Minnesota Press, 1997).

38. Guido Brignone; from Hay, *Popular Film Culture in Fascist Italy: The Passing of the Rex,* 192.

39. James Hay introduces this reading, among others, in *Popular Film Culture in Fascist Italy.*

40. For an impeccably researched history of Italian colonization in East Africa encompassing debates about race, laws on miscegenation, and the positions on colonialism adopted by prominent figures in the Fascist hierarchy,

among other topics, see Del Boca, *Gli italiani in African Orientale*, vol. 3. John Sorenson examines diversified positions on the racial identity of Ethiopians in the interwar years as well as the lasting effects of Italian colonial intervention, in *Imagining Ethiopia: Struggles for History and Identity in the Horn of Africa* (New Brunswick, N.J.: Rutgers University Press, 1993).

41. See Wahneema Lubiano, "Don't Talk with Your Eyes Closed: Caught in the Hollywood Gun Sights," in *Borders, Boundaries, and Frames: Essays in Cultural Criticism and Cultural Studies*, ed. Mae G. Henderson (New York: Routledge, 1995); and Judith Butler, *Gender Trouble: Feminism and the Subversion of Identity* (New York: Routledge, 1990). See also Jane Marcus's suggestive examination of Nancy Cunard's forms of drag performance in "Bonding and Bondage: Nancy Cunard and the Making of the *Negro Anthology*," in *Borders, Boundaries, and Frames: Essays in Cultural Criticism and Cultural Studies*, ed. Mae G. Henderson (New York: Routledge, 1995).

42. Lubiano, "Don't Talk with Your Eyes Closed," 192.

43. Butler, *Gender Trouble*, 137.

44. I borrow this term from Frantz Fanon's *Black Skin, White Masks*, trans. Charles Lam Markmann (New York: Grove Press, 1967).

45. See James Hay, *Popular Film Culture in Fascist Italy;* and Ruth Ben-Ghiat, "Envisioning Modernity: Desire and Discipline in the Italian Fascist Film," *Critical Inquiry* 23, no. 1 (1996): 109-144, for further readings of Mailù's Western and non-Western looks.

46. Astuto, "La donna italiana nelle nostre colonie," 119.

47. Karen Pinkus has recently scrutinized this subject in her important study, "'Black and Jew': Race & Resistance to Psychoanalysis in Italy," *Annali d'Italianistica* 16 (1998): 145-167.

48. For a salient analysis of literary representations of biracial identity developed in the specific context of Italian colonization, see Graziella Parati, "Italian Fathers and Eritrean Daughters: Women without Nationality," in *Gendered Contexts: New Perspectives in Italian Cultural Studies*, ed. Laura Benedetti, Julia L. Hairston, and Silvia M. Ross (New York: Peter Lang, 1996). Of related interest are also Graziella Parati's "Italophone Voices," *Italian Studies in Southern Africa* 2 (1995): 1-15; and "Scrittura meticcia," *Via Dogana. Rivista di politica* 9 (1993): 10-11, which make an important contribution to this growing area of study.

49. Astuto, "La donna italiana nelle nostre colonie," 119.

50. Ibid., 120.

51. Del Boca, *Gli italiani in Africa Orientale*, 238.

52. Ibid., 249.

53. The male *meticcio* drag act, which I can only sketch here, warrants further attention for the visual images constructed and how they may inscribe fears and anxieties as challenges to Western masculinity.

54. Laura Mulvey, "Pandora: Topographies of the Mask and Curiosity," in *Sexuality and Space*, ed. Beatriz Colomina (New York: Princeton Architectural Press, 1992), 60.

55. The articles I examine carry a full array of photographic materials. See Giuseppe Piazza, "La donna nelle nostre colonie africane," *Almanacco della donna italiana* (1921): 233–241, for examples of typical Western poses, especially the photo of the young Arab women from Tripoli (234).

56. Landy, *Fascism in Film*, 154–155.

57. See Pinkus, *Bodily Regimes;* and bell hooks, *Black Looks: Race and Representation* (Boston: South End Press, 1992), for analyses of the eroticization of the black female body in Italian advertising of the interwar years, performance art, and film culture.

58. hooks, *Black Looks*, 72.

59. Donald Bogle, *Toms, Coons, Mulattoes, Mammies, and Bucks: An Interpretive History of Blacks in American Films*, 3rd ed. (New York: Continuum, 1994), 152. Additional issues associated with visual and verbal representations of race, such as colorism, passing, and black female spectatorship, are interrogated in, for example, Alice Walker, *In Search of Our Mothers' Gardens* (San Diego: Harcourt Brace Jovanovich, 1983); Frances Stubbs and Elizabeth Hadley Freydberg, "The Mulatto Woman—Color and Caste in American Films," in *Multiple Voices in Feminist Film Criticism*, ed. Diane Carson, Linda Dittmar, and Janice R. Welsch (Minneapolis: University of Minnesota Press, 1994); and Jane Gaines, "White Privilege and Looking Relations: Race and Gender in Feminist Film Theory," in *Multiple Voices in Feminist Film Criticism*, ed. Diane Carson, Linda Dittmar, and Janice R. Welsch (Minneapolis: University of Minnesota Press, 1994).

60. *Cinema* 2 (1937): 378.

61. Ibid.

PART III
Fascism and Cinema in (Con)texts

8

Seeing Red

The Soviet Influence on Italian Cinema in the Thirties

Piero Garofalo

Commenting upon the state of Italian cinema, Mussolini once stated: "The Russian film is at the foremost post. In Italy, we shall in no time have the means for that too."[1] As a cultural practice, cinema occupied a privileged space in the National Fascist Party's efforts to develop a palingenetic Italian society. Mussolini's oft-cited dictum, "Cinema is the strongest weapon," implicitly recognized that film, as a locus for the production of particular desires and discourses, provided an effective mass medium for the regime's rhetoric of regenerative ethos. By appropriating cultural institutions such as film for the propagation of Fascism's foundational aspirations, the government attempted to mold and manipulate social subjects. To achieve these goals, Fascism publicly promoted the impression of an autochthonous cinema while privately acknowledging the industry's assimilation of successful non-national models. As Mussolini's admiration for the USSR's film industry made clear, Russia's model was the one to emulate.

Although Hollywood exerted the most visible foreign influence on Italian film production, it was only one among several cinematic traditions that Italian directors incorporated in their films.[2] Scholarship has neglected the relevance of Soviet cinema to the development of the domestic feature film in the 1930s. While only a very limited selection of the Soviet avant-garde production circulated in Italy, these texts resonated among Italian cineastes of the period. This crucial exposure to the Soviet film scene was possible because Fascism took a broadly pragmatic approach to the emergence of the Leninist state, which the Italian regime perceived as paralleling its own seizure of power. In fact, the

Bolshevik Revolution provided a functional example of societal interpellation from which Fascism transposed practices to its own consensus-generating machinery. Mussolini's above-mentioned cinematic stock phrase was none other than a rehashing of Lenin's "Of all the arts for us the most important is cinema."[3]

This essay explores how both Italy's sociopolitical interest in Russia and the ideological relationships between the two states led to the development of a certain Italian cinema inspired by the Soviet model. Four films stand out as early efforts to incorporate Soviet-style cinema into Fascist production: Alessandro Blasetti's *Sole* (*Sun*, 1929) and *Terra madre* (*Mother Earth*, 1931), Mario Camerini's *Rotaie* (*Rails*, 1930), and Walter Ruttmann's *Acciaio* (*Steel*, 1933). These films fall in the mid-range of a period of expanded Italian interest in the Soviet Union that spanned roughly a dozen years, from Mussolini's diplomatic recognition of the Leninist state in 1924 to the hostilities of the Spanish Civil War in 1936.[4] During this increased awareness of the USSR, film constituted but one element in the circulation of multiple discourses that informed the development of this new Italian cinema. Political constraints often prevented the screening of Soviet films in Italy so that exposure to secondary sources, criticism, and theoretical manifestos formulated many Italian impressions of this cinema.

The formal and thematic experimentalism of these four texts contrasted sharply with the contemporary features that were circulating and indicated a new direction for Italian cinema. In fact, critics' reactions were generally positive about these innovations, which they saw as a welcome change from the dominant bourgeois productions. They found this new cinema to be extremely Fascist and hoped that it might inaugurate a new era in the industry. While all these expectations were not realized, the films did lend themselves to a philo-Fascist interpretation and succeeded in transforming Soviet aesthetics into a filmic representation on Italian soil. What differentiates these texts from Soviet films, however, is their lack of revolutionary fervor—an essential component of Soviet film theory and practice. Ultimately, *Sole, Terra madre, Rotaie,* and *Acciaio* serve only to reinforce rather than challenge classical narrative paradigms and rigid class hierarchy.

Fascist Italy and Communist Russia

From the end of the 1920s to the mid-1930s, the Fascist regime displayed a vivid interest in the USSR in an effort to determine any similarities between their respective revolutions. This apparent ideological incongruity can be explained as a vestige of Italian foreign policy before the March on Rome and was entirely consonant with Mussolini's realpolitik. In fact, one of Mussolini's initial forays into international diplomacy involved the recognition de jure of Soviet Russia as part of the commerce and navigation treaty that the two nations signed on 7 February 1924.

From a domestic perspective, this renewed governmental concern manifested itself frequently in the press. Italian newspapers and magazines devoted ample space and regular columns to events in the Soviet Union.[5] The numerous journalists serving as correspondents provided special-interest features on every aspect of the Soviet system. Between 1928 and 1934, for example, *La Stampa* had no less than five Russian correspondents, among whom were Pietro Sessa, Curzio Malaparte, Corrado Sofia, and Corrado Alvaro, while *Il Tevere* boasted the services of poet Vincenzo Cardarelli, who arrived in Moscow in September of 1928.[6]

The public interest generated by the USSR in the Italian press can be best understood by the marginalized positions that the two nations occupied in the balance of world power. Although the Soviet regime was the ideological antithesis of the Fascist regime, the Italian press often compared their shared opposition to the decadence of the "Old Order" and its commitment to a degenerative form of capitalism. Furthermore, with the failure of the Third International to foment revolution and the subsequent diffusion of the Communist threat, Fascism pursued a foreign policy in which the USSR, regardless of its internal governing, was judged solely on its geopolitical and economic relevance.

In his desire to assume a prominent role in both European and Mediterranean affairs, Mussolini recognized the strategic importance of the Soviet Union for establishing a feasible balance of power in Europe. In addition, given the precarious condition of the Western economies, he realized that favorable relations with the USSR were essential to bolstering Italy's economic base. Pragmatically refuting the dominant Western policy of effecting change through isolation, Rome moved to solidify its relations with Moscow. In fact, on 2 August 1930, the two countries signed a favorable commercial treaty granting each other special trade privileges; they expanded this initial agreement with another trade treaty on 28 April 1931. This rapport culminated in the pact of friendship, neutrality, and non-aggression signed on 2 September 1933.

Fascism's realpolitik distinguished between ideology and political strategy and, on the basis of the latter, sought to improve relations with Soviet Russia. Mussolini thought that the pact with the Soviet Union could be used, as the need arose, either to keep Germany in check or to lessen French influence in Central Europe. In this respect, Mussolini considered the internal politics of the USSR to be a matter of domestic policy with which Italy need not concern itself. As he stated in 1933:

> We cannot ignore Russia's potential. A population of 164 million must be treated as a world power. Italy has recognized Russia's right to assume the position that it is due. An unbridgeable distance separates us from Russia in political theory, but these political theories mostly address internal governing, in which Italy does not intend to interfere now, nor ever. We do not have hostile intentions against any nation.[7]

Fascism set aside pragmatically ideological differences to pursue its own self-interest. Despite the discomfiture that both this attitude and the pact of friendship caused other Western nations, Mussolini now presented himself in the international political arena as a primary artificer of European politics.

This détente strategy also had a domestic component. Special correspondents' reports promoted the state's cautious interest in the Soviet Union to the Italian public. For the *Popolo d'Italia*, Mirko Ardemagni and Luigi Barzini, in 1931 and in 1934 respectively, regularly conveyed the USSR's strategic importance as well as its exotic fascination.[8] In 1934, Barzini wrote of a country "fierce and human, paradoxical and reasonable, barbarous and progressive, absurd and logical."[9] These continuous contradictions—replete with extreme imagery—captured the public's imagination and allowed the Fascist regime more maneuverability in addressing Soviet affairs. In fact, the single most recurring theme in the press of the period was the effort to bridge the ideological gap in order to find affinities between the Fascist and Bolshevik revolutions.

Ideological Relationships between the States

Beyond a general recognition of the need for the two countries to live in peaceful coexistence, within Fascism there were divergent views about how the two nations could relate to each other. While recognizing the inherent affinities between the two revolutions (both of which were situated beyond traditional political systems), the most dominant tendency —not surprisingly—was to consider Fascist doctrine indisputably superior to Soviet doctrine. In 1934, Renzo Bertoni went so far as to suggest that the only possibility for "saving" Russia lay in the Soviets' abandonment of Communism and embracement of Fascism.[10]

More interesting is the sector that considered the Soviet system valid within its historical context and therefore sought to understand it objectively. The writings of such critics as Vincenzo Cardarelli, Ugo D'Andrea, Giuseppe Gregoraci, Ettore Lo Gatto, Curzio Malaparte, and Rodolfo Mosca exposed the contradictions between Marxist-Leninist doctrine and the current Soviet state. Their critique, however, was not geared toward elevating Fascism at the expense of Communism; rather, they attempted to maintain objectivity by attributing these inconsistencies to the perceived utopian tendencies of Marxism. Stemming from these analyses was the pragmatic conclusion that the USSR had consolidated its political position to such a degree that, despite Western illusions, there could be no imminent return to pre-socialist Russia. Whatever the merits of the Soviet system, the consensus that emerged from the press was that Mussolini's inclusive policy was the most productive one to pursue because it increased both the international prestige of Italy and the stability of Europe.

In addition to the differences between the two countries, there also existed numerous affinities that the press explored. For example, both nations were late arrivals to the world of modern industrialization, to whose perceived decadence they juxtaposed their own vigorous energy —one through corporatism, the other through collective Bolshevism. And while the distinctions between extreme corporatism and socialism were at times blurred, they remained the defining characteristics of the two systems. In fact, for Fascism, collectivism in the sense of standardization was not limited to the Soviet system but was also associated with the United States: both countries had created an enormous capitalist machinery founded on class (as opposed to caste) and both were driven by extreme mechanization. However, while communism was geared toward the collective, capitalism was geared toward the individual. Fascism saw itself as superseding both systems because its collectivism subordinated individual concerns to the needs of the nation while maintaining individuality and differentiation, culminating in the importance of the hierarchy. From this perspective, the theory of corporatism sublimated the economic and social concerns of particular groups into a superior spiritual sphere in the service of the nation, while collectivism was devoid of spiritual authority because it served class. The conclusion was that Fascism had united all classes through corporatism, while the USSR's foundation was the proletariat class.[11]

In the 1920s and early 1930s, *Critica fascista*, the journal founded by Giuseppe Bottai in 1923, dedicated many pages to the affinities and divergences between Rome and Moscow. *Critica fascista* examined a broad range of political, economic, social, and cultural issues, including the power struggle between Trotsky and Stalin, contrasting the former's ideological intransigence with the latter's political realism. In fact, at one point Bottai himself risked being associated with Trotsky-ism.[12] Although careful to distinguish the political-ideological aspects of Trotskyism from the state and economic apparatus, these contributions considered the October Revolution to supersede the decadent liberal-democratic system. From this common premise, some even extended the argument that Bolshevik Russia represented "the prelude of Fascism,"[13] while others thought that the Soviet state represented the final stage of capitalism.[14] For the latter, the actual irreconcilability between the two revolutions lay in their conceptualizations of life and of the world: Fascism was the "religion of spirit" while Bolshevism was the "religion of matter."[15] From this debate, two affinities emerged: the revolutions were both anti-liberal and anti-democratic, and they both pursued a totali-tarian state model. Of course, what remained unstated was that under-lying both systems was the cult of personality. In these discussions, Mussolini evolved into a metonymical figure who was rhetorically iden-tified with all things Italian both within Italy and in the international arena. As undersecretary of press and propaganda Dino Alfieri affirmed in 1935: "Mussolini incarnates . . . the sublime myth of the Fatherland and of the Nation. No one today equals him. . . . He is the *only* one to whom the new generations, anxious for freedom, look. He is the master of life . . . the expression of national genius, even in its universal as-pects, the greatest of the Italians, the Italian in the world."[16] Mussolini was no longer merely the national leader but also a political and spiritual prophet. Stalin cultivated a similar larger-than-life image of himself through which he became the figurative father of the state.

Although it recognized the innovative aspects of Soviet society, the general consensus in the Fascist press was that in 1917 Russia had passed from one form of slavery to another because its power base re-mained the police and the bureaucracy. And yet, Fascism remained cu-riously open to the Soviet experiment. Regarding this issue, Giacomo Gandolfi wrote in 1935:

> We Western Europeans have to admit that not all people have reached the same level of civilization and that the systems that would be inexplicable and unjust to us can be indispensable to lesser-developed nations.
>
> And since communist theorists commit the error of believing that regimes and political opinions can be built in a row, let us not fall into the opposite heresy, presuming that our way of thinking and of living is the only one applicable to all people in all situa-tions. And last, let us not forget that the Soviet regime, by doc-

trine, has to battle all customs and to search within each order of
ideas the most new and rational solutions.[17]

In generating consensus for Mussolini's foreign policy, the press promoted a version of cultural pluralism that explained and justified the
government's political strategy. The suggestion that not all countries
were sufficiently developed for the Fascist revolution explained how
Italy could continue to interact with nations whose goals were at odds
with its own. Such opportunistic open-mindedness characterized much
of Fascism's relations with the USSR.

Soviet Cinema in Italy

In general, Soviet avant-garde cinema was concerned with aesthetic, political, economic, and social issues as well as more personal ones, which
varied among directors. This confluence of subject matters prevented
the cinema debate of the period from being reducible to an extension of
the political command. In fact, the dominant discussion was animated
by efforts to assess cinema's specificity in relationship to the theatre. Of
course, Soviet cinema was not a monolithic entity. In particular, its
montage tradition (itself widely diverse), as opposed to that of narrative
cinema, spearheaded the Soviet influence in Italy and Europe.[18]

Soviet avant-garde films were received with great interest in Italy because they seemed to represent the new order that the Bolshevik Revolution had created, an order in which art assumed a more prominent
position than it held under capitalism. This new cinema, an art of the
machine age, made manifest its pedagogic possibilities—an aspect of
film that attracted and intrigued Italian filmmakers. However, neither
for the Soviets nor for the Italians did this exploration of cinematic potential reduce itself to a facile equation with political engagement. For
film directors committed to the social and aesthetic revolutions implicit
in modernist movements, such as Futurism, in which art and science
converged, Soviet cinema presented an art of the new age freed from
liberal-democratic values of the fin de siècle. Embodying new relations of both production and consumption, this cinema exemplified the
means of social representation to which Fascism aspired.

Soviet films first began to be screened abroad in 1921, through the
Berlin-based Internationale Arbeiterhilfe, or Workers' International
Relief (WIR). The WIR helped to produce and distribute the films internationally in the early 1920s through Workers' Film Societies. As
the primary venue outside the USSR for screening Soviet films, the

Berlin Film Festival generated publicity for those avant-garde texts as well as an opportunity to view them. From Germany, the Soviet films often moved on to Paris, to London, and then to the United States. While the Berlin screening of Sergei Eisenstein's *Bronenosets Potëmkin* (*The Battleship Potemkin*) on 29 April 1926 inaugurated the Soviet cinema's dramatic impact on the international community, Italian spectators had to wait three more years to enjoy Eisenstein's work. Because of the limited viewing possibilities, the Venice International Film Festival developed into an important vehicle for the dissemination of Soviet filmic texts in Italy.

At the first Venice International Film Festival, held in 1932, forty-two films were screened. Among these were Nikolai Ekk's *Putyovka v zhizn'* (*The Path to Life*, 1931), which received both great acclaim and a referendum prize, Ivan Pravov and Olga Preobrazhenskaya's *Tikhif Don* (*The Cossacks of the Don*, 1930), and Alexander Dovzhenko's *Zemlya* (*The Earth*, 1930), which, while not rewarded by the jury, still left an indelible impression on Italian filmmakers.[19] At the next Festival in 1934, the USSR received a Biennial Cup for the best national presentation with Grigori Alexandrov's *Vesyolye rebyata* (*Jazz Comedy*, 1934), Dovzhenko's *Ivan* (*Ivan the Terrible*, 1932), Alexander Ptushko's *Novyi Gulliver* (*New Gulliver*, 1934), Mikhail Romm's *Pyshka* (*Boule de suif*, 1934), Grigori Rashal's *Petersburgskaya noch'* (*Petersburg Night*), Y. Poselsky's documentary *Chelyuskin*, Vertov's *Tri pesni o Lenine* (*Three Songs of Lenin*, 1934), and Vladimir Petrov's *Groza* (*The Storm*, 1934). This prominent Soviet presence is not surprising, since the inspiration for the Festival came from Luciano De Feo, director of the Istituto Internazionale della Cinematografia Educativa (International Institute of Educational Film), who, in 1928, traveled to the Soviet Union, where he viewed the films of Eisenstein, Pudovkin, Dovzhenko, and Vertov.[20]

Prior to this direct exposure, Soviet cinema had entered Italy indirectly through France, Germany, and, to a lesser degree, Britain. Without immediate access to Soviet texts, Italian filmmakers contented themselves with the critical evaluations of René Marchand and Pierre Weinstein's *L'Art dans la Russie nouvelle: Le Cinéma* (1927), Léon Moussinac's *Le Cinéma Soviétique* (1928), and the French journals *Ciné-ciné* and *Le Revue de cinéma*. To a lesser degree, English studies such as Bryher's *Film Problems of Soviet Russia* (1929) and Huntly Carter's *The New Theatre and Cinema of Soviet Russia* (1924) also circulated among Italian cineastes. In addition, specialized journals in Italy were initiating original criticism. For example, *Cinematografo, Cinemalia, Close-Up, Rivista del cinema educatore,* and *Lo Spettacolo d'Italia* provided a space for the articulation of Soviet montage theory. The journal *Inter-*

cine contained monthly updates on Soviet productions, and *L'Italia letteraria* ran a two-part essay from Eisenstein's "Della forma cinematografica" ("Film Form") in its 28 May 1932 and 4 June 1932 issues. Even Eugenio Giovanetti's early theoretical analysis, *Il cinema e le arti meccaniche* (1930), devoted considerable space to both Pudovkin and Vertov.

In Italy, the dissemination of Soviet films occurred primarily through private cinema clubs such as the Cine Club Italiano and Cineguf (film clubs sponsored by the Gruppi Universitari Fascisti, or GUF—Fascist University Groups) rather than through public projections. In addition to promoting cinema and cultivating film professionals, the GUF organized local film festivals and special screenings. Non-GUF film clubs also provided a space for viewing and discussing film. For example, Massimo Bontempelli, head of the Cine Club Italiano, sponsored a screening of Konstantin Eggert's *Medvezh'ya svad'ba* (*The Bear's Wedding*, 1926) for the membership in 1930. Though less influential than the private cinema clubs, exclusive public screenings of these texts did occur in Italy; however, the general distribution of Soviet films remained problematic. In 1929, select Italian audiences enjoyed *The Battleship Potemkin* as well as Pudovkin's films *Konets Sankt-Peterburga* (*The End of St. Petersburg*, 1927) and *Potomok Chingis-khana* (*Storm over Asia*, 1929). In 1930, several more films were shown, including Olga Preobrazhenskaya's *Baby ryazanskie* (*Women of Ryazan*, 1927) and two by Fyodor Otsep: *Kollezhskii registrator* (*The Station Master*, 1925) and *Zhivoi trup* (*The Living Corpse*, 1929).[21]

The Italian film industry's cultural aperture to non-national modes of cinematic production was part of a preexisting social trend that sought to incorporate European and American innovations into Italian society. Known as *Stracittà* (ultra-city), this avant-garde urbanistic movement, spearheaded by Massimo Bontempelli's *Novecento* group, promoted modernism as the most effective instrument for representing national-popular culture. In the Soviet Union, Russian Futurism and filmmaking movements such as FEKS (Factory of the Eccentric Actor) extolled similar ideals because the USSR was also attempting a rapid economic modernization. Much of Fascism's modernist rhetoric coincided with *Stracittà* precepts, and this celebration of the machine age outweighed base ideological considerations. Similarly, curiosity about and a fascination with the modern (in contrast to the self-awareness of a certain provincialism) inspired cineastes to turn their gaze abroad. For Fascism and filmmakers alike, politics and aesthetics justified the need to establish contacts and exchanges with the Soviet cinema.

In 1927, articles on Soviet cinema began to appear in *Rivista inter-*

nazionale del cinema educatore and in *Cinemondo*. These studies emphasized film's pedagogical potential and drew upon Russia's mastery of
this strategy to urge Italy to do likewise.[22] Three years later, in the pages
of *Cinematografo*, Mario Serandrei discerned in the Soviet film industry
a synthesis of culture and politics that he perceived to be absent from
Italian cinema: "The Russian Revolution could not have a cinematic art
different from that which it had and has. And if any one artist may err,
all the artists of a nation do not err. Nor can all of art be placed at the
service of an idea, if this idea were not truly felt by the artists."[23] In his
view, Fascism needed to establish a similar symbiotic rapport between
art and the State.

Just as the October Revolution articulated Fascism's opposition to a
degenerative capitalism, the Soviet film industry articulated Fascism's
interest in reeducation and the organization of mass culture. To that
end, different ministries took measures to secure a national cinema. An
important aspect of increasing government involvement in the industry
occurred in 1926, with the nationalization of L'Unione Cinematografica
Educativa (Educational Film Union, also known as the Light Institute
or LUCE). This institute produced newsreels that exhibitors were required to screen as well as documentaries that extolled the achievements
of Fascism.

In 1932, LUCE's president Alessandro Sardi visited the USSR to
learn about the organization of Russian cinema and returned from this
experience determined to centralize the entire industry. In particular,
his exposure to Moscow's State Film School, established by Vladimir
Gardin in 1919, convinced Sardi of the need for a similar entity in Italy.
The State Film School provided a model for the formation, in 1932, of
the Scuola Nazionale di Cinematografia (National Cinema School), out
of which emerged the Centro Sperimentale di Cinematografia (Experimental Film Center) in 1935. The Soviet model was instinctively attractive to Fascist hierarchs both because Russian production conveyed
a sense of unity between nation and film that Italian cinema lacked
and because Russian film was politics as well as art. These characteristics were what made Russian film such an effective pedagogical tool.
Corrado Pavolini, a journalist who was the brother of the future Minculpop minister Alessandro Pavolini, wrote:

> Film, which is both art and an instrument of propaganda, needs a
> collective consciousness in order to achieve all its potential. . . .
> The success of American, German, and Russian productions de-
> rives from film in those countries being based on a national psycho-
> logical feeling, expressed in its own appropriate cinematic form. . . .

In Moscow, there is such a close and spontaneous relationship
between the nation and film that these two merge into one. . . .
Cinema is . . . a unique, modern expression of national collectivity,
profoundly differentiated from one people to another.[24]

Throughout the 1930s, articles in cinema journals continued to address
the need to emulate the Soviet model. Between 1930 and 1932, Ettore
Margadonna's numerous essays on Soviet cinema in *Comoedia* examined
Italy's potential to surpass the USSR's film industry. Sharing a similar
perspective with Malaparte, Margadonna professed in 1930: "Understand Russia! . . . because to comprehend means to surpass."[25]

In 1933, Margarita Sarfatti, a cultural promoter of the *Novecento*
movement best remembered for her relationship with Mussolini, picked
up the theme of cinema's potential as an instrument capable of exercis-
ing immense influence. She claimed that, for the Russians, film was the
"revolutionary fifth power."[26] Sarfatti's declaration clearly echoes Mussolini's Leninist evocation that "cinema is the strongest weapon." This
appeal for a more propagandistic cinema repeated itself in the pages of
Il Cantiere (1934)—a journal dedicated to, among other things, the poli-
ticization of film along the Soviet model. What emerged from these frequent interventions was the recognition, from both the political right
and the political left, of cinema's potential.

Perhaps the most influential figure in the promotion of Soviet cinema
in Italy was the leftist critic Umberto Barbaro. Through his translations
of Russian, German, and French texts and through his acute critical
contributions, he affirmed the imperative to expose Italy to European
culture. Although their motivations differed, Barbaro's cultural activ-
ism was consonant with *Stracittà*'s aims. As a film critic, he debuted in
1928 with "Morality and Immorality of Cinema" and swiftly rose to
prominence.[27] His frequent interventions became necessary points of
reference for the new generation of filmmakers. In fact, he was one of
the original professors at the Centro Sperimentale di Cinematografia
(CSC), where he screened Soviet films for his students. Between 1930
and 1935, Barbaro also translated Eisenstein and Semyon Timoshenko,
as well as Béla Balázs, Rudolf Arnheim, and Raymond Spottiswoode.
Barbaro's translations of Vsevolod Pudovkin's theoretical writings, including *Il soggetto cinematografico* (1932) and *Film e fonofilm* (1935), and
his discussions of Eisenstein's dialectic montage significantly influenced the formation of a new critical conscience in Italian cinema.[28]
The CSC used his texts to influence a generation of filmmakers. Of
course, the emergence from the CSC of the film journal *Bianco e Nero*
also contributed to the dissemination and critical examination of Eisen-

stein's and Pudovkin's theories. These texts expanded the boundaries of filmic discourse in Italy. For example, several critics discerned a challenge to Fascist hegemony in Pudovkin's exposition of the need for coherence between signifier and signified in the formal composition of film. As Barbaro later recalled: "Pudovkin's arguments swept away the entire cultural foundation upon which I too had been raised. . . . [He showed] a direct road, a different way of understanding art, opposed to that which had dominated unchallenged in Italy."[29]

Interestingly, Italy's screening of the avant-garde Soviets postdated the development of sound. The premiere of Alan Crosland's *The Jazz Singer* in October 1927 immediately provoked an overwhelming demand for synchronized sound in the United States and western Europe, thereby shifting interest away from Soviet montage cinema. In Italy, however, technical and financial constraints prolonged the industry's transition to sound so that the appearance of Soviet films alongside the publication of Eisenstein's and Pudovkin's theoretical texts provided a space for studying and incorporating aspects of the Soviet cinema into national productions. Nevertheless, despite the following examples, revolutionary montage never displaced bourgeois narrative, since Italian audiences also preferred "Charlie [Chaplin]'s arse to Eleonora Duse's hands."[30]

Alessandro Blasetti, Ruralism, and Soviet Formalism

Alessandro Blasetti was one of the first Italian directors to interpret and attempt to incorporate the dynamic principles of Soviet cinema into Italian filmmaking. Blasetti's cinematic debut occurred in August 1919, not as a director but rather as an extra in Mario Caserini's film, *Anima tormentata* (*Tortured Soul*). Finding himself on the wrong end of the camera, he quickly abandoned acting in favor of critiquing. As a writer for the hard-line Fascist *L'Impero*, he contributed a regular film column, "Lo schermo" ("The Screen"), which blossomed into the full-length journal *Cinematografo*. In *Cinematografo*, militant Fascists and anti-Fascists shared a forum in which they discussed the technical and material aspects of movie-making at the expense of Crocean aestheticism. In fact, Umberto Barbaro and other leftists such as Libero Solaroli and Aldo Vergano contributed regularly to Blasetti's journal. Still anxious to be involved actively in the film industry, Blasetti co-founded a cooperative production company in December 1928, Augustus, named in recognition of Augusto Turati's financial support and geared toward both revitalizing the Italian film industry from the inertia of the Pittaluga company and promoting a national cinema. Goffredo Alessandrini, Umberto Barbaro, Corrado D'Errico, Umberto Masetti, Gino Mazzucchi, Mario Serandrei, Libero Solaroli, and Aldo Vergano were some of the principal figures who collaborated on the Augustus projects. Although lacking any clear position toward the film industry other than a desire to see it grow and evolve, these enterprises provided a forum for discussing the status of cinema.

Out of this innovative collaboration, and benefiting from Bottai's tacit support, emerged the idea for *Sole* (*Sun,* 1929), which Blasetti formulated with a script developed by Vergano. They based this feature film on one of the regime's vaunted initiatives: the draining of the Pontine marshlands. In the narrative, the reclamation of the land is linked to the reconciliation of the two competing factions (the local inhabitants and the redevelopers) through the marriage of Rinaldi (Marcello Spada), the head of the redevelopers, and Giovanna (Dria Paola), the daughter of the local leader. *Sole* represented a current social issue in juxtaposing terms in which youth overcomes conservatism to promote national progress.

When *Sole* was released on 16 June 1929, Mussolini enthusiastically proclaimed "the dawn of the Fascist film."[31] However, as Carlo Lizzani noted, Blasetti's style emphasized the representation of formal qualities over the exploration of the social drama itself:

> The fast-paced editing of the images, the audacious framing and the preference for considering bodies and faces more as still lives, as beautiful objects rather than as centers of emotions and passions, shifted the center of attention to the form, to the composition and away from the conflict, from the discovery of human nature.[32]

What distinguished *Sole* from other patriotic rural tributes was its integration of the realistic tradition in Italian silent cinema (best expressed in the Neapolitan school) with the newly experienced dramatic Soviet cinema. The novelty of this approach was evident in the ideological and aesthetic representation of the harsh, stagnant conditions under which the residents of the region existed. Blasetti's use of rapid montage, his penchant for extreme long shots, his representations of mass action, the use of an Eisensteinian typology, and his ability to establish correspondences between the form and the content of the shots suggest a familiarity with Soviet aesthetics. In discussing the cinema of the late 1920s, Blasetti acknowledged his debt to the Soviet filmmakers:

20. *Sole* (Alessandro Blasetti, 1929).
Courtesy of the Museum of Modern Art Film Stills Archive

We read with interest and attention what reached us from the Russians Eisenstein, Pudovkin, and Nikolai Ekk, but we still had some years to wait before we could actually see *Potemkin, The General Line, Storm over Asia*, and *Road to Life* [*Putevka v zhizn'*]. Then, they immediately won the admiration of all Italian film-makers, who devoted careful study to them.[33]

Sole's many formal innovations attest to the filmmaker's awareness of Soviet montage theory and other principles of expression, albeit through initial exposure to the written as opposed to filmic texts.

In his next film, *Terra madre* (*Mother Earth*, 1931), Blasetti exploited the tension between urban and rural societies evident in Soviet cinema to a very different end. This film tells the story of a rich proprietor who at first neglects his holdings but then renounces his luxurious and decadent life in the city to respond to the call of working in the fields. This typical *Strapaese* (ultra-country) tripartite narrative reflected that aspect of Fascism that had incorporated into its rhetoric the ideological refutation of chaotic modern life in favor of simple and noble country living. The emphasis was thus placed on the importance of origins and establishing common identities. In this sense, the film fed the anxieties of the burgeoning bourgeoisie torn between the rapid modernization of urban living and the stable security of rural continuity.

In *Terra madre*, the city/country dichotomy weighs in heavily in favor of the rural element, particularly on the formal level. The Soviet-inspired shot composition of the outdoor scenes integrates the peasants with the landscape in a symbiotic relationship suggesting a natural order. In contrast, the shot composition of the demimonde sequences emphasizes the stifling, corrupt, and artificial space in which these people exist. This clash between urbanism and ruralism also raises issues of class, constituting a major point of bifurcation between Italian and Soviet cinemas. An exchange between Duke Marco (Sandro Salvini) and the steward's daughter Emilia (Leda Gloria) reveals the need to maintain the class distinctions that Soviet films sought to corrode. The duke overhears Emilia pray that he remain permanently on the estate. When, without revealing his identity, he confronts her, she says, "If [the duke] were of our kind [*razza*], he would agree with me," to which he responds, "But he isn't of your kind." At the end of the film, Marco maintains this distinction. Returning to the estate, the duke reaffirms his ownership: "These lands and these houses are still mine and will remain mine. . . . Everyone return to your duty!" The duke's return restores the social order, which retains class hierarchy.

Furthermore, while Marco and Emilia's marriage seems to suggest the possibility of a classless society, the conclusion challenges this utopian unification for two reasons. First, their relationship obeys the Fascist precepts of the proper role for a married woman—her place is in the home. Second, it is the duke who inaugurates the modern era in the rebuilding of the estate, thereby reinforcing the necessity of an authoritarian presence to ensure social justice. The notion of class is challenged, but it is exchanged for another form of hierarchy in which meritocracy supplants aristocracy.

The tensions between town and country and between modernity and tradition are present in both *Sole*'s and *Terra madre*'s assimilation of the Soviet cinematic avant-garde. Although *Terra madre* incorporates dynamic shot selection and rhythmic editing as well as thematics and imagery common to Soviet cinema, it remains firmly rooted in the Fascist cult of the hearth. However, this celebration of rural regeneration is subverted by the same formal techniques on which it is founded. The most evocative scenes (the opening sequence, the fire, the demimonde soirée, the feast at the estate, and the confrontation between the duke and Emilia) are long sequences without dialogue. These scenes fetishize the characters and their society rather than engage them in a critical

21. *Rotaie* (Mario Camerini, 1930).
Courtesy of the Museum of Modern Art Film Stills Archive

discourse. The folkloric world that *Terra madre* celebrates is a romanticized caricature of a rapidly vanishing reality, while the road to modernization that the film extols runs inexorably through the city. The reconciliation of these tensions is never complete.

Mario Camerini and Urbanism

Mario Camerini's *Rotaie* (*Rails*, 1930) also reflects a cinematic preoccupation with modernity and its effects on the everyday citizen. Camerini began directing in 1923 with *Jolly, clown da circo* (*Jolly the Circus Clown*). Seven more silent films followed this debut until, in 1929, Camerini directed *Rotaie*, with a script developed by Corrado D'Errico, for the Sacia studios. Along with Blasetti's *Sole*, *Rotaie* occupies a liminal position marking the conclusion of the silent film era in Italy. Re-released in 1931 with a limited sound track, Camerini's film bears the influence of German, American, and Soviet cinema. Mira Liehm describes *Rotaie*'s formalism as an accumulation of disparate techniques: "*Rails* emerges in a sense as an anthology of cinematic expression in the silent era by indulging in long takes of rails running, in interplays of light and shadow and in a parallel rhythmical montage that creates an intensely emotional mood."[34] This assimilation of avant-garde experimentalism, however, contains a formal justification: the film's tripartite structure reflects the three dominant stylistic interpretations.

Rotaie traces the melodramatic motif of two young lovers, Giorgio (Maurizio D'Ancora) and Maria (Käthe von Nagy), who are temporarily lured into the (pre-)jet-set lifestyle only to realize that true happiness does not come from material wealth. The opening sequence, in which the couple is huddled in the oppressive squalor of a hotel room contemplating suicide as the only escape from their economic woes, is indebted to German expressionism. While the *Kammerspiel* technique accentuates the play of light and shadow in the room, the camera lingers on inanimate objects (the clock, the glass, the city lights), imbuing them with symbolic value. The restricted space also reinforces the reduction of the global economic crisis to that of isolated individuals.[35] When chance upsets their ill-planned attempt, the couple flees the hotel. Happening upon a cash-laden wallet, they decide to take the next train out—first-class.

As the couple's fortune changes, so do the cinematic aesthetics. At first, luck is kind to the lovers as they try their chance in the casinos of Stresa; then fortune's flighty nature takes their winnings and challenges their commitment to each other. Marquis Mercier (Daniele Crespi), a decadent Frenchman who had befriended the couple on the train, loans Giorgio money to gamble so that he can seduce Maria. This representation of the escapist world of high society, in contrast to the travails of the protagonists, suggests the influence of the American comedies of the 1920s, such as Erich Von Stroheim's *Foolish Wives* (1922), which takes place in the hotels and casinos of the Riviera and features a seduction. In a similar vein, Cecil B. DeMille's *The Affairs of Anatol* (1921) and Ernst Lubitsch's *The Marriage Circle* (1924) are social satires that capture the vacuousness of the filthy rich.

In the final sequences of *Rotaie*, the two young lovers return home, this time riding the rails in a third-class car, penniless but committed to rebuilding their lives. Rejecting the fantasies and immorality of the casinos, Giorgio decides to take a job in the local factory, which is by contrast concrete and earnest, and Maria assumes the role of dutiful spouse. Gambling has no labor value; it produces only ephemeral wealth. In contrast, the factory produces tangible goods through calculable labor. The editing, the close-ups of the workers' faces on the train —one of the first times that Italian cinema profiles the proletariat—and the representation of the factory as a symbolic communion between man and machine acknowledge class issues and the indirect awareness of Soviet-style cinema. The closing scenes of modernity (turbines spinning, human solidarity) promise a new dawn for those who eschew illusory wealth for honest, productive labor.

This celebration of the worker and of the workplace, however, restores the traditional social order in which the husband works and the wife serves, thereby retaining class and gender distinctions. While *Sole* and *Terra madre* valorize ruralism, *Rotaie*'s celebration of urbanism promotes the same return to traditional values as Blasetti's films. The concluding portrait of domestic bliss suggests that the societal critique resides more in knowing one's station than in condemning the vacuousness of the upper classes. *Rotaie* denigrates the desire for social status rather than the status itself. The social order functions and society prospers when each cog in the wheel is properly maintained.

Walter Ruttmann: East Meets West

Industry, machinery, and social order are fused in Walter Ruttmann's *Acciaio* (*Steel*, 1933), based on Luigi Pirandello's short story "Giuoca, Pietro!" ("Play, Peter!").[36] In 1932, when the Cines studio bought the rights for 70,000 lire, Pirandello, with his son Stefano, revised the story expressly for cinema. To complement the illustrious screenwriter, the studio, with government pressure, sought a foreign director, preferably German, in order to promote a new vision of Italy abroad. At the end of May 1932, Georg Wilhelm Pabst was engaged, but within a month he withdrew from the project. Then the playwright pressed unsuccessfully for Eisenstein to direct the film.[37] Ultimately the contract went to the German documentary filmmaker Walter Ruttmann, whom Emilio Cecchi, director of production at Cines, chose because he thought Ruttmann capable of infusing a greater cosmopolitan sensibility into Italian cinema while still capturing the music of the factory. Best known for such films as *Die Melodie der Welt* (*World Melody*, 1929) and *Berlin, die Symphonie einer Großstadt* (*Berlin, Symphony of a Great City*, 1927), Ruttmann found himself with a sentimental script which was out of character with his previous work. Along with Mario Soldati—the latter performed the bulk of the revisions—he rewrote the story so that the final product hardly resembled Pirandello's original subject. Accordingly, Ruttmann and Soldati even changed the title from *Giuoca, Pietro!* to *Acciaio*.[38]

The film was shot almost entirely on location, although a few interior scenes were filmed in the Cines studios in Rome. This re-elaboration permitted Ruttmann to take advantage of scenery and movement in order to construct a rather lyrical representation of Terni, the "Italian Manchester"—a technique that owed more to his documentary experience than to any Italo-German collaboration. Nevertheless, the film manages to retain the rhythmic elements that Pirandello had infused in the script. In particular, the steel mill and dam scenes capture the lyrical harmony that the playwright sought to convey. In 1932, Pirandello expressed this concern in an interview: "The soundtrack will be very important in the film. At a certain point the rhythm of the machines becomes human; thus a perfect synchronism is achieved between the movement of the machines and the energy of human life."[39] Ruttmann had already experimented with this synchronization of the visual with the aural when he worked on *Berlin, Symphony of a Great City* with Edmund Meisel, who had composed the *Battleship Potemkin* score for Eisenstein. In *Acciaio,* Ruttmann refined his formalist rhythmic montage to a level of expertise not previously produced in Italy, reflecting the influence of Dziga Vertov. With mixed results, he reduced the dialogue to a minimum to accentuate the contrapuntal effect of sound and image.[40] Ruttmann's conflicts with Gian Francesco Malipiero, who composed the musical score for *Acciaio,* and the banality of the story line prevented the film from achieving symphonic "organicity," to borrow Eisenstein's term.[41] However, in certain sequences—the footage at the Terni steel mill and Marmore Falls—sound and image construct symbolic meanings through vertical montage. These scenes were camera-recorded and then edited to re-arrange the sequences into expressive recreations of modernity. As one reviewer observed: "*Acciaio* is the opposite of an American film."[42]

Starring Piero Pastore (Mario Velini), Vittorio Bellaccini (Pietro Ricci), and Isa Pola (Gina), *Acciaio* fuses a melodramatic romance with a documentary on steel production.[43] Mario's return home from the military is spoiled by the discovery that his best friend Pietro is engaged to his former fiancée Gina. When Pietro dies in a mill accident, the town ostracizes Mario, whom it holds responsible for the tragedy. However, Pietro's father, Giuseppe (Alfredo Polveroni), intercedes on behalf of Mario, who is then reunited with Gina.

While the sentimental subplot finds its resolution in the restoration of social order and harmony, the representations of modernity are anything but consoling. Dramatic angles, the juxtaposition of shots, the expressionistic play of lights, composition, rapid editing, the metaphorical substitution of objects, and stylized and mechanical movements—all reinforced by the rhythmic pounding of the soundtrack—suggest an uneasy tension between man and machine.[44] For example, the amusement park sequence is intercut with factory scenes. The accelerating

22. *Acciaio* (Walter Ruttman, 1933).
Courtesy of the Museum of Modern Art Film Stills Archive

juxtaposition of images parallels the escalating tension between Mario and Pietro as well as the increasing exertion of the workers in the mill.

Despite the formal pyrotechnics, *Acciaio*'s experimentalism failed to open new cinematic venues because these innovations were subsumed within Fascism's critique of modernity. The montage sequences are primarily audiovisual analogies: the children playing with the maul and the factory press, the mother closing the shutters and the factory gates opening, and the carousel and the factory. While sustaining a frenetic rhythm, this montage method mitigates the potential "Kuleshov effect" of the sequences by deferring responsibility for generating meaning to the spectator. The unequivocal analogies and the frenetic rhythm with which they are edited account for viewing that is mesmerizing but ultimately tedious.

Perhaps the most famous sequence, the "symphony of the machine" that follows the children playing outdoors in part one, illustrates the cinematic limitations of *Acciaio*. Beginning with the children's pretend pounding of the maul, the scene parallel-cuts into the mill and the pounding of the machines. Lasting nine minutes, the diegetic sound of the factory and Malipiero's musical score alternate, forming an audio analogy. The soundtrack divides the sequence into three movements: the first, lasting one minute, and the third, lasting three and a half minutes, are diegetic while the second, lasting four and a half minutes, is commentative. In the transition between the first two movements, the sounds of both the factory and the musical score blend to form a modern symphony. The second transition is an abrupt break marked by the factory whistle. Within the first minute of the sequence there are a total of thirty-seven shots—the other two movements are comprised of fifty-nine shots and of forty-nine shots, respectively. In this first minute, the rhythm of the editing and of the sound escalate at a feverish pitch. Despite the dizzying effect of sensory overload, the sequence lacks the engagement between shots that could imbue the text with additional meanings. When the symphony ends, the spectators are exhausted, but the rewards for their efforts are minimal.[45]

The result of this sequence is the realization that the factory has become a superhuman force that forges into the modern soul to celebrate the triumph of machinery and steel over the frailty of humanity. As long as individuals occupy their proper place in society—men in the factory and women in the home—then the well-oiled machinery of capitalism will run with Fordist efficiency. Pietro's inability to "mechanize" himself disrupted the harmony of the workplace and resulted in his death. In *Acciaio*, individuals must conform to their station (owner, worker, etc.) to transform society into a superhuman machine. Whether through their sweat or through their blood, the workers keep the machinery of capitalism running. *Acciaio*'s celebration of the machine poses the subject in an imaginary identification with the community and, synecdochically, with the nation. The mythologizing of the machine reinserts the individual into the collective while maintaining gender and class distinctions. Any lingering tensions are resolved in the final shots of the factory, which conveys the sense of a renewed spiritual communion between man and machine.

In an era when most European countries, both to protect and to promote cultural heritage, established strict quota systems against American films, Italy remained exceedingly receptive to foreign products through the mid-1930s—its primary restriction being that all films screened had to have a soundtrack in Italian. This openness extended to experimentalism with avant-garde aesthetics. Blasetti's integration of Soviet thematics and style paralleled Camerini's—the former using farmers, the latter using factory workers. Ruttmann represented a conscious effort to internationalize and revitalize Italian cinema. *Sole, Terra madre, Rotaie,* and *Acciaio* were hailed as inaugurating a new era in Italian cinema in both form and content. Furthermore, they broadened the base of cinematic representation to encompass social strata previously excluded or marginalized.

Though less overt, the Soviet influence on Italian cinema continued throughout the Fascist era. Two films framing the period and servicing the propagandistic needs of the regime illustrate how this influence was subsumed, devoid of political impetus, into the collective unconscious of filmmaking. At one end, Giovacchino Forzano's editing in *Camicia nera (Black Shirt,* 1933), which LUCE produced for the tenth anniversary of Fascism's triumph, betrays Vertov's lessons. At the other end, Augusto Genina's *Assedio dell'Alcazar (Siege of Alcazar,* 1940), which celebrates Franco's triumph in Spain's Civil War, models its underground sequence on Eisenstein's *The Battleship Potemkin.* In the twelve-year period from 1929 to 1940, adherence to Soviet filmic precepts was mollified by Fascist spiritualism, which purged the films of any suggestion of Marxist praxis.

Disciplinary oppositions do not suffice to explain the relationship between Italian and Soviet cinema during the *ventennio.* The Russian Revolution provided an organizational model that appealed to both Fascist and anti-Fascist critics. Fascism built rhetorically on Soviet revolutionary achievements as a means of invoking a regenerative ethos. While the regime did not consider Bolshevism to be a socio-political model to be emulated literally, Fascism's rhetorical appropriation of the Russian Revolution blurred the boundaries between subversive representations of Communism and panegyric representations of Fascism. Indeed, the regime accommodated various aesthetic creeds as long as they shared a common perspective of culture's role in the regeneration of the nation. The cohesiveness of Fascist cultural policy lay in its relationship with the myth of ultra-nationalism. Thus, any appropriation of perceived Marxist aesthetics lent itself to an ambiguous reading that could insert itself into the rhetoric of the State. Devoid of praxis, Soviet aesthetics provided Italian audiences with rose-colored glasses.

Notes

1. Cited in Mira Liehm, *Passion and Defiance: Film in Italy from 1942 to the Present* (Berkeley: University of California Press, 1984), 6.

2. While Hollywood's influence on Italian cinema is often assumed, few studies have pursued this intuition to demonstrate how the influence manifests itself. For a general approach to this issue, see David W. Ellwood and Rob

Krees, eds., *Hollywood in Europe: Experiences in Cultural Hegemony* (Amsterdam: VU University, 1994).

3. Lenin's remark, from a conversation with Anatoli Lunacharsky in 1922, has been frequently quoted and subjected to diverse interpretations. The original context is provided in Richard Taylor and Ian Christie, eds., *The Film Factory: Russian and Soviet Cinema in Documents* (Cambridge, Mass.: Harvard University Press, 1988), 56–57.

4. In a broad sense, these same years also marked the most active period of the American public's fascination with the Soviet Union. There were two clamorous events that seemed to frame Americans' interest in the USSR. The terminus a quo was the executions of Sacco and Vanzetti in 1927, and the terminus ad quem was the execution of Nikolai Buckarin in 1938. The former elicited sympathy for leftist causes and provided an impetus to explore socio-cultural alternatives to capitalism while the latter marked the disillusionment with this fascination—a disillusionment which would be amplified by the Russian-German pact of 1939.

5. This discussion on the representation of the Soviet Union in the Italian press is indebted to Rosaria Quartararo's *Italia-URSS, 1917-1941. I rapporti politici* (Napoli: Edizioni Scientifiche Italiane, 1997); and Giorgio Petracchi's *Da San Pietroburgo a Mosca. La diplomazia italiana in Russia, 1861/1941* (Roma: Bonacci Editore, 1993).

6. See Pietro Sessa, *Fascismo e bolscevismo* (Milano: Mondadori, 1934); and Curzio Malaparte [pseudonym of Curzio Suckert], *Intelligenza di Lenin* (Milano: Treves, 1930) and *Il Volga nasce in Europa* (Milano: Bompiani, 1943).

   Corrado Alvaro first traveled to the Soviet Union in 1932 and then returned in the spring and summer of 1934 for *La Stampa*. He collected and published his articles in the volume *I maestri del diluvio. Viaggio nella Russia Sovietica* (Milano: Mondadori, 1935). Subsequently, he reissued the collection under the title *Viaggio in Russia* (Firenze: Sansoni, 1943). See Corrado Alvaro, *Quasi una vita: giornale di uno scrittore* (Milano: Bompiani, 1950), 124–140.

   Vincenzo Cardarelli arrived in Moscow just when festivities were getting under way to celebrate Leon Trotsky's fiftieth birthday. He participated in these proceedings along with Ettore Lo Gatto, the doyen of Slavic studies in Italy. See Vincenzo Cardarelli, *Viaggio di un poeta in Russia*, reprinted in *Opere complete* (Milano: Mondadori, 1962).

7. "Italia e Russia," *Il Popolo d'Italia*, 30 September 1933 (my translation). The translations of all texts cited in this essay are mine unless otherwise noted.

8. See Mirko Ardemagni, *Russia. Quindici anni dopo* (Milano: Istituto Editoriale Nazionale, 1932); and Luigi Barzini, *Urss. L'impero del lavoro forzato* (Milano: Hoepli, 1935).

9. Luigi Barzini, "Impressioni sulla Russia sovietica. Varcando una porta di ferro," *Il Popolo d'Italia,* 18 July 1934.

10. Bertoni bases his analysis on the consideration that both Fascism and Bolshevism shared the dual objectives of raising the standard of living and renovating society. See Renzo Bertoni, *Il trionfo del fascismo nell'Urss* (Roma: Signorelli, 1934); and Renzo Bertoni, *Russia: trionfo del fascismo* (Milano: La Prora, 1937).

11. Of particular interest in this regard is the attention that the Italian press devoted to the Five Year Plan, with its central themes of industrialization, self-sufficiency, and agricultural collectivization, to see to what degree it might be emulated. See Malaparte, *Intelligenza di Lenin;* Ugo D'Andrea, *Le alternative di Stalin* (Milano/Roma, 1932); Giuseppe Gregoraci, *Riuscirà la Russia?* (Roma: Maglione, 1932); Ettore Lo Gatto, *URSS 1931. Vita quotidiana—Piano quinquennale* (Roma: Anonima Romana, 1932); and Rodolfo Mosca, *URSS 1932—Verso il secondo piano quinquennale* (Milano: Giacomo Agnelli, 1932).

12. See Giuseppe Bottai, "Il nuovo corso di Trotski," *Critica fascista,* 15 November 1924. From 1930 to 1935, Tommaso Napolitano served as the Soviet specialist to *Critica fascista.* Bottai also edited the journal *Archivio di Studi Corporativi,* which devoted considerable attention to the economic aspects of corporatism/Bolshevism.

13. Bruno Spampanato, "Equazioni rivoluzionarie dal bolscevismo al fascismo," *Critica fascista,* 15 April 1930.

14. Sergio Panunzio, "La fine di un regno," *Critica fascista,* 15 September 1931, 342–344.

15. Ibid., 343.

16. Dino Alfieri, "L'Italiano nel mondo," *L'Illustrazione italiana* 52.51 (22 December 1935).

17. Giacomo Gandolfi, "Lettere dalla Russia. Da una schiavitù all'altra," *Corriere padano* (3 October 1933).

18. When film critics assess the influence of Soviet cinema in this period, they tend to limit the canon to Sergei Eisenstein, Dziga Vertov, Vsevolod Pudovkin, and Alexander Dovzhenko; Lev Kuleshov and Alexander Medvedkin are intermittent presences on this list. With the exception of *Aleksandr Nevskii (Alexander Nevsky,* 1938), *Ivan (Ivan the Terrible,* 1932), *Simfoniya Donbassa (Enthusiasm,* 1930), and *Tri pesni o Lenine (Three Songs of Lenin,* 1934), all the canonical films are silent. Consequently, these are the only films that achieved significant international distribution.

19. In fact, Ekk's influence can be seen in both the thematics and the aesthetics of Ivo Perilli's *Ragazzo (Boy,* 1933), while Vittorio Cossato's documentary *Risveglio (Reawakening,* 1936) owes much to Dovzhenko's cinematography. However, unlike the warm reception of Ekk's film, Mussolini himself intervened to block *Ragazzo*'s release.

20. Gian Piero Brunetta, *Storia del cinema italiano*, vol. 2, *Il cinema del regime 1929–1945* (Roma: Riuniti, 1993), 41.

21. Although Eisenstein's films did not achieve general distribution in Italy, they were frequently exhibited in the private cinema clubs—especially *The Battleship Potemkin*, *General'naya liniya* (*The General Line*, a.k.a. *Staroe i novoe—The Old and the New*), and *Stachka* (*The Strike*, 1925). See Libero Solaroli and Giovanni Vento, "Vita italiana del cinema sovietico," *Cinema sovietico* 2, no. 4 (July–August 1955): 43–54.

22. "La cinematografia russa," *Cinemondo* 1 (1927); "Film culturale e film d'insegnamento," *Rivista internazionale del cinema educativo* 1 (January 1930); and "Vita cinematografica sovietica," *Rivista internazionale del cinema educativo* 6 (June 1930).

23. Mario Serandrei, "Ancora sulla cinematografia russa," *Cinematografo* 7 (30 July 1930).

24. Corrado Pavolini, "Dare all'Italia una coscienza cinematografica," *Il Tevere*, 1 May 1930.

25. Ettore Margadonna, "La linea generale del cinema russo," *Comoedia* 12, no. 6 (June–July 1930).

26. Margherita Sarfatti, "Il rivoluzionario quinto potere," *Rivista internazionale del cinema educativo* 1 (January 1933).

27. Umberto Barbaro, "Moralità e immoralità del cinematografo," *Cinemalia* 2, no. 13–14 (July 1928).

28. Pudovkin, *Il soggetto cinematografico* (Roma: Le Edizioni d'Italia, 1932); and Pudovkin, *Film e fonofilm* (Roma: Le Edizioni d'Italia, 1935). Some of the earliest explications of Soviet montage came in 1929, from Libero Solaroli. His essays "Should Italian Cinema Imitate Soviet Cinema?" (1929) and "Notes on Montage" (1929) provided an impetus and a context for the cinematic discourse that Barbaro propounded. See Libero Solaroli, "Il cinema italiano deve imitare quello russo?" *Cinematografo* 3, no. 5 (March 1929), and "Appunti intorno al montaggio," *900* 4, no. 5 (1929).

29. Umberto Barbaro, *Poesia del film* (Roma: ed. Filmcritica, 1955), 62.

30. Grigori Kozintsev, "Eccentrism" [1922], in Taylor and Christie, eds., *The Film Factory*, 58. The reference is from a manifesto of FEKS (Factory of the Eccentric Actor), a Petrograd filmmaking group that extolled popular art and the machine.

31. Cited in Liehm, *Passion and Defiance*, 25. *Sole* received wide critical acclaim; see Alberto Cecchi, "*Sole*," *L'Italia letteraria* 4 (23 May 1929); Corrado Pavolini, *Il Tevere*, 17 June 1929; and Alberto Frateili, *La tribuna*, 18 June 1929. An anthology of *Sole*'s press reviews was published in *Cinematografo* 3, no. 22 (10 November 1929) and in Alberto Boero, Alessandro Blasetti, and Aldo Vergano, *Sole. Soggetto, sceneggiatura, note per la realizzazione*, ed. Adriano Aprà and Riccardo Redi (Roma: De Giacomo Editore, 1985), 113–120.

32. Carlo Lizzani, *Storia del cinema italiano, 1895–1961* (Firenze: Parenti, 1961), 51.

33. Alessandro Blasetti, "Italian Cinema Yesterday," reprinted in *The Fabulous Thirties: Italian Cinema, 1929–1944*, ed. Adriano Aprà and Patrizia Pistagnesi (Milano: Electa International Publishing Group, 1979), 40. See Blasetti's interview with Francesco Savio in Francesco Savio, *Cinecittà anni trenta. Parlano 116 protagonisti del secondo cinema italiano (1930–1943)*, 3 vols., ed. Tullio Kezich (Roma: Bulzoni, 1979), 109.

34. Liehm, *Passion and Defiance*, 30.

35. Gian Piero Brunetta notes that *Rotaie* is the only Italian film of the era to acknowledge the global economic crisis of 1929. Gian Piero Brunetta, *Storia del cinema italiano*, vol. 1, *Il cinema muto 1895–1929* (Roma: Riuniti, 1993), 330.

36. Letter to Marta Abba dated 6 May 1932, in Luigi Pirandello, *Lettere a Marta Abba*, ed. Benito Ortolani (Milano: Mondadori, 1995). The original motivation for the film stems from Mussolini's personal request in 1928 for Pirandello to pitch a story celebrating work in Fascist Italy. An exhaustive treatment of the filmic adaptation of Pirandello's short story is contained in Claudio Camerini, ed., *Acciaio. Un film degli anni trenta. Pagine inedite di una storia italiana* (Torino: Nuova ERI—Edizioni Rai, 1990).

37. Pirandello had met Eisenstein several times, including at the 1929 Berlin premier of *General'naya liniya (The General Line)* and shortly thereafter in La Sarraz, Switzerland, at the Conference of Independent Filmmakers (2–9 September 1929). In fact, Eisenstein traveled from Berlin to La Sarraz with none other than Walter Ruttmann, with whom he had become friends in Germany. These events also marked Pirandello's first meetings with Ruttmann. On at least two other occasions, the playwright encountered Eisenstein in Berlin: once in 1930, and then again in the fall of 1932, when Pirandello returned to the German capital to meet with Paramount Studio executives. See Francesco Callari, "S.(ua) M.(aestà) Ejzenštejn a tavola con Pirandello," *Sipario* 476–477 (May–June 1988).

In Pirandello's letter to Eisenstein (June 1932) urging the director to accept the commission, the playwright states: "The complexity of the plot, which involves large crowd scenes, and the rapidity of the cuts, necessitated by the pressing nature of the action, require the magisterial hand of a great director." The letter is reprinted in Camerini, *Acciaio*, 239–240.

38. On 25 February 1933, Cecchi hosted a special screening for, among others, Margherita Scarfatti, whose negative assessment of *Acciaio* precipitated Mario Soldati's firing. Cines released him on 2 March 1933—even though the film was not released until 30 March 1933. *Acciaio* premiered in Trieste and Bologna, where it stayed in theaters for a week. It opened in Rome on 15 April 1933 and lasted five days. Despite positive public reviews, the film was a box-office failure. See Camerini, *Acciaio*, 46.

39. Enrico Roma, "Pirandello e il cinema," *Comoedia* 7 (15 July–15 August 1932): 22.

40. Libero Solaroli, who worked on *Acciaio* as the director of services and organization, recalls that Umberto Barbaro came to watch Ruttmann's editing process. See Libero Solaroli, "Ricordo di Barbaro alla vecchia Cines," *Filmcritica* 118 (March 1962): 83.

41. On the strained rapport between Ruttmann and Malipiero, see "Carteggio Malipiero-Cecchi-Pirandello-Ruttmann," in Camerini, *Acciaio*, 237–265.

42. Francesco Pasinetti, "*Acciaio*," *La gazzetta di Venezia*, 1 April 1933.

43. Pirandello had written the role of Gina for Marta Abba; however, Ruttmann decided against casting her. Pirandello unsuccessfully argued about this decision with Emilio Cecchi. The playwright refers to this incident in his letter to Marta Abba dated 11 August 1932. Ruttmann first offered the role to Cecchi's 18-year-old daughter Suso, but she turned down the part. See Suso Cecchi d'Amico, "Cecchi e il cinema," *Emilio Cecchi. Quaderni della Antologia Viesseux* 2 (1985): 40. Public mores prevented the casting of a local woman in the starring role, so Ruttmann and Soldati settled on Isa Pola (the stage name of Luisa Maria Betti di Montesano), whose acting credits included *Terra madre* and *La canzone dell'amore* (*The Song of Love*, dir. Gennaro Righelli, 1930)—a film based on Pirandello's short story "In silenzio." In general, Ruttmann deferred the casting decisions to Mario Soldati, who recruited the inhabitants of Terni and the steel-mill workers—including Vittorio Bellacini and Alfredo Polveroni. Piero Pastori, the "new Valentino," was a friend of Soldati's and the ex–center forward for the Lazio Football Club.

44. Marcia Landy discerns the influence of Vertov's *Enthusiasm* in *Acciaio*'s editing; see *Fascism in Film: The Italian Commercial Cinema, 1931–1943* (Princeton: Princeton University Press, 1986), 252–254.

45. See Pier Marco De Santi, "A proposito di rumori," in Camerini, *Acciaio*, 179–185.

9

Theatricality and Impersonation

The Politics of Style in the Cinema of the Italian Fascist Era

Marcia Landy

The Italian popular cinema's preoccupation with theatricality in the 1930s and early 1940s was a form of politics—a politics of style rather than one of doctrinal and polemical substance. The films are reflexive about performance and in their play with intertextuality, and their emphasis on fictional narratives is drawn from theater, opera, literature, and folklore. Nevertheless, the films are often trivialized as "escapist" and written off as Fascist because in their fascination with wealth, upward mobility, and security, they are said to have diverted audiences from the harsh realities of life under Fascism.[1] These conflicting views cannot be harmonized, but the notion of "escapism" can be enlarged to a level of complexity that redeems it from the familiar charge of vacuity, frivolity, and evasion of conflict. Never totally removed from everyday or social conflicts, the texts draw on the folklore of sexual politics— familialism, gendered and sexual identity, work, leisure, and conflicts over power and authority—coded in the conventions of genre.[2] Through their focus on theatricality, the films share with their audiences knowledge of their status as commodities, a slippery relationship to conformity and opposition, and a simultaneous sense of involvement and detachment. Their treatment of spectacle is aligned to a reflexive use of gesture, costume, and mise-en-scène, stressing artifice of setting and highlighting impersonation, disguises, doubling, carnival, and spectacle.

In this essay, I discuss six exemplary films of the era to identify the ways in which they address and exploit "theatricality," the term I use to designate a mode of escapism in which life is equated with performance —not authenticity. While the narratives remain attached to familiar images of gender, sexuality, and work; conflicts between the home and the world; the public and private spheres; and personal desire and perceived social imperatives, their reflexivity about performance produces an ambivalent and dialectical interplay between realism and fiction, social conflict and fantasy, entertainment and seriousness, and affective involvement and distanciation. I examine how their allusions to live entertainment and the presence of role-playing are essential to the films' conception of community, and how impersonation, doubling, and disguises are central to the development of images of life as amenable to control and management. The sixth and final film that I discuss, *Sorelle Materassi*, is, I argue, a dissection and mordant critique of escapism.

Life, Opera, and "Putting on a Show"

The cinematic form most identified with escapism is the film musical, where song and dance are considered to be evasions of the hardships of life—failure, aggression, unrequited interpersonal relations, and abuses of power. The prime characteristic of musicals is their emphasis on a show within a film, which serves to mirror art as life ,and to celebrate performance over naturalism.[3] Their escapism is mainly identified in their exaltation of artifice, romance, and resolution of conflict. One of the first Italian sound films was *Figaro e la sua gran giornata* (*Figaro's Big Day*, 1931), a musical directed by Mario Camerini. In the tradition of musicals, the film parallels life and art.[4] *Figaro* is indebted to Rossini's *The Barber of Seville* and to a play by Arnaldo Fraccaroli, *Ostrega che sbrego!* (*Oh, What Fun!*). The narrative is structured around the attempts of a baritone, Basoto (Gianfranco Giachetti), to insert himself into a performance of *The Barber of Seville* to be given by a visiting opera troupe. His boasting about his once-great career is not matched by his singing performance. By contrast, Nina (Leda Gloria), a victim of parental control, is vocally talented, and Basoto and Rantolini, the manager, seek to enlist her as their Rosina in the performance of the opera. Her father is opposed to her performing in public, and, for reasons of jealousy, so is her lover, Chiodini (Maurizio D'Ancora). Her life is also complicated by the refusal of her parents to approve her marriage to Chiodini. The film relies on counterparts in romance and theatrical performance—between the Rossini opera and the trials and tribulations of Nina and her relationship to Chiodini. However, just as obstacles to artistic achievement in the film's treatment of opera are eliminated, so also are obstacles to romance overcome.

As is characteristic of film musicals, "the symbolic wedding celebrates the ongoing relationship between film and spectator as much as it celebrates the union of the couple,"[5] and, thereby, the union of art and life. *Figaro* blurs the distinction between life and opera by also consistently calling attention to the role of spectatorship, involving several audiences in the film—the townspeople, the opera troupe, parental figures, and Basoto and Chiodini as eavesdroppers to Nina's singing. Through the operatic performance, the film "seeks to bridge the gap between audience and performance by setting up 'community' as an ideal concept" in ways consonant with those described by Jane Feuer in her analysis of the Hollywood film musical.[6] The focus on "live entertainment," as in the case of *Figaro* and its uses of opera, serves "to speak more directly to the spectator. . . . Maybe that's why so many musicals are about putting on a show rather than about making films."[7]

The plight of beleaguered and helpless feminine figures beset by irate parents and jealous spouses, a traditional source of melodramatic conflict, is overcome through performance not only for the characters but presumably also for internal and external audiences. In the context of entertainment, the misunderstandings, misrecognition, deception, and prohibitions associated with "real life" are complicated, suggesting the reality and power of illusion through the valorization of artifice. Escapism in this film can be construed as the transformation of life into theater where all problems can be resolved. However, the "coincidence" of the parallel between the opera and the film, the consequence of "putting on a show," has a more substantial and contradictory valence. While the film eschews a realist form of representation in favor of illusion, its reflexivity in calling attention to the parallels between art and life ironically suggests an absence of consonance between social reality and representation. Theatricality (in this case, melodrama), the acknowledgment of the necessity of performance, becomes a strategy for exposing and contending with, not denying, conflict, taking a number of directions in the cinema of the era.

An Exemplary Fiction

Based on common sense as folklore, popular narratives focus on theatricality as a way of calling attention to the necessity of withholding information. Escapism relies on the clever and subtle management of knowledge, hence the predominance of masks, disguises, and impersonation. However, certain characters within the text expose secrets to the external audience, ostensibly placing the audience in a position superior to many of the characters. *Una moglie in pericolo* (*A Wife in Danger*, 1939), directed by Max Neufeld,[8] is an exemplary text with which to explore the forms of escapism of the so-called white-telephone films because it highlights not only the ubiquity of deception but also its necessity for social harmony. In its predilection for upper-class subjects and an upper-class environment, the film appears to have no direct connection with Fascist politics—or any politics, for that matter. The comedy is set in a mythical world that highlights sexual intrigue. However, in assessing the film's theatrical character and its reflexivity, unexceptional attributes among the films of the era, the critical viewer cannot miss the familiar scenarios with their strategies that have their roots, by way of folklore, in the everyday world of sexual politics. A union of Hungarian and Hollywood comedy with Italian comedy, the film focuses on the world of the middle class and on threats to domestic harmony. In its brittle dialogue, its reliance on double entendre and in its reflexivity, *Una moglie* produces an anti-sentimental and pragmatic resolution of the requisite sexual intrigue, after first presenting a potentially destabilizing and threatening domestic scenario reminiscent of such comic operas such as *The Marriage of Figaro* and *Die Fledermaus.*

The family constellation involves an absent mother; an inept aunt, who stands in as a mother-surrogate; a womanizing father; Mary, a childlike wife whose role is to maintain the fiction of an ideal marriage; and a son-in-law, Pietro, who is redeemed from being a cuckold. With his wife Mary's complicity, Pietro emerges as hardworking, sincere, and responsible. Giorgio, Pietro's colleague and the irrepressible Don Juan of the film, who threatens the family by his amorous designs on Mary, is chastened for his exploits by being threatened with exposure and, hence, with social ostracism. The maidservant, Lina, mistaken for Mary as the object of Giorgio's seduction, never confesses her impersonation of Pietro's wife in the conspiracy to maintain Mary's integrity, nor does she implicate others. Not only does Lina tidy the house but she also orders the family's sexual affairs.

The domestic politics of the film center on the drama of "diplomacy" and "intrigue" as a central feature in the negotiation of social life. The emphasis on concealment is reinforced by the vocation of the masculine characters. Ironically, Pietro and Giorgio are diplomats, though the real diplomats turn out to be the women who keep the men pacified and monogamous. The women are the ones who channel the narrative from melodrama into comedy. The common sense of the comedy, its pragmatic and theatrical nature, is apparent in the film's access to and management of cultural knowledge, specifically the knowledge of marriage as a masculine encumbrance and of femininity as the guarantor of domestic order, legitimacy, and social continuity. The comic elements revolve around the danger of the husband's potential cuckoldry, hence the possibility of insult to his honor and the necessity of neutralizing promiscuity.

The setting is Budapest in a lavish home. A photograph of a woman, his wife Mary (Marie Glory), sits on Pietro's (Antonio Centa) desk. He goes to switch off a phonograph player as Mary approaches him to divert him, and he tells her to let him work. Having lured her husband to bed, she again interrupts him with her curiosity about a book he is reading, *A Wife in Danger*, about a wife who gets into trouble, though not of her own making. She responds that a "good wife never gets into trouble." This prologue sets the terms for the marital intrigue to come. The motif of infidelity and womanizing is developed through Giorgio and through Mary's father, who spends his time and money on women. By contrast, Pietro is committed to his work as a diplomat, having little time to pursue such pleasures.

At home, a forlorn Mary wants to go to a masked ball, but Pietro is unavailable. She tries to convince her father to accompany her, but he tells her he's going to bed. Aware of his subterfuge, Lina complains to Mary that "all men are cheats." In disguise, mistress and servant both go to the ball, where Mary sees her father. There she also makes Giorgio's acquaintance and he becomes enamored of her, though because of her disguise he cannot ascertain her identity. In his enthusiasm, he telephones Pietro to inform him that he has met his ideal woman and is determined to pursue her, thus unwittingly threatening Pietro with becoming a cuckold. Giorgio follows Mary home, and his presence creates sufficient disturbance in the household before he finally leaves.

The following day, Giorgio arrives at a reception to celebrate Pietro and Mary's anniversary. Threatened with exposure, Mary gets faint; Lina also sees him and drops a tray, while Giorgio brags to Pietro about his escape. He informs him that the woman he was chasing never removed her mask, so that he is still uncertain about her identity. Oblivious to the fact that Giorgio presents a potential threat to his own honor, Pietro tells him that if he were the cuckolded husband he would kill Giorgio. When Mary is introduced to Giorgio, he tries unsuccessfully to ferret out if she was the woman with whom he danced at the ball, only to learn that the only other women in the house are an older aunt and the maid. Through Lina's machinations, the aunt appears wearing the dress that Mary wore the previous evening, sprayed by Lina with Mary's perfume, and Giorgio is completely duped. As Mary and Pietro dance, they discuss the ending of the novel, *A Wife in Danger*, and Pietro decides that, although in the novel the husband and wife separate, it is better not to confess. She, however, decides to "confess." The confession?—her love for him.

The world in which the characters move alternates between work and parties, receptions, and balls. The film focuses on consumer objects—clothing, handkerchiefs, perfume, expensive fans, and the signposts of wealth and leisure. They are the source of tricks the characters play on each other. They signify the fetishized character of this world, the interchangeability between women and objects, the conduits through which misunderstanding and misperception circulates. The emphasis on disguises and on diplomacy elevates the notion of impersonation that provides the necessary ingredients of comic misperception, serving to underscore and minimize the potential consequences of the sexual games that are being played. But the impersonation has a more serious side insofar as it highlights artifice, providing a defense against the possibility of confrontation with and legitimation of socially transgressive behavior.

Thus, the film entertains the possibility of promiscuity while at the same time containing it. The seductions are never consummated, but there is a great deal of posturing and many double entendres about sexual games. The three women in the film, while differentiated according to social class and age, are, in fact, the same, united in their roles to maintain domestic harmony and respectability. Finally, the ending of the film also serves as a disclaimer for the film, reinforcing not only the sense that nothing untoward has happened but that the essence of "fiction" (and hence, cinema) is concealment. Despite its ostensible frivolity, the film is saved from vacuousness by its reflexivity, its acknowledgment of the necessity of fictionalizing and of impersonation for maintaining the fiction of domestic concord. The theatricality inherent to escapism requires a certain "realism" in the acknowledgment of performance and its connection to the maintenance of social appearances.

Escapism and Carnival

Carnival is fundamental to comedy and satire, and many of the comedies of the era are set within the context of the carnivalesque, a portrait of a world turned upside down. Familiar behavior is suspended; roles are interchanged and reversed. Instead of impersonation, there is masquerade. Instead of collectivity and community, there is romantic coupling as escape when the protagonists flee the chaos of the world that has been exposed as threatening. Comedy is often predicated on a familiar hypothetical question designed to overturn existing social roles.

In the case of Mario Camerini's *Darò un milione* (*I'd Give a Million*, 1935), the premise is: "What would happen if you met a millionaire who was willing to bankroll you?" The film begins with Blim, a hobo (Luigi Almirante), who, in disillusionment with the world, tries to drown himself by tying a weight around his leg. (Blim is reminiscent of Boudu in Renoir's *Boudu Saved from Drowning* [1932] and also of Chaplin's tramp.) On a yacht, a tuxedoed man, Gold (Vittorio De Sica), observes the hobo seeking to end his existence and he jumps into the water to rescue him. The men struggle and Gold restrains Blim. The scene cuts to a room where elegant people are gathered by the radio listening to news of Gold's disappearance, while the hobo and the millionaire are seen sitting by the fire. Gold tells the beggar that he "would give a million" if he could find a person interested in him for reasons other than his money. When Blim awakens in the morning, his clothes are gone and so is Gold, but not Gold's clothes or his money.

The scene dissolves to a carnival and to a clothesline, a recurrent image in this film and also in Camerini's *Il cappello a tre punte* (*The Three-Cornered Hat*, 1935). In his films, objects, especially clothing and sheets, are of paramount importance, serving to identify attachment to or detachment from commodities and often functioning reflexively as an allusion to performance and to the deceptive character of vision. Gold is asleep, with a dog by his side, another allusion to *Boudu*. As he awakens, he sees a shadow of a slim woman on a sheet. He looks again, then sees a heavyset woman, not the same as the shadow figure. Finally a young woman appears out of the shadows: it is Anna (Assia Noris), Gold's destined mate. He assists her in chasing a circus dog, Bob, a mathematical whiz who has run off after a cyclist.

Blim, meanwhile, has gone to the newspapers with his story, informing them about the millionaire's offer. A lengthy sequence introduces the editor's interview of the beggar and his plans for capitalizing on the story, which involves a montage of photographs and headlines, culminating in an image of the headline, "I'd give a million to whoever makes a disinterested and generous gesture toward me." People are shown reading the paper and then passing the information on to others, thus emphasizing the role of media in transmitting misinformation and in creating confusion. Beggars are shown helping each other in the hope that one of them is the millionaire. Suddenly, they are no longer social undesirables: a sign from a store window that reads "Beggars forbidden to enter" is removed. Beggars are shown being overwhelmed by people wanting to do good deeds. Also, at the point that Anna and Gold are about to recapture Bob, dogcatchers grab the dog. Heroically, Gold grabs Bob, freeing the other dogs as well, but then is arrested. Given the ambiguity about who is a beggar and who is a millionaire, Gold is released. Thus, this prologue to the film has stressed role reversal between rich and poor, the blurring of class identities, and the notion of the carnival as the site for such reversals. The characters are typed in terms of occupation and gender and the film involves a journey through a gallery of social types—mendicants, entrepreneurs, hustlers, self-styled millionaires, and romantic lovers.

At the circus, after a Grand March, a banquet for the beggars is set up (reminiscent of Blasetti's *La tavola dei poveri* [*The Beggar's Table*, 1932]). The camera travels around the table capturing the beggars in various postures. The management surveys them in the hope of locating the actual millionaire. The feast serves several functions in the film. It satirizes the role of charity; it offers an image of the poor without idealizing their image or, conversely, making it appear grotesque; and it reinforces the notion of saturnalia, the idea of the suspension of the normal and everyday. The feast also satirizes public spectacle as a medium for images of benevolence toward the poor and needy that were characteristic of 1930s propaganda and underlines the politics of style as theatricality.

The stage is set for a lottery to be held as planned by the manager. Gold, thanks to Anna, has been hired as a lottery attendant. The scene is crowded with equestrians, acrobats, floats, and beggars as a billboard with a million-lire note painted on it is lowered. The spectacle in this scene involves a musical number miming the beggars and millionaires. The draw takes place, and the number called is "32," Gold's number. When the beggars discover that Gold has the winning number, they douse him with water. Anna takes him to her room to help him dry his clothes. Outside, the world has gone mad. Gold's "abdication" has turned the world upside down, destabilizing social relations and producing greed masked as altruism. While Anna irons his clothes, she finds a diamond ring. He approaches her and kisses her, offering her the ring, which she refuses. Suspicious, she interrogates him, wondering why he doesn't work. The manager enters and expels Gold from the circus, thinking that he has compromised Anna. Gold returns to see Anna again, but with the same shadow technique as at the opening of the film, he sees Anna and the manager talking and assumes that they are plotting against him.

As Gold leaves, he encounters Blim, who tells the millionaire that Gold did him no favor. Gold, having decided to return to his yacht, explains to Blim his disillusionment with society. Life is beginning to normalize as people return to their habitual dismissive behavior toward the poor. Gold tells Anna that since he is not the millionaire, there is no reason for her to pursue him. In his rage at her, he breaks some dishes, but Anna pays the woman for the damage. As he prepares to get into a boat to row to his yacht, she tells him good-bye, turns to leave, but then turns back and presses ten francs into his hand to help him. This gesture melts his anger. He kisses her and says that he has finally found a truly generous friend. He takes her with him to the yacht and places his ring on her finger. The scene cuts to the beggars and Blim, who are having their own party. With the money that Gold had left him, Blim pays for rides for the beggars, and the film ends on a carnivalesque note.

As with all satiric allegory, the film relies on role-playing, role reversal, irony, burlesque, and hyperbole. Gold, like the meaning of his English name, is the force that sets these agencies into motion and that also disrupts their normal functioning. The film, like most of Camerini's films, does not resort to a utopian vision, offering instead a cynical view of competition as a destructive quest for wealth and power and a critique of the misguided operations of institutionalized altruism. The narrative suggests that the vision of a transformed society is illusory. The exceptions to this view reside in the notion of pleasure as exemplified by the beggars, who with Blim enjoy the amusement rides at the end, perhaps an ambiguous comment on bread and circuses. The notion of escape pervades the film, beginning with Blim's suicide attempt, Gold's disappearance from his yacht, the dog's attempt to escape from the circus, Blim's escape from the newspaper editor, and Gold and Anna's escape from the "circus." The romantic element with Anna and Blim balances the portrait of greed and opportunism. In the conventions of romance comedy, Anna becomes the saving remnant, the one truly worthy person. The poor woman and the rich man are united; their bonding based on their shared indifference to wealth and their quest for authenticity. Anna is put on trial and, of all the needy people in the film, she is deemed the most worthy and rewarded. As each group in the film finds its own counterpart, Anna finds hers with Gold. The sexual conflict in the film not only serves to mate the compatible couple but also suggests that there is an inverse connection between the competition for wealth and sexual desire exposed through the strategic use of impersonation.

The image of clothing is the signifier of the film's preoccupation with masquerade, fetishism, and the confusion between money and needs, objects and people, highlighting disguises and role reversals. At the outset Gold exchanges clothes with Blim. Later, clothing comes to be associated with Anna, who is a maker of costumes. Her silk slip becomes an object of contemplation for Gold as she irons his clothes. He strokes it as if it were Anna, even though Anna is in the room. Shadows, too, are central to the film's preoccupation with masquerade and the quest for authenticity. Blim first encounters Anna as a shadow. Later, he misperceives her motives as he looks at her as a shadow figure as she talks with the manager. This film, like Camerini's others, appears to be uneasy about spectacle and spectatorship. A preoccupation with the illusory nature of appearance, a suspicion of looking, governs the text. In its treatment of femininity, the film seems to equate woman with spectacle, and, as we have seen, spectacle with confusion, hypocrisy, and deception. The coupling of Anna and Gold is a necessary convention of romantic comedy, but their escape functions less as a celebration of romantic love and more as a reproach to the status quo as the film dissects and exposes the threadbare quality, the frailty, of performance. Like *Una moglie*, the film is reflexive, acknowledging the power of performance, but, unlike the Neufeld film, it is suspicious of theatricality, using masquerade to undermine the powerful sway of role-playing.

Regarding Friendly Fascism

Escapism in popular films is often identified with playful immorality, a flouting of romance and heterosexual coupling and of marital and familial responsibilities, as well as a disregard of polemic and formal politics. The reflexivity, intertexuality, and incorporation of conventions that are characteristic of genre films can be construed as a disregard for reality, even a reassertion of conventional values. Yet an examination of so-called escapist films, their evasion of censorship and their ostensible claims to entertainment, reveals that their stance of indifference often masks knowledge of and an investment in social realities. In the case of *Batticuore* (*Heartbeat*, 1939), also directed by Camerini, the film's archness and theatricality entertain a more serious notion, inherent in political economy, that "property is theft." The "escapism" challenges fundamental issues about the hypocrisy of the upper classes and the ambiguous nature of the law as it defines crime.

The film is set in Paris, offering a satiric excursus into the world of the upper class. At the outset, in voyeuristic fashion, the camera moves to a window, remaining outside as a professor (Luigi Almirante) lectures. Another window is half shaded, obstructing vision, and soon the professor pulls the shade on the other window, momentarily excluding the spectator. So far, the scene seems innocuous, suggesting nothing disreputable. Like any respectable teacher, the professor is testing his pupils, while a stuffed mannequin is evident as the focal point of testing and interrogation. Later, on the street, Arlette (Assia Noris) and a young man discuss the professor's assignments and his high expectations. She takes a letter from her purse to mail, and as the couple walks, they talk about gaining employment. However, the narrative takes an unexpected turn as Arlette's colleague approaches a fat man with a cigar and tries to pick his pocket. The affair backfires, and the victim calls for help. People gather, and Arlette and her companion escape.

Returning to the school, Arlette hides behind a door and peers through the window opening, observing the professor and his students, recapitulating the opening scenes that involve the dichotomy between inside and outside and highlighting the issue of surveillance. She enters the room and joins the others as Professor Comte lines up his pupils. He drills them through various movements, asking them to look to the right and the left and having them raise their hands, palms out. The camera pans their faces, and the professor praises them as the group practices pickpocketing on the mannequin. Some are too fast; others are "not bad." For their final exercise, the "students" pretend they are riding on the bus and plying their trade. Their practice is cut short by the entry of the professor's wife, who reminds them of a graduation celebration in the evening as their send-off into the world. At the party, the professor further observes Arlette to make sure she looks sufficiently innocent. He has her practice an alibi should she get caught, namely that she is basically an honest and virtuous person, that she has never had any conflict with the law and therefore begs leniency. Satisfied with her performance, he prophesies a promising career.

After attempting to find legitimate work and failing, Arlette finds herself on an elevator with a well-to-do-looking man wearing a jeweled stickpin. A series of cuts between her in close-up to a close-up of the stickpin leads to a shot of the man's cravat minus the pin. On the street, she opens her hand, which is holding the pin. Seeking to evade her victim, she goes to a movie theater where a Ginger Rogers–Fred Astaire film is playing, only to find the man in the seat next to her. She rehearses her innocent-victim routine, while the film on the screen replays the same scenario. The man, Count Maciaky (Giuseppe Porelli), orders her to come with him to the Stivonian Embassy, where she is ordered to impersonate a Stivonian baroness. She arrives at a ball set in lavish surroundings in clothes provided by Maciaky, who introduces her as a baroness. Maciaky tells her to dance with Jerry, Lord Salisbury (John Lodge), an English nobleman, and steal his pocket watch.

The professor and his students, learning of Arlette's success at the embassy, are duly excited about her future prospects. After the ball, Jerry insists on escorting Arlette home. She stops at a hotel where she claims she will stay, pretending to take a room. Thinking Jerry is gone, she exits only to find him waiting outside. He invites her to a restaurant, the Lapin Rouge, and tries to pry information from her about the secrecy he "sees in her eyes." They have their picture taken and again Jerry comments on her eyes, telling her she does not look like a sinner, thus highlighting vision as a problematic in the film. When they exit, they are observed by the professor, who is hiding in the bushes, disguised behind a beard. Jerry tries to catch him, but all he finds is a discarded beard. Arlette returns to the hotel, takes a room, and the following day Jerry calls her. She tells him she cannot see him, since she does not have her baggage from Stivonia. At his residence, Jerry tells his butler (coincidentally, the victim of Arlette's companion earlier), that he is in love with Arlette but that he plans to teach her a lesson. Maciacky sends her a bracelet with a request for her to return the borrowed clothing.

The professor arrives and offers to help Arlette. He takes the bracelet and in return gives her the money to pay her hotel bill. When Jerry returns for her, she tries to dissuade him from any future relations with her, saying that he knows nothing of her past. In the lobby, her former companion in crime is plying his trade, and Jerry discovers that his watch is missing, thinking that Arlette is the culprit. Incompetent as always, Arlette's colleague is caught by hotel security, and Jerry insists that the man be tried and punished. The scene shifts to police headquarters, where Arlette tries to confess to her crimes. When called to testify, the count disavows her confession, asserting that nothing of his has been stolen and revealing that he is in possession of the stickpin that Arlette claims she stole from him. Privately, he confesses to the commissioner that the theft of the watch was a secret matter of state involving political motives. There were secret plans in the watch. After prying the watch open, it is revealed that the only thing in it is the photo of Jerry and Arlette taken earlier. Jerry and Arlette are reconciled as she begins to recount a narrative of her life. The film ends with their wedding and with the professor and his students enjoying the opportunity to fleece the rich guests; however, since they agree it is a special day, they return the stolen items.

The element of thievery is potentially the material of melodrama, linked as it is to notions of the sanctity of the law and the protection of property, but melodramatic expectations are short-circuited through comedy. Negative associations with criminals are subverted by the comparison of the school for thieves to a respectable pedagogical enterprise. The incompetent nature of the crooks also mitigates the usual association of thievery with malevolence: the thieves are, after all, only trying to earn a living. The home-like atmosphere of the thieves' community evidenced by the relationships between the professor, his wife, and their charges militates strongly against negative identification with the thieves. Most of all, Arlette, as their "star" pupil, is attractive and desirable, as the romance plot demonstrates. And when placed against the image of the foreign diplomats and their knavery, the boundary between the thieves and respectable folk further blurs. The thieves' society seems more interesting and variegated than that of the upper classes, reminiscent of Camerini's continuing predilection for the "ordinary" folk.

The film plays on the possibility that crime and impersonation is profitable.[9] They are the entrée into the upper reaches of society. In being presented as a form of work, as a "profession," crime stands in contrast to the leisure and machinations of the upper class. Crime appears to be useful to the upper classes, as the count's hiring of Arlette indicates. The film's seemingly "light" comedy (which is underestimated as such) touches at the heart of basic social structures. The film reproduces conventional voyeurism, allowing a window onto the world of wealth and luxury, but the mechanisms of spectatorship are such that this view into the life of the other half exposes its moral imperfections. From the opening shots, the issue of surveillance is highlighted. The inside-outside images play with the audience, withholding and then revealing what goes on inside this society. The audience is playfully indicted as a voyeur and then invited to participate. Arlette is observed by her first victim. Maciaky surveys Arlette as she steals the watch. Jerry observes Arlette. The professor spies on Jerry and Arlette. That Arlette is "caught" by Maciaky while watching a film is not an empty reflexive device but another indication of an urban world where looking has primacy: looking enhances the desire to be and to possess what one sees.

The connection to cinema as a consummate purveyor of these images is central to Camerini's films, offering a meditation on media representation as unstable currency. Impersonation, that is, performance, is thus more than a convention. As in so many melodramas of the era, impersonation begins to resonate with supplementary meanings involved in cultural politics. It raises the question of authenticity and of the primacy of illusion. In *Batticuore*, the film undermines confession as truth-telling, which is exemplified by the fact that the film ends with the withholding of the count's motives for his "crime." Also, Jerry and the police thwart Arlette's attempts at confession. In foregrounding looking and linking it to crime, the film undermines any simplistic notion of escapism. Instead, it offers an insight into the cinema of the era, exceeding intentionality and becoming part of the dense texture of a world devoted to spectacle and thus a challenge to reductive conceptions of Fascism and its relationship to the cinema.

Theatricality and Maternity

These films produced during the *ventennio* do not, despite their stance of escapism, escape Fascism; in fact, they have much to illuminate about the importance of role-playing and impersonation in relation to the Fascism of everyday life. The films offer a different perspective than "fascinating Fascism" and its emphasis on public spectacle and formal politics. Escapism as theatricality, as role-playing and performance, is revealed to be necessary and even inevitable. Theatricality appears to be particularly associated with femininity, with maternity, and with an emphasis on masquerade and impersonation. The films that feature feminine figures offer a repertoire of maternal figures and maternal surrogates who, in their excessiveness, appear to be caricatures of service and self-abnegation. While the maternal figure, whether as a paragon of self-abnegation or as errant and destructive, is ubiquitous, her portrait is not seamless and unproblematic.

Even when the mother is not directly invoked, the scenario of maternity guides the narrative, the images, and relationships among characters, drawing on a traditional iconography embellished and brought up to date to conform to modern aspirations.[10] Magazines, newspapers, and documentaries by LUCE were increasingly devoted to this project, aligning it with government campaigns to enhance the birth rate in particular as well as with the battle to restore the primacy of the family, which was presumed to be under siege.[11] The image of woman is identified with the maintenance of the family which is, in turn, identified with melodramatic images of loss and compensation for sacrifice. The theatrical as operatic is the mainstay of such fictions; it is identified with performance and not with authenticity. As is often the case in advertising "the product itself gains power and prestige over the means of production [and] . . . the human subject is gradually elided, mechanized, or annihilated by a violent representational act."[12]

If there was a fantasy of the coming into being of a "new man," there was also an attempt to produce a "new woman."[13] An examination of the attention paid to maternity reveals that the regime was zealous in seeking to reinvent the family. Corresponding to the production of new men and new women was an emphasis on the "new family." Common to all these conceptions was the attempt to align the family with the nation: "The state claimed that the family was sacrosanct and indivisible, yet, in the name of nation, the dictatorship justified every kind of intrusion," which produced a number of tensions.[14] While propaganda insisted on the sexual puritanism, economic frugality, and austere leisure habits associated with early industrialism, the creation of a modern consumer society created contradictions between past and present social practices.

A singular focus on Fascist institutions, however, does not adequately reveal the character of representations of femininity. "If we want to gain a less limited understanding of all the levels and complexities of the cultural construction of gender in the Fascist era," writes Lucia Re, "we need to consider the ways in which the hegemonic discourse of the regime finds philosophical as well as political and ideological grounding in its *theories* of gender."[15] Examining the writings of such philosophers as Giovanni Gentile, Re probes the contradictory ways in which the theorization of sexual difference must be accounted for; she highlights its modernity, its culturalist bent, and its insistence on motherhood as "something innate, original, and essential to woman."[16] For example, in relationship to representation, Re cites modernist and avant-garde writings that denaturalize the biological and maternal by means of the techniques of estrangement, irony, and satire, indicating that even in the midst of totalizing rhetoric and practices, there were fissures in the cultural fabric. An examination of popular commercial films reveals fissures in their mode of escapism, the theatricality that calls attention to the blurring of boundaries between theatricality and life. As Karen Pinkus has written, "At times, the body seems to erase any traces of its own gender—to masquerade or cross-dress—as a security measure, almost as if to escape the controls of the regime."[17]

Maternal sacrifice emphasizes form over content, style over substance, and femininity thereby becomes a strategy, a performance with a pre-scripted scenario. *Il carnevale di Venezia* (*Carnival in Venice*, 1940) is an exemplary film with which to examine the highly theatrical character of maternal discourse and how it draws on a form of escapism that is tied to affect identified with the reigning folklore of motherhood and the family. Through its uses of opera, the film offers images of femininity and maternity that ultimately reveal the Janus face of escapism. Directed by Giuseppe Adami and Giacomo Gentilomo, the film contains a mélange of opera arias (orchestral work by the Royal Opera of Rome), folk songs, and ballet (performed by the Corps de Ballet of La Scala). The central figure, a mother and an entertainer, is the opera singer Toti Dal Monte, a renowned lyric soprano. The city of Venice also figures largely in the film. More than backdrop, the city is central to the spectacle and theatricality of the text, especially to the folklore of carnival as liberating.

The film opens with images of Venice, the Grand Canal, palaces, bridges, and people scurrying about. A title, "The Bridge of Sighs," givcs way tu the pages of a musical score and then to a view of musicians under the direction of a conductor, Montini. The conjunction of the city with musical culture provides a prolegomena to the ways the film seeks to establish the relationship between urban life and performance. Montini's appearance introduces a necessary tension in the film between definitions of success and failure through operatic spectacle and melodramatic performance. Montini's rehearsal is interrupted by a gust of rain that blows in from an open window and scatters the musical scores. We also learn that his daughter, an opera singer, is not a success on the stage but works as a foreman in a tobacco factory. The factory where she works is also associated with music as she and the other women sing as they work. Conflict erupts when Ninetta warns one of the women that she will have to work more responsibly or be reported. In response, the woman informs on Tonina (Junie Astor), Ninetta's daughter, saying that she is carrying on with Paolo, Count Sagredo (Guido Lazzarini). Tonina is studying music at a conservatory. A fight, reminiscent of the opening scenes in Bizet's *Carmen*, ensues between the two women, and others join the fray.

Thus, the film poses a number of oppositions between upper-class and lower-class existence, the visual splendor of Venice and familial constraints, relations between mothers and daughters, success and failure, and everyday life and theatrical spectacle. Misrecognition and confusion multiply as Ninetta assumes that her daughter is actually having an affair with a baker, Marchetto (Stefano Sibaldi), who is in possession of a scarf of Tonina's which he found on the street. Tonina does nothing to dispel her mother's suspicions, thus concealing that she is actually involved with Paolo. Disaffected with her family and with the neighbors, she tells Paolo that she is going to run away. He urges her to think of her mother. Marchetto is making preparations to celebrate his engagement to Tonina at the Feast of the Redeemer, which is to be held that evening. Ninetta is morose, and Tonina is angry for being questioned concerning her activities. After the family is dressed for the feast, Ninetta discovers that her daughter has left home. Stoically, she goes to the festival. Asked to sing by her father, she at first refuses but relents after he commands her to hide her feelings. As she performs, the editing intercuts between her and the numerous assembled groups in the boats and on the shore (among which is Tonina with Paolo). When she performs a traditional lullaby that Tonina recognizes from her childhood, the daughter decides to return to her mother and finds her praying before an image of the Madonna.

Tonina makes an attempt to improve her singing. Discouraged, she tells her mother, "I must succeed," but Ninetta does not understand her daughter's ambition, though she acknowledges that Tonina is no longer her little girl. Here the contrast between mother and daughter is most apparent, Ninetta embodying an acceptance of her social class and style of life, Tonina struggling against her mother's values and seeking to escape into a life of romance through artistic success. She asks Ninetta to perform for her, and Ninetta sings arias from *Lucia di Lammermoor* and *La Sonambula*. The mother's exemplary performance does not encourage the daughter, though it provides Montini with another opportunity to lament that Ninetta's voice is wasted in her work at the factory. Paolo, zealous for Tonina to perform, plans for her to appear in Venice as "the nightingale of San Marco." Posters and signs advertise the appearance of the "nightingale." Confusion escalates as Marchetto seeks restitution for the money he has expended for the engagement party; he threatens to appropriate Montini's piano as compensation.

The carnival, the climax of the film, highlights spectacle once again, beginning with an elaborate ballet sequence and mingling it with the dancing of crowds. Tonina's performance is endangered when she loses her voice, but Ninetta, concealed within, sings in her stead as Tonina mimes the words. The audience is wildly enthusiastic. Tonina tries to confess but is stopped by Paolo, who drags her away to his friends. The final shots of the film take place indoors with Ninetta alone at the piano until joined by Montini, who tells her that he alone knows that she was the singer. She comments, "But he'll marry her," as she leans against Montini. On the surface the film provides a narrative of reconciliation. Marchetto has relented in his claim, Tonina will marry well, and the secret of the fraudulent performance is safe.

Il carnevale di Venezia offers an affectively intense and ambiguous version of the benign and selfless face of maternal femininity, reenacting the melodramatic motif of a mother who devotes herself totally to her daughter to the point of self-abnegation, subordinating her own career to further her daughter's ambitions. However, the daughter's "career" turns out not to be a musical one but marriage to a nobleman. The film does not reconcile talent, success, and domesticity. Rather, creativity is subordinated, in the case of both mother and daughter, to work and to the domestic sphere. Though the film has certain classic elements of the opera and the musical—romance, spectacle, the struggle to succeed in the world of entertainment, and self-reflexivity about performance and spectatorship—its treatment of spectacle does not overwhelm the conflicts but highlights their incommensurability, exposing a disjunction between performance and social life.[18] The festive aspects of carnival that usually function as vehicles for undermining conventional behavior and restraints are complicated and diluted by the knowledge of Ninetta's fraudulent act of ventriloquism.[19]

Unlike Victor Savile's British melodrama *Evergreen* (1934), in which the heroine impersonates her mother, is forced to confess in order to be absolved for her crime of fraudulence, and hence is enabled to continue as a performer in her own right, *Il carnevale* suppresses the confession and, hence, the requisite absolution.[20] Ninetta uses her vocal talent to conceal her daughter's inadequacies. In the final analysis, she not only "gives up her child to the social order," but in so doing she also negates her own identity.[21] The film can be seen to reiterate the pathos of a film such as *Stella Dallas* (1937), where maternal desire is "displaced onto the daughter."[22] The film's silences—like Ninetta's—argue for the premise that the text is working on commonsense assumptions shared with the audience; for example, playing with the subordination of the public to the private sphere, of collective submission to individual action, and of self-expression to suppression and repression. The viability of the private sphere is maintained by suppressing truth, by keeping the secret of impersonation intact. Melodrama as the language of muteness serves common sense in *Carnevale:* at the same time that it enacts the paradigm of maternal service it also—intentionality aside—exposes how common sense is based on maintaining silence and, therefore, how this silence is the instrument of consensus.

In the context of escapism, this emphasis on silence can be read in ambiguous terms as prescriptive or as cynical revelation. However, the mother-and-daughter relationship, which operates within the conventions of the musical, remains fractured through the conspiracy of silence, despite several attempts at reconciliation. This silence, which is not obscured from the external audience, undermines the conventional characteristics of the musical. The musical's reflexivity depends on performance to create a sense of shared community between internal audience and external audience. In this film, the exposure of secrecy works on several levels to impair the semblance of unity. The genre itself is undermined by subverting claims to the intactness and inviolability of spectacle. The narrative is exposed as relying on fraudulence. Most especially, the film denaturalizes femininity by inadvertently revealing how the maternal figure serves as the determinant of social value while receiving nothing in exchange but an image of its sacrifice, reinforcing the notion that escapism in terms of its theatricality and reflexivity is not devoid of a knowledge of its contradiction that it shares with its audiences. Yet there is still another (ironic) twist to the film's reliance on theatricality. As the recognized star of opera and of the film, Toti Dal

Monte's role serves both to reinforce the image of maternal sacrifice in the narrative and at the same time intertextually undermine it through the audience's knowledge of her own success as a performer.

Dissecting Escapism

Not all of the films are cast in the ambiguous mold of the "escapist" films discussed above; some appear to directly address and dissect the tendency to valorize romance, upward mobility, material rewards for the deserving, and service. However, given the tension in the culture and in the cinema of the era between tradition and modernity, essentialism and culturalism, ideology and opportunism, it is not surprising that films other than musicals and comedies should address the issue of escapism and link it to profound psychological questions about conformity and social accommodation. In a striking and unsettling vein, Poggioli's *Sorelle Materassi (The Materassi Sisters,* 1943) is a dissection of the sexual politics of power and the power of sexual politics, exposing images of the self-sacrificing nature of maternal behavior, the sanctified haven of the family, the fictions of masculinity and femininity, and the vain and destructive desire to be mastered.

Poggioli utilizes the Gramatica sisters, who were popular in the theater and on screen, in roles that are satiric and melodramatic. The film is a portrait of a world gone berserk, where accumulation, venality, hypocrisy, and exploitation are commonplace. Consisting of three sisters, an assistant to the sisters, a cook, a princess, and an American woman from Argentina, this harem-like world is invaded by a man, Remo (Massimo Serrato), the nephew of the Materassi sisters, whose presence transforms the home into bedlam. Based on a novel by Aldo Palazzeschi, the film begins on a street where a car turns into a gate bearing the sign "Materassi Sisters." Women gape out of the window excitedly as the car arrives. The visitor, a priest, goes to a workroom, where two of the sisters, Teresa and Carolina, are fitting a customer with lingerie. When the priest enters, one of the sisters discreetly covers the customer's body. At Teresa's request, Carolina gives the priest vestments they have made for the church, and he commends them for their excellent work, telling them that they have been honored for their work by a visit to the pope. Niobe, the cook (Dina Romano), rushes out, shouting the good news for all to hear.

In a highly choreographed scene at the Vatican, the sisters walk down a long hall decorated with murals and paintings until they reach an ornate door and are stopped. When the pope is announced, the sisters kneel as he blesses them and others. In stark contrast to this scene of hard work rewarded, Remo is seen on a train, traveling in a first-class compartment with a third-class ticket. When confronted with this discrepancy by the conductor, he is saved by a young woman who offers to the pay the difference between the tickets as an older man observes the transaction, shaking his head. When the sisters return home, they are again observed by others from the window and on the street. The element of voyeurism, the film's recurrent use of mirrors and windows to highlight spectatorship and opposition between inside and outside, looking and being looked at, will become a leitmotif for the film. Inside, the sisters babble about their visit to the Vatican, but their narrative is interrupted by the sounds of crying. The two sisters walk upstairs to enter the room of their bedridden third sister, Giselda (Olga Solbelli), who from her bed complains that they have fun while she languishes. She accuses them of being ignorant of life, and when Teresa and Carolina leave, she picks up a photo of a man, her husband who deserted her, kisses it, and cries. This photo is her weapon against the unmarried sisters. The preoccupation with inanimate objects—photos, bikes, cars, clothing, and money—will gain in intensity through the narrative.

When Giselda ventures downstairs, she finds Teresa; Carolina; Laurina, their assistant (Anna Maria); and Niobe hovering around Remo, who has arrived on the scene. He tells the women a sad story of maltreatment at the hands of an uncle while leering seductively at Laurina. He complains of being forced by his uncle to take work that was unworthy of him. Teresa and Carolina invite him to stay with them, while Giselda adamantly refuses to have a man in the house. Against her wishes, he stays, and Teresa and Carolina offer him a bike for transportation. Six months later, Remo is still with them, and the two sisters rave about their nephew to the priest, calling him a "perfect saint." The "perfect saint" is at that moment putting on his jacket while a woman on the bed takes out money from a wallet to pay him for his services. The sisters continue to wait servilely on Remo and refuse to believe anything negative about his behavior. When a mother comes to the house to complain of Remo's taking advantage of her daughter, Teresa and Carolina angrily send her away. After seeing a motorcycle that he covets, he asks the sisters for money to buy it and they refuse. He punishes them by withholding affection and they relent, but Remo has already charmed Niobe, who, fearful that he might leave, gets him the money.

Remo's conquests with women now include the sisters, a sculptress, Niobe, and Laurina. In the hope of placating Remo, the sisters now buy him a car. Thus, Remo's rise in this world is marked by his graduation from a bike to a motorcycle to a car. The situation of the two sisters is characterized by increasing fear and desperation over the possibility of losing Remo. The more they suffer, the more Gisela gloats. When the princess, who has also been supporting Remo, comes to the house to pick up lingerie, Teresa and Carolina tell her they no longer want her business. Giselda shows the sisters a card from the sculptor she has found in Remo's jacket, another indication of her constant spying and of her desire to torture them. Remo, appearing to be grateful for the gift of the car, invites the sisters to dinner at a restaurant. He sits down one sister before a mirror and fashions a new hairdo for her as the other looks on jealously. At the restaurant, Remo's regular haunt, a place where he meets his cronies and engages in shady transactions, he cavorts with the men while the sisters sit alone at a table looking at him admiringly and giggling. They end up paying for the meal, but they are unperturbed. At home, they wax enthusiastic about him, seeing him as a prince, a soldier, or a bishop. When they learn that Laurina is pregnant and that Remo is the father, their shining image of him remains untainted. He brings his cronies to the house, and the aunts are displaced. They sit on the stairs, observing the men carouse and giggling at Remo's antics. Only Giselda complains of the noise. Remo makes fun of them as he parades around for his friends in lingerie he has taken from the workroom, but still the aunts are not offended. When the friends leave, Teresa and Carolina confront him with Laurina's situation. When he disingenuously says he will marry her, they offer to find her a more suitable husband.

The sisters' relationship with Remo reaches new heights when he, pressed to pay back a loan, asks the sisters for the money. Despite the fact that the sisters' property is totally mortgaged, he insists that they sign a promissory note. They refuse, and he locks them in a closet, pocketing the key. Smoking indifferently in the doorway, he meets Niobe, who also seems unperturbed by the aunts' incarceration. She informs him that she has found a man who will marry Laurina. He opens the closet, and the sisters file out with the signed note. Giselda is pleased, thinking that they have seen the end of Remo. However, the sisters behave as if nothing unusual has happened. At the automobile showroom where he works, Remo waits on a client, a rich American woman, Peggy (Clara Calamai), and makes a sale. She insists on going for a test drive in the car, and as a result of her machinations, the two are forced to spend the night at an inn.

At the Materassi house, the sisters wait impatiently for news of Remo, who has not bothered to inform them that his escapade will deter him from returning to their house in the evening. A telegram arrives, announcing Remo's marriage to Peggy. The sisters accuse Peggy of be-

ing old and a witch. A dissolve to the street near the Materassi establishment reveals a group gathered to see the arrival of Peggy and Remo.
Their arrival is also observed from the window by the sisters, and Peggy
turns out to be young and beautiful, not at all as the Materassi sisters
have imagined her. Teresa and Carolina greet her stiffly. At the church,
where again a crowd is assembled, Peggy appears radiant as a bride.
Teresa and Carolina arrive next—also dressed as brides, to the amusement of the crowd. After the wedding, the two sisters, still in their bri-
dal finery, learn from Remo that he is leaving. In a scene that borders on
the surrealistic, the women, like deserted brides, part with Remo. He
says his farewell as the camera pans to the window. The aunts look out
at a show of fireworks, and the film ends with the sisters again at work.

The film's satire develops through excessively stylized characterization. Each character—particularly Teresa, Carolina, Giselda, and Remo
—is drawn in caricature to the straining point of credibility. Their
speech, gestures, and movement convey their self-imprisonment, obsession, and inability to hear or see. Remo is the focus of their obsession,
the source of their impossible desires. The consummate exploiter of
women, he is portrayed as entrapped in a fetishized relation to the
world, a caricature of the commodification of social relations. To say
that he is cruel and sadistic would make him a melodramatic villain.
What negates such identification is the film's portrait of the sisters, who
are portrayed as equally fetishistic, with Remo their fetish. They are
complicit in their treatment of Remo, in their blindness to his manipu-
lations.

The film valorizes looking in ways that also undermine melodrama or
at least make it appear self-consciously theatrical. Theresa and Carolina
observe the world through their window. They observe Remo's every
movement even when what they see is designed to make them look ridiculous. Giselda observes her sisters and Remo through peepholes. The
crowds watch the comings and goings at the Materassi house, amused
by the events they see. The sisters are voyeurs, gratifying their desire
through viewing photographs and especially through constant scrutiny
of their nephew. The number of spectators on the street, which in-
creases as the film progresses, serves as an ambiguous and ironic surrogate for the external audience, a distancing device that permits sardonic
laughter. By extension, the external audience is implicated in the voyeurism. The emphasis on looking is a means of distanciation, undermining identification with the characters and affect. Looking functions
as a way of underscoring the disjunction between desire and attainment,
heightening the sense of their incommensurability. The shifting perspectives inhibit the stabilization of one spectatorial position. Where an

unchanging perspective might ensure an affective involvement with the character, the shifting of positions draws identification away from any one character, dispersing attention among the various characters and directing it toward the situation. Spectatorship in the film is triangulated, shifting from the characters to the internal audience and from them to the external audience.

The characters' mechanical gestures and responses are like dream condensations, contributing to a sense of the de-realization and the masquerade-like character of their world. The objects in the film—the clothing, the bicycle, the motorcycle, and the car—are more substantial than the people. The metamorphosis of the characters into puppet-like creations and their interchangeability with objects serve to dramatize the film's preoccupation with power as sexual politics exemplified in the characters' manipulation of each other. Teresa and Carolina seek to control Giselda and Laurina. Giselda in turn seeks to undermine that control through her own machinations. Remo seeks to control his aunts, his mastery over them predicated on his ability to play on their desire to possess him and on the threat of withdrawal of affection. The essential force that animates their interactions with each other and with others is their fear of isolation. Locked into their sexual fantasies, vainly waiting for someone to free them, their desire for affection and recognition plunges them into degradation, violence, and exploitation. The sisters' entrapment is made literal when Remo locks the sisters in a closet until they accede to his financial demands. Through Remo's character, the film probes the excessive and destructive side of bourgeois attitudes toward family and respectability. Economics and sexuality (money, cars, and sex) are the terrain on which the game of dominance and subordination is played out between Remo and the sisters. The job Remo finally acquires is as an automobile salesman, and motor vehicles become signifiers of his sexuality. If he is the women's object of desire, their fetish, locomotory objects are his fetishes, corollaries of his inability or his exploitation of people for the acquisition of material goods. In this film, basic thematic elements of many of the films that address familial virtues are overturned—the sanctity and security of family relations, the elevation of industriousness, and the imperative of loyalty and service.

The melodramatic conflicts are orchestrated in several ways: in the sisters' aggressive and competitive relationship with each other, in their "adoption" of and conflict with Remo, and in their competition with Peggy, who wins Remo. The petit-bourgeois world they inhabit can be read in the sisters' conspiracy with Remo to maintain the ideal of being "useful," even to the point of tolerating verbal and physical debasement. The emphasis on looking underscores the film's obsession with vicarious experience. The excessive style of acting and the claustrophobic mise-en-scène create an alienating effect, producing an uncomfortable relationship to the events viewed. The ending of the film is an ironic commentary on the fantasy of the happy ending. Remo is successful in finding a rich woman to gratify his economic and sexual aspirations, and the sisters are freed of his tyranny. However, the sisters are once again alone, their illusions intact, as they were at the beginning before Remo's arrival. Nothing appears to have changed, but the internal as well as the external audience has witnessed their consummate degradation.

In the sisters' situation, the film obliquely invokes a reminder of the war and of the scarcity of men, who were away fighting in Greece, Russia, Africa, and even in sections of Italy. In the interactions between Remo and the sisters, the film also provides an unsettling portrait of masculinity as violent and exploitative that runs counter to the official legitimation of virility, sexuality, and power. But the binarism of melodrama is undermined by the excessiveness of the women's desperate attachment to a dominant masculine figure, their endowing that person with great power, and their willingness to endure any humiliation to maintain that relationship. The stylized acting of the female protagonists and the claustrophobic mise-en-scène unsettle a univalent reading of the sisters. Desperate and fragile, they are victims of desire who are culpable in their willingness to endow Remo with power over them.

All the characters dramatize the desire to possess, to manipulate, and to control through the obsession with money, respectability, and the terrifying fear of isolation. The lingerie and linen, the house, the objects of locomotion, the photograph, and the clock that signifies Remo's absence and the sisters' longing for him testify to the film's exploration of the commodification of desire. In its negative and interrogative view of this topsy-turvy world, the film orchestrates a connection between familialism, sexuality, and power. The inclusion of Peggy is no exception, augmenting the chain of exploitation, inviting reflection on marriage as another dimension of the exchange of commodities and of the transformation of the human into inanimate objects. Everyone is corrupt, but none is beyond empathy. The film offers the remote possibility, through its focus on spectatorship, that seeing, not merely looking, might offer an avenue of escape, if only for the audience. The film has all the appurtenances of melodrama—obsession, consuming and endless but ungratified desire, and misperception—but the characters' opaqueness and invulnerability temper the pathos. Nothing enters to disturb this enclosed world except the possibility of recognition, and the only locus for such perception is the external audience. The film appears overtly to complicate escapism, suggesting through its portrait of obsessional behavior and the self-deceptions that it generates that it is possible to gain an insight into the nature of escapism and, in particular, its investment in performance.

Thus, while theories of "fascinating Fascism" call attention to the ritualistic and spectacular manifestations of Fascism—its public spectacles and political rhetoric—they underplay the immediate, everyday, and dynamic dimensions of representation characteristic of many of the films produced. The film texts discussed above are clever about politics and self-conscious about their need to be entertaining, present themselves in terms of genre, and stress spectatorship, artifice, doubling, disguises, and impersonation. The theatricality of the films merges with images of quotidian life to offer clues that, for better or worse, invoke the fantasies, needs, and aspirations of their audiences in ways that complicate and force a modification of notions and judgments of escapism. Through theatricality, escapism reveals itself as entailing identification and participation as well as a cynical awareness of the posturing necessary to "keep the show going." Rather than dismissing these films as trivial escapist texts or as legitimations of Fascism, the texts should be regarded as sources of new insights into the complex character of Fascist representation that modify notions of coercion or consensus.

Notes

1. Gerald Mast, *A Short History of the Movies* (New York: Macmillan, 1986); David A. Cook, *A History of Narrative Film* (New York: W. W. Norton, 1996); and, from another vantage point, the writings of G. P. Brunetta, "The Long March of American Cinema in Italy," in *Hollywood in Europe: Experiences of a Cultural Hegemony,* ed. David W. Ellwood and Rob Kroes (Amsterdam: VU University Press, 1994), 139–155.

2. James Hay, *Popular Film Culture in Fascist Italy: The Passing of the Rex* (Bloomington: Indiana University Press, 1987).

3. Jane Feuer, *The Hollywood Musical* (London: BFI, 1982).

4. Elaine Mancini, *Struggles of the Italian Film Industry during Fascism, 1930–1935* (Ann Arbor: UMI Research Press, 1985).

5. Feuer, *The Hollywood Musical,* 82.

6. Ibid., 3.

7. Ibid., 23.

8. Max Neufeld has been described as a master, as practically the inventor of white-telephone films, and as a "miracle of efficiency." He was a "hands-on" director who paid careful attention to the ambiance of the film, to the photography, and especially to the clarity of the lighting. Francesco Savio,

*Cinecittà anni trenta. Parlano 116 protagonisti del secondo cinema italiano,
1930–43,* 3 vols. (Rome: Bulzoni Press, 1979), 3: 1068 and 989.

9. Marcia Landy, *Fascism in Film: The Italian Commercial Cinema, 1930–1943*
(Princeton: Princeton University Press, 1986), 265–269.

10. Victoria de Grazia, *How Fascism Ruled Women: Italy, 1922–1943* (Berkeley:
University of California Press, 1991), 75–115; Lesley Caldwell, "Madri
d'Italia: Film and the Fascist Concern with Motherhood," in *Women and
Italy: Essays in Gender, Culture, and History,* ed. Zygmunt G. Baranski
and Shirley W. Vinall (New York: St. Martin's Press, 1991), 43–64; and
Jacqueline Reich, "Reading, Writing, and Rebellion: Collectivity, Specularity, and Sexuality in Italian Schoolgirl Comedies," in *Mothers of Invention: Women, Italian Fascism, and Culture,* ed. Robin Pickering-Iazzi (Minneapolis: University of Minnesota Press, 1995), 220–251.

11. De Grazia, *How Fascism Ruled Women,* 78–215.

12. Karen Pinkus, *Bodily Regimes: Italian Advertising under Fascism* (Minneapolis: University of Minnesota Press, 1995), 16.

13. The emphasis on the valorization of motherhood corresponded to the de-
valorization of feminist aspirations. Toward the ends of making motherhood attractive and profitable, the regime offered honorific and monetary
incentives. Writing of the character and effects of maternity practices under the regime, de Grazia says, "The fascist family services offered the
allure of the modern without its underpinnings. These set new standards,
interfered with old customs, and stigmatized traditional practices. Yet they
failed to provide the wherewithal to feel empowered by a modernized maternal craft—either as the providers or as the beneficiaries of new services,
Italian mothers of all classes were made to feel inadequate, anxious, and
dependent." *How Fascism Ruled Women,* 60.

14. Ibid., 81.

15. Lucia Re, "Fascist Theories of 'Woman' and the Construction of Gender,"
in Pickering-Iazzi, *Mothers of Invention: Women, Italian Fascism, and Culture,* 80.

16. Ibid., 81.

17. Pinkus, *Bodily Regimes,* 154.

18. Christian Viviani, "Who Is Without Sin: The Maternal Melodrama in
American Film, 1930–1939," *Wide Angle* 4 (1980): 4–17.

19. Victoria de Grazia, *The Culture of Consent* (Cambridge: Cambridge University Press, 1981), 215.

20. Marcia Landy, *British Genres: Cinema and Society 1930–1960* (Princeton:
Princeton University Press, 1991), 200–203.

21. Mary Ann Doane, *The Desire to Desire: The Woman's Film of the 1940s*
(Bloomington: Indiana University Press, 1987), 74.

22. Ibid., 73.

10

Shopping for Autarchy

Fascism and Reproductive Fantasy in
Mario Camerini's Grandi magazzini

Barbara Spackman

If Fascist ideology bound together heterogeneous and often incompatible elements, its interpellation of those it constructed as women presents an especially knotted case of how such elements compete and collide. Fascism at once relegated women to the roles of wife and fecund mother, deprived them of the rights and jobs they had only recently and fleetingly acquired, and at the same time called them to participate in political life, devote themselves to good works, and appear in mass demonstrations. Fascist topography thus at once insisted on the boundary between heavily gendered spheres of public and private space and called for its transgressive crossing. Figures such as the Fascist feminist Teresa Labriola (who would argue for the virilization of the Fascist mother) or the women athletes of the Scuola di Orvieto (working out for the fatherland) are responses to this divided call. Announcing themselves to be "virile yet feminine," they attempt to keep one foot in the maternalist sphere of reproductive duty while standing on tiptoe with the other in the masculinized sphere of political participation and public exhibition.[1] But this already divided interpellation is itself riven by the still-debated and conflictual relation between Fascism and modernization. The Fascist regime fostered the industrialization, the economic rationalization, and, to a lesser extent, the secularization that are characteristic of modernization but, especially in the years of the demographic campaign, rejected the urbanization that is inseparable from it.[2] Here one might say that the specifically Fascist interpellation addressed women as rural mothers—in Fascist discourse, city life brings with it sterility, prostitution, and the lure of foreign goods—whereas modernization and the consumer culture that accompanies it increasingly addressed women as urban consumers.[3] In competition throughout the *ventennio*, these ideological imperatives collided most dramatically during the late 1930s, when the policy known as economic autarchy was introduced, first as a necessity due to the economic sanctions imposed by the League of Nations after the 1935 invasion of Ethiopia, and later as permanent policy. Italy was to be self-sufficient, and foreign imports, material as well as cultural and linguistic, were to be eliminated. "Buy Italian" was the slogan of the day, and autarchic fabrics and fashions were created to tempt the woman whose patriotic duty it was to shop for autarchy at the same time as she continued to reproduce *piccoli fascisti*.[4]

It is within this context that I would like to place Mario Camerini's 1939 film, *Grandi magazzini* (*The Department Store*), in order to read it as a text of mass culture that works on and with ideological materials of the *ventennio*. More specifically, I want to argue that in it we find a condensation of the multiple interpellations issued by Fascism, and an attempt, through narrativization, to reconcile some of the contradictions arising from the presence of competing elements. Apparently a politically indifferent, escapist film shaped by the conventions of classic Hollywood narrative cinema, *Grandi magazzini* follows the romance of a salesgirl, Lauretta (played by Assia Noris), and a delivery-truck driver, Bruno (played by Vittorio De Sica, at the end of his matinee idol days), as it unfolds almost entirely on the set of a large, generically modern department store, presumably in Milan.[5] Its generic modernity is underscored by the fashion plates that serve as background to the opening credits, and many of the film's themes and ideologemes (if not their specific articulation) can be found in earlier representations of commodity culture and the department store, such as Emile Zola's *Au bonheur des dames* (*The Ladies' Paradise*).[6] One shot alone locates it explicitly within the Fascist period and suggests that escape may not be what the film has to offer: in the background of the millinery department hangs a sign that reads: "*tessuti autarchici del primato italiano*" [autarchic fabrics of Italian supremacy], a reminder that in 1939 Italy was at the height of the campaign for autarchy and the first hint that the film will turn out to be an autarchic one, given over to imagining the store itself as a self-sufficient economy. Engagements and pregnancies are celebrated in its locker rooms and its female vendors dream of buying what they sell, while its managers scheme to seduce those they manage and steal what they oversee. Even the black market comes not from the outside but rather from the "inside job" of the pilfering scheme. In fact, the absence of an outside is nicely figured when Bruno mistakenly ends up driving the truck that contains the goods the managers have stolen for themselves.[7] Hours later he returns to the store with the packages and reports to the anxious culprits that the addresses written on them didn't exist. There is no economic outside, and even in the final scene, the protagonists, now a happy couple accompanied by other happy couples, leave the store only to turn around and gaze into its display windows, where they see themselves reflected. This autarchic structure is further strengthened by the striking number of exclusively Italian brand names that appear on the walls, on products, and on signs throughout the film: Oliofiat, Mirelli, Motta, Cinzano, Galtrucco, Gancia, Raion, and so on; the film itself is one long advertisement whose message says, loud and clear, "Buy Autarchic."[8]

Who answers? I would like to suggest that through its riven address to women, as "sterile" urban consumers on the one hand and as faithful wives and fecund mothers on the other, the film attempts to reconcile these contradictions and produce a fertile urban consumer-mother. The divided interpellation produces a range of female characters who hear one or the other strain: the hefty countrywoman who appeals to the night watchman Gaetano is clearly the rural mother, but with her ample bosom and broad hips she is clearly also too rural to be desirable or to fit into the fashions displayed throughout the film. Anna, the salesgirl in millinery, is the figure of the so-called luxury woman whose too-conspicuous consumption is marked by white furs, feathery bedroom slippers, and lascivious behavior; too urban a consumer, her consumption must be represented as theft. Indeed, she appears to be the ringleader of the manager's illicit scheme, and her "romantic" attachments appear to be prostitution.[9] The sweet Emilia, abandoned by her husband in the beginning of the film only to reunite with him later, is the model of the young woman who properly leaves the store upon discovering that she is pregnant.[10] Each of these answers a part of the call, but none manages to become the urban yet fertile consumer.

The salesgirl Lauretta instead is the node around which the competing imperatives collect and the character through whom the film will attempt to produce a figure of resolution between consumer and mother, public and private. Her character stands at the intersection of two different economies: one, the specifically Fascist autarchic economy in which she must learn to be a proper consumer, and the other, the familiar homosocial economy in which, as salesgirl, she herself is one of the commodities on the market, and she must learn how properly to sell, or not to sell, herself.[11] This latter conflation of seller and object of sale comes as no surprise, for it would appear to accompany consumer culture. A fully developed topos in the department-store novels of the late nineteenth century, it was already firmly in place in representations of boutique culture in seventeenth- and eighteenth-century France. In an essay on the ancien régime, Jennifer Jones has noted that shopping was, for much of the seventeenth and eighteenth centuries, "considered a form of male entertainment in which the line between the licit pleasure of luxury consumption and the illicit pleasures involved in the sexual consumption of women was often blurred."[12] The model was long-lived, surviving the nineteenth-century feminization of consumption and lingering on even in 1939 in Italy. That women are among the goods shopped for in the *Grandi magazzini* is thematized from the moment Bruno enters the store.[13] Lauretta is metonymically identified with the goods she sells ("You're wasting your time with sporting goods," Anna will say to Bertini, the frustrated, sexually harassing boss), and, in case we didn't get the point, Assia Noris plays an entire scene with a price tag dangling from her jacket.[14] Lauretta herself is on display, and the film sets about trying to figure out how to differentiate between what is presented as "prostitution" and a proper bill of sale, between licit and illicit economic transactions, a distinction that, as Jones's analysis suggests, is blurred at the origins of consumer culture itself.[15] Indeed, one might add that it is blurred at the origins of French and Italian, insofar as they, in the first case, confuse, and in the second, conflate, the distinction between the Latin *consumo, consumere,* and the Latin *consummo, consummare.*

Grandi magazzini, in fact, is entirely centered on the distinction between licit and illicit economic and sexual transactions, and all interactions among characters turn on it. If consumption (of commodities) and consummation (of sexual relations) are inextricable for consumer culture, the specifically Fascist imperative aims to introduce a splitting and rebinding such that licit autarchic consumption is bound to properly Fascist consummation for reproductive ends, and illicit luxury consumption, codified as "theft," is bound to illicit consummation, codified as "prostitution." This splitting and rebinding in turn produces a splintering of plot and character common to several of Camerini's films, including *Il signor Max, Batticuore, Darò un milione,* and *Grandi magazzini.* This splintering is, again not surprisingly, a gendered one that accounts for the older model that figures the consumer as male as well as the newer one that figures her as female. The male protagonist will literally be split in two by competing class interpellations. The various so-called doubles of Camerini's films—the working-class Gianni masquerading as the upper-class Max of *Il signor Max* or the millionaire masquerading as down-and-out bum of *Darò un milione,* for example—might be said to embody both what Ernesto Laclau has called the popular-democratic interpellation of Fascism on the one hand

(Gianni and the down-and-out bum), and the call to the modernized, urban consumer on the other (Max and the millionaire).[16] As we shall see, De Sica will be similarly doubled in *Grandi magazzini*, with Bruno the deliveryman embodying the populist male, and Bruno's look-alike mannequin, dressed first for a weekend on the slopes and later in coat and tails, figuring the consumer of leisure goods. The splintering of the female character produces not doubles but narratives of crime and punishment; over and over again, the Assia Noris character will be found innocent of one crime (of consumption or consummation) and guilty of another (also of consumption or consummation). Though more frequently represented as a narrative sequence, the woman's innocence and guilt are, in the most interesting cases, figured simultaneously, thereby giving form to the paradoxical interpellation that founds the Fascist female subject. So, for example, *Grandi magazzini* opens with Bruno's successful attempt to con compensation for a faked injury, supposedly suffered while in the service of the store. With 6,000 lire in his wallet, he descends in a crowded elevator in which he and Lauretta are thrown together; he feels for his wallet and, finding it missing, demands that the culprit reveal herself and accuses Lauretta. It turns out, of course, that the wallet was not stolen after all; honest, virtuous Lauretta is falsely accused by Bruno the con man. The melodramatic plot of *Grandi magazzini* turns on the reversal of this recurrent setup, for by the end of the film, Lauretta will truly have stolen, and Bruno will truly have been injured for the sake of the store; Lauretta will have "given" herself to Bruno, and Bruno will have generously decided to make an "honest woman" out of her. In order for this reversal to take place, Lauretta must become a criminal, something that is foreshadowed not only by Bruno's initial accusation but also by an interfilmic reference that would not have escaped viewers in 1939: Assia Noris had only months before appeared in Camerini's *Batticuore*, where she played the almost anagrammatic Arlette, a pickpocket who first plies her trade in an elevator.[17] The uncanny repetition iconographically suggests Lauretta's guilt, even as the narrative asserts her innocence.[18] (Similarly, in *Darò un milione*, the Assia Noris character will be falsely accused of being on the take by the De Sica character, who is himself the millionaire masquerading as pauper, and again in *Il signor Max*, her character will be falsely accused of illicit consummation by the De Sica character, who this time plays the working man masquerading as the idle rich. This last case provides another example of the simultaneity of guilt and innocence, for De Sica as Gianni accuses Assia Noris of giving in to De Sica as Max; Noris is guilty as charged, and yet at the same time innocent, since Max and Gianni are one and the same.) One might say, in fact, that Camerini's films repeatedly stage the production of the subject through scenes of accusation and acquittal that, as Judith Butler has recently argued, inhere in Althusser's own example of interpellation as hailing by the police.[19] The mise-en-scène also joins in her criminalization. Shot from a high angle that suggests a panopticon, the elaborate mezzanines mimic nothing so much as the structure of a prison, and the uniformed shopgirls are overseen by similarly uniformed matrons who, as the film progresses, more and more resemble wardens keeping watch over their uniformed prisoners. And we first see Bruno as he emerges from behind bars: the sinuous bars of the elevator frame his denunciation of Lauretta as well as the final tussle and capture of the thieving Bertini, which again takes place in the elevator. If, figurally speaking, Lauretta is already in prison, then it is only logical that she should commit a crime—but the crime, paradoxically, is that of becoming the consumer that the film's autarchic address wants her to become.

It is because of the imbrication of sexual and consumer economies that Lauretta will succumb to temptation, but only after the De Sica character will himself prove vulnerable to a seduction by class. A recurrent concern in Camerini's comedies, the seduction by class takes precedence over that by gender, though its consequences would appear initially to be the same. At once unwitting participant in the managers' illicit trafficking and not entirely unwilling visitor to the luxury woman's apartment, Bruno enters into both economies simultaneously and is transformed. The morning after, he is the object of a verbal exchange between Anna and Lauretta:

> Lauretta: That guy's been hanging around me for fifteen days, and I've had nothing to do with him. If you're interested, I'll give him to you as a gift.
> Anna: I'd need something else, of a completely different class.
> Lauretta: Oh come on, if it's what comes along, don't take so long choosing.
> Anna: Ah, my dear, it seems that he has chosen this time.
> Lauretta: Everyone has her own method.
> Anna: What do you mean by that?
> Lauretta: I mean it's easy enough for you to add to your collection.
> Anna: You'll pay for that.

What makes this dialogue interesting is that the referent of its pronouns is equally Bruno and a new "character" on the set, a mannequin made to resemble him that had appeared next to Lauretta's station that very morning. It is as though Bruno's entrance into both sexual and consumer economies has transformed him and placed him among the goods to be bought and sold. Having accepted Anna's invitation to accompany her on a skiing trip, Bruno is led by her to Lauretta's station and finds himself face to face with his look-alike mannequin. In an almost parodic example of successful interpellation, Bruno explicitly recognizes himself—*"ma, questo sono io!"* [But that's me!], he exclaims, even before Anna has directed his desire to adopt the mannequin as ego ideal by buying the ski jacket it wears. That this recognition is also a misrecognition will become clear later when, in the scene at the train station, the physical humor deriving from Bruno's awkwardness with his skis and his clumsiness with his mittened hands signal the gap between the delivery truck driver's *corps morcélé* and the apparent integrity of the urban consumer. (It is more than a little ironic, of course, that the body that represents unity in relation to Bruno's should be a mannequin's, itself, as a later scene reveals, a body routinely dismembered and toted about in fragments. The gap between the two bodies is, furthermore, marked as one of class; Bruno's awkwardness with his skis is mocked by a group of well-dressed young people clearly more accustomed to leisure-time activities.) But this moment of identification also marks the appearance of a kind of ghost narrative in which the characters are transformed into mannequins, and the problem of reconciling urban consumer with rural mother is displaced onto them.

Almost mechanically, in fact, Lauretta follows suit; as if following the conventional wisdom, newly recycled by the science of advertising in the 1930s, that jealousy makes women buy, it is at this moment that Lauretta's resistance breaks down.[20] Having overheard Anna make a date with Bruno for midnight at the station, Lauretta resolves to meet him herself; glancing from the Bruno mannequin to a female mannequin also dressed for the slopes, Lauretta decides to take up Bertini's offer of overtime so that, in the darkened store, she might supply herself with the appropriate outfit for the trip. She slips away from the other women, and finds herself, and the store, fully in the thrall of what Marx called the magic of commodity fetishism. A long shot shows her mounting the grandiose stairs; she arrives at her station, peopled only by mannequins, and fumbles nervously with the boxes. Cross-cutting shows Gaetano mounting the stairs more slowly, and the musical score marks his actions, including his startled turn at the sound of a falling box. When the lights come on (accompanied by an annunciatory, extra-diegetic chord), Lauretta, now wearing ski jacket and hat, assumes a smiling pose among the other mannequins, to the musical punctuation of a "ping." The scene calls to mind the fantasy, especially common in children's books, of toys and mannequins that come to life in stores at night, a fantasy that is the acting out of the logic of commodity fetishism itself, according to which relations among human beings assume the fantastic form of relationships among the products of their labor, and human agency is given over to those products. Produced not by a subject but in and through the act of exchange itself, this fetishism is one that already in Marx's text secreted a phantom-like reality in which tables danced and commodities talked. What one might call its "secondary elaboration" in cultural fantasy, and hence on the part of subjects, retains and reinforces "magic" as the tip-off to the presence of the fetishistic structure. "Magic," in both Marxist and psychoanalytic discussions of fetishism (as well as in the anthropological discourse that provided both the term and its enduring assumptions), names this displacement and, later, misrecognition of agency. And that children's literature should serve as the repository of the fantasy, and thus as the support of our disavowed belief in that agency, is consistent with Octave Mannoni's analysis of the logic of fetishism in his classic essay "Je sais bien, mais quand même. . . ."[21] Here that fantasy is predictably reversed along the axis of figural exchange, for if mannequins may come to life, then humans may equally well become mannequins, the very image of the urban consumer. Lauretta herself becomes a mannequin, mimics the mannequin in the moment in which she becomes a consumer of fashion, *and* assumes her place among the goods for sale. Walter Benjamin's suggestion, in the *Passagenwerk*, that the woman who adopts the newness of fashion mimics the mannequin and enters history as a "gaily decked-out corpse" finds visual confirmation in the image of the petrified Lauretta, price tag dangling from her ski jacket.[22] In both Fascist discourse and in Benjamin's *Passagenwerk*, that turning of the body into a sexual commodity is associated with prostitution and sterility. For Fascist discourse, it is the urban environment itself that is to blame; for Benjamin, it is a question of fashion prostituting the "living body to the inorganic" realm and a substitution of the newness and transience of the commodity for the older transience of nature. Women and their reproductive power are the chief figures for that older, organic cycle, and their fecundity stands, in Benjamin's understanding, as antagonistic to mechanical productivity. When the woman becomes a mannequin, therefore, she has submitted to that productivity and, in the words of Susan Buck-Morss, must repress her own reproductive power and become instead a prostitute.

In the case of *Grandi magazzini*, "prostitution" and the answer to the call to be an urban consumer are inseparable; illicit consummation follows upon illicit consumption, as Lauretta waits, unaccompanied, for Bruno in the railway station, with the price tag still dangling from the jacket. Bruno is buying, and after a weekend spent alone together in the mountains, both Lauretta and the jacket are tainted goods: "*Sai, ci dob-biamo sposare*" [We have to/are supposed to get married] she announces ambiguously to Emilia, and immediately thereafter cries out that the jacket has a little tear in it that must be repaired before it can be re-turned to the store.

The narrative, too, has a little tear in it, for at this point its condem-nation of consumption is total. Reparations must be made, if consump-tion and reproduction, urban consumer and rural mother, are to be reconciled. Here again the narrative splinters; the sub-plot of middle management's thievery is enlisted in order to reinstate a distinction be-tween illicit consumption and consumption in the name of reproduc-tion, and the ghost narrative of the mannequins works to recode the association of sterility and commodification such that fertility might stand in its place.

Bruno's offer of marriage begins to mend the tear and magically rec-onciles consumption and reproduction, public and private space. Here the magic is worked by the camera itself. In the scene that immediately follows Lauretta's announcement to Emilia, we see Bruno and Lauretta seated together in a living room. For the first time dressed neither in their "*grandi magazzini*" uniforms nor in their mannequin look-alike ski jackets, they appear to be at home, a young couple making plans for their future, discussing, predictably, what they will need to buy for their new apartment. Then, having lingered long enough to establish the set-ting, the camera pans right and pulls back to reveal that this domestic space is in fact a display within the furniture department of the store, and Lauretta and Bruno had been trying out the wares. The scene thus offers a visual reconciliation of domestic and commercial spaces and the woman's place within them.

The sub-plot of the thieving middle managers, however, reopens the tear only to suture it again. About to be discovered himself, Bertini re-ports to Bruno that Lauretta stole not only the ski jacket but also expen-sive stockings (whose brand name, Raffaella, is angled clearly into view of the spectator, thereby visually encouraging the very act of consump-tion the film's narrative condemns). In relation to this latter act, clearly illicit both economically and ideologically, the theft of the jacket is pro-nounced a foolish but not unforgivable act done as it was out of love, "*una ragazzata*," one of those things young girls do. That Bertini him-self planted the stockings is clear enough to the viewer but not to Bruno who, though willing to excuse the theft of the jacket that was lifted for love in order to go on the "*treno per la neve*," a popular initiative organ-ized by the Dopolavoro to allow workers leisure activity, cannot pardon the theft of stockings, in 1939 clearly a luxury item and one that allows

Bertini to insinuate that Lauretta is one of "those." Bruno accuses her pitilessly and, as the spectator knows, unjustly, thereby staging the falseness of the necessary association of prostitution and consumerism. So unjust is the accusation that Lauretta is brought to the brink of suicide. In the magic of the department store at night, the store and its mannequins acquire an agency of their own and act both as her temptation and her salvation. The door to the elevator, in which she had already once been falsely accused, swings slowly open of its own accord to reveal an empty shaft; on the opposite side stands the Bruno mannequin, with a sign in hand reading "*auguri*" [Best wishes]. The simultaneous interpellation and prohibition issued by the store (and the possibilities of social "ascent" punningly represented by the elevator, in Italian an "*ascensore*") are nicely embodied in Lauretta's swoon, first toward the shaft itself and then away from it, saved, it would seem, by the shock of seeing the Bruno mannequin with his darkly funny message. Here again, an interfilmic reference produces an uncanny reminder of another Camerini film: the tuxedoed Bruno mannequin visually recalls De Sica's role in *Il signor Max* (1937), where he played the working-class Gianni who masquerades as the English-speaking, Scotch-drinking, tuxedo-wearing upper-class Max. And a second interfilmic reference puts a definitive end to the manager's scheme. The car crash that ends the chase scene, in which Bruno pursues one of the pilferers, takes place beneath a billboard that reads "*Terra madre*," or "Mother earth." If the reference to "mother earth" weren't already enough, it turns out that *Terra madre* was the title of Alessandro Blasetti's 1931 film extolling the virtues of agrarian existence; it is as though urban corruption were brought to a halt by rural virtue. And indeed, Lauretta will later be hoisted up by the crowd, victorious and once again virtuous.

If consumerism and prostitution are uncoupled through this superposition of plots, sterility and urban consumerism will be uncoupled through the ghost narrative of the mannequins. Mannequins would seem to be the perfect figure of the sterile urban consumer, lacking, as we know, the genitalia necessary for reproduction. Nor would these mannequins seem to be an exception, for we do see them naked and dismembered when Emilia and her husband Maurizio return to the store, now reunited, in order to dress new displays. But in the same scene we discover that there is an anatomical distinction between the sexes of mannequins; the male mannequins all have little trap doors in their chests, the female mannequins do not. What could the psychological consequences of this curious distinction be? Here we can return to the scene in which the Bruno mannequin appeared for the first time. In that scene, Anna directs Lauretta to unzip the Bruno mannequin so that the real Bruno can admire the zipper. What Anna admires, instead, is the trap door, which she opens, asking, *"Dove avrà il cuore, a destra o a sinistra?"* [Where do you suppose his heart is, on the right or on the left?]. While the question is most readily understood as a way of asking which of the two women will win his heart, the one on the right or the one on the left, it is also, within the context of a man shopping for clothing, an upward displacement of a question that regards the member that stands as that more familiar figure for the difference between the sexes.[23] And several of the consequences of this difference are displayed in the final scene of the film.

Reconciled, and having just been promised the furniture for an entire apartment by the store president, Bruno and Lauretta leave the store, accompanied by Maurizio and Emilia, who has recently discovered she is pregnant (in fact, her pregnancy is revealed immediately after Lauretta has spent the weekend with Bruno, as though it were the displaced result of their lovemaking). Gaetano, the night watchman, also accompanies them, and the object of his affections, the hefty woman who is the figure of the rural mother throughout the film, passes by as the couples stop to admire the new window display. In a shot–reverse shot, we first see the display from outside, with and from behind the characters, then from inside the display itself, we look out at the couples. In the window, doll babies slowly turn on a kind of lazy susan, and the whirling dolls are reflected in the window, superimposing the dolls and the couples on the other side of the glass. Inside and outside, public display and private relations, consumption and reproduction are visually reconciled by the camera.[24] What is more, in the final shot, the eye of the camera identifies itself with the position of the doll who, assuming that the display is symmetrical, would be standing in the right rear corner of the window, thereby making it one of the few optical point-of-view shots in the entire film. That the subjective shot should be the doll's has consequences both for the relation between cinema and the commodity form and for the resolution of the contradictory interpellations at play in the film. On the one hand, the identification of camera and commodity points to the film's own participation in the production of a mode of perception belonging to the commodity and reminds us that, as Mary Ann Doane has put it, "the film frame is a kind of display window and spectatorship consequently a form of window shopping."[25] On the other hand, the dolls, we are to think, are the simulacra of the babies that the couples will soon produce. But they are also, fantasmatically, baby mannequins, and the attribution to them of point of view underscores their acquisition of agency. Indeed, the mannequins turn out not to have been sterile after all; under the spell of the commodity, they have managed to reproduce, and the baby mannequins, the manne-quins' babies, *are* the children of the autarchic urban consumer. The rural mother fades into the background, no longer in the picture of me-chanical fertility.

This reproductive fantasy evolves out of the wooden brain of the com-modity, as Marx would say, and gives the lie to that other fantasy that evolved out of the woolly brain of Il Duce, namely the reproductive fan-tasy that drove the demographic campaign. That fantasy, as I have tried to demonstrate elsewhere, was not only that more and more bodies would be produced, but that the offspring would organically embody a political doctrine, a conflation of social and biological reproduction that constitutes Fascist racism (rather than, as in the case of Nazism, a be-lief in "racial purity").[26] For Mussolini, Fascists are born and not made, and the *razza italiana* should be born in the countryside, far from the city, figure for the social, political and cultural consequences of mod-ernization. But modernization has a mind of its own, and the fecundity it knows is that of the commodity. As James Hay has noted, the recon-ciliation of Bruno and Lauretta takes place against the background of festivities in the store, festivities that celebrate a new season that is not an agrarian one that inaugurates a new cycle of planting but rather a commercial one that inaugurates a new shopping season.[27] Commodity culture is the new nature, and in that nature there is but one religion, that of the commodity itself. One final shot sums it up: surrounded by mannequins, and thinking themselves alone, Emilia and Maurizio stand, side by side, man and wife, before one of the male mannequins. His wooden hand raised, his index finger slightly higher than the middle finger, ring finger and pinkie slightly lower, thumb folded against the palm, the gesture of the mannequin might be taken as a limp Roman salute or, as Emilia and Maurizio in fact take it, as the sign of benedic-tion. *"Questa è mia moglie. Benedici questa coppia felice"* [This is my wife. Bless this happy couple], says Maurizio. The mannequin mutely com-plies.

Notes

1. On Teresa Labriola, see Sara Follacchio, "Conversando di femminismo. 'La donna italiana,'" in *La corporazione delle donne. Ricerche e studi sui modelli femminili nel ventennio fascista*, ed. Marina Addis Saba (Florence: Vallecchi, 1988); Victoria de Grazia, *How Fascism Ruled Women: Italy 1922–1945* (Berkeley: University of California Press, 1992); and Barbara Spackman, "Fascist Women and the Rhetoric of Virility," in *Mothers of In-*

vention: Women, Italian Fascism, and Culture, ed. Robin Pickering-Iazzi (Minneapolis: University of Minnesota Press, 1995), 100-120. On the "Scuola di Orvieto," see Rosella Isidori Frasca, . . . *e il duce le volle sportive* (Bologna: Pàtron, 1983); and Rosella Isidori Frasca, "L'educazione fisica e sportiva, e la 'preparazione materna'" also in *La corporazione delle donne.*

2. For an overview of the various interpretations of the relation between Fascism and modernization, see Stanley G. Payne, *A History of Fascism, 1914-1945* (Madison: University of Wisconsin Press, 1995), 471-486. As Payne writes, "The balance is neither one of unalloyed modernization nor of pure anti-modernism, but a complex mixture distinct from either of these. In industrialization and technology, Fascist ideology was at least moderately successful. The broader Fascist cultural ideals, rebelling against the priorities of the nineteenth century, were opposed to urbanism, rationalism, and true secularism (however anticlerical and anti-Christian), devoted to achieving a new twentieth-century counterculture that was modernist in some ways but Roman and military in others" (479).

   As Payne notes, some of the conflict in interpretation has to do with a failure to distinguish between German Nazism and Italian Fascism. In my experience in consulting these interpretations, I have also found a confusion of terms, such that "modernism," "modernization," and "modernity" are sometimes used interchangeably. Here I have found Fredric Jameson's distinction to be useful. In *Postmodernism, or, The Cultural Logic of Late Capitalism* (Durham, N.C.: Duke University Press, 1991), Jameson writes: "If modernization is something that happens to the base, and modernism the form that superstructure takes in reaction to that ambivalent development, then perhaps modernity characterizes the attempt to make something coherent out of that relationship" (310). Various modernisms come into being precisely as protests against modernization, while others replicate the values and forms of modernization, creating both "modern modernisms" and "anti-modern modernisms." Ruth Ben-Ghiat offers a richly detailed analysis of the relation between Fascism and modernization in *Fascist Modernities* (Berkeley: University of California Press, 2000). On Fascism as a secular religion, see Emilio Gentile, *The Sacralization of Politics in Fascist Italy,* trans. Keith Botsford (Cambridge, Mass.: Harvard University Press, 1996).

3. See Victoria de Grazia, "La nazionalizzazione delle donne. Modelli di regime e cultura commerciale nell'Italia fascista," *Memoria* 33, no. 3 (1991): 95-111; de Grazia, "Nationalizing Women: The Competition between Fascist and Commercial Cultural Models in Mussolini's Italy," in *The Sex of Things: Gender and Consumption in Historical Perspective,* ed. de Grazia (Berkeley: University of California Press, 1996), 337-358; and David G. Horn, "Constructing the Sterile City: Pronatalism and Social Sciences in Interwar Italy," in *American Ethnologist* 18, no. 3 (1991): 581-601, as well as his *Social Bodies: Science, Reproduction, and Italian Modernity* (Princeton, N.J.: Princeton University Press, 1994).

4. On fashion during the *ventennio*, see Natalia Aspesi, *Il lusso e l'autarchia* (Milan: Rizzoli, 1982). Aspesi reports that after the sanctions were imposed, numerous exhibitions devoted to Italian textiles were organized, among them the spectacular "Mostra del tessile italiano," organized by Fascist party secretary Achille Starace and inaugurated by Mussolini on 18 November 1937, in Turin, on the occasion of the second anniversary of the sanctions.

5. Based on the Rinascente in Milan, the *grandi magazzini* were reconstructed at Cinecittà. In a 1974 interview, Camerini notes somewhat apologetically that his department store was larger and better than anything that then existed in Italy, and hence perhaps somewhat "unreal." See Francesco Savio, ed., *Cinecittà anni trenta. Parlano 116 protagonisti del secondo cinema italiano, 1930-43*, 3 vols. (Rome: Bulzoni, 1979), 1: 218. On Assia Noris, see Nunzia Messina, *Le donne del fascismo. Massaie rurali e dive del cinema nel ventennio* (Rome: Ellemme, 1987), 36–44.

The notion that such "escapist" comedies were politically innocent has effectively been put to rest by Marcia Landy in *Fascism in Film: The Italian Commercial Cinema, 1931-1943* (Princeton: Princeton University Press, 1986) and her *The Folklore of Consensus: Theatricality in the Italian Cinema 1930-1943* (Albany: State University of New York Press, 1998); and by the Italian scholars collected in *Risate di regime. La commedia italiana 1930-1944*, ed. Mino Argentieri (Venice: Marsilio, 1991). See especially Simona Argentieri, "Il ridicolo e il sublime," 19–33; Lino Miccichè, "Il cinema italiano sotto il fascismo. Elementi per un ripensamento possibile," 37–63; and Vito Zagarrio, "La commedia non riconciliata," 275–287.

6. The articulation of ideologemes in Camerini's film differs significantly from their articulation in Zola's novel. *Au bonheur des dames* is a tale of social mobility, whereas *Grandi magazzini* reasserts immobility; an economic outside—the pre-department store shops and economy—is crucial to Zola's representation of the colonialist expansion of capital and destruction of a previous way of life. Octave Mouret is a successful predator, unlike Bertini, and, unlike Lauretta, Denise Baudu is a shrewd businesswoman who holds out for the highest price: marriage to Mouret. On *Au bonheur des dames* and commodity culture, see Rachel Bowlby, *Just Looking: Consumer Culture in Dreiser, Gissing, and Zola* (New York: Methuen, 1985); Anne Friedberg, *Window Shopping and the Postmodern* (Berkeley: University of California Press, 1993); and Kristin Ross, "Shopping," Introduction to Emile Zola, *The Ladies' Paradise* (Berkeley: University of California Press, 1992), v–xxiii. Ross reports that three French film versions of *Au Bonheur des dames* were made between 1913 and 1943.

7. The only other sets, briefly seen, are the apartments of Lauretta and Anna, the train station of the *treno per la neve*, and a few staged street scenes that feature various vehicles at night. That the vehicles that circulate "outside" bear the inscription "*Grandi magazzini*" has the effect of reabsorbing that

"outside" back inside the store. I am grateful to Dana Crudup for this observation.

8. Sergio Grmek Germani suggests that Camerini only reluctantly included the very large number of commodity tie-ins demanded by producer Giuseppe Amato. See Grmek Germani, *Mario Camerini* (Florence: La nuova italia, 1980), 83. Germani also comments on the "autarchic" structure of the film: "And *Grandi magazzini*, which, in a transitory year like 1939, provisionally realizes the desire of a classic, 'autarchic' perfection in Italian cinema, mirroring the characters' dreams with those of the spectators" (85).

9. On the "luxury woman," see de Grazia, *How Fascism Ruled Women*, 223–234. Though when she is in uniform Anna would appear to be of the same class as Lauretta and Bruno, when she is out of uniform we find that her apartment, maid, and furs recode her as of the same class as Bertini, who, when first seen with his shiny automobile, announces *"fuori l'ufficio, sono tutt'altro uomo"* [Outside of the office, I'm an entirely different man]. Other resemblances also mark this double class affiliation; for example, like Bertini, Anna will first make advances while driving at night.

10. As de Grazia notes, the regime tolerated women working when young, but then induced them to leave the official labor market when they married and had children. See *How Fascism Ruled Women*, 168.

11. For an extended analysis of commodification and female subjectivity in *Grandi Magazzini*, see Jacqueline Reich, "Consuming Ideologies: Fascism, Commodification, and Female Subjectivity in Mario Camerini's *Grandi magazzini*," *Annali d'italianistica* 16 (1998), 195–212 (ed. Robert Dombroski and Dino S. Cervigni). In *Popular Film Culture in Fascist Italy: The Passing of the Rex* (Bloomington: Indiana University Press, 1987), James Hays also notes that the film dramatizes the process of learning to become consumers; he takes the context to be that of the Fascist corporativist economy.

12. See Jennifer Jones, *"Coquettes* and *Grisettes:* Women Buying and Selling in Ancien Régime France," in de Grazia, *The Sex of Things*, 25–53. Jones points out that the model of shopping as heterosexual courtship functions to rationalize the consumption of the male shopper: "Men did not shop to buy clothing, and they did not shop because they were irrationally seduced by goods and shop displays; men shopped for women" (35).

13. On novelistic representations of the department store, see Bowlby, *Just Looking*. At the beginning of the film, Gaetano recognizes in Bruno "a ladies' man" (*un tipo donnesco*) and issues a truncated warning about women in the store: *"Perchè la donna"* (Because women).

14. This metonymical conflation of subject and object of the transaction (seller and object of sale) is replicated in the experience of the female spectator. In *The Desire to Desire: The Woman's Film of the 1940s* (Bloomington: In-

diana University Press, 1987), Mary Ann Doane discusses women's role as consumers in relation to cinema, noting that the woman is "the subject of a transaction in which her own commodification is ultimately the object" (30).

15. The managers' thievery involves precisely the legal bill of sale: at the end of the chase scene, in which Bruno and Gaetano pursue Remo, we discover that the stolen goods are the "Grandi Magazzini" stamps used to validate receipts.

16. See Ernesto Laclau, "Fascism and Ideology," in his *Politics and Ideology in Marxist Theory* (London: Verso, 1977). Mary Ann Doane remarks on a similar "split subjectivity" that motivates the representation of twin sisters in the film *A Stolen Life*. See her "The Economy of Desire: The Commodity Form in/of the Cinema," *Quarterly Review of Film and Video* 2 (1989): 23–33. Marcia Landy addresses the function of impersonation in relation to social class in Camerini's other comedies in *The Folklore of Consensus*, 85–106.

17. It has been noted that a poster for *Batticuore*, which was in distribution as *Grandi magazzini* was being filmed, appears twice in the film itself. See Elaine Mancini, *Struggles of the Italian Film Industry during Fascism, 1930–1935* (Ann Arbor: UMI Research Press, 1985), 67–68.

18. I owe the notion of interfilmic references as uncanny reminders to Tom Conley's *Film Hieroglyphics: Ruptures in Classical Cinema* (Minneapolis: University of Minnesota Press, 1991). Conley's analysis of such references in the films of Renoir offers a particularly rich model for discussing Camerini's practice of self-citation. Other such references in *Grandi magazzini* would include the initial appearance of De Sica; with arm in sling, De Sica's Bruno recalls De Sica's Gianni in *Il signor Max*. Injured while chasing the cab containing Assia Noris, Gianni's arm served as the visual marker of class difference, allowing Noris to distinguish between the working-class Gianni and the Max he pretends to be. The repeated coupling of De Sica and Noris in Camerini's films is yet another such uncanny reminder that, in Conley's words, "beckon[s] across the barrier of one film to gain an identity recently lost in another" (2). Conley's analysis of letters in filmic images, and hence of the image as rebus, would also find fertile terrain in Camerini's films. I think, for example, of the shots of Noris and De Sica in *Il signor Max* against the background of an awning bearing the words "Caffè nazionale"; framed in medium close-up, the letters that appear behind their heads are "nazion," labeling them as the national couple.

19. See Judith Butler, *The Psychic Life of Power* (Stanford: Stanford University Press, 1997). Butler writes: "To become a 'subject' is thus to have been presumed guilty, then tried and declared innocent. Because this declaration is not a single act but a status incessantly *reproduced*, to become a 'sub-

ject' is to be continuously in the process of acquitting oneself of the accusation of guilt" (118).

20. On women and the science of advertising, see Karen Pinkus, *Bodily Regimes: Italian Advertising under Fascism* (Minneapolis: University of Minnesota Press, 1995), 153.

21. See Octave Mannoni, "Je sais bien, mais quand même . . . ," in *Clefs pour l'imaginaire ou l'autre scène* (Paris: Seuil, 1969).

22. Quoted in Susan Buck-Morss, *The Dialectics of Seeing: Walter Benjamin and the Arcades Project* (Cambridge, Mass.: MIT Press, 1989), 101. Interested in the "liberatory" possibilities of consumption, Jacqueline Reich proposes a "transgressive" reading of this image: "Lauretta, now sexually and socially 'deviant,' becomes a counter commodity to be consumed by the spectator" (207).

23. Although this reading is suggested more by the question than by the zipper itself, the philologically curious may want to know that zippers were indeed beginning to replace buttons and fly fronts in the mid-1930s. See Mario Sichel, *History of Men's Costume* (New York: Chelsea House, 1984), 66.

24. James Hay also notes the inside-out structure: "They have become insiders standing on the outside looking in." See his *Popular Film Culture in Fascist Italy,* 111.

25. Doane, *The Desire to Desire,* 27. On the relation between cinema and the commodity, see also Friedberg, *Window Shopping and the Postmodern.* Reich's already cited analysis of *Grandi magazzini* is particularly astute in addressing this aspect of the film; she also notes that the mannequins themselves are a commodity tie-in, and their supplier is duly recognized in the credits.

26. See Spackman, *Fascist Virilities: Rhetoric, Ideology, and Social Fantasy in Italy* (Minneapolis: University of Minnesota Press, 1996), 153.

27. See Hay, *Popular Film Culture,* 108.

11

The Last Film Festival

The Venice Biennale Goes to War

Marla Stone

On 30 August 1942, Joseph Goebbels, the Nazi minister of public enlightenment, and Alessandro Pavolini, the Fascist minister of popular culture, together inaugurated the Tenth Venice Biennale International Film Festival.[1] The Festival opened with a large and tightly regimented rally dedicated to "The Armed Forces."[2] "An inauguration in perfect harmony with the severe and ardent atmosphere of the moment in which we live," wrote a reviewer in *La rivista cinematografica*. "An homage from Cinema to the Nation at Arms," he added.[3] The Festival itself commenced with a special screening for sailors, aviators, and infantrymen of *Three Young Cadets* (*Tre aquilotti*), hailed as "an aeronautical film . . . exalting the courage and heroism of young aviators."[4]

Two years earlier, in honor of the common military effort, the Venice Film Festival had been reconstituted as a joint Nazi-Fascist celebration; as such, the 1942 edition was the second and final "Italian-German Film Festival."[5] The film festival of 1942, aptly titled the Mostra di Guerra (War Festival) and celebrated as a cultural manifestation of the Axis-dominated "New Europe," would be the last of the Fascist era. Held in the Mussolini regime's final year and at the moment when Axis armies had achieved their greatest reach across Europe, this Nazi-Fascist event reveals the impact of World War II on cultural production and display. In less than a year, Allied troops would land in Sicily and the Fascist Grand Council would depose Mussolini.

For many in Italy, the collapse of Fascism was not yet a foregone conclusion and conditions remained stable enough to mount a film festival, but the regime's failures and fragility were visible in both the form and content of this last Fascist Venice Biennale International Film Festival.[6] In 1942, the film festival was reconceived and restructured in order to mirror the militarization of the larger Italian society. As discussed below, the films shown in 1942, the nations attending, and the rhetoric of the event reflected both an Italian Fascist attempt to project unity with and faith in the Nazi-Fascist project and the fractures and ambivalence already present in that project. Moreover, the narrative strategies of the prize-winning Italian films of 1942 reveal, in their depictions of the enemy and of resistance to that enemy, anxiety and dissonance in the face of the national struggle.

In addition to providing a vision of the Fascist regime in its last months, the tenth annual Venice Biennale Film Festival offers an opportunity to assess the changes that had transpired in Fascist official culture between 1932 and 1942.[7] When the event was founded in the early 1930s, the Fascist-appointed Biennale staff promoted the film festival— the first in Europe—as an example of Fascist innovation and cultural experimentation.[8] This popular event represented a focal point and object of pride for much of the Fascist cultural bureaucracy, which hailed it as an example of Fascism's international taste and of its openness to the world. At its 1932 inauguration, the film festival made a splash, projecting forty films from nine nations and attracting 25,000 spectators.[9] The film festival showed two films per night for twenty nights on the glamorous seaside terrace of the Excelsior Hotel.[10] A Hollywood-infused spectacle with an international following, the Festival lent the regime an aura of sophistication, modernity, and style.

In 1934, the Fascist government declared the film festival a permanent annual event: that year, seventeen nations participated and fifty-eight production companies showed films to 41,000 people.[11] The film festival attracted a large and loyal following, with attendance figures rising continually through the 1930s. In 1935, 38,500 viewers attended; in 1936, the event boasted 50,000 spectators; and the 1937 version counted 60,000 viewers.[12]

In the 1930s, the film festival stressed variety and entertainment, especially multiplicity of genre and nationality. At Venice, the Fascist regime demonstrated its embrace of new cultural forms and of the world while also celebrating the vitality of Italian film. For the 1932 debut, showings included E. Goulding's *Grand Hotel*, Leni Riefenstahl's *Blue Light*, Dziga Vertov's *Toward Life*, and René Clair's *Our Liberty*.[13] American films predominated through the middle 1930s: at the inaugural Fascist-sponsored event *Doctor Jekyll and Mr. Hyde*, *The Champion*, *Frankenstein*, *The Cry of the Crowd*, *Forbidden*, *Grand Hotel*, and *The Man I Killed* were screened. In 1935, juries honored films as aesthetically, ideologically, and thematically diverse as Germany's *The Triumph of the Will*, America's *Becky Sharp*, and Palestine's *Promised Land*.[14] Jean Renoir's *The Grand Illusion*, controversial for its pacifist and Popular Front sentiments, was awarded an honor two years later.

The regime's pursuit of a large and diverse audience and official desire to market a groundbreaking event gave the film festival a diverse and open character. In addition to a range of melodramas, historical dramas, musicals, situation comedies, documentaries, and animated shorts, the program "include[d] films of unusual characters: avant-garde, surrealist, musical light symphonies."[15] The composition of the audiences mirrored the diversity of the offerings: Italian and international vacationers could be seen sharing a screening with stars, starlets, and Fascist officials.

Until the pressures of cultural autarchy and war shifted the regime's cultural priorities away from inclusion, appropriation, and consensus, American films and Hollywood stars dominated the festivities and the prizes. The film festival merged a number of spectacular elements, such as nighttime film premieres, the romantic ambiance of Venice, the dramatic appearances of "stars," and the titillating excitement of treating cinema as a fine art. The Biennale's promoters eagerly cultivated the drama and "hype" available in the film festival. Internationally staffed juries awarded the prizes in tense and staged ceremonies; the Festival's premieres and closings were carefully orchestrated, and the whole of the event was tied to the glamour and fantasy of Hollywood.

As the 1930s progressed, the content of the film festival reflected larger alterations in Fascist cultural politics. After 1935, with the conquest of Ethiopia and the declaration of empire, Fascism's foregrounding of "empire" as a way to convey messages about the nation and race was reflected in the prizes given: in this period, the Biennale introduced a prize for best colonial film, and films of bombastic propaganda received the bulk of the prizes. Two of the most celebrated propaganda films of the Fascist era won the Duce Cup for Best Italian Film at the film festivals of 1937 and 1938. In 1937, *Scipione l'africano* (*Scipio, the African*) re-invented the conflict between Rome and Carthage as the battle of authoritarianism against democracy, action against debate and irresolution. This 1937 film, directed by Carmine Gallone, stressed an emergent racialized politics, depicting the Carthaginians as uncivilized and "Semitic."[16] Goffredo Alessandrini's *Luciano Serra, Pilota* (*Luciano Serra, Pilot*) won the 1938 prize for its celebration of soldiers who fought in the Abyssinian War.[17] This film emphasized the qualities of the Fascist "new man"—heroism, love of risk, adventure, and male comradeship.

The Venice Biennale Film Festival evolved alongside the changing priorities of its government and Fascist party organizers. By 1938, political exigencies overshadowed aesthetic or audience-attracting concerns, and the "relative autonomy of the juries, up until then respected," waned.[18] After 1937, the prize for best foreign film went without exception to Nazi Germany. Leni Riefenstahl's documentary of the 1936 Berlin Olympics, *Olympia,* took the 1938 honors. Following the screening, Fascist Minister of Popular Culture Dino Alfieri and the head of the Nazi delegation cabled Mussolini to celebrate the film's "brilliant first showing."[19] One of the most powerful signs of the cultural coordination of the two fascist regimes and of the integration of the film festival into the regime's propaganda apparatus was the world premiere of the infamous Nazi anti-Semitic film *Jud Süß* (*Jew Süss*) by Veit Harlan at the 1940 film festival.[20]

World War II and the film festival's connection to the Ministry of Popular Culture encouraged its full appropriation by the regime's propaganda machine. For pro-Nazis, such as Alessandro Pavolini at the Ministry of Popular Culture, who had witnessed the Nazi cultural *gleischaltung,* a propaganda weapon as powerful as the film festival could not be left outside the war effort. The growth of the film festival, its obvious propaganda value, and Fascism's revised patronage style led to the festival's legal and organizational redefinition after 1936. As part of its growing control over the creation and dissemination of films, the Ministry of Popular Culture under Dino Alfieri expanded its role in the festival. A law of 13 February 1936 severed the film festival from the Biennale administration and decreed it an *ente autonomo,* which gave it an equivalent and autonomous legal status with the Biennale as a whole.[21] As opposed to a committee selected in Venice by the Biennale administration, after 1936, committees of appointed party and government officials coordinated the film festival. The head of the Department of Cinema of the Ministry of Popular Culture, the president of the LUCE, and the president of the Fascist National Federation of Entertainment Industries held government-appointed posts at the film festival.[22] A law determining annual financial contributions to the newly independent institution followed: the Biennale contributed 10,000 lire, the city of Venice 20,000 lire, and the Ministry of Popular Culture 30,000 lire.[23] Thus, as of 1935, the regime's propaganda ministry donated the majority of the money and expected the majority of the influence. A final reorganization came in 1940, when the film festival was renamed the Manifestazione Cinematografica Italo-Germanica (Italian-German Film Festival).[24] As late as June 1943, Mussolini's office authorized planning for that year's film festival, which was also organized with Goebbels's ministry.[25]

The final film festival of 1942 bore little resemblance to its origins. Only Axis powers, their satellites, puppet states, and fellow-traveler nations participated in the Mostra di Guerra. The festival was predominantly a showcase for Italian and German films: each nation projected six films, with other Axis nations such as Slovakia, Croatia, Romania, and Hungary screening two to three films each. Spain, Portugal, and Switzerland constituted the remainder of the attendees. Documentaries celebrating the military victories of Fascist Italy and Nazi Germany preceded each feature film.

The war and the commitment of the two regimes to mobilize film in that struggle determined the form and content of the event. Reporters cloaked their coverage of the festival in inflated militarist bombast. The press hailed the film festival as a sign of the strength of the Axis, and it stressed the role of cinema in an Axis victory. "From its opening moments," cheered the *Rassegna dell'oltremare*, "the Venice Festival has presented a profoundly military face. . . . This year, European cinema has appeared at the Venetian event with a unitary character, as severe as it is interesting."[26] The Roman paper *Tribuna* interpreted the Festival as a portent of the future: "But the Venetian exhibition has another purpose: to reveal the spiritual character that the Axis nations will give to the Europe of the future; thus, Italy and Germany dominate the event."[27] Even specialized cinema journals such as *Primi piani* saw the festival's coordination with the war as an improvement and as a healthy rejection of the Hollywood-inspired superficialities of the 1930s. The *Primi piani* reviewer was glad that "the usual divas, half divas, and the little divas in shorts . . . imported by the Hearst company" had been replaced by "our own well-bred and creative people."[28]

Taking a cue from Nazi Germany's requirement that art and film criticism be replaced by what Goebbels called "art reporting," many Italian newspapers merely reported and described the films screened at Venice. Nazi cultural ideology rejected art criticism as a Jewish and modernist hoax designed to deflect the public from the natural and authentic aspects of art. With this in mind, the Biennale staff canceled the practice of prior screenings for critics and journalists, because the "inexact and premature judgments" of critics would cloud the inherently healthy tastes of the public.[29] As revived Fascist populism dictated, "The public's own judgments are almost always correct, because they are collective."[30]

Despite the restrictions, some reviewers in the cinematic press continued to level more critical judgments than did daily newspapers, but they often focused on technical questions rather than on narrative choices. Magazines such as *Cinema*, which was edited by Mussolini's son Vittorio, who was a proponent of Fascist cultural autarchy, lauded the technical acumen of German color feature films, such as Veit Harlan's *The Great King*, a celebration of Frederick the Great.[31] Other reviewers praised the achievements of Italian color cartoons—which critics patriotically noted as "color cartoons capable of competing with those from America."[32] The press stressed the appearance and success of Italian-made color cartoons, which were produced by Bassoli Film and designed by Sgrilli, as demonstrative of a domestic ability to challenge banned Disney productions.[33] "[That] the 1942 Festival marks the onset of Italian cartoon production cannot but be crowned as a great success," wrote *Italia-Roma*.[34]

But unanimity in the press proved impossible, especially given the startling changes in the shape of the festival. *Cinema*, generally supportive of government efforts to mobilize film for official purposes, lamented the deadening conformity of the event:

> The war has dictated its iron laws even at Venice. It has put in place a silent and harmless unity. Thus, it has ended those struggles and polemics that had [once] animated a now dead corpse. It would be useless today to look for that enthusiasm and those long debates which had stimulated the spirits of critics and spectators.[35]

The *Mediterraneo* reviewer sarcastically compared the early festivals, which had featured "appearances of Marlene Dietrich and the Duchess of Windsor," to the 1942 edition, about which attendees could "now say that we are familiar with the rural and coastal life of Portugal, Spain, Finland, Sweden, and Hungary."[36]

The genres of the films screened in the summer of 1942 were markedly different than what had predominated in the 1930s. The program consisted mostly of dramas; it had very few comedies, and the white-telephone films that had been so popular in the mid-1930s had disappeared. White-telephone films were depression-era situation comedies with luxurious settings and glamorous stars. One reviewer lamented the "total absence of the thrillers, society dramas, seductive costumes, white telephones, from which we must distance ourselves for essential and constructive reasons."[37]

Anti-Communist films dominated in the summer of 1942, followed by a number of historical dramas of a nationalist bent.[38] "The concomitance," wrote the *Fiamma* of Parma, "of anti-Bolshevik films has been striking; they have been made by all the Nations which fight on the Russian front."[39] Italy screened *Noi Vivi* (*We the Living*). Hungary showed *Atonement*, Spain offered *Marriage in Hell*, Romania (as a coproduction with Italy) produced *Odessa in fiamme* (*Odessa in Flames*), and Finland brought *Beyond the Frontier*. These films of the War Festival presented no detailed evocation of the New Europe; instead, they offered the common enemy of Bolshevism and the promise of a glorious past.

The two Italian films that were most loudly hailed by the critics and which received the top prizes at Venice offer a lens into Fascism at war. Through *Bengasi*, which won the Coppa Mussolini (The Mussolini Cup), and *Noi vivi* (*We the Living*), which received the Premio della Biennale (Biennale Prize), the fault lines of the Fascist regime at its moment of greatest crisis emerged. In these two films, we find two depictions of the enemy—the "other" against whom Fascism measured itself—but an absence of Fascism itself. Both films offer a vision of that which must be fought against but not that which is to be fought for. Read together, these wartime films reflect the regime's failure to create deeply rooted Fascist identities and commitments. The two films bespeak the dictatorship's need to fall back on pre-Fascist categories of identity and socio-cultural bonds to explain "why we fight."

Augusto Genina's *Bengasi* premiered on the film festival's opening night at the San Marco theater in Venice. A full house, according to critics, cheered the film and its director. At the festival's conclusion, the jury awarded it the Mussolini Cup. This 1942 production by Bassoli Films represents an expansion of Genina's war/propaganda films. By 1942, Genina had a reputation as the director of "virile" propaganda films that idealized Fascism at war. In *L'assedio dell'Alcazar* (*The Siege of the Alcazar*) of 1940, he romanticized the Falangist fight against Communism. For *L'assedio dell'Alcazar*, filmed in Spain just after Franco's victory, Genina used the struggle of a small group of Spanish Fascists and their families to celebrate resistance, heroism, and family unity.[40] Soon to become one of Fascist Italy's most important war films, *L'assedio dell'Alcazar* received significant critical and popular acclaim in 1940/41.[41] Like *Bengasi*, *L'assedio dell'Alcazar* focused on the besieged in a situation that called for heroism and self-sacrifice.[42] Offering a formula that Genina would develop further in *Bengasi*, the film combined "the tones of a dramatized documentary" with "romantic conventions."[43]

In *Bengasi*, Genina brought his talent for personalizing and dramatizing war and the individual's struggle in war to the battle between the Axis and the Allies in North Africa. In this, the last of Genina's war films, he told the story of the 57-day British occupation of the North African town of Bengasi. Genina filmed *Bengasi* at lightning speed in the brief period between the British withdrawal from the town in 1942 and its recapture in early 1943. Rejecting traditional plot or unified narrative, Genina wove together vignettes to depict the life of Italian settler-citizens in the British-occupied town. The film pivots around four interwoven stories, involving Italian settlers from all classes and walks of life. From the separate stories emerge messages about what must be fought against and what in Italian life must be defended. It is highly sentimental; the besieged Italians are uniformly represented as noble, self-sacrificing, and innocent victims and the British as duplicitous, corrupt, and amoral oppressors.

Shot at Cinecittà in cheap orientalized North African sets which claimed to faithfully reconstruct a neighborhood of the town, the film shows the signs of both time and money constraints.[44] The speed of its production notwithstanding, *Bengasi* attempted a grand scale. As one critic mused: "From the technical point of view, *Bengasi* represents an extremely impressive achievement: 150,000 meters of film . . . 50 tanks, 12 airplanes, 5000 soldiers, and 60,000 man hours of extras."[45] Genina was completing the film when the town fell again to the Allies; *Bengasi* was not widely distributed because of further Italian losses in North Africa.

Bengasi's narrative depends on tropes about gender, identity, and ideology in wartime Italy. The film's dominant purpose is to contrast the Italian civilians with their British occupiers. The film provides its moral and ideological message through the dichotomy of "us" versus "them." The actions and behavior of the Italians are determined by the values of family, community, and humanity, while the British occupiers are motivated by self-indulgence and cruelty. Genina represents these differences through gender stereotypes, and it is gender which gives shape to the polarities. The gendered nature of resistance is made explicit with the film's opening credits which explain that it is "Dedicated to the Women Who Suffered Silently" and that the film is based on "real events."

The film pivots around the heroic Captain Enrico Berti and his young wife, Carla. Captain Berti was played by Fosco Giachetti, whose rugged masculinity triumphed at the Venice film festival in a number of films that year and won him the award for best actor. In the wake of the defeat of the Italian army, Captain Berti returns clandestinely to the besieged city to find his wife and to convince her to flee. After much pressure, she agrees. While escaping the falling city, she and other refugees are strafed by British aircraft. As a result of British targeting of civilians, her baby dies in her arms, and she returns to conquered Bengasi. Later, Berti escapes from the British prisoner-of-war camp in order to find his family; despite his wife's attempts to shield him from the tragedy, he discovers the truth of his child's death and vows to revenge him.

The sub-plot that explicitly evokes patriotism involves an Italian double agent, Filippo, who appears to be collaborating with the British; Filippo suffers the taunts of his fellow Italians, even being spat upon. He bears the ostracism of the community for the higher good and is finally caught and shot by the British for his devotion to the *patria*. Berti's last words to Filippo assure him that he will not die in vain; as Berti, the patriarchal figure and head of the community, says, "You have been the best among us." The other stories focus on the plight of a peasant family whose life and livelihood are destroyed by the occupiers and a group of single women of questionable reputations living together in the city.

Women hold together the community of the besieged; at the core of *Bengasi* is a community of Italian women of all classes and ages, from the bourgeois wife and mother Carla to the peasant mother to the noble prostitutes. In one vignette, soldiers in hiding, after having refused to turn themselves in to the occupiers, take refuge with a group of women of ill repute who nurse them and hide them. These women stand stoically in the face of the violent British soldiers who come to search for the hidden Italian men. While of dubious moral character, these women "protect" their men. In this film, resistance to the enemy is feminine. The women are strong, but they are also feminine and maternal. The women of *Bengasi* are strong because of their devotion to the patriarchal moral order; their strength derives from their roles as mothers, wives, and women who protect men. The main character, Carla, is shown repeatedly with her child in her arms—the film opens with a shot of Enrico and Carla in a "Holy Family" pose, with mother, father, and child united in a pyramid. In the sub-plot that focuses on a settler family, the mother is reunited with her son, who was blinded in the battle for the town. *Bengasi* celebrates the family, as held together by women standing in for absent men.

The gendered discourse of *Bengasi* reflects an adjustment to earlier Fascist uses of gender to conflate sexual and social power.[46] As Ruth Ben-Ghiat has written, Fascist ideology depended upon the opposition of

> ideal, male-bounded modernity marked by discipline, hierarchy, and the subordination or exclusion of women, and a negative modernity that linked female strength to moral corruption, political impotence and social turbulence.[47]

Films from the early and mid-1930s demonstrated the dangers of destabilizing or threatening the established gender/social order. However, by the early 1940s, gender became a location for the revelation of the inability to maintain social hierarchies. In the films discussed here, the gendered nature of power was in flux and unpredictable. In the case of *Bengasi*, women took on new functions and roles, and the film ended without a full reconstitution of the social order.

If resistance is gendered in *Bengasi*, so are the dichotomies of enemy and friend. In contrast to the solid values of family, loyalty, and home represented by the Italians of Bengasi, the enemy is weak and covers its weakness with arrogance and decadence. The British and their imperial troops flout international law, loot, vandalize, and terrorize. The British soldiers are effeminate and old; the British officers have high-pitched voices and weak facial features. The film shows them fortifying themselves with liquor. The Australian troops, whom it is implied must do the British's fighting for them, are brutal and vulgar. According to the film, healthy societies have clear gender lines. British degeneracy and weakness is implied in a scene which juxtaposes British officers getting drunk in a fancy club with Italian women, children, and elderly queueing for bread and soup at a *cucina popolare* (soup kitchen), where they are served by nuns.

In a scene that opposes the enemy's destructive and violent impulses with the nurturing ones of the Italian settlers, Australian troops enter the home of an elderly Italian settler. Despite the promises of the British officers, the troops harass and loot for the joy of destruction; they shoot down the farmer's accordion (his symbol of the old country) from the wall, and they shoot at birds in the farmer's beloved garden. When the Australians begin to destroy his fruit trees, the farmer cries, "You do not touch the land!" and picks up a shovel with which to defend his land. The Australians shoot him in cold blood. The not-so-subtle message asserts that Italians came to "make the desert bloom," while the Allies come to pillage it.

The social bonds of *Bengasi* are all familial, and the duties are all local—a husband to his wife, a mother to her son, women to endangered men, a farmer to his land. Italian masculinity is tied to protection of the family rather than to commitment to an ideology. At the same time that the film attempts to affirm the patriarchal order and the importance of gender roles, it reconfigures them. In addition to the fact that women are the resisters in the film, most of the male protagonists are in some way emasculated or damaged. When Berti clandestinely returns to Bengasi, he does so with his arm in a sling—a "signal" of his castration.[48] The blind soldier rescued from the hospital by his mother is led home to the farm as an invalid. Italy/*La patria* is represented through a discourse of family, but it is a family in crisis, desperately trying to hold on to traditional hierarchies even as those hierarchies are collapsing.

Bengasi's representation of national identity and its explanation of the conflict between the Allies and the Axis are its most salient components. Fascism is absent from the film, as is the Italian state. In fact, the film focuses on the community once official institutions of the state and the military are gone. No symbols of Fascism appear nor is Fascism explicitly cited by any of the characters. The Italian armed forces are absent for most of the film because the men are either in hiding or in prisoner-of-war camps until the film's close. According to *Bengasi*, Italians fought for community and out of responsibility to family and neighbors. Patriotism and allegiance to the Axis were not articulated as reasons to fight. Instead of a call to defend Fascism or Il Duce, the film mobilizes preexisting categories of identity, such as family and local community.[49] The regime had been unsuccessful in conflating patriotism and Fascism, instead creating a war propaganda that turned to older, local, and preexisting categories. The film includes no representation of "what" is being fought for ideologically, only what is being fought against. The enemy is clear, but the New Europe of the Axis powers is neither mentioned nor articulated. Finally, the film's displacement of the national struggle onto the colonial landscape further bespeaks the instability at home.

Nonetheless, as scholarly work on film in other contexts, such as Nazi Germany or the United States, has shown, the absence of political symbols or slogans does not imply the lack of propaganda intention or impact. Calls for defense of the national community can be and have been made using a wide range of rhetorical and narrative strategies. As Eric Rentschler and Linda Schulte-Sasse argue for Nazi Germany, the vast majority of films sanctioned by the Nazi regime had the intended goal of entertainment.[50] "[The] most important 'political' lesson in Nazi Cinema," writes Schulte-Sasse, "is not to be found in its political content, but in its generation of a subject effect that would seem to have little to do with politics."[51]

Casablanca, Michael Curtiz's epic declaration of American anti-Fascism, produced the same year as *Bengasi* and also set in North Africa (but obviously excluded from the Venice film festival), offers an interesting counterpoint to *Bengasi*'s narrative. In *Casablanca*, the ideas being fought for are clear: America equals freedom and democracy. Rick's conversion to active anti-Fascism comes from his realization that without the triumph of American values, the world would be an unlivable place and he would have lived a life without meaning. In the end, Rick sacrifices his personal fulfillment so that the struggle for freedom, so much greater than any individual's needs, can continue. In the case of *Casablanca*, the protagonist moves from the margins, that is, the isolation of possessive individualism, to the center of engagement in the national/patriotic project.[52]

Bengasi's theme that most directly presents official ideology is that of varieties of imperialism. The film stresses the hypocrisy and corruption of British imperialism, comparing it to the civilizing nature of Italian imperialism. According to this reading, Italian imperialism in North Africa was creative: it built cities and made the desert fertile. British imperialism was destructive, dependent upon raping the land and abusing the natives. As the Italian troops retreated and promised to return, the natives thanked them and bade them a sad farewell. The film patently erases the brutality and atrocity that characterized Italian Fascist imperial rule.

The war delimited the spaces available to critics, and much of the popular and critical cinematic press followed the lead of the regime in calling for cinema to support the war effort.[53] The reviews in the daily press tended toward puffed-up patriotic rhetoric. In this context, *Bengasi*'s sentimentality and melodrama gave reviewers much to work with. They celebrated the film as a great contribution to the war effort: "A beautiful film which speaks to the heart of all Italians," wrote the *Popolo di Roma* reviewer.[54] "He [Genina] knew," claimed *L'Avvenire*, "with his feverish evocation, how to bring to life all our best feelings for our brave brethren—soldiers and those waiting on the fourth shore of *our sea*."[55] *La voce cattolica* passionately praised the film: "For now, we speak only one name, a great and unforgettable name, which clouds the eyes with emotion and fills the soul with pride: *Bengasi*."[56] In sum, effused this reviewer, *Bengasi* "demonstrates all the healthy developments in cinema."[57] For *La rivista cinematografica*, *Bengasi* was "the Festival's victor," because of "the artistic perfection of all its elements."[58]

Along with the praise, the press also qualified its celebration of *Bengasi*: *La voce cattolica* found the structure "episodic and fragmentary, and without a central subject"; yet, the reviewer hailed the scenes of family devotion, such as that of the mother of the blind soldier who escorts her wounded son home.[59] The film's fragmentary character irritated a number of reviewers, such the *Settegiorni* critic, who said, "Perhaps it is a bit too fragmentary and anecdotal. The characters are not connected to one another."[60] Perhaps, sensing Alessandrini's ambivalence in *Bengasi*, the reviewer in *Il regime fascista* found it "distant from the outstanding beauty of *L'assedio dell'Alacazar*."[61]

Bengasi's fragmentary structure and documentary-like qualities raise interesting questions. As contemporary scholars have suggested, rather than emerging after or in opposition to Fascism, many of neorealism's roots lay in the Fascist era.[62] While the film's narrative remained traditional, its failure to propose a single dominant story, its attention to the "ordinary citizens" of Bengasi, and its focus on all the social classes resident there—from bourgeois to peasant to prostitute—hint at the priorities of neorealism. In addition, Genina's emphasis on open-air shots, such as those of wounded soldiers in the hospital garden or the pivotal scene in the farmer's garden, marks the realist style.

The film that closed the film festival offers a complimentary view of Fascism in crisis. *Noi vivi* (*We the Living*), directed by Goffredo Alessandrini, screened the festival's final night, from 7:30 to midnight. Perhaps to lift the mood of the audience after a long and heavy film, a cartoon entitled *Nel paese dei ranocchi* (*In the Land of the Frogs*) followed the four-and-one-half-hour film. This adaptation of Ayn Rand's novel *We the Living* employed the techniques of Hollywood melodrama to critique Bolshevism and celebrate individualism. It won the highest honor at the film festival, the Premio della Biennale (Biennale Prize).

Noi vivi tells the story of three characters—Kira, Leo, and Andrei—whose lives have been destroyed by the repression and corruption of Bolshevism. *Noi vivi* conveys its narrative through exaggerated emotions, close-up shots, and "star" performances. The film's action centers on two top box-office attractions—Fosco Giachetti (who also played Captain Berti in *Bengasi*) and Alida Valli—who play the central characters. Rossano Brazzi made one of his first screen appearances. Because of his roles in *L'assedio dell'Alacazar*, *Bengasi*, and *Noi vivi*, Giachetti has been seen as "the 'Fascist' Italian actor par excellence"; as Adriano Aprà writes, Giachetti was "a masculine, paternal figure—dark and self-reflective, but responsible, courageous and decisive, but without smirks or weakness."[63]

Noi vivi recounts the romantic tale of great love against the turmoil of war and revolution. The plot depends on stock melodrama, such as a series of near-captures, copious tears, and continual life-or-death choices. The melodrama reaches a climax in the last scene as Kira, the protagonist, tries to flee across the border in the wedding dress (chosen because the white blends with the Russian snow) she never wore as a bride. She is shot at the border, destined never to reach freedom. In a nod to the Hollywoodization of Italian film and despite the film's attempt to show the desperate conditions of post–Civil War Russia, *Noi vivi* is rife with art-deco interiors and high-fashion costumes.

Noi vivi centers on Kira, the daughter of an industrialist who returns to Petrograd in 1921. She is, above all else, a woman who creates her own morals, who eschews systems and is able to see through the hypocrisy of Bolshevism. Kira dreams of being an engineer because "engineering is the only profession for which you don't have to lie." But in the context of Soviet decadence and destruction, her dreams are dashed. There is nothing for an individual to create in a Russia eviscerated by Bolshevism. In the film's decisive scene, she meets Leo, the son of an executed aristocrat, and seduces him: Kira is drawn to Leo because she sees a spark of resistance in him. When Leo becomes sick with tuberculosis, the only way for him, as a former aristocrat, to go to a sanatorium is to pay with money they do not have. Kira gets the money by becoming the mistress of a high-ranking member of the secret police, Andrei. Leo comes back from the sanatorium healthy in body but sick in mind. He takes to speculation and is arrested, but he is saved by Andrei, who intercedes on Leo's behalf out of deep, abiding love for Kira. In the end, Andrei, at first the true believer, makes the long voyage through Communism to individual conscience. Faced with the emptiness of the Communism to which he devoted his life, Andrei shoots himself.

The film's overarching theme is the deadening effect of Communism on the individual. With the exception of Andrei, the hero, the film portrays Bolsheviks as corrupt, abusive, and vulgar. They are weak opportunists who use ideology for personal gain. Russia under Communism is depressed and empty. Bolshevism has sucked the blood out of society; everyone has been driven either into an amoral collaboration with the devil or numbed resignation. In this context, Kira, the heroine, motivated by her individual conscience and her love of Leo, represents a spark of hope.

Noi vivi sympathizes with the bourgeoisie who have suffered as a result of the Revolution; it underlines the injustice of punishing individuals according to class. At this level, the rejection of a class definition of society, *Noi vivi* coincides with Fascist ideology. Further, mirroring Fascist puritanism and the Fascist notion that Bolshevism meant the collapse of morality, the film stresses the decline of morals and the threats to women's purity that come with Communist collectivism. At one point, the former peasant in charge of the collectivized apartment building comes to Kira's family and says "two to a room, even if of opposite sexes." Alessandrini also employed the moral breakdown of life under Bolshevism as titillation, as in the scene when Kira and Leo first meet; Leo takes Kira for a prostitute and puts his hand up her skirt. Because of her depressed isolation and her hope that he, like her, has transcended the parasitism of Bolshevism, she lets him.

Alessandrini used the film set to convey the stultifying atmosphere of life in Soviet Russia. Most of the scenes take place in cramped, dark, and run-down quarters, especially in overcrowded communal living spaces. Kira and Leo's attempt to escape on a departing merchant vessel is filmed in the tiny cabin in which they hide. Many scenes take place at night, conveying a feeling of tension and subterfuge, such as that of Andrei's nocturnal trial, which is held in a dark and dank room in which the only ray of light shines from behind the now redeemed former-Bolshevik-turned-martyr. Alessandrini also employed repeated close-up shots to give the film a claustrophobic, shut-in quality.

Noi vivi contains both dominant and alternative narratives and remains controversial as a veiled condemnation of Fascism. Critics at the time and since the film's debut have read it against the grain and as an example of the cultural *fronde* that produced anti-Fascist work from within official culture.[64] Because the representation of Bolshevism is so multi-valenced, the film is easily read as a critique of all systems that force the individual into submission. In a fairly obvious challenge to Fascism, Kira delivers a speech in which she says that the state is never more important than the individual. She says that no one should subordinate themselves to the state, any state. While the dominant message is anti-Communist, not very far below the surface the film asserts the destructive force of all systems. The fact that it is ideology that destroys the love between Kira and Leo and that makes the love between Kira and Andrei impossible suggests that all totalizing ideologies are corrupt because they ruin the deepest bonds between people.

Without a doubt, the fact that the central hero—Andrei—was a believing Bolshevik who comes to reject the ideology to which he has devoted his life, finding the only true knowledge in love, opens spaces for multiple readings, if not for an explicit critique of Fascism. In the end, it is not the state or the nation for which he dies; he dies of unrequited love and an awareness of the crimes he has committed in the name of the state. Andrei was the successful thinking Bolshevik who, in the course of the film, learns a lesson deeper and truer than any politics. The powerful rejection of submission to the state and the elevation of an individual's absolute commitment to his fellow human being in the midst of the war reflected both Alessandrini's anxieties about Fascism and those in the larger society.

As in *Bengasi*, in *Noi vivi*, women hold together family and community, and resistance is female. The only true voice and the only character consistently above ideology and invincible to the seductions of power and money is Kira. The film portrays Kira as both feminine and as the possessor of a higher truth. She is a real woman who is driven by love and who gives her only asset, her body, for Leo. She makes her own morality. Leo emerges as weak and corruptible, but Kira protects him. As he adapts to the corrupt culture around him, turning to speculation and gambling, Leo becomes weaker and more feminine. In an opposite trajectory, as Andrei abandons the false system, he becomes increasingly masculine.

While Kira embodies the heroic fight against Bolshevism and, as such, is the central protagonist, she also remains an object of desire. It is ultimately through her desirability as a woman that Kira achieves her agency. Throughout the film, Kira is dressed, posed, and shot as the object of the sexualized gaze of the spectator and of the two male leads, Andrei and Leo. If *Noi vivi* challenges dominant gender codes by using a female lead as the true resister, it does so without fully disrupting the norms of the gender hierarchy.

Noi vivi conveys the destabilizing impact of Bolshevism through gender confusion. Sonia, the calculating apparatchik, is a symbol of how Bolshevism distorts gender: it has made women into men and men into women. Sonia is short and heavyset, with dark beady eyes and a gruff voice. She is power-hungry and uses her power to capture and control a man she is too ugly to get on her own. Bolshevism has masculinized the women and emasculated the men. Here, "appropriate" gender behavior is the measure of the morality or immorality of a system.

Anti-Bolshevism dominated the 1942 film festival, and it signaled the unity of the Fascist and Nazi worldviews. Nearly every participating nation presented an anti-Bolshevik film. Anti-Bolshevism had been at the core of Fascist ideology since its inception in the 1920s, but, in the course of World War II, domestic anti-Communism appropriated elements of Nazi anti-Communism, which gave it a racial reading. By the late 1930s, Fascist anti-Communism was racialized, often depicting Communists as subhuman or barbarian and moving closer to Nazi conceptions that linked Jews and Bolsheviks as *untermenschen*. Yet, challenging Fascist propaganda, the anti-Communism of *Noi vivi* is complex and human; in Corrado Alvaro's script based on the Ayn Rand novel, Bolshevism is oppressive, but one could have followed it for the right reasons.[65] The hero, Andrei, is a Bolshevik who comes to understand the system and rise above it.

As in *Bengasi*, *Noi vivi* presents the enemy—that which must be fought—but little, other than individual loyalty and love, to defend. And, like *Bengasi*, *Noi vivi* offers no resolution. The fates of Andrei, who takes his own life rather than live a lie, and Kira, who meets her death while escaping, imply the dead end of totalizing systems. This recognition in the summer of 1942 that no triumph lay ahead hints at the fragility of the Italian commitment to the war.

The press, controlled by and sympathetic to the regime, read *Noi vivi* and *Addio Kira* (it was divided into two parts due to its length) as seamlessly anti-Bolshevik. The reviewer in *Brenero-Trenti* cheered the film, saying: "From the point of view of polemic, the film is perfect. Through the stories of Kira, Leo and Andrea the monstrous creation of Bolshevism is captured in all its fatal absurdity. Only in death will Kira find peace."[66] Carlo Viviani, in *Gazzetta di Venezia*, found the depiction of life under the "blows of the violent storm destroying Russia" particularly powerful.[67] "The film's best aspect," continued Viviani, "is its depiction of the tragic atmosphere of decay which drowns men and things, [producing] the desperate and useless protests of some and the resigned acquiescence of others."[68] *La tribuna* welcomed the anti-Bolshevik message as salutary but found the personal tragedy of unrequited love to be the dominant message. No political system has the right to conquer love: "Romantic characters against a background of brutal realism. They seem to be endlessly pulled down by the gusts of the furious storm. . . . But Kira and Andrei are illuminated by the flame of their respective love that consumes them and carries them to death."[69]

Reviews celebrated the performances of Alida Valli and Fosco Giachetti, but they often found Rossano Brazzi inadequate in the part of Leo. Some, such as the reviewer in *Popolo d'Italia*, lamented Alessandrini's decision to faithfully follow the novel's detailed plot, suggesting that a shorter, condensed version would have achieved an equally felicitous result.[70] G. Hartsarich, in *La tribuna*, concurred, "Goffredo Alessandrini has burdened the plot with a profusion of useless details; perhaps, in order to remain true to the original."[71]

The jury and the audiences at the 1942 Venice Biennale International Film Festival celebrated *Noi vivi* and *Bengasi* as critically and popularly triumphant films. They have much in common: both are survival narratives in which the main characters must defend themselves from devastating threats from the outside. In both cases the enemy, either the wild, depraved Bolshevik or the degenerate and effeminate British, represent a profound challenge to the established social order. In these films, the audience is given Fascism's two great ideological enemies: *Bengasi* shows the degenerate liberal democracies (weak and feminine, forced to act cruelly out of their weakness) and *Noi vivi* presents the Communist Soviet Union (evil, corrupt, and empty). The threats are palpable, but neither film offers resolution or reinscription of the traditional order.

Bengasi and *Noi vivi* materialize the deep contradictions driving Fascism in 1942. On the one hand, Fascist officials desperately sought to mobilize cinema for the war effort and to create a domestic consensus in favor of the war. Vocal elements in the Ministry of Popular Culture—which administered the film festival as of 1938—demanded an emulation of Nazi culture. Reviewers turned to puffed-up rhetoric, hoping that the tales told in the documentaries would come to pass. "Rest assured," wrote Giannino Omero Gallo, "that the German documentaries give the profound impression of great glories in a war already won."[72] The film festival's structure fit the new mold; only sympathetic nations attended, and the government tightly controlled the selection of films. The entire event was couched in inflated and bombastic language hailing the "New Europe" and condemning the twin evils of Anglo-American weakness and Bolshevik tyranny.

On the other hand, the gaps, tensions, fractures, and *frondes* that always had existed in Fascist culture became more visible and pronounced during the war. Rather than project unity in the face of war, the prize-winning films at the last Fascist-administered Venice film festival reveal that Fascist consensus was merely a façade and that the regime was about to collapse.

Notes

1. "La giornata di Goebbels e Pavolini a Venezia," *Il gazzettino*, 31 August 1942.

2. "La X Mostra Internazionale d'arte Cinematografica," *La rivista cinematografica*, 15 September 1942.

3. "La X Mostra Internazionale d'arte Cinematografica."

4. "La X Mostra Internazionale d'arte Cinematografica." "I tre aquilotti" was directed by Mario Mattoli and was designated as "*fuori concorso*" (out of competition).

5. *Gazzetta di Venezia*, 1 October 1940. The Italian title of the event was *Manifestazione cinematografica italo-germanica*.

6. On the conditions and character of the film industry during World War II, see Mino Argentieri, *Il cinema in guerra. Arte, comunicazione e propaganda in Italia, 1940–1944* (Rome: Riuniti, 1998); and Mino Argentieri, ed., *Schermi di guerra* (Rome: Bulzoni Editore, 1995).

7. On the phases and character of Fascist official culture and state patronage, see Marla Stone, *The Patron State: Culture and Politics in Fascist Italy* (Princeton, N.J.: Princeton University Press, 1998). For histories of the Venice Biennale of International Art, see Romolo Bazzoni, *Sessant'anni della Biennale di Venezia* (Venice: Lombroso Editore, 1962); and *Storia della Biennale*, ed. Paolo Rizzi and Enzo di Martini (Milan: Electa, 1982).

8. For an analysis of the Fascist creation of the Venice Biennale International Film Festival, see Marla Stone, "Challenging Cultural Categories: The Transformation of the Venice Biennale International Film Festival Under Fascism," *Journal of Modern Italian Studies* 4, no. 2 (1999): 184–208; and Francesco Bono, "La Mostra del cinema di Venezia. Nascita e sviluppo

nell'anteguerra (1932–1939)," *Storia contemporanea* XXII, no. 3 (June 1991): 513–549.

9. Elio Zorzi, "Inaugurazione della III Mostra Internazionale del Cinema," *L'Illustrazione italiana*, 18 August 1935, 345, and "La prima Esposizione Internazionale d'arte Cinematografica," *Gazzetta di Venezia*, 24 May 1932. The films at the first show came from Germany, the United States, France, the Soviet Union, Great Britain, Italy, Czechoslovakia, Poland, and Holland; the largest number of entries came from the United States and Germany. "Un elenco di films," *Gazzetta di Venezia*, 24 July 1932.

10. Zorzi, "Inaugurazione della III Mostra Internazionale del Cinema," 345.

11. *L'arte nelle mostre italiane* IV, no. 1 (January 1939): 7 and 24.

12. *L'arte nelle mostre italiane* IV, no. 1 (January 1939): 7; "Appunto per S.E. il Capo del Governo," September 9, 1935, Archivo Centrale dello Stato (hereafter ACS), Presidenza Consiglio dei Ministri (hereafter PCM) (1934–36), 14.1.4677. The figure of 55,237 for 1937 was also cited by Maraini in a telegram to Mussolini on September 9, 1937. See *ACS*, PCM (1937–39), 14.1.2966, sottofascicolo 5.

13. "Un elenco di films," *Gazzetta di Venezia*, 24 July 1932. "Referendum Pubblico—Iᵃ Esposizione Internazionale d'Arte Cinematografica," *ACS*, PCM (1934–36), 14.1.4677; Gian Piero Brunetta, *Cinema italiano tra le due guerre* (Milano: Mursia, 1975), 67, 71; Marcia Landy, *Fascism in Film: The Italian Commercial Cinema, 1931–1943* (Princeton, N.J.: Princeton University Press, 1986), 15. See also Vito Zagarrio, "Il modello sovietico: tra piano culturale e piano economico," in *Cinema italiano sotto il fascismo*, ed. Riccardo Redi (Venice: Marsilio, 1979), 185–200.

14. Letter and attachment, September 3, 1935, Maraini and Volpi to Mussolini, ACS, PCM (1934–36), 14.1.4677. *Triumph of the Will* won the prize offered by the Istituto LUCE for best foreign documentary; *Becky Sharp* won the Biennale prize for best film in color; *Promised Land* was given a diploma of honorable mention by the jury. *Promised Land* was produced by Urim Palestine F.C.

15. "Relazione per l'assegnazione dei premi alla Mostra Internazionale d'Arte Cinematografica," ACS, PCM (1934–36), 14.1.4677.

16. Geoffrey Nowell-Smith, "The Italian Cinema under Fascism," in *Rethinking Italian Fascism*, ed. David Forgacs (London: Lawrence and Wishart, 1986), 154; *Il Gazzettino*, 11 July 1937. According to James Hay, it "met with only lukewarm critical reaction" at the Cinema Show, and according to Gian Piero Brunetta, it failed "because of blocks of dialogue which broke up its internal rhythm, as well as [because of] the silliness of its expression and technique." James Hay, *Popular Film Culture in Fascist Italy: The Passing of the Rex* (Bloomington: Indiana University Press, 1987), 115; and Brunetta, *Cinema italiano tra le due guerre*, 77.

17. Nowell-Smith, "The Italian Cinema under Fascism," 150. Roberto Rossellini worked as co-scriptwriter on this film.

18. Gian Piero Brunetta, *Storia del cinema italiano* (Rome: Riuniti, 1979), 313.

19. Telegram, 31 August 1938, Biennale to Mussolini, ACS, PCM (1937–39), 14.1.2966, sottofascicolo 6.

20. For an interpretation of the meanings of *Jud Süss*, see Linda Schulte-Sasse, *Entertaining the Third Reich: Illusions of Wholeness in Nazi Cinema* (Durham, N.C., and London: Duke University Press, 1996), 47–91; and Eric Rentschler, *The Ministry of Illusion: Nazi Cinema and Its Afterlife* (Cambridge, Mass.: Harvard University Press, 1996), 149–169.

21. *Gazzetta Ufficiale del Regno D'Italia*, no. 122 (27 May 1936), 1758–1759.

22. Ibid.

23. ACS, PCM (1937–39) 14.1.2966, sottofascicolo 4.

24. *Gazzetta di Venezia*, 1 October 1940.

25. "Appunto per il Duce," 13 June 1943, ACS, PCM (1937–39) 14.1.2966, sottofascicolo 8.

26. Umberto De Franciscis, "Caratteri della Xª Mostra Internazionale d'Arte Cinematografica," *Rassegna d'oltremare* (Roma) 31 (August/September 1942).

27. "Fervida vigilia della Mostra del cinema," *Tribuna*, Roma, 21 August 1942.

28. Giannino Omero Gallo, "Vitalità della Mostra," *Primi piani*, Milano, August 1942.

29. *La domenica del lavoro fascista*, Rome, 27 September 1942.

30. Ibid.

31. On support within the cinematic press for the regime's centralization and coordination of the film industry during World War II, see Argentieri, *Il cinema in guerra*, 1–46.

32. Ercole Patti, "Bengasi il nuovo successo italiano," *Il popolo di Roma*, 6 September 1942.

33. "Chiusura della Mostra del Cinema," *Italia*, Roma, 17 September 1942.

34. Ibid.

35. Massimo Mida, "Rivelazioni veneziane," *Cinema*, 10 September 1942.

36. Maria Del Corso, "Fine della mostra," *Mediterraneo*, 19 September 1942.

37. Ibid.

38. *Odessa in fiamme* was directed by Carmine Gallone as a joint Italian-Romanian production; it told the story of a woman's struggle to save her family during the Bolshevik invasion of Bessarabia.

39. "Insegnamenti di una mostra," *Fiamma*, Parma, 21 September 1942.

40. This film won the Coppa Mussolini in 1940.

41. Argentieri, *Il cinema in guerra*, 55–60.

42. Pierre Leprohon, *The Italian Cinema* (London: Secker and Warburg, 1942).

43. Argenticri, *Il cinema in guerra*, 58.

44. Sergio Grmek Germani and Vittorio Martinelli, *Il cinema di Augusto Genina* (Rome: Edizioni Biblioteca dell'Immagine, 1989), 267.

45. Ercole Patti, "Bengasi il nuovo successo italiano," *Il popolo di Roma*, 6 September 1942.

46. Ruth Ben-Ghiat, "Envisioning Modernity: Desire and Discipline in the Italian Fascist Film," *Critical Inquiry* 23 (Autumn 1996): 113.

47. Ibid., 113.

48. Schulte-Sasse, *Entertaining the Third Reich*, 88.

49. Mabel Berezin discusses the official wartime attention to earlier structures of identity in *Making the Fascist Self: The Political Culture of Interwar Italy* (Ithaca and London: Cornell University Press, 1997).

50. Rentschler, *The Ministry of Illusion;* and Schulte-Sasse, *Entertaining the Third Reich*.

51. Schulte-Sasse, *Entertaining the Third Reich*, 17.

52. On American wartime film production, see Clayton Koppes and Gregory Black, *Hollywood Goes to War: How Politics, Profits and Propaganda Shaped World War II Movies* (Berkeley: University of California Press, 1990).

53. In "La critica cinematografica in tre settiminali: 'Illustrazione italiana,' 'Oggi,' 'Tempo,'" Massimo Garritano discusses the relationship among the popular press, film reviews, and the war. In *Schermi di Guerra*, ed. Mino Argentieri (Rome: Bulzoni Editore, 1995), 239–284.

54. Ercole Patti, "*Bengasi* il nuovo successo italiano," *Il popolo di Roma*, 6 September 1942.

55. Mario Milani, "Il film italiano *Bengasi* trionfa," *L'Avvenire*, Rome, 8 September 1942.

56. Giannino Omero Gallo, "Vitalità della mostra," *Primi piani*, Milan, August 1942.

57. "Alla decima mostra cinematografica Veneziana," *La voce cattolica*, Brescia, September 19, 1942.

58. "La X Mostra Internazionale d'arte Cinematografica," *La rivista cinematografica*, 15 September 1942.

59. "Alla decima mostra cinematografica Veneziana."

60. "Cinema senza pietà," *Settegiorni*, 12 September 1942.

61. Giuseppe Avon Caffi, "*Bengasi* di Genina e *Andreas Sclutter*," *Il regime fascista*, 6 September 1942.

62. See, among others, Brunetta, *Cinema italiano tra le due guerre*, 55–59; and Ruth Ben-Ghiat, *La cultura fascista* (Bologna: Il Mulino, 2000), 83–120.

63. Adriano Aprà and Patrizia Pistagnesi, *I favolosi anni trenta. Cinema italiano, 1929-1944* (Milan: Electa, 1979), 96.

64. Davide Turconi and Antonio Sacchi, ed., *Bianconero rosso e verde* (Florence: La Casa Usher, 1983), 75. Turconi and Sacchi write, "in *Noi vivi* and *Addio Kira*, [where] Alessandrini projects the preoccupations and the sense of an inevitable end to Fascism onto a *papier-mâché* Russia."

65. Corrado Alvaro had a varied and productive career during the Fascist era. For details, see Ben-Ghiat, *La cultura fascista*, 106–112.

66. Alberto Albani-Barbieri, "Una spietata requistoria antibolscevica. *Noi vivi*," *Brennero Trenti*, 17 September 1942.

67. Carlo Viviani, "Il cineromanzo *Noi vivi*," *Gazzetta di Venezia*, 16 September 1942.

68. Ibid.

69. G. Hartsarich, "*Noi vivi* e *Addio Kira*," *La tribuna*, 17 September 1942.

70. Dino Falconi, "Spettacolo di chiusura alla mostra cinematografica," *Il popolo d'Italia*, 16 September 1942.

71. G. Hartsarich, "*Noi vivi* e *Addio Kira*," *La tribuna*, 17 September 1942.

72. Giannino Omero Gallo, "Vitalità della Mostra," *Primi piani*, Milano, August 1942.

12

Film Stars and Society in Fascist Italy

Stephen Gundle

From the mid-1930s on, Italian Fascism engaged in a concerted effort to build up the film industry, raise its standards, and turn it once more into an international force. Like other European governments, it sought, as part of this effort, to place restrictions on the activities of American film companies by introducing taxes, quotas, and regulations relating to the import of foreign movies. In general, the regime's interventions in this sphere were motivated by economic considerations, that is, by the desire to ensure that profits earned in Italy remained, as far as possible, in the country and benefited national industrial development. But, given Fascism's totalitarian pretensions, broader cultural and political considerations played a part. Few wished to turn cinema into an overt tool of propaganda, but all Fascists felt that cinematic entertainment should contribute to the national rebirth and at least offer amusement that was dignified and not trivial or demeaning.

The issue of stars was bound up with these moves. It was obvious to all that one of the great sources of Hollywood's appeal was its magnificently good-looking and perfectly presented stars. Unlike the great Italian *dive* of the silent era, American stars of the 1930s were not extreme but realistic; they represented alluring yet accessible types whose ways of behaving, dressing, and appearing were widely copied by young people. Fascists, and Italian producers and directors, were unsure whether stars were a good thing and whether they were a necessary part of any film industry. Although there were some Italian stars in the early 1930s, the phenomenon was still considered to be mainly an American one. Thus, between the early 1930s until the fall of the regime, the question was debated repeatedly, and sometimes contradictory *dictats* and measures were adopted.

Few people in Italy in the 1930s fully perceived the way stars were implicated in social, economic, and cultural processes. But on the part of Fascists, there was a dim sense that they were codifiers of gender roles, value systems, and certain ideas about national identity. The aim of this essay is to investigate these aspects of stardom and also to consider stars as promotional tools, objects of desire and imitation, and potential supporters of a political project. Particular attention will be paid to the relationship between American and Italian stars and to the place of stars in popular culture.

Fascism and Stars

Were there any stars in Fascist Italy? It is necessary to begin by posing this basic question, because Franco Rositi argued in an article published in 1967 that there were not.[1] The purpose of the article was to investigate how Italian Fascism was able to allow the film market to be dominated for most of the 1920s and 1930s by American cinema when, according to the hypothesis advanced by Francesco Alberoni,[2] dictatorships cannot tolerate the existence of elite groups which are separate from political power. Rositi argued that because Italy was still at a low level of economic development, education was not widespread and substantial parts of the country were virtually untouched by mass communications; traditional forms of social interaction and communication continued to dominate. Social and political control was exercised largely by direct and interpersonal means. Cinema and other commercial media did not represent any threat to the regime because they occupied a relatively peripheral place in the cultural system. In particular, Rositi argued, they failed to generate any star cults which might have posed a challenge by presenting models of behavior or systems of values at variance with those approved by the regime.

Rositi based his conclusions about the absence of star phenomena largely on an empirical survey of the periodical press. An examination of every third issue of *La domenica del corriere, Il secolo illustrato, Illustrazione italiana, Novella, Eva,* and *Lei* published between 1924 and 1938 revealed a low level of personalization in the coverage of all subject areas from politics and religion to cinema and entertainment. The press was narrowly informative; it offered no models of behavior, did not report on private lives, and promoted no collective gossip. Although there was coverage of American cinema, Rositi argued, there was no attempt to link it to realistic contexts in which imitative mechanisms and consequently dissonance from officially approved values might arise. Insofar as individual Italians were singled out for praise in the press—and many were—they were lauded for their hard work, seriousness, sense of duty, and love of home and family.

Rositi argued that this lack of personalization was general; it was not that adulation of political figures took the place of the cult of entertainment personalities, for the press showed no special interest even in Mussolini or other Fascist leaders. He asserted that no particular star veneration could be found even in women's magazines; that is, in a subordinate sector of the press where deviations might have been more easily tolerated. From this, he drew the conclusion that economic development in Italy had not advanced sufficiently for mass commercial culture to take on the star characteristics that had arisen in more advanced countries.

It is remarkable that Rositi's analysis has remained unchallenged for over thirty years, for his methodology was imperfect and his argument far from persuasive. The first problem concerns periodization. His study dealt only with the period between 1924 and 1938. The cutoff date of 1938 was never explained or justified, yet it is odd because the years between 1938 and 1945 are recognized to be ones in which cinema and mass culture became a part of the experience of a wider range of Italians than ever before. The withdrawal of major American studios from the Italian market following the institution of the state distribution monopoly meant that although the quantity of American films in circulation was much reduced, national film production underwent a tremendous expansion to fill the gap. Moreover, it was during this phase that the regime first moved systematically to restrict or suppress manifestations of star culture by limiting the salaries of film actors, insisting that they use public transport, banning the publication of biographies, and controlling and suppressing magazines such as *Omnibus* and *Le grandi firme*, in which "dissonant personalization" was present. In addition, restrictions were placed on the beauty contests and look-alike competitions that had flourished in earlier years. Such measures provide evidence that a star culture had developed in Italy.

A second problem concerns sources. The decision to focus on the press follows Alberoni's observation that it is this parallel medium, rather than the cinema or radio themselves, which is decisive in creating and perpetuating star cultures. Yet the titles chosen for the survey were perhaps not the most appropriate. *La domenica del corriere*, *Il secolo illustrato*, and *Illustrazione italiana* were quite conservative family magazines directed mainly at the middle classes. At no point in their histories (either before or after the war) did they pay much attention to stars.

In other words, it would be quite possible to replicate Rositi's survey using the issues published in, say, the 1950s and reach the same results. Yet no one would argue that there was no star veneration in the 1950s. The women's magazines *Eva* and *Lei* were quite emphatically publications for the "modern woman"; they stressed not family, duty, and sacrifice but "selfishness"; that is to say, they gave much space to discourses on work, to the "spirit" of the modern woman (her enthusiasm and versatility), and to her interests in beauty and fashion. Within this approach, all sorts of modern images found a place, including advertisements for Fiat cars with women at the wheel and women airplane pilots. Among these were many images of American actresses and other pictures of Hollywood derivation. The amount of material on single women stars was perhaps limited (although Joan Crawford, Jean Harlow, and many others appeared on covers), but the social consequences of star culture are plain to see.

The point becomes clearer if a wider range of women's magazines is drawn into the equation and a broader time scale is considered. After World War II, there was actually *less* focus on stars in women's magazines than previously, due to both economic circumstances and to neorealism. In contrast to the covers of the 1930s, covers in the 1940s often featured ordinary women in accessible dresses. *Lei* (from 1938 *Annabella*) contained roughly the same coverage of stars in the 1950s as it did in the 1930s. *Grazia,* a slightly older publication than both *Eva* (founded in 1933) and *Lei* (founded in 1932), increased its focus on cinema around 1941, when stories about Italian stars were regularly published, including features on them in their homes and discussions of their trademark styles.

In the 1930s, the stars were most visible in the widely read movie magazines that constituted the staple diet of the keen filmgoer. Although Rositi excluded them from his survey, *Cinema illustrazione, Stelle, Primi piani,* and *Cinema* offered a steady stream of news, photographs, and stories about movie stars.[3] They supplied mechanisms such as look-alike competitions and quizzes, which stimulated an identification with stars and some merging of star culture and everyday life. The correspondence columns were also important. Figures with exotic-sounding names such as Knight of Hearts, Dona Dolores de Panza, and Aladin gave people advice on all manner of aspirations and personal problems, including looks, courtship, dress, how to attract attention, and so on. As Victoria de Grazia points out, this was tremendously important at a time when such matters were simply not discussed within families or often even between friends. The culture of film was a sphere in which people could find some possibility of self-definition.[4]

A further problem with Rositi's methodology concerns his failure to explore posters and publicity material, to inquire into audience responses to stars, and to examine the roles of single actors and actresses who in both popular memory and histories of film are considered to have enjoyed the status of stars.[5] While Rositi's focus on the press is necessary and fruitful, it is by no means the only source, and it cannot be analyzed solely quantitatively.

Italy's lower level of development meant that star-related phenomena were less widespread and played less of a central part in collective life there than in the United States or northern Europe, but there was nonetheless much interest in celebrities. The question that will be addressed here, therefore, is not whether or not a star culture existed but rather what its extent and nature were, how it interacted with other social processes, and what its specific characteristics were.

The Fascist Star System

The discussion of stardom in Italy in the 1930s cannot but begin with Mussolini. The country's ruler from 1922, Il Duce was a constant presence, a figure whom it was impossible to ignore and who accompanied Italians in many spheres of their lives. His portrait and sayings were featured in public places, and his activities were regularly reported in the daily press. He inspired imitation in speech, appearance (in particular the shaved head and the jutting jaw), gestures, attitude, and enterprises. Rositi seems to have discounted the Mussolini cult by saying that there was relatively little veneration of him in the press organs he studied.[6] Alberoni, for his part, downplayed the spectacularization of Mussolini's private life by arguing that it was stage-managed in order to reaffirm conventional family values.[7] The first point is true but proves little, for the cult of Mussolini was encouraged and reinforced in myriad ways. The second point implies that the coverage of the private lives of stars is not normally managed and manipulated, which is obviously false. Although Mussolini had no Goebbels to mold and promote his image, only the much-ridiculed secretary of the PNF, Achille Starace, and the newsreels of the Istituto LUCE ensured that Il Duce's every enterprise was familiar to a substantial proportion of the population. Particularly well known are the sequences of a bare-chested Mussolini helping out with the harvest in the "battle for grain," but there were many more examples of the exaltation of his physical and sporting activities. Il Duce was not just a political leader but the best representative of the new spirit of vigor and energy that the Fascists wished to instill in the Italians (Italian men in particular). Although the ideology of the family was of great importance, there was also an emphasis on the masculinity and the virility of Il Duce, whose reputed prowess as a lover was the subject of much myth-making.

The construction and projection of the Mussolini personality occurred within a framework in which the collective consciousness had already been shaped and conditioned by certain real enterprises and by certain archetypes of popular literature and film. In the urban centers of Italy, where cinema was already a mass phenomenon in the pre–World War I era, the impact of stars on social behavior was considerable. No matter how exaggerated their gestures, Francesca Bertini, Pina Menichelli, Carmen Boni, Leda Gys, and Lyda Borelli were much imitated. Although they were condemned at the time by conventional arbiters of taste, Irene Brin wrote in 1943 that the "masculine curls" of Carmen Boni and "the mink borders on black velvet dresses" of Borelli were copied by petit-bourgeois women who visited the cinema in the afternoons. They no longer copied aristocrats; instead, they copied the "false duchesses" of the screen.[8] It was a sign that the rigid hierarchical society was giving way to a mass society in the turbulence of the postwar era. Yet at just this time, Italian cinema, having known an early splendor, was declining due to a weak industrial and financial footing and the retirement and marriage of many *dive*. "The grand *dive* of the silent era were either getting old or getting married: Francesca Bertini was about to become Countess Cartier; Lyda Borelli had just become Countess Cini," wrote Dino Biondi. "Practically the only star left was Mussolini; indeed, one evening at the theatre he was even introduced to the audience, much to the amazement of the applauding public up in 'the gods.' The language the newspapers used to describe him was taken directly from the 'star system.'"[9]

The Fascists created their own system of heroes and idols beneath Il Duce. They were without exception masculine and heroic, examples of daring and risk, individuals who by their achievements brought luster to the image of Italy abroad. Italo Balbo, the Fascist *ras* of Ferrara who crossed the Atlantic by plane in 1933 and was given a resounding reception in New York, was one such case. Alongside such figures, there were also a number of sports champions, including Primo Carnera and Tazio Nuvolari. In general, however, there was more emphasis in these cases on the collectivity, the team, and the nation than on the individual. Male sports figures were lauded for their specific talents in their chosen fields and because they were positive examples of Italianness.

The national space of stardom therefore was filled by the regime itself to some degree in the 1920s and early 1930s. But beneath these official figures there was a range of alternative figures who were featured in the

American films which flooded into Italy following the collapse of the national film industry. Because they were outside a national space and appeared to be ideologically neutral, these personalities were often viewed as not influential or significant. However, there can be little doubt that young people living in urban centers were greatly fascinated by them.

The Lure of American Commercial Culture

There is little reason to believe that, in the mid-1930s, American film constituted a full-fledged alternative pole of attraction to the regime and its models, although there were certainly contradictions that became more pronounced toward the middle of the decade. Viewed as a sop to the masses and as a quick and ready way of broadening the basis of consent on which the regime rested, film actually constituted something of an obstacle to the realization of some of the regime's propaganda goals.

To understand the impact of American films, it is necessary to look beyond film content and at the way movies changed everyday life. The American star system was promoted in Italy by local agencies of the major U.S. film studios, by the film press that the agencies supplied with photographs and copy, by posters, and by related minor parallel media ("signed" photographs for fans, chocolate cards, etc.). Also, a range of techniques was employed to enhance the identification of young people, and especially girls, with stars and the star culture. Even though the typical female movie star in the 1930s had little to do with Italian physical types, many women attempted to imitate the hair, make-up, attitude, and dress of stars, especially, but by no means only, women among the lower middle classes. Following the example of Jean Harlow, the platinum blonde, who was dubbed "the most beautiful woman in Hollywood" by *Eva* in 1935, some young women were tempted to bleach their hair. Competitions of one sort or another linked to particular films were commonplace, as were beauty and look-alike contests.

Convinced that Italy was the breeding ground of beauty and talent, the major Hollywood film studios indulged in periodic searches. These began after the death of Rudolph Valentino in 1926. Twentieth Century Fox launched a hunt for "the new Valentino" and held a competition for this purpose. The winner, Alberto Rabagliati, went to Hollywood and made one silent film, but his career there, like that of many foreign actors, ended with the arrival of the "talkies."[10] He later made a successful career in Italy as a crooner of swing songs. In 1932, MGM held a Greta Garbo look-alike competition for promotional purposes (it was won, as is well-known, by Sophia Loren's future mother, Romilda Villani, who did indeed bear a striking resemblance to the Swedish actress). More commonplace than these exceptional, much-publicized initiatives, though, were the look-alike competitions and "photogenic" contests that the film magazines ran. These competitions were held constantly and often each one ran for months on end; each week or month a regular page would be devoted to news, comments, and photographs about the event.

Very often the competitions were publicized with photographs of starlets to give people an idea of the sort of look that was desirable and current. One in *Cinema illustrazione* in October 1930, for example, featured Leila Hyams, Mary Philbin, and Alice White. The pictures sent in by readers provide a remarkable testimony of the penetration of star culture into everyday life. These photographs exhibited much attention to hairstyle, pose, and expression. Permed hair (which was sometimes bleached), plucked eyebrows, and make-up were common among women, although there were also photographs of simple girls who used little or no artifice to improve on their natural appearance. Young men often appeared with their hair brushed straight back and Brylcreamed, Valentino style, or in a wavy perm. They often had cigarettes dangling from their mouths, pencil moustaches, and a passionate look in their eye. Hollywood toothy smiles, halfway between a laugh and a smile, were common. Most of the photographs were of face only or of head and shoulders but there were also a few full-length portraits of their subjects—both girls and boys—wearing swimming costumes. This was a reflection of the image the magazines conveyed of Hollywood life; leisure, sport, healthy outdoor pursuits, and worship of the body and the body beautiful.

It is clear from all this that the whole idea of beauty and of attractiveness was being redefined in a way that tended to displace traditional evaluations. Emphasis was placed on exteriority, on the physical, on the body. New non-national or regional standards were being introduced. Interestingly, people were also being empowered to alter and shape their appearance to some degree, to choose an image and to make the best of themselves. As Jackie Stacey has observed in her study of women and stars in Britain, people copied stars not just to try to be thought of *as* them (like the Ronald Colman type in Fellini's *Amarcord*), they also took stars and star looks as a starting point to redefine their own appearance and hence sometimes their identity.[11] The direction in which this process went was the one mapped out by the new standard and producer of beauty: Hollywood. Confirmation that centuries-old standards of beauty were being displaced by new, cosmopolitan ones was offered by the publication in 1931 of an image of the Mona Lisa on whose features had been superimposed those of Marlene Dietrich.[12]

Whereas the Italian stars of the silent era had been remote, fantastic creatures who were exotic and extreme, the American stars of the 1930s were more realistic. The great names (Gary Cooper, Errol Flynn, Clark Gable, and Ronald Colman for the men; Jean Harlow, Greta Garbo, Joan Crawford, Carole Lombard, and Myrna Loy for the women) conformed to types and were manufactured by a remarkable industrially organized studio system in which every aspect of the process of recruiting stars, grooming them, launching their careers, eliciting the desired response to their images, and using them in the studios was meticulous and scientific. Audiences in Italy, as elsewhere, loved them and admired them, even if they had difficulty pronouncing their names and the process of dubbing leveled out some of their individuality. The letters and columns of fan magazines revealed frustrations with the language barrier that made it impossible for Italians to communicate directly with their favorites. Yet the success of Rudolph Valentino (even if his alleged effeminacy provoked criticism and his renunciation of Italian for American citizenship the year before his death drew anger from the regime) showed that even an Italian from the backwaters of Puglia could aspire to join the elite of elites. This was important, for one of the reasons stars appealed to fans rested on the assumption by the fans that they too, given the right luck, could join an elite for which no special qualifications were required.

Although American stars were remote and frustratingly out of reach, save the rare occasions when they visited Italy for promotional or vacation purposes, they introduced a set of codes, rituals, and genetic traces that determined how people understood stardom. Stars were defined by beauty, youth (or, sometimes for men, youthful maturity), a good physique, excellent grooming and tailoring, attractive moral qualities, wealth, happiness, a leisure-oriented lifestyle, good humor, charm, and so on and also by a capacity to arouse collective interest in their publicly projected private lives. There were familiar star poses and attitudes, including ritual protestations of ordinariness and so on, and a series of recognizable lifestyle traits and expressions.

The cult of American stars continued well after the withdrawal of the major U.S. film studios in 1938 and was never entirely eradicated. *Cinema illustrazione* still featured American actors on the cover in 1939, and in *Film* as late as August 1940 there were pictures of stars such as Joan Crawford and Maureen O'Hara. The quantity, however, was reduced, because the agencies were no longer supplying new material, and sarcastic captions were often placed beneath the images. In *Cinema illustrazione* on 1 March 1939, for example, it was said that Joan Bennett "is considered most elegant of the actresses of Hollywood, but this elegance is often artificial, 'sophisticated'; it is very different from the spontaneous elegance of our actresses." Without a regular supply of material, the film magazines grew poorer, they printed fewer photographs, they dropped two-tone color prints, and they reduced the number of pages. Yet for real fans, the American cult went on, in part because there was never a total break—throughout the war years there were always some American films in circulation, and the surrogate nature of some Cinecittà products kept alive nostalgia for the originals. Fanatics continued to adore their idols in secret, Viniccio Marinucci confessed in August 1944; they whispered items of news to each other and passed postcards around. They also lovingly leafed through their collections of past issues of film magazines.[13]

Italian Screen Stars

Italian screen actors and actresses occupied at best a marginal position. When one looks through fan magazines such as *Cinema illustrazione*, it is striking just how few pictures and articles in the early 1930s deal with Italians. There were occasional pictures of the actress Dria Paola (who took the lead role in the first Italian sound film, *Canzone dell'amore*), sometimes in a swimsuit, or of Alberto Rabagliati, who cultivated the look and dress of a film star even after his return from America. From his debut in the 1932 film *Gli uomini, che mascalzoni!*, Vittorio De Sica became, despite his physical ordinariness, a focus of attention. He was a sort of "ordinary Joe," the typical lower-middle-class or working-class guy. Elsa Merlini, the star of Goffredo Alessandrini's 1932 success *La segretaria privata*, became an idol for working girls and for those who aspired to be such. Chirpy and spirited, with a constant spring in her step, her frivolous manner and trademark fringe were much imitated. For the most part, though, Italians were given scant treatment and were considered as substitutes for, or equivalents of, the more attractive and powerfully projected, but faraway, American stars. They were regarded as second rate above all by the audiences of first-run cinemas, who viewed Italian films in general in the same way. Maria Denis was dubbed the Italian Janet Gaynor, Gemma Bolognesi the Italian Mae West; Assia Noris was equated to Claudette Colbert, Mino Doro to Clark Gable, Macario to Eddie Cantor, and so on. Italians emerged within, and were viewed in terms of, a lexicon of stardom that was of unequivocally American origin.

This point can be illustrated most clearly in relation to the one actress to be given a "proper" launch: Isa Miranda. There was no studio system in Italy, and in general there was no systematic process of selecting, grooming, and launching stars. These matters were handled in a more rudimentary fashion and were left largely to chance. The one exception was Miranda. A Milanese typist, model, and sometime prose actress who had appeared in bit parts in a few films, she won the competition launched by the publisher Rizzoli to find a young woman to play Gaby Doriot in the Max Ophuls film *La signora di tutti* (1934). She was given star treatment in the Rizzoli magazines, which played a coordinated part in the promotion of the film. In the wake of its success, Miranda became a recognized star figure, the only one in Italy who acquired an international dimension; she also made films in Germany, Austria, and France.

Miranda became a symbol of the possibility of existence of a full-fledged Italian star figure. She enjoyed much popularity and was invested with hopes which reached their highest point when she was offered a contract by Paramount and invited to Hollywood in 1937. There she made two films, *Hotel Imperial* and *Adventure in Diamonds*. A car accident prevented a third, after which deteriorating relations between Italy and the United States led her to return home. Her films received positive reviews in the United States, where she was hailed as a good dramatic actress (even the bizarre description of her as the "blonde Venus from Mussolini-land" by William Boehnel in the *New York World Telegram* of 4 April 1940 was not intended to be derogatory). But reactions in Italy among specialized observers were divided. G. V. Sampieri, writing in the Fascist organ *Lo schermo,* hailed the improvement that her transfer to Hollywood signaled (presumably on the basis of pictures and reports; Miranda's American films were not released in Italy until 1947). She was "miraculously rejuvenated by the ocean breeze that has liberated her of the make-up forced on her in Italian and international films." "Max Factor and his collaborators have made her over as new, removing the covering of antiquity and discovering finally her true face. It is not so much a star that has been born in Hollywood but a woman," he wrote.[14] This view was not shared by others, who felt, as Miranda herself did, that she was reduced in Hollywood to merely being a Marlene Dietrich look-alike or stand-in; for her, the experience meant not rejuvenation but mortification.

In fact, part of Miranda's identity was always set in these terms. She was, Caldiron and Hockhofler have written, "a sort of Italian reply to Hollywood, something half way between the undisguised sexual provocation of Marlene Dietrich and the undisguised spiritual depth of

Greta Garbo, the epochal legs of Marlene and the disquieting eyes of Greta."[15] Her birth as an actress, they wrote, "took place within the contradictory and prejudicial framework of an idea of stardom that, despite its 'autarchic' aspirations (or perhaps really because of these), was wholly geared towards American models, preferred and pursued precisely because they were far off and unreachable." Yet although she often played the femme fatale type on screen and became stuck in the cliché of the decadent vamp, there was always a strain of wholesomeness to Miranda that allowed Italians to identify with her and share in her endeavors and her successes. Her eyes, Giuseppe Turroni has written, were "more romantically alive than those of the 'corrupt' Marlene."[16]

The division of opinion over Miranda bore witness to a real problem in the attitude toward cinema under Fascism. On the one hand, there was a great admiration for American cinema, for its quality, its industrial system, its charm, and its universal appeal. It was thought that Fascist Italy, another young country on the rise, could learn a great deal from America and indeed should do so in order to launch a national cinema. Others took the view that America was a thoroughly negative influence and that the task was to produce something national and different by combating corrosive American elements. These opposing attitudes mixed and clashed and were sometimes contradictorily held by the same person. The problem concerned the whole of the drive to establish a national cinema industry in Italy that was expressed in the foundation of the Centro Sperimentale, the opening of Cinecittà in 1937, and the restrictive measures which led to the boycotting of the Italian market by the American major film studios in 1938. As far as the question of stars was concerned, the problem was relatively straightforward. Was the principal aim to create an Italian star system to challenge and replace the American one, or was it rather to abolish star veneration and overcome this corrupt feature of the use of cinema?

This question would never be answered unequivocally, with the result that male and female actors in the late 1930s and 1940s were caught between American models and Fascist and traditional pressures. In essence, it may be said that America functioned as the matrix—in other words, as the reference point in the selection and determination of screen character types and in some of the mechanisms of relationships between stars and public—but that pressures were bought to bear to render actors bearers of national qualities and virtues in terms of masculinity and femininity, morality, looks, names, commitment to collective purposes, frugality, and so on. There was, in short, an aesthetic battle in which stars were pulled in different directions as the regime looked to the cinema for ideal racial types and expressed a desire to make cinema the "strongest weapon" of its propaganda.

Sampieri was one of those who took the view that stars were the key to the success of American film; indeed, Hollywood had transplanted its stars to Italy, leaving no space for homegrown products. "There is a great deal to be done to create a true, genuine Italian star culture," he wrote in July 1939.[17] Three things needed to be done, he felt. First, the circulation of news and photographs about American stars needed to be stopped because it was defeatist and cultivated nostalgia for the absent U.S. stars; second, photos of Italian actors had to be circulated in order to make them desirable and interesting. Third, actors had to be persuaded to stop getting angry if they were approached to do bathing-costume shots or if news and gossip was circulated about imaginary love affairs, as this type of publicity was necessary if curiosity was to be aroused. The last point was the most controversial, not only because actors were extremely sensitive, but because official opinion took a dim view of the sort of gossip that occasionally appeared in the press. A note in *Lo schermo* of November 1940 called for the interruption of a series of articles published in the Trieste newspaper *Il piccolo* under the title "Storielle dello schermo" ("Tales of the Screen") because it suggested that "a manicurist with good legs was promoted to the level of star thanks to her love affair with Commendatore So-and-so, executive director of Ipsilonfilm." "All this just covers the cinema world with discredit in the eyes of the public," the author wrote. "Real actresses are not born on the knees of Commendatori."[18]

Constructing a National Star System

Despite these reservations, Italian studios had considerable success in giving rise to stars who could prosper in the absence of the Americans. People grew to like Italian stars, who were familiar, individual, sometimes plain-looking, human, and tender. Some, like De Sica and the blonde ingenue Assia Noris, retained their following from earlier years, although De Sica's appeal to young girls diminished over time. In addition, there was a whole category of names whose pictures appeared frequently in the film press and who became familiar.[19]

The stars of the late 1930s and 1940s were recruited in various ways. Many actors, including Amedeo Nazzari, Fosco Giachetti, Elsa Merlini, and Gino Cervi, had a theatrical background. Singers and actors who had acquired their popularity in variety theatres and in the *café chantants* also made films. Others, particularly some of the young

23a. Assia Noris   23b. Amedeo Nazzari

**Chocolate cards of the Russian-born actress Assia Noris and the
"Italian Errol Flynn," Amedeo Nazzari, two popular actors who
embodied gender stereotypes in the 1930s and early 1940s.
From the author's private collection**

women, who embarked on film careers won competitions organized by
commercial companies to find protagonists for given films. Dina Sas-
soli, who won the competition launched by Lux film in 1940 to find a
Lucia for the film version of *I promessi sposi*, provides an example.

In the early 1940s, it was much less common for actresses to be recruited simply by being spotted casually by producers or directors as
had occurred a decade previously. (The 16-year-old Assia Noris, at the
time resident in France, was, according to her own testimony, spotted
while on holiday by producer Peppino Amato.)[20] Instead, the structures
established by the state undertook the tasks of selection and grooming.
It was the Centro Sperimentale which acted as the main forging ground
for new talent. Together with Cinecittà, it functioned as the equivalent
of a big film studio (Ufa in Germany, the majors in the United States).
Luisa Ferida, Alida Valli, Carla Del Poggio, Luisella Beghi, Elli Parvo,
and many others undertook courses there on generous grants and in

some cases began film careers before terminating their studies. Articles about the Centro regularly appeared in the press, and it acquired a mythical aura.

There was certainly an attempt to give rise to direct replacements for Americans, just as in earlier years the American matrix had functioned as a grid in the selection and launch processes. But very often Italian tastes intervened here to underpin certain options. For example, adolescent Canadian actress and singer Deanna Durbin attracted enormous admiration in Italy (as she did in Britain), more so than she did in America. She served as the model for a whole series of Italian adolescent actresses who populated the schoolgirl comedies.[21] Chiaretta Gelli and Lilia Silvi were probably the nearest equivalents because they also sang, but Irasema Dilian, Carla Del Poggio, and Valentina Cortese were also Durbin types.

Despite the more systematic approach to recruitment, in the absence of proper studios and of exclusive contracts (for the most part), star careers were not planned or constructed in the way they were elsewhere. It was largely up to the individual, therefore, to work to sustain the admiration of the public by insisting on roles, budgets, and promotions that reinforced and perpetuated the qualities that had won that admiration. And some individual actors or actresses deliberately cultivated traits the public liked. "Some journalists wrote that I was bit doll-like, a bit affected," Noris told Savio in the 1970s. "Well, I'm not really like that, but I pretended to be because the public liked it."[22]

The spontaneous nature of the Italian star system was largely responsible for the comparative ordinariness of the stars. In America, every studio had its own photographers and its own photographic style, just as each studio had a costume department that created the on- and off-screen elegance of its "properties." Clothes and star portraits were crucial signifiers of star glamour—of that "hyper-perfect," beautiful look which people associated with stardom. In Italy, because there were no studios in the American sense, there were no studio photographers, full-time costume designers, or fashion consultants. Nor was much attention paid to health, fitness, diet, or even make-up. Production companies used freelance photographers who ran portrait studios in Rome. Italo Zannier has shown that the best of the largely foreign freelance portrait photographers whom production companies used for stills oscillated between two styles, neither of which was cinematographic: the heroic, bottom-up portrait favored by Fascist officials, which mirrored the official Istituto LUCE style, and the soft-focus, heavily retouched kitsch style that was designed to turn the defects of bourgeois and aristocratic subjects into an idealized, abstract beauty.[23] The only portrait photographers who grasped the needs of cinema and who therefore quickly established a specialty in star portraits were Arturo Ghergo and Brazilian Elio Luxardo. According to Giuseppe Turroni, Luxardo, influenced by Futurism and Hollywood, was more modern and dynamic than his contemporaries: he used wind machines to introduce elements of movement and rhythm into photographs.[24] He also made use of dark as well as light and cast shadows across the features of his subjects in order to add depth and "culture." His use of light, while intriguing and expressionist in its effect, "muddied" the portraits and deprived them of the uncomplicated euphoria of the sheer light and glistening aura that was lent to American stars by photographers such as George Hurrell and Clarence Sinclair Bell.

Fashion and costume reached respectable standards in Italy as far as historical films were concerned, thanks to much-admired costume designers such as Nino Novarese and Gino Sensani, but they were a weak point of contemporary Italian films. Fashion magazines and fashion journalists such as Irene Brin and Vera often complained of the tastelessness and, more frequently, sheer ordinariness of the dress of screen actresses, who were treated as gauche upstarts lacking the poise and manners of some of the great dames of the theatre who inspired bourgeois women in the way they dressed. In the absence of costume departments headed by the likes of Adrian (MGM) or Edith Head (Paramount), actresses were allowed to choose their own clothes, often with disastrous results. It was not unknown in the 1930s for well-to-do audiences to whistle and laugh at fashions that were either out of date by the time they made it onto the screen or which, because they were intended for everyday wear, looked plain. Although this problem was the subject of continuous debate and it was widely agreed that what was needed was a systematic linkup between the film industry and the fashion world, this never came about because of the desire of the former to economize on costumes and the unwillingness of the latter to accept that it would benefit if it donated time, skills, and costumes. Thus, with the partial exception of Clara Calamai (who was seen as the glamour queen of Cinecittà) and Vivi Gioi (a famously elegant actress who was dressed by the Milanese designer Biki), there was little manufactured allure.

It should also be mentioned that the luxuriously hedonistic, leisure-oriented lifestyle which lent American stars an escapist dimension was missing with Italian stars. The pictures of Italian performers at home which appeared with some regularity in magazines in the 1940s revealed that their standard of living was modest. Their well-furnished flats and cozy living rooms may have represented an aspiration for lower-middle-class and working-class cinema audiences, but they were really quite ordinary. Indeed, there was even a complaint to this effect in the *Domenica del corriere.*[25]

Fans and Audiences

This does not mean that public interest was also understated. After 1938, much of the U.S. star culture—especially, but by no means only, among those too young to have taken a serious interest in the Americans before the embargo—was transferred to Italian stars. People looked to stars as models and as bearers of their hopes and fears, and they also looked to them for ideas and models in terms of dress, appearance, and hairstyles.

The relationship with the audience was quite intense and took various forms. Both female and male stars received many letters, requests for autographs, and even marriage proposals. Noris claimed to receive 400 or 500 letters per day at the height of her popularity and employed three secretaries to deal with them.[26] Episodes of what might be called movie-star mania were on the whole rare but by no means unknown. Autograph hunters descended on Venice in large numbers at the time of the festival and laid siege to the hotels of the stars. When the premiere of *Piccolo mondo antico* was held in Vicenza in April 1941, *Film* reported that a mass of students tried to force their way into Alida Valli's hotel, even though the actress was not there.[27]

Star culture was fueled by the press, which mentioned the family lives of stars, their places of origin, their living conditions, their wardrobes, and so on. In August 1940, *Film* published on its back cover a map of Rome with the faces and addresses of the stars, indicating where they lived (like *Novella 2000* does from time to time today). There were numerous articles focusing on Cinecittà, on what was going on there, what was being filmed, and so on. The magazines also published caricatures of stars. Cinecittà became a mecca, like Hollywood; many people wanted to become actors and were obsessed with the idea of an easy life and limitless earnings.

To examine more closely the relationship between stars and their admirers, let us look at two of the articles by Alessandro Ferraù published by *Film* in 1941 under the title "Lettere d'amore" ("Love Letters"). In these articles, Ferraù read and analyzed a sample of fan letters written to actors. He deduced that the authors were drawn largely from the audiences of first-run cinemas because the quantity of letters received went up when the recipient was appearing in a film engaged in a first run and it declined after the film closed. Authors also seemed to be young and educated to some degree, suggesting that they were middle class. Actor Roberto Villa, a Leslie Howard *signorino* type, who appeared in *Luciano Serra, pilota* alongside Nazzari, received letters mainly from schoolgirls who tended to write in twos and threes after having been to the cinema together several times to see one of his films. Villa's appeal derived in part from *Maddalena—zero in condotta* in which his character fell in love with a schoolgirl. If a girl was especially timid, an older person would write on her behalf. Letters were addressed "to the nicest actor in the world," "my beloved actor," "illustrious actor," "to Roberto," suggesting different levels of presumption of intimacy. Authors asked which shoe size he wore, which brand of toothpaste he used, and the like. One of the letters from which Ferraù quoted passages was obviously written during school lessons and informed Villa that "your photograph did the rounds of the class between the pages of a Latin textbook."[28] Actress Carla Candiani received letters from students and soldiers, who wrote to her from the front confessing their love, asking for signed photographs, or offering advice. Some confessed to having been tempted to steal posters of her, Ferraù wrote, while "others declare that they do not want actresses who are blonde 'like your American colleagues' on the screen and who sing the praises of brunettes. 'Now we want stars that belong to us, to our country: beautiful brunettes like you who are endowed with the charm of our peninsula.'"[29]

Stars and the Regime

The question of the relationship of stars to the regime is one that has conventionally been treated in terms of the "scandalous" liaisons between actresses and senior fascists. Goebbels's affair with the Czech actress Lidia Baarova found an almost exact parallel in the liaison between Alessandro Pavolini and Doris Duranti—with the difference that whereas Goebbels obeyed his master's order to break off the relationship and return to his family, Pavolini refused point blank to do so.[30] There was also gossip concerning the rumored relationship of Vivi Gioi with Ciano and of Valli with Bruno Mussolini and/or Il Duce himself (which were always denied by the actress).[31] In none of these cases, however, was the actress's career the result of, or dependent on, the real or alleged affair. The sole instance of an actress whose career was entirely the fruit of her association with the Fascist elite was Miriam Di San Servolo, sister of Mussolini's lover Claretta Petacci.[32]

More significant were the attempts by the regime to profit in some way from the successes of actors by association or to utilize them in propaganda productions. It is worth noting that some of the biggest successes of Amedeo Nazzari (*Luciano Serra, pilota, Bengasi, Quelli della*

24. Publicity postcard
of Doris Duranti, an
actress who specialized
in exotic femme fatale
roles and who was also
the lover of culture
minister Alessandro
Pavolini.
From the author's
private collection

montagna) and Fosco Giachetti (*L'assedio dell'Alcazar, Bengasi, Giarabub*) were propaganda-oriented war films. Although these films accounted for only a small proportion of the overall output of these actors, they were sufficient to qualify them to some degree as representatives of Fascist heroism and masculinity. This meant that the regime took an interest in the roles they chose. Giachetti, for example, told Savio that Vittorio Mussolini was unhappy that he had been given the role of the strangely positive Communist Andrei in Alessandrini's adaptation of *We the Living* (*Noi vivi*).[33] Nazzari was also invited personally by Mussolini to join the PNF in 1939 after *Luciano Serra, pilota*, but he refused. On the whole, there was a negligible level of political involvement on the part of stars. As actors, they took pride in their independence and were careful not to compromise their popularity by too explicit an identification with the regime.

In the late 1930s, the regime took an interest in the appearance of stars. There was an assumption that actors should be ideal types of the Italian race, that their Italian qualities should be underlined, and that the corrupting foreign influences of previous years should be eliminated. As far as the men were concerned, there was general satisfaction with the results that had been reached. The humiliating effeminization of the Latin male for which Valentino and Novarro had been responsible was deemed to have been corrected by Nazzari and Giachetti, the two actors who were most representative of Italian virility. Nazzari in particular, although wooden and inexpressive in some ways, constituted a sort of "super-Italian," not a typical man but an ideal one. Tall, curly haired, and strong, with dark eyes, he was rugged masculinity incarnate. He was helped, no doubt, by a certain resemblance to Errol Flynn, although he told Savio that his own model was Gary Cooper. However, in Nazzari the delicate features and suave manner of Flynn were missing. He projected not charm but honesty and reliability. His was a masculinity that belonged more to the war and costume genres than to the sophisticated comedy (although he did make a few of the latter, including Poggioli's *La bisbetica domata*).

For women, the problem was much greater. Many actresses did not conform to Italian standards of beauty. At a time when the northern European type of looks associated with Garbo, Harlow, and Dietrich was current, the platinum blonde was also common in Italian cinema. Miranda, Noris, and Gioi bear witness to this. Moreover, many were either foreign (Noris, Dilian, Mercader) or partly foreign (Valli, Gioi, Parvo, Berti). They were exotic looking and as such were well suited to the unreal atmosphere of the white-telephone films, which tended to be set in Budapest or other cosmopolitan locations. There were some darker, more Mediterranean types (although some, like Luisa Ferida and Doris Duranti, had a distinctly oriental or Gypsy appearance). Dissatisfaction was often voiced with the standards of beauty offered by actresses on screen—both that they were not beautiful enough and that they did not look Italian enough. The success of Maria Denis in the 1936–1942 period is probably due to the fact that she, although no great beauty, was a recognizable Italian type, a lively, dark-haired girl next door who was regarded as an ideal daughter or sister.

Film stars interviewed by Savio in the 1970s denied that in the Fascist period there had been much star veneration and said that they had been able to lead normal lives. But these post-facto statements which inevitably include comparisons with the postwar years cannot be accepted at face value. What is probably true is that stars did not function at all fully as a "transgressive elite." Although some of them offered images of subjectivity which went beyond the regime's gender ideology, they did so within certain limits. For example, no stories were planted in the press about their private lives. "I think we expressed the Italians of that time," Maria Denis said later, "and in those days the consciousness of the individual was a bit underdeveloped. We did nothing to try and say anything new; we were not encouraged to say new things."[34]

That there was a cult of stars which had significant if not immediate or always readily discernible effects can be illustrated by the clampdown on it that occurred in 1941–1942. In the middle of 1942, the Miniculpop introduced a ban on the publication of biographies of screen and popular music stars. Ceilings were introduced for show-business earnings (which Nazzari got around by securing a percentage of box-office takings on his films) and chauffeur-driven cars for actors and personnel at Cinecittà were withdrawn (ostensibly because of fuel shortages, but this was probably not the only reason). Privileges, in short, were under attack, and those who adapted well and, like Alida Valli, took the tram to the studio were singled out for praise.[35]

These measures were greeted with relief by the Catholics. In several articles in their *Rivista del cinematografo* in 1942–1943, they attacked the damaging influence of the cult of stars, drawing attention to the attack on decency that occurred when actresses were photographed wearing bathing costumes at the Venice festival.[36] There was also great concern that cinema was fundamentally subversive because it created a new awareness and dissatisfaction among the poor, who in increasing numbers were forming its audience. Quietly and tacitly it was eroding social distinctions and creating expectations of a social leveling.[37]

Stardom at the End of the Regime

The fall of Mussolini in July 1943 and subsequent dramatic events in Italy had a profound impact on the star system. Film production in Rome came to a standstill and did not recommence on any sort of normal footing until 1948. The collective mobilization of the population, including women, during the war; the experience of German and Allied occupation; the Resistance; and the massive influx of American films all affected public consciousness and perceptions of stars. With the return of democracy and abolition of many of the procedures and some of the institutions that had governed the film business under Fascism, a situation came about that presented few continuities with the past.

The partisan execution of Il Duce and Claretta Petacci in 1945, and the terrible spectacle of their bodies being kicked and spat on in Milan's Piazzale Loreto before being strung up above a petrol station, signaled at once the end and the exorcism of the cult of the biggest star of the Fascist period. A few film stars faced the same fate. The popular screen "bad guy" Osvaldo Valenti and his partner Luisa Ferida, who were suspected of having belonged to the band of the infamous torturer Pietro Koch in Milan, were shot in late April 1945 as symbols of the cinema of the regime.[38] The same end would undoubtedly have befallen Doris Duranti had she not succeeded in escaping over the Swiss border.[39]

Most film personnel were careful to distance themselves from Fascism in 1943 and turned down invitations to join the cinema of the Republic of Salò in Venice. Thus they did not run foul of the young turks who led the internal political reckoning within the film community in 1944–1945. But if the stars could not be faulted explicitly on ideological grounds, they could certainly be criticized on professional and aesthetic ones. In two incisive articles published in *Star*, Antonio Pietrangeli dissected the talent that had been available to Italian cinema. On the whole, performers were dismissed as inexpressive and superficial, lacking in moral and artistic sensitivity. Nazzari, who was compared unfavorably with Errol Flynn, was described as a static figure who had neither developed nor improved over time (a "wooden, clumsy star"). Giachetti was dubbed as immobile save for a few nervous twitches, which made him appear implacable and ridiculous at the same time. As for the women, particular venom was reserved for Assia Noris ("always the same and unpleasantly simpering, sickly sweet and artificial . . . , with frenetic little sentimental shouts and the unbearable bleats of her constant accent that lies somewhere between the exotic and the mannered . . . monotonous and doll-like"). Others, such as Maria Denis, were denounced as lacking authenticity or talent.[40] Those who, by contrast, could in Pietrangeli's view be utilized effectively were sincere, humane, and moral; these included Miranda, De Sica, Valli, Cervi, and Calamai.[41]

In the long view, while some big stars such as Nazzari, Miranda, and Valli survived reasonably well into the postwar years, and others, such as Anna Magnani and Totò, who had enjoyed minor celebrity under the regime, saw their careers take off in a spectacular way, most stars failed to find regular screen work after the war. Some, including Giachetti and Doro, continued in minor roles; Dilian and Duranti went to Spain or South America; and Villa worked in radio. Many others, including Noris and Denis (the former died only in 1998; the latter was still alive in 2000), reluctantly withdrew into private life. Yet it should not be imagined that the public was indifferent to their demise. After 1945, Italian stars continued to be viewed with affection. Magazines such as *Star* and *Hollywood* often published letters asking for news of favorites such as Denis and Giachetti, who had slipped out of view. Their names continued to appear in popularity polls. They also constituted a reference point for those fans who sent in photographs to the look-alike competitions that were so popular in the postwar period. It is striking to find pictures side by side of girls who modeled themselves on both Luisa Ferida (despite her execution) and Anna Magnani in the pages of magazines. There was great stability of tastes from this point of view. There were always crowds present whenever film actors appeared in the theatre (as many did, for example in the *Za Bum* variety shows during the inactivity of the film industry) or at the publicity football matches featuring teams of actors and actresses that occurred from time to time in 1945–1946. These actors were an important part of the personal history of Italians who were young in the 1930s or 1940s, and they would continue to bathe in the afterglow of celebrity for many decades, even though their names would mean nothing to later generations.

Notes

1. Franco Rositi, "Personalità e divismo in Italia durante il periodo fascista," *IKON* 17, no. 62 (1967): 9–48.

2. Francesco Alberoni, *L'elite senza potere* (1963; reprint, Milan: Bompiani, 1973), 25.

3. The stories were sometimes completely invented by Italian journalists with fertile imaginations. For a selection of Cesare Zavattini's fictitious gossip pieces, see *Cronache da Hollywood* (Rome: Lucarini, 1991).

4. Victoria de Grazia, *How Fascism Ruled Women: Italy 1922–1945* (Berkeley: University of California Press, 1992), 133–135.

5. Several books which seek to document cases of stardom under Fascism have been published since 1967. Of particular interest are Stefano Masi and Enrico Lancia, *Stelle d'Italia. Piccole e grandi dive del cinema italiano dal 1930 al 1945* (Rome: Gremese, 1994), and the monographic volumes on single stars also published by Gremese. For a contemporary reflection on the phenomenon of stardom, see Lucio Ridenti, *Il traguardo della celebrità* (Milan: Ceschina, 1931).

6. Rositi, "Personalità e divismo," 37.

7. Alberoni, *L'elite senza potere,* 57.

8. Irene Brin, "La moda nel cinema" (1943), in *La moda e il costume nel film,* ed. Mario Verdone (Rome: Bianco e Nero, 1950), 52–53.

9. Dino Biondi, *La fabbrica del duce* (Florence: Vallecchi, 1973), 88–89.

10. Rabagliati recounted his experiences in Hollywood in *Quattro anni con le stelle* (Milan: Bolla, 1932).

11. Jackie Stacey, *Star Gazing: Hollywood Cinema and Female Spectatorship* (London: Routledge, 1994), 126–175.

12. *Cinema illustrazione,* 26 August 1931, 6.

13. Viniccio Marinucci, "Cinema proibito," *Star,* August 1944, page unnumbered.

14. G. V. Sampieri, "Isa di Hollywood," *Lo schermo,* January 1938, 19.

15. Orio Caldiron and Matilde Hockhofler, *Isa Miranda* (Rome: Gremese, 1978), 12.

16. Giuseppe Turroni, *Luxardo. L'italica bellezza* (Milan: Mazzotta, 1980), 12.

17. G. V. Sampieri, "Divismo," *Lo schermo,* July 1939, 18-20.

18. g.v.s., "Come s'inventa una stella," *Lo schermo,* November 1940, p. 19.

19. State film boss Luigi Freddi was behind the development of a Cinecittà press office which distributed vast quantities of publicity material on single actors. See his *Il cinema* (Rome: L'Arnia, 1949), 1: 408-410.

20. Testimony of Assia Noris in Francesco Savio, *Cinecittà anni trenta* (Rome: Bulzoni, 1979), 832.

21. On this genre, see Jacqueline Reich, "Reading, Writing, and Rebellion: Collectivity, Specularity, and Sexuality in the Italian Schoolgirl Comedy, 1934-1943," in *Mothers of Invention: Women, Italian Fascism, and Culture,* ed. Robin Pickering-Iazzi (Minneapolis: University of Minnesota Press, 1995), 220-251.

22. Savio, *Cinecittà anni trenta,* 833.

23. Italo Zannier, *Storia della fotografia italiana* (Bari: Laterza 1986), 273-274.

24. Turroni, *Luxardo,* 24-25.

25. Jori, "Attori . . . fuori schermo," *La domenica del corriere,* 13 April 1941, 16. The article observed, in an admonishing tone, that "there is nothing exceptional to report on the off-screen activities of our film actors. They display none of the hundreds of oddities that we [have] learned to expect from American stars. They seem like nothing more than fine lasses and well-behaved boys." On a more positive note, the article concluded by asking if this modesty was not "perhaps an additional reason why we like them."

26. Savio, *Cinecittà anni trenta,* 843.

27. Bort, "Alida Valli trova un personaggio," *Film,* 19 April 1941, 5.

28. Alessandro Ferraù, "Lettere d'amore a Roberto Villa," *Film,* 27 February 1941, 11.

29. Alessandro Ferraù, "Lettere d'amore," *Film,* 5 April 1941, 8.

30. See Archivio Centrale dello Stato, Rome, Italy, Segreteria particolare del Duce, folder: Pavolini, Alessandro. Also relevant is Doris Duranti, *Il romanzo della mia vita,* ed. Gian Franco Vené (Milan: Mondadori, 1987), 140-141.

31. See Lorenzo Pellizzari and Claudio M. Valentinetti, *Il romanzo di Alida Valli* (Milan: Garzanti, 1995), 119-120.

32. This episode is recounted in detail in Freddi, *Il cinema,* 1: 353-374.

33. Savio, *Cinecittà anni trenta*, 580.

34. Ibid., 468.

35. *Lo schermo* (July 1941), 24–25.

36. See G. S. Ch., "Difendere il popolo dal divismo," *Rivista del cinematografo*, June 1942, 77 and G. S. Ch., "Saggio di divismo," *Rivista del cinematografo*, September 1942, 101.

37. a.s.m., "Cinema sovvertitore," *Rivista del cinematografo*, May 1943, 49–50.

38. See Romano Bracalini, *Celebri e dannati: Osvaldo Valenti e Luisa Ferida— storia e tragedia di due divi del regime* (Milan: Longanesi, 1985).

39. Duranti, *Il romanzo della mia vita*, 15.

40. Antonio Pietrangeli, "Gli attori," *Star*, 23 September 1944, 3–4.

41. Antonio Pietrangeli, "Gli attori," *Star*, 30 September 1944, 14.

Selected Bibliography

Addis Saba, Marina, ed. *La corporazione delle donne. Ricerche e studi sui modelli femminili nel ventennio fascista*. Firenze: Vallecchi, 1988.

Affron, Matthew, and Mark Antliff, eds. *Fascist Visions: Art and Ideology in France and Italy*. Princeton, N.J.: Princeton University Press, 1997.

Alberoni, Francesco. *L'elite senza potere*. Milano: Bompiani, 1973.

Aldrich, Robert. *The Seduction of the Mediterranean: Writing, Art and Homosexual Fantasy*. New York: Routledge, 1993.

Allen, Beverly, and Mary Russo, eds. *Revisioning Italy: National Identity and Global Culture*. Minneapolis: University of Minnesota Press, 1997.

Aprà, Adriano, and Patrizia Pistagnesi, eds. *The Fabulous Thirties: Italian Cinema, 1929–1944*. Milano: Gruppo Editoriale Electa, 1979.

Araldi, Paolo. *La politica demografica di Mussolini*. Mantova: Mussolinia, 1929.

Argentieri, Mino. *La censura nel cinema italiano*. Roma: Riuniti, 1974.

——. *Il cinema in guerra. Arte, comunicazione e propaganda in Italia, 1940–1944*. Roma: Riuniti, 1998.

——. *L'occhio del regime. Informazione e propaganda nel cinema del fascismo*. Firenze: Vallecchi, 1979.

——, ed. *Risate di regime. La commedia italiana, 1930–1944*. Venezia: Marsilio, 1991.

——, ed. *Schermi di guerra*. Roma: Bulzoni Editore, 1995.

Aristarco, Guido. *Storia delle teoriche del cinema*. 2nd ed. Torino: Einaudi, 1963.

341

Aspesi, Natalia. *Il lusso e l'autarchia. Storia dell'eleganza italiana 1930–1944*. Milano: Rizzoli, 1982.

Barbaro, Umberto. *Il film e il risarcimento marxista dell'arte*. Roma: Riuniti, 1960.

Barbina, Alfredo, ed. *Sperduti nel buio*. Roma: Nuova ERI, 1987.

Bazzoni, Romolo. *Sessant'anni della Biennale di Venezia*. Venezia: Lombroso Editore, 1962.

Bencivenni, Alessandro. *Luchino Visconti*. Milano: Editrice Il Castoro, 1994.

Benedetti, Laura, Julia L. Hairston, and Silvia M. Ross, eds. *Gendered Contexts: New Perspectives in Italian Cultural Studies*. New York: Peter Lang, 1996.

Ben-Ghiat, Ruth. "Envisioning Modernity: Desire and Discipline in the Italian Fascist Film." *Critical Inquiry* 23, no. 1 (Autumn 1996): 109–144.

———. "Fascism, Writing, and Memory: The Realist Aesthetic in Italy, 1930–1950." *Journal of Modern History* 67, no. 3 (September 1995): 627–665.

———. *Fascist Modernities: Italy, 1922–1945*. Berkeley: University of California Press, 2001. (Translated into Italian as *La cultura fascista* [Bologna: Il Mulino, 2000].)

Benjamin, Walter. "The Work of Art in the Age of Mechanical Reproduction." In *Illuminations*, trans. Harry Zohn, 217–251. New York: Schocken Books, 1968.

Berezin, Mabel. *Making the Fascist Self: The Political Culture of Interwar Italy*. Ithaca, N.Y.: Cornell University Press, 1997.

Bernardini, Aldo, and Vittorio Martinelli, eds. *Il cinema italiano degli anni venti*. Roma: Cineteca Nazionale-CNC, 1979.

Bergonazzi, Giampaolo. *L'immagine del mito*. Bologna: CLUEB, 1983.

Bertelli, Pino. *La dittatura dello schermo. Telefoni bianchi e camicia nera*. Catania: Anarchismo, 1984.

Bertellini, Giorgio, and Saverio Giovacchini. "Ambiguous Sovereignties: Notes on the Suburbs in Italian Cinema." In *Suburban Discipline*, ed. Peter Lang and Tam Miller, 86–111. New York: Princeton Architectural Press, 1997.

Biondi, Dino. *La fabbrica del duce*. Firenze: Vallecchi, 1973.

Black, Gregory D. *Hollywood Censored: Morality Codes, Catholics, and the Movies*. Cambridge: Cambridge University Press, 1994.

Blasetti, Alessandro. *Il cinema che ho vissuto*. Edited by Franco Prono. Bari: Dedalo, 1982.

———. *Scritti sul cinema*. Venezia: Marsilio, 1982.

Bolzoni, Francesco. "La commedia all'ungherese nel cinema italiano." *Bianco e nero* 49, no. 3 (1988): 7-41.

———. *Il progetto imperiale. Cinema e cultura nell'Italia del 1936.* Venezia: Ed. La Biennale di Venezia, 1976.

Bondanella, Peter. *Italian Cinema: From Neorealism to the Present.* 2nd ed. New York: Continuum, 1990.

Bono, Francesco. "La Mostra del cinema di Venezia. Nascita e sviluppo nell'anteguerra 1932-1939." *Storia contemporanea* 22, no. 3 (June 1991): 513-549.

Bordoni, Carlo. *Cultura e propaganda nell'Italia fascista.* Messina: D'Anna, 1974.

———, ed. *Fascismo e politica culturale. Arte, letteratura e ideologia in Critica fascista.* Bologna: Brechtiana, 1981.

Borghini, Fabrizio. *Fosco Giachetti.* Firenze: Ed. Play Time, 1984.

Bragaglia, Anton Giulio. *Il film sonoro.* Milano: Edizioni Corbaccio, 1929.

Brunetta, Gian Piero. *Buio in sala. 100 anni di passione dello spettatore cinematografico.* Venezia: Marsilio, 1989.

———. *Cent'anni di cinema italiano.* Roma-Bari: Laterza, 1991.

———. *Cinema italiano tra le due guerre.* Milano: Mursia, 1975.

———. *Intelletuali, cinema e propaganda fra le due guerre.* Bologna: Pàtron, 1972.

———. *Storia del cinema italiano, 1896-1945.* Roma: Riuniti, 1979.

———. *Storia del cinema italiano.* 4 vols. Roma: Editori Riuniti, 1993.

Bruno, Giuliana. *Streetwalking on a Ruined Map: Cultural Theory and the City Films of Elvira Notari.* Princeton, N.J.: Princeton University Press, 1993.

Caldiron, Orio, ed. *Il lungo viaggio del cinema italiano. Antologia di Cinema 1936-1943.* Padova: Marsilio, 1965.

———. *La paura del buio. Studi sulla cultura cinematografica in Italia.* Roma: Bulzoni, 1980.

———, and Matilde Hockhofler, eds. *Isa Miranda.* Roma: Gremese, 1978.

Caldwell, Lesley. "'Madri d'Italia': Film and Fascist Concern with Motherhood." In *Women and Italy: Essays on Gender, Culture and History,* ed. Zygmunt G. Baránski and Shirley W. Vinall, 43-63. London: Macmillan, 1991.

Camerini, Claudio, ed. *Acciaio. Un film degli anni Trenta. Pagine inedite di una storia italiana.* Torino: CSC/Nuova ERI, 1990.

Campari, Roberto. *Il fantasma del bello. Iconologia del cinema italiano.* Venezia: Marsilio, 1994.

Cannistraro, Philip V. *La fabbrica del consenso. Fascismo e mass media.* Roma: Laterza, 1975.

Carabba, Claudio. *Il cinema del ventennio nero.* Firenze: Vallecchi, 1974.

Carpi, Fabio. "Il cinema rosa del ventennio nero." In *Antologia del cinema nuovo (1952–1958).* Vol. 1, 170–173. Firenze: Guaraldi, 1975.

Casadio, Gianfranco. *Il grigio e il nero. Spettacolo e propaganda nel cinema italiano degli anni trenta 1931–1943.* Ravenna: Longo, 1991.

———, Ernesto G. Laura, and Filippo Cristiano. *Telefoni bianchi. Realtà e finzione nella società e nel cinema italiano degli anni quaranta.* Ravenna: Longo, 1991.

Castello, Giulio Cesare. *Il divismo. Mitologia del cinema.* Torino: Ed. Radio Italiana, 1957.

Chiarini, Luigi. *Cinematografo.* Roma: Cremonese, 1935.

Cinema italiano: 1929–1943. Rassegna retrospettiva a cura del Centro Universitario Cinematografico. Firenze, 1958.

Il cinema sui muri. Tarento: Mostra catalogo, 1983.

Clark, Martin. *Modern Italy, 1871–1995.* London and New York: Longman, 1996.

Dalle Vacche, Angela. *The Body in the Mirror: Shapes of History in Italian Cinema.* Princeton, N.J.: Princeton University Press, 1992.

De Felice, Renzo. *Fascism: An Informal Introduction to Its Theory and Practice.* Edited by Michael Ledeen. New Brunswick, N.J.: Transaction Books, 1976.

———. "Fascism and Culture in Italy: Outlines for Further Study." *Stanford Italian Review* 8, no. 1–2 (1990): 5–11.

———. *Le interpretazioni del fascismo.* Revised ed. Bari: Laterza, 1989.

De Grand, Alexander. *Italian Fascism: Its Origins and Development.* 2nd ed. Lincoln: University of Nebraska Press, 1989.

———. "Women under Italian Fascism." *Historical Journal* 19, no. 4 (1976): 947–968.

De Grazia, Victoria. *The Culture of Consent: Mass Organization of Leisure in Fascist Italy.* Cambridge: Cambridge University Press, 1981.

———. *How Fascism Ruled Women: Italy, 1922–1943.* Berkeley: University of California Press, 1991.

———. "Nationalizing Women: The Competition between Fascist and Commercial Cultural Models in Mussolini's Italy." In *The Sex of Things: Gender and Consumption in Historical Perspective,* ed. Victoria De Grazia, 337–358. Berkeley: University of California Press, 1996.

———. "La nazionalizzazione delle donne: Modelli di regime e cultura commerciale nell'Italia fascista." *Memoria* 33, no. 3 (1991): 95–111.

Del Boca, Angelo. *Gli italiani in Africa Orientale. La caduta dell'Impero.* Vol. III. Bari: Laterza, 1982.

Del Monte, Peter. "Le teoriche del film in Italia dalle origini al sonoro." *Bianco e nero* 30, nos. 1–2, 5–6, and 7–8 (1969): 19–28, 21–35, and 2–37.

De Miro, Ester, et al., eds. *Il cinema italiano dal '30 al '40*. Genova: Tilgher, 1974.

Di Giammatteo, Fernaldo, ed. *La controversia Visconti*. Roma: Bianco e Nero, 1976.

———. *Lo sguardo inquieto. Storia del cinema italiano 1940–1990*. Firenze: La Nuova Italia, 1994.

Doane, Mary Ann. "The Abstraction of a Lady: *La signora di tutti*." *Cinema Journal* 28, no. 1 (Fall 1988): 65–84.

Duranti, Doris. *Romanzo della mia vita*. Milano: Mondadori, 1987.

Ellwood, David W., and Rob Krees, eds. *Hollywood in Europe: Experiences in Cultural Hegemony*. Amsterdam: VU University Press, 1994.

Falasca-Zamponi, Simonetta. *Fascist Spectacle: The Aesthetics of Power in Mussolini's Italy*. Berkeley: University of California Press, 1997.

Faldini, Franca, and Goffredo Fofi, eds. *L'avventurosa storia del cinema italiano raccontato dai suoi protagonisti 1935–1959*. Milano: Feltrinelli, 1979.

Fasoli, Massimo, Giancarlo Guastini, Bruno Restuccia, and Vittorio Rivosecchi. *La città del cinema. Produzione e lavoro nel cinema italiano 1930–1970*. Roma: Casa Ed. Roberto Napoleone, 1979.

Ferrero, Adelio, ed. *Visconti. Il cinema*. Modena: Ufficio del Cinema del Comune di Modena, 1977.

Ferretti, Gian Carlo. "Gramsci e il cinema." *Cinema nuovo* 4, no. 60 (6 October 1955): 427–429.

Forgacs, David. *Italian Culture in the Industrial Era, 1880–1980: Cultural Industries, Politics, and the Public*. Manchester: Manchester University Press, 1990.

———, ed. *Rethinking Italian Fascism: Capitalism, Populism and Culture*. London: Lawrence and Wishart, 1986.

Freddi, Luigi. *Il cinema. Miti, esperienze e realtà di un regime totalitario*. 2 vols. Roma: L'Arnia, 1949.

Friedberg, Anne. *Window Shopping: Cinema and the Postmodern*. Berkeley: University of California Press, 1993.

Gambetti, Giacomo. *Cinema e censura in Italia*. Roma: Edizioni Bianco e Nero, 1972.

Garofalo, Piero. "Myths and Countermyths: The Making of America in Fascist Italy." *Italian Culture* 15 (1997): 91–103.

Gentile, Emilio. "Fascism in Italian Historiography: In Search of an Individual Historical Identity." *Journal of Contemporary History* 21 (April 1986): 179–208.

———. *The Sacralization of Politics in Fascist Italy.* Trans. Keith Botsford. Cambridge, Mass.: Harvard University Press, 1996.

Germani, Sergio Grmek. *Mario Camerini.* Firenze: La Nuova Italia/Il Castoro, 1980.

———, and Vittorio Martinelli, eds. *Il cinema di Augusto Genina.* Roma: Edizioni Biblioteca dell'Immagine, 1989.

Ghergo, Arturo. *Dive degli anni '30 agli anni '60.* Milano: Sugar Co., 1984.

Gili, Jean. *L'Italie de Mussolini et son cinéma.* Paris: Veyrier, 1985.

———. *Stato fascista e cinematografia. Repressione e promozione.* Roma: Bulzoni, 1981.

Gori, Gianfranco. "Condottieres, artistes et saints: le film biographique en vingt années de fascisme." *Les Cahiers de la Cinématheque* 45 (March 1986): 81–92.

———. *Patria Diva. La storia d'Italia nei film del ventennio.* Firenze: La casa Usher, 1989.

———. "Le thème du Risorgimento dans le cinéma italien des années vingt." *Les Cahiers de la Cinématheque* 49 (1988): 37–41.

Gramsci, Antonio. *Letteratura e vita nazionale.* Roma: Riuniti, 1987.

Graziani, Gianfranco, ed. *Pratiche basse e telefoni bianchi. Cinema italiano 1923–1943.* Pescara: Tracce, 1986.

Griffin, Roger. *The Nature of Fascism.* New York: St. Martin's Press, 1991.

Gromo, Mario. *Davanti allo schermo. Cinema italiano 1931–1943.* Torino: Stampa, 1992.

Hay, James. "Piecing Together What Remains of the Cinematic City." In *The Cinematic City,* ed. Dave Clarke. London/New York: Routledge, 1997.

———. *Popular Film Culture in Fascist Italy: The Passing of the Rex.* Bloomington: Indiana University Press, 1987.

Hewitt, Andrew. *Fascist Modernism: Aesthetics, Politics, and the Avant-garde.* Stanford, Calif.: Stanford University Press, 1993.

———. "Fascist Modernism, Futurism, and Post-modernity." In *Fascism, Aesthetics, and Culture,* ed. Richard J. Golsan, 38–55. Hanover, N.H.: University of New England Press, 1992.

———. *Political Inversions: Homosexuality, Fascism, and the Modernist Imaginary.* Stanford, Calif.: Stanford University Press, 1996.

Horn, David G. "Constructing the Sterile City: Pronatalism and Social Sciences in Interwar Italy." *American Ethnologist* 18, no. 3 (1991): 581–601.

———. *Social Bodies: Science, Reproduction, and Italian Modernity.* Princeton, N.J.: Princeton University Press, 1994.

Immagini e movimento. Memoria e cultura. Catalogo mostra. Mostra bibliografica ed iconografica sul cinema italiano dal 1905 al 1943. Roma: La Meridiana, 1989.

Isnenghi, Mario. *Intellettuali militanti e intellettuali funzionari. Appunti sulla cultura fascista.* Torino: Einaudi, 1979.

Laclau, Ernesto. *Politics and Ideology in Marxist Theory: Capitalism, Fascism, Populism.* London: Verso, 1977.

Landy, Marcia. *Fascism in Film: The Italian Commercial Cinema, 1931–1943.* Princeton, N.J.: Princeton University Press, 1986.

———. *The Folklore of Consensus: Theatricality in the Italian Cinema 1930–1943.* Albany: State University of New York Press, 1998.

Laura, Ernesto G. *Alida Valli.* Roma: Gremese, 1979.

Liehm, Mira. *Passion and Defiance: Film in Italy from 1942 to the Present.* Berkeley: University of California Press, 1984.

Lizzani, Carlo. *Il cinema italiano dalle origini agli anni ottanta.* Roma: Riuniti, 1982.

Luciani, Sebastiano. *L'antiteatro. Il cinematografo come arte.* Roma: La Voce, 1928.

Magrelli, Enrico, ed. *Cinecittà 2. Sull'industria cinematografica italiana.* Venezia: Marsilio, 1986.

Mancini, Elaine. *Struggles of the Italian Film Industry during Fascism, 1930–1935.* Ann Arbor: UMI Research Press, 1985.

Il manifesto cinematografico dal '30 al '60. Foggia: Catalogo Mostra, 1981.

Martini, Andrea, ed. *La bella forma. Poggioli, i calligrafici e dintorni.* Venezia: Marsilio, 1992.

Masi, Stefano, and Enrico Lancia. *Stelle d'Italia. Piccole e grandi dive del cinema italiano dal 1930 al 1945.* Roma: Gremese, 1994.

Messina, Nunzia. *Le donne del fascismo. Massaie rurali e dive del cinema nel ventennio.* Roma: Ellemme, 1987.

Miccichè, Lino. "L'ideologia e la forma. Il gruppo *Cinema* e il formalismo italiano." In *La bella forma. Poggioli, i calligrafici e dintorni,* ed. A. Martini, 1–28. Venezia: Marsilio, 1992.

———. *Visconti e il neorealismo.* Venezia: Marsilio, 1990.

Micheli, Paola. *Il cinema di Blasetti, parlò così . . . Un'analisi linguistica dei film 1929–1942.* Roma: Bulzoni, 1990.

Mida, Massimo, and Lorenzo Quaglietti, eds. *Dai telefoni bianchi al neorealismo.* Bari: Laterza, 1980.

Mosse, George L. *Nationalism and Sexuality: Respectability and Abnormal Sexuality in Modern Europe.* New York: Howard Fertig, 1985.

Mostra Internazionale del Nuovo Cinema. *Cinecittà 1. Industria e mercato nel cinema tra le due guerre.* Venezia: Marsilio, 1985.

Nowell-Smith, Geoffrey. "The Italian Cinema under Fascism." In *Re-thinking Italian Fascism*, ed. David Forgacs. London: Lawrence and Wishart, 1986.

———. *Luchino Visconti*. London: Secker & Warburg, 1967.

Nuovi materiali sul cinema italiano, 1929-1943. Quaderno 71. Pesaro: Mostra del cinema di Pesaro, 1976.

Payne, Stanley G. *A History of Fascism, 1914-1945*. Madison: University of Wisconsin Press, 1995.

Pellizzari, Lorenzo, and Claudio M. Valentinetti. *Il romanzo di Alida Valli*. Milano: Garzanti, 1995.

Pickering-Iazzi, Robin, ed. *Mothers of Invention: Women, Italian Fascism, and Culture*. Minnesota: University of Minnesota Press, 1995.

———. "The Politics of Gender and Genre in Italian Women's Autobiography of the Interwar Years." *Italica* 71, no. 2 (Summer 1994): 176-197.

———. *Politics of the Visible: Writing Women, Culture, and Fascism*. Minnesota: University of Minnesota Press, 1997.

———. "Structures of Feminine Fantasy and Italian Empire Building, 1930-1940." *Italica* 77, no. 3 (Fall 2000): 400-417.

———. "Unseduced Mothers: The Resisting Female Subject in Italian Culture of the Twenties and Thirties." University of Wisconsin—Milwaukee Center for Twentieth Century Studies (Fall–Winter 1990-91), Working Paper 1.

———, ed. *Unspeakable Women: Selected Short Stories Written by Italian Women during Fascism*. Translated with an introduction and afterword by Robin Pickering-Iazzi. New York: The Feminist Press, 1993.

Pinkus, Karen. *Bodily Regimes: Italian Advertising under Fascism*. Minneapolis: University of Minnesota Press, 1995.

———. "'Black and Jew': Race & Resistance to Psychoanalysis in Italy." *Annali d'Italianistica* 16 (1998): 145-167.

Pividori, Bianca ed. "Critica italiana primo tempo: 1926-1934." *Bianco e nero* 34, nos. 3-4 (March–April 1973): 5-179.

Quaglietti, Lorenzo. *Storia economico-politica del cinema italiano. 1945-1980*. Roma: Riuniti, 1980.

Quargnolo, Mario. "Un periodo oscuro del cinema italiano. 1925-1929." *Bianco e nero* 25, nos. 4-5 (1964): 16-32.

Quartermaine, Luisa. "Tempo di storia e tempo di miti. Teoria e prassi nel cinema durante il fascismo." In *Moving in Measure: Essays in Honour of Brian Moloney*, ed. Judith Bryce and Doug Thompson, 152-168. Hull: Hull University Press, 1989.

Redi, Riccardo, ed. *Cinema italiano sotto il fascismo*. Venezia: Marsilio, 1979.

————, ed. *Cinema scritto. Il catalogo delle riviste italiane del cinema, 1907–1944.* Roma: Associazione italiana per le ricerche di storia del cinema, 1992.

————. *Ti parlerò . . . d'amor. Cinema italiano fra muto e sonoro.* Torino: ERI, 1986.

Reich, Jacqueline. "Consuming Ideologies: Fascism, Commodification, and Female Subjectivity in Mario Camerini's *Grandi Magazzini.*" *Annali d'Italianistica* 16 (1998): 195–212.

————. "Reading, Writing, and Rebellion: Collectivity, Specularity, and Sexuality in the Italian Schoolgirl Comedy, 1934–1943." In *Mothers of Invention: Women, Italian Fascism, and Culture,* ed. Robin Pickering-Iazzi, 220–251. Minnesota: University of Minnesota Press, 1995.

Reich, Wilhelm. *The Mass Psychology of Fascism.* Translated by Vincent R. Carfagno. New York: Farrar, Strauss & Giroux, 1970.

Risate del regime. La commedia italiana, 1930–44. Quaderno edito in occasione del V Evento Speciale. Pesaro: Ente Mostra Internazionale del Nuovo Cinema, 1991.

Rentschler, Eric. *The Ministry of Illusion: Nazi Cinema and Its Afterlife.* Cambridge, Mass.: Harvard University Press, 1996.

Ridenti, Lucio. *Il traguardo della celebrità.* Milano: Ceschina, 1931.

Rizzi, Paolo, and Enzo di Martini, eds. *Storia della Biennale.* Milano: Electa, 1982.

Rondolino, Gianni. *Luchino Visconti.* Torino: UTET, 1981.

————. *Roberto Rossellini.* Torino: UTET, 1989.

Rositi, Franco. "Personalità e divismo in Italia durante il periodo fascista." *IKON* 17, no. 62 (July–September 1967): 9–48.

Sarti, Roland, ed. *The Ax Within: Italian Fascism in Action.* New York: New Viewpoints, 1974.

Savio, Francesco. *Cinecittà anni trenta. Parlano 116 protagonisti del secondo cinema italiano, 1930–43.* 3 vols. Roma: Bulzoni, 1979.

————. *Ma l'amore no. Realismo, formalismo, propaganda e telefoni bianchi nel cinema italiano di regime 1930–43.* Milano: Sonzogno, 1975.

Schifano, Laurence. *I fuochi della passione. La vita di Luchino Visconti.* Translated by Sergio Ferrero. Milano: Longanesi, 1988.

Schnapp, Jeffrey T. "Epic Demonstrations: Fascist Modernity and the 1932 Exhibition of the Fascist Revolution." In *Fascism, Aesthetics, and Culture,* ed. Richard J. Golsan, 1–37. Hanover, N.H.: University Press of New England, 1992.

————. *Staging Fascism: 18BL and the Theater of Masses for Masses.* Stanford, Calif.: Stanford University Press, 1996.

Schulte-Sasse, Linda. *Entertaining the Third Reich: Illusions of Wholeness in Nazi Cinema.* Durham, N.C.: Duke University Press, 1996.

Sessa, Pietro. *Fascismo e bolscevismo*. Milano: Mondadori, 1934.

Skinner, James M. *The Cross and the Cinema: The Legion of Decency and the National Catholic Office for Motion Pictures, 1933–1970*. Westport, Conn. and London: Praeger, 1993.

Sontag, Susan. "Fascinating Fascism." In *Movies and Methods: An Anthology*, ed. Bill Nichols, 31–43. Vol. I. Berkeley: University of California Press, 1976.

Spackman, Barbara. "The Fascist Rhetoric of Virility." *Stanford Italian Review* 8, nos. 1–2 (1990): 81–101.

——. *Fascist Virilities: Rhetoric, Ideology, and Social Fantasy in Italy*. Minneapolis: University of Minnesota Press, 1996.

——. "Fascist Women and the Rhetoric of Virility." In *Mothers of Invention: Women, Italian Fascism, and Culture*, ed. Robin Pickering-Iazzi, 100–120. Minneapolis: University of Minnesota Press, 1995.

Spinazzola, Vittorio. *Cinema e pubblico. Lo spettacolo filmico in Italia, 1945–1965*. Milano: Bompiani, 1974.

Stirling, Monica. *A Screen of Time: A Study of Luchino Visconti*. New York: Harcourt, Brace, Jovanovich, 1979.

Stone, Marla. "Challenging Cultural Categories: The Transformation of the Venice Biennale International Film Festival Under Fascism." *Journal of Modern Italian Studies* 4, no. 2 (1998): 184–208.

——. *The Patron State: Culture and Politics in Fascist Italy*. Princeton, N.J.: Princeton University Press, 1998.

——. "Staging Fascism: The Exhibition of the Fascist Revolution." *Journal of Contemporary History* 28, no. 2 (April 1993): 215–243.

Sternhall, Zeev, with Mario Snajder and Maia Asheri. *The Birth of Fascist Ideology: From Cultural Rebellion to Political Revolution*. Translated by David Maisel. Princeton, N.J.: Princeton University Press, 1994.

Tannenbaum, Edward R. *The Fascist Experience: The Italian Society and Culture 1922–1945*. New York: Basic Books, 1972.

Theweleit, Klaus. *Male Fantasies*. Vol. I, *Women, Floods, Bodies, History*. Minneapolis: University of Minnesota Press, 1987.

Thompson, Doug. *State Control in Fascist Italy*. Manchester: Manchester University Press, 1991.

Tinazzi, Giorgio, ed. *Il cinema italiano dal fascismo all'antifascismo. Testi e documenti dello spettacolo*. Padova: Marsilio, 1966.

Trasatti, Sergio. *Renato Castellani*. Firenze: La Nuova Italia/Il Castoro, 1984.

Turconi, Davide, ed. *Il cinema nelle riviste italiane dalle origini ad oggi*. Roma: Associazione per le ricerche di storia del cinema, 1972.

———, and Antonio Sacchi, eds. *Bianconero rosso e verde*. La Casa Usher: Firenze, 1983.

Turroni, Giuseppe. *Luxardo. L'italica bellezza*. Milano: Mazzotta, 1980.

Venè, Gian Franco. *Mille lire al mese. La vita quotidiana della famiglia nell'Italia fascista*. Milano: Mondadori, 1988.

Verdone, Luca. *I film di Alessandro Blasetti*. Roma: Gremese, 1989.

Verdone, Mario, and Leonardo Autera, eds. *Antologia di* Bianco e nero: *1937–1943*. 5 vols. Roma: Edizioni di Bianco e Nero, 1964.

———. *La moda e il costume nel film*. Roma: Bianco e Nero, 1950.

Villien, Bruno. *Visconti*. Translated by Salerio Esposito. Milano: Garzanti, 1987.

Wagstaff, Christopher. "The Italian Cinema Industry during the Fascist Regime." *The Italianist* 4 (1984): 160–174.

Wanrooij, Bruno P. F. "Il 'casto talamo.' Il dibattito sulla morale sessuale nel ventennio fascista." In *Cultura e società negli anni del fascismo*, ed. Luigi Ganapini and Camillo Brezzi, 533–561. Milano: Cordani, 1987.

———. *Storia del pudore. La questione sessuale in Italia 1860–1940*. Venezia: Marsilio, 1990.

Contributors

Giorgio Bertellini is with the Society of Fellows at the University of Michigan, where he is also a Visiting Assistant Professor in the Department of Film & Video Studies. He is the author of a monograph on Bosnian film director Emir Kusturica (1996) and the editor of a special issue of *Film History* on "Early Italian Cinema" (Fall 2000). His essays have appeared in numerous journals and he has contributed to various anthologies such as *Suburban Discipline* (1997), *American Movie Audiences: From the Turn of the Century to the Early Sound Era* (1999), *Le Cinéma en histoire. Institution cinématographique, réception filmique et reconstitution historique* (1999), *Storia del cinema mondiale* (1999), and *Fritz Lang's* Metropolis: *Cinematic Views of Technology and Fear* (2000).

Ennio di Nolfo is Professor of History of International Relations at the University of Florence. He is the author of *L'Italia e la politica di potenza in Europa, 1938–40; Le paure e le speranze degli italiani; La Repubblica delle speranze e degli inganni; L'Italia dalla caduta del fascismo al crollo della Democrazia cristiana;* and *Storia delle relazioni internazionali, 1918–1999.*

David Forgacs is Professor of Italian at University College London. His publications include *Rethinking Italian Fascism* (ed. 1986); *Italian Culture in the Industrial Era* (1990); and the book on *Rome Open City* in the BFI Film Classics series (2000).

Piero Garofalo is Assistant Professor of Italian at the University of New Hampshire.

Stephen Gundle is Senior Lecturer in Italian at Royal Holloway, University of London. He is the author of *Between Hollywood and Moscow: The Italian Communists and the Challenge of Mass Culture, 1943–91,* and many articles on Italian cinema, television, politics, and popular culture. He also co-edited *The New Italian Republic: From the Fall of the Berlin Wall to Berlusconi* (1996).

James Hay is Associate Professor in Speech Communication, the Graduate Program in Cultural Studies, the Unit for Criticism and Interpretive Theory, and the Unit for Cinema Studies at the University of Illinois-Urbana. He is author of *Popular Film Culture in Fascist Italy;* co-editor of *The Audience and Its Landscape;* and co-author of *The Companion to Italian Cinema.* He has written numerous articles on Italian cinema and television and currently is completing a book, *Articulated Places: Cultural Technology, Governmentality, and the Production of Social Space.*

Marcia Landy is Distinguished Service Professor of English/Film Studies at the University of Pittsburgh. Her book publications include *Fascism in Film: The Italian Commercial Cinema, 1931–1943; British Genres: Cinema and Society, 1930–1960; Film, Politics and Gramsci; Cinematic Uses of the Past;* and *Italian Film.* She has also published essays in film journals and teaches courses on European and American cinema.

Robin Pickering-Iazzi is Professor of Italian and Comparative Literature at the University of Wisconsin–Milwaukee. She is author of *Politics of the Visible: Writing Women, Culture, and Fascism,* and editor of *Mothers of Invention: Women, Italian Fascism, and Culture.*

Jacqueline Reich is Assistant Professor of Italian and Comparative Literature at the State University of New York at Stony Brook.

Barbara Spackman is Professor of Italian Studies and Comparative Literature at the University of California, Berkeley. She is the author of *Fascist Virilities: Rhetoric, Ideology, and Social Fantasy in Italy* (1996); and *Decadent Genealogies: The Rhetoric of Sickness from Baudelaire to D'Annunzio* (1989).

Marla Stone is Associate Professor of History at Occidental College. Her book *The Patron State: Culture and Politics in Fascist Italy* was awarded the Marraro Prize from the Society for Italian Historical Studies for the best work on Italian history. She has published articles on cultural politics in *The Journal of Contemporary History; The Journal of Modern Italian Studies;* and *Tikkun.*

William Van Watson is currently Visiting Assistant Professor of Italian at the University of Arizona at Tucson. He is author of *Pier Paolo Pasolini and the Theatre of the Word* and articles on theatre, film, and MTV that have appeared in *Theatre Insight; Romance Languages Annual; Semicerchio; Il Veltro; Theatre Journal;* and *Annali d'Italianistica.*

Index

Page numbers in italic type refer to illustrations.

Index

357

www.ingramcontent.com/pod-product-compliance
Ingram Content Group UK Ltd.
Pitfield, Milton Keynes, MK11 3LW, UK
UKHW030111220225
455422UK00007B/43